Saving Miss Oliver's

A novel of leadership, loyalty and change

Stephen Davenport

H.H. BONNELL, PUBLISHER
P.O. BOX 11220
OAKLAND, CA 94611-1220

Publisher's Cataloging-in-Publication
(Provided by Quality Books, Inc.)

   Davenport, Stephen.
      Saving Miss Oliver's : a novel of leadership, loyalty
   and change / Stephen Davenport
      p. cm.
      LCCN 2005930202
      ISBN-13: 978-09769255-2-1
      ISBN-10: 0-9769255-2-4

      1. Women school principals--Fiction. 2. Teaching--
   Fiction. 3. Boarding schools--Connecticut--Fiction.
   4. Girls--Fiction. 5. Connecticut--Fiction.
   6. Organizational behavior--Fiction. 7. Psychological
   fiction.   I. Title.

   PS3604.A9437S28 2006   813.6
                 QBI05-600114

Library of Congress Control Number today 2005930202

PERMISSIONS

Excerpt from "Home Burial," copyright © 1969 by Robert Frost. Reprinted by permission of Henry Holt
and Company, LCC.

"Two Voices in a Meadow" from *Advice to a Prophet and Other Poems,* copyright © 1957 and renewed 1985
by Richard Wilbur. Reprinted by permission of Harcourt, Inc.

To J.T.D.

IT'S NO SURPRISE that *Saving Miss Oliver's* is informed by a compassionate knowledge of the lives of all people who inhabit independent schools. After all, the book's author spent years teaching at and leading this kind of institution, and later was one of the nation's top school consultants. He knows the territory.

What may be a surprise, though, is that the book is such a strong, beautifully wrought, engaging novel. As one reads along, it becomes clear that Davenport writes much too well and feels far too deeply for his complex, passionately human characters to resort to the hype and melodrama that so often maim "school novels." Rather, he creates his figures and then lets them live, struggle, and develop in ways that are frequently moving and always honestly related.

In other words, the book steps beyond its genre. And in so doing it powerfully reminds us that real people are at the heart of any first-rate school. Their integrity, strength of character, hope for the world, and courage are the capital good schools are always built on. Davenport knows this. At the end of *Saving Miss Oliver's,* so will you.

—PETER TACY, FORMER EXECUTIVE DIRECTOR OF THE CONNECTICUT ASSOCIATION OF INDEPENDENT SCHOOLS AND HEAD OF THE MARVELWOOD SCHOOL, KENT, CONNECTICUT

THIS BOOK CAUGHT me by surprise—a surprise I would recommend to everyone. On the face of it, the story is about a difficult leadership transition in a well-established girls' school that is experiencing hard times. It is much more. Mr. Davenport weaves an intricate tapestry of personal intrigue, educational excellence, institutional and cultural history, and minefields in independent school leadership. His characters jump off the page and made me keep reading to find out what they were thinking, how they developed, and what they did next. I was enthralled by the stories within the story and moved to tears by the strength and bravery of the characters who so quickly became my friends and acquaintances. This is a story of struggle and disappointment, but most of all, it is a story about wisdom and hope. "

—JESSIE-LEA ABBOTT, HEAD OF SCHOOL, KATHERINE DELMAR BURKE SCHOOL, SAN FRANCISCO, CALIFORNIA

STEVE DAVENPORT is a consummate schoolmaster and a gifted writer. In this splendid first novel, Davenport builds on all the other exceptional "school" novels: *The Prime of Miss Jean Brodie, The Rector of Justin, The Headmaster's Papers*, and *The River King. Saving Miss Oliver's* is a must read for anyone who appreciates the seasons of a school's life and the lives of people who make schools work.

—PETER BUTTENHEIM, SANFORD SCHOOL,
HOCKESSIN, DELAWARE

STEVE DAVENPORT'S novel is fast-paced, entertaining and singularly evocative of the pressure-cooker atmosphere of a boarding school. Steve knows schools, and he brings us face to face with their passions, their absurdities and their virtues – especially when it comes to schools for girls.

—RACHEL BELASH, FORMER HEAD OF MISS
PORTER'S SCHOOL, FARMINGTON, CT

SAVING MISS OLIVER'S is a fascinating novel, a school story vibrant with personalities, crises, hopes, idealism, laughter, tears, struggle and soaring spirit. Anyone who has ever been a student or administrator or trustee or parent in a school will find the book riveting, and will stop again and again with recognition, shock and delight. The reader will care intensely about the persons and events in this book, the drama and comedy vividly alive in it.

—DAVID MALLERY, SEMINAR LEADER
AND CONSULTANT TO SCHOOLS IN
THE U.S. AND ABROAD.

IF YOU ARE AN EDUCATOR and care about leadership and the role played by change in the life of a school, read this wonderful book.

—ROD NAPIER, PRESIDENT OF THE NAPIER
GROUP, CONSULTANT, AND AUTHOR OF *THE
COURAGE TO ACT* AND *INTENTIONAL DESIGN
AND THE PROCESS OF CHANGE*

BOOK ONE

SUMMER

O N E

EVEN IN THIS, the last year of her reign, Marjorie Boyd has insisted that the graduation exercise take place *exactly* at noon.

"When the sun is at the top of the sky!" she has declared—as she has every year for the thirty-five years she has been headmistress of Miss Oliver's School for Girls. "Time stands still for just a little instant right then. And people notice things. They *see!* And what they see is the graduation of young women! Females! From a school founded by a woman, designed by women, run by a woman, with a curriculum that focuses on the way *women* learn! I want this celebration to take place exactly at noon, in the bright spangle of the June sunshine, so the world can see the superiority of the result!" Marjorie Boyd has demanded once again, still dominant at the very end in spite of her dismissal. She will be the headmistress till July 1, when her contract expires. Until then her will prevails.

Even her opponents understand that it is Marjorie's vivid leadership that has made the school into a community so beloved of its students and alumnae (who are taking their seats now in the audience as the noon hour nears) that it must be saved from the flaws of the very woman who has made it what it is. Founded by Miss Edith Oliver in 1928, and standing on ground once occupied by a Pequot Indian village in Fieldington, Connecticut, a complacent suburb twenty miles south of Hartford on the Connecticut River, the school that Marjorie has created is a boarding school, a world apart, whose intense culture of academic and artistic richness is celebrated in idiosyncratic rituals sacred to its members.

"But it will be too hot at noon," the more practical-minded members of the faculty have objected once again in an argument that for senior faculty members Francis and Peggy Plummer has become an old refrain. They are like theatergoers watching a play whose ending they have memorized.

"No, it won't," Marjorie has replied.

"How do you know it won't?"

"I just do," she said, standing up to end the meeting. For meetings *always* end when Marjorie stands up—and begin instantly when she sits down. Francis and Peggy understood that what Marjorie means is that she would cause the weather to be perfect for their beloved young women by the sheer power of her will. The weather has been perfect for each of the thirty-three graduation ceremonies in which Peggy and Francis have been on the faculty—and today, June 10, 1991, is no exception.

The clock in the library's steeple chimes the noon hour now, and Marjorie Boyd is standing. She strides across the dais to the microphone. The graduating class sits in the honored position to the left of the dais, their white dresses glistening in the sunshine. The sky is an ethereal blue, cloudless, and under it, the green lawns sweep to the river. Behind the dais a huge three-hundred-year-old maple spreads its branches, and Francis imagines a family of Pequot Indians sitting in its shade. The scent of clipped grass rises. In the audience the mothers wear big multicolored hats against the sun, and behind them the gleaming white clapboards of the campus buildings form an embracing circle.

Standing at the microphone, Marjorie doesn't look much older to Peggy and Francis than when she first hired them thirty-three years ago immediately after their marriage, Peggy as the school's librarian, Francis as a teacher of math, and soon after also of English, assigning them too as dorm parents in what was then a brand-new dormitory. She still wears her long brown hair, now streaked with gray, in a schoolmarmish bun at the back of her neck. Her reading glasses still rest on her bosom, suspended from a black string around her neck. "You *were* Oliver girls," they hear Marjorie say, and Francis reaches to hold Peggy's hand. They know what she is going to say next, and when she says it: "Now you are Oliver *women!*" giving the word a glory, Peggy starts to cry. She is surprised at her sudden melting. For up to this moment she has managed to assuage her grief over Marjorie's dismissal by reminding herself that she had agreed with the board's decision.

But *Francis* isn't crying! He's too angry to cry, won't give his new enemies the satisfaction—for that's how he thinks of those colleagues, old friends, whom he suspects of optimism over the dismissal of his beloved leader. He grips Peggy's hand, squeezes hard, makes her wince. It's *her* school! he wants to shout. Marjorie's! Not theirs! He doesn't want Peggy to cry; he wants her to be angry, to be obstreperous at every opportunity, to express disgust at the notion that schools bear any resemblance to businesses, as he does; he wants her to say rebellious things in faculty meetings, the way he's been doing, surprising everyone, including himself, by seeming out of control.

Still sobbing, Peggy yanks her hand away. She's been over this so many times before. You can be loyal without being stupid, she wants to yell. She was your boss, not your daddy. But of course she doesn't. It's not the time to tell her husband that maybe his ardent following of Marjorie was his way of escaping the dominance of a father who couldn't be more different than Marjorie—*he* would have fired her years ago! She keeps her mouth shut. It's bad enough that people see her sobbing.

Marjorie sits after exactly four minutes during which she has told her audience that now *they* must take care of the school. All of her thirty-five graduation speeches have been exactly four minutes long. She practices them—first in her bathroom—"I love to hear the words bouncing off the tile," she tells Francis and Peggy every year when she starts working on her speech weeks before the event. Francis and Peggy know that she times herself with the same stopwatch she brings to the track meets so that she can congratulate any girl who has improved her time. In this last year of her reign she has been taking the stopwatch to faculty meetings so she can time the windy ruminations of Gregory van Buren, head of the English Department, who, second in seniority only to Peggy and Francis, sits today immediately to Peggy's right in the front row of the graduation audience, smirking as if he has discovered a grammatical error in Marjorie's speech. Gregory doesn't even try anymore to disguise his joy at what he loves to call "Marjorie's expulsion"—or the "demise of the monarchy at Miss Oliver's School for Girls."

There is an instant of silence after Marjorie sits, and then, simultaneously, Francis and the graduating class stand up. In an instant Peggy is up too, taller than her husband. The audience rises. Their applause swells. The block of undergraduates sitting right behind the faculty is chanting, "Yay, Marjorie! Yay, Marjorie!" On the dais, the trustees stand too, their board chair, Alan Travelers, looking uncomfortable.

To Peggy's right, Gregory van Buren rises too slowly. She turns to him, grabs his elbow, pulls him upward. "Stand straight, windbag!" she whispers through her sobbing. "Stand straight and clap!"

Gregory's too smart; he doesn't even turn his head to her. He's gazing up over the podium as if he were watching a bird, his hands coming together so softly they don't make a sound, and Peggy is amazed to hear herself hissing: "Louder, you *politician!* Louder! Or I swear to God I'll poke out both your eyes right here in front of everybody!"

For an instant as the words fly out, she feels wonderful, a prisoner released. But then stupid. This isn't her. She doesn't insult people, she's never been involved in the school's politics. And she doesn't have Francis's talent for effective goofiness. She thinks maybe she's going to lose control permanently, wonders if everything is falling apart: Marjorie's leaving and the resultant division in the faculty, and equally pressing, Francis's leaving tomorrow on a trip that will last all summer, the first time in their thirty-three-year marriage they'll be apart for more than a week. It's the final straw. So she makes up her mind: she'll stay in control. Not just for herself. For Francis too—until he's able to control himself again.

Gregory still does not turn his face to her. He stares straight ahead, places his right hand on Peggy's, lifts her hand from his elbow, places it at her side as if he were putting something back in a drawer, and whispers: "I thought *you* understood, unlike your husband—who only understands the past. Actually, I *know* you understand."

Gregory's right. She does understand. It was the newer members of the board who forced the issue. The era is passed, they pointed out, when being a great educator is enough. No longer do certain kinds of families automatically send their children away to boarding school; and besides, just as boarding school grows too expensive for many families, single-sex education for women seems to be losing its allure. So pay more attention to the business side: to marketing scenarios, strategic plans, financial projections. That's the road to survival.

Peggy tried hard to persuade her friend to pay attention; and when rumors began to fly that the school was so strapped that it might have to make the one decision no one could even dare imagine, the one that would destroy the reason for the school's existence—namely, to admit *boys*—to survive, she barged right in to Marjorie's office and told her that if she, Peggy Plummer, the school's librarian for the past thirty-three years, were on the board, she would vote for Marjorie's dismissal in spite of their ancient friendship, unless she changed her ways and started to act as if her profession, for all it was a calling, were a business too. But nobody gives Marjorie advice. It's the other way around. So Peggy wasn't surprised when, six months later, the board, whose chair, Alan Travelers, was the first male board chair in the school's history, screwed its courage to the sticking place and demanded Marjorie's resignation.

Peggy stops crying by the time she and her friend Eudora Easter, chair of the Art Department, have to go up front and confer the diploma on the first student. The order was determined the night before when the president of the junior class picked the graduates' names out of the tall silk hat that is brought out of safekeeping once a year, according to ritual. The hat is rumored to have belonged to Daniel Webster. At Miss Oliver's it is a sign of loyalty to believe myths that lesser schools would scorn.

Facing the audience beside Eudora, Peggy is calm again. She's tall, slim, full breasted, her short black hair not covered by a hat, and she wears a trim business suit—librarian's clothes. Eudora is much shorter than Peggy, very round, her beautiful African features shadowed under a huge red hat, and her red slippers are pointed upward at the toes like a genie's. The students cheer her costume.

The ceremony goes on for several hours. For the graduates the teachers recite poems, sing songs, perform dances, even put on little skits. Francis confers the diploma on several girls by himself, and he and Peggy together do so for three girls who have lived in their dorm. For each, he spins the amazing tale of their blossoming, thus blessing their parents. Gregory van Buren's one girl gets a long poem that nobody understands. She tries hard not to show her disappointment. When Gregory hugs her, he bends his middle away from her, sticking his butt out behind as if he were wearing a bustle.

LATER THAT DAY in the desolate silence that overcomes the school when the last girl has left for the summer, Peggy roams her empty dormitory. For the past four years at exactly this time, their son, Sidney, would return from college, and she and Francis would focus on him all summer, feasting on his presence. But Siddy, who finished college a year ago in June, left for Europe in September to wander for an indeterminate time. He's figuring out who he is, what he wants to do with his life, Peggy tells herself over and over, seeking comfort. All the young ones do that these days. The mantra brings her no more comfort than knowing that young people don't bother getting married anymore before they live with each other. To Peggy, whose school is a home away from home for 345 students, wandering is an anathema.

So, she asks herself, why does her husband insist on this trip that he will start tomorrow, the first day of summer vacation? He will be away not only from her for the entire summer—but also from the new head who needs the senior teacher's help in getting acclimated—and has every right to expect it. Francis has a big responsibility to fulfill right here this summer—one that he can fulfill better than anyone. So why does he choose to wander? *He's* not just out of college; he's fifty-five, for goodness sake!

She knows Francis's response would be that he won't be wandering. He'll be chaperoning a group of students from schools all over the East on an archeological dig in California—what's wrong with that? Isn't Miss Oliver's School famous for its anthropology courses; isn't that what makes us different from all those *other* schools? "If our girls can learn to look objectively at other cultures," he reminds her, "then they can look at their own with open eyes, instead of the way they have been indoctrinated to see—by men. That's how we change the world! We're going to live in a reconstructed Ohlone

Indian village on the shoulder of Mount Alma while we do the dig to find the real village they lived in," he tells her—as if she didn't know!

If he would just admit to himself the real reason, that he wants to *be* like an Indian, she could object—and remind him that Indians made their vision quests when they were fourteen years old! For that's what they're trying to do: be like Indians. Otherwise, why not just live in tents?

But chaperoning an exercise in anthropology? How can Peggy argue with that? She's the who one who, thirty years ago, started the tradition of cultural relativism that makes Miss Oliver's unique. For it was she who discovered the jumble of Pequot Indian artifacts in a closet of the little house that then served as the school's library and persuaded Marjorie to raise the funds for a new library in which the Pequot artifacts, and several small bones of a young Pequot woman unearthed when the library's foundation was dug, are now respectfully displayed. It is lost on no one that the library—which many of the faculty think of as Peggy's Library—is situated exactly at the center of the campus.

Peggy walks slowly down the hall of her dormitory, entering each girl's room as if it were ten-thirty in the middle of the school year and she were saying goodnight. Even though she knows the girls won't be in their rooms to turn their faces to her as she stands in the door, she is surprised to discover how lonely she feels in this sudden barrenness where the sound of her footsteps echoes off the walls.

She moves from room to room. It doesn't surprise her that Rebecca Burley's left the poster of Jimi Hendrix on the wall; she and Francis have told each other more than once that this kid needs to try on lots of different coats before it's too late, but further down the hall, when she discovers a well-used bong sitting squarely in the middle of the desk of Tracy Danforth—who just graduated and was president of the Honor Council—she wants to get Francis, bring him here to show him how Tracy was trying to show them who she really was. But she doesn't get Francis. Because he's too busy. Packing for his trip.

She thinks: he can't possibly pack for a whole summer without her help, he's helpless about such things, doesn't know where anything is, he'll go off with no underwear and ten pairs of pants. She turns away from the empty dorm.

SHE FINDS FRANCIS in their bedroom. He's on the other side of the bed from where she stops in the doorway the instant she sees him putting a big duffel bag on the bed. He's holding his hiking boots in his hands and is about to stuff them in.

"Oh!" she says. "I've never seen that before."

"It's new."

"When'd you buy it?" Its ugly, she hates it.

He shrugs. "The other day."

"Oh!" she says again. She takes one step back, almost out the door. Why does seeing him pack disturb her so? She wonders if she's going to cry for the second time that day.

He notices the movement, stops packing, his attention full on her. "I got it at Le Target." He pronounces it *"targay,"* looking for her smile.

It doesn't work. But his little joke does stop her retreat. "Maybe you should pack later, Francis," she says, taking several steps back into the room. "The reception for the new headmaster starts in half an hour." She knows it's dumb to think he'll change his plans and stay home where he belongs if he defers packing until after the reception. Nevertheless, the thought flashes.

"I'm not going to the new head's reception," he says.

"Say that again." She's standing perfectly still now.

"I'm not going," he says again. But already he's beginning to relent. He knows how foolish it is to stay away, how churlish it will seem. But in Marjorie's house! It's her home, he wants to say, no one else's. But of course it isn't her house; it's the school's.

"Yes, you are, Francis," Peggy says. "You're going. You're not childish enough to stay away," and immediately regrets using that word.

He drops his gaze to the bed. Now he's tossing in his shaving things and his toothbrush and toothpaste. Loose. All jumbled up with everything else.

"Oh, for goodness sake!" she says. "You can't pack like this!" She reaches in, pulls out a wad of shirts, tosses them over her shoulder. "Or this!" tossing a crumpled pair of chinos in another direction. "Or this!" Three big paperback books go flying, their pages fluttering. She's got her hand back in the bag again, she's going to empty the whole damn thing. She knows perfectly well she's not helping him pack, she's *un*packing him, and she *is* crying now, his clothes flying all over the room.

He puts his hand on hers, stops its motion. "All right," he says. "I'll go."

She stands still in the midst of the strewn clothes, her hand in his grip poised motionless over the duffel, and stares across the bed at him. Then she tries to reach in for the rest of his stuff.

"Peg! I said I'll go!" He's gripping both her wrists now, one in each hand.

She lets him hold, keeping her hands still, forces herself to stop crying. "You know," she says, "sometimes I think we're as married to the school as we are to each other." It's the first time she's dared to put the thought into words.

"No," he says. "No way, Peg."

"So when you risk your place here, I wonder what other seams will start to tear."

"Peggy, I said I will go."

She feels a huge relief growing, as if maybe she doesn't have so much to worry about after all. "You know, he's been very considerate," she says, speaking of the new head. She's looking at Francis again because now, with victory, she can't resist explaining her point. "He refused the invitation to speak at graduation."

"I know all about it," Francis says.

She sees Francis trying not to look irritated, persists anyway. She wants so much to convince! "He said it was inappropriate. He said it was Marjorie's moment, not the new head's. That's pretty nice, you know."

"I don't want to talk about him, "Francis says. "I'm not going to his reception for *him*. I'm going for you," and she realizes that the other part of her relief is that of the mourner who doesn't want the wake to end because then she'll be alone.

FIVE MINUTES BEFORE they leave for the reception, Francis stands in front of the mirror above his bureau, putting on his tie. Peggy comes up beside him, kisses him on the cheek. Leaning against him, she feels his body soften. "Indians don't wear ties," she says, trying for a joke. Right away she wishes she could take the joke back when she feels his shoulders stiffen. He turns his head just slightly away so that her kiss doesn't linger, and she steps back, feeling her anger flame. Why right now? she suddenly wants to ask again, to hell with jokes. On top of everything else! Don't you know we're too old to believe in different things? Francis moves away, leaving her framed in the mirror, and for an instant she doesn't recognize the tense woman who stares back at her.

Francis still thinks he's going on an archeological dig, the face in the mirror tells her. He's not ready to admit he's going on a vision quest. It's much too far out for Francis, too over the top, too *embarrassing,* to imagine himself, a middle-class white man in a tweed sports coat, a boarding school teacher, for goodness sake! chasing Indian visions. In California, too, where *every*body's weird! But that's what's happening. And she thought for years that her vision and his were the same! She's known almost from the day they met thirty-three years ago that Francis is a spiritual man. That's the deepest of the reasons she loves him so much. So it wasn't hard to believe that the reason he asked her to join in his family's staunch Episcopal faith when they were married was that he believed in it. He thought so too, she understands, for the force of that belief was so strong in the family that he couldn't believe he was different enough not to share it. But what she knows now, better than he does, is that the real reason he asked her this favor is that he couldn't imagine explaining to his father that he cared so little for his religion that he wouldn't ask his wife to join it. Even though she had none of her own to relinquish if she did.

I've been hoodwinked, she wants to say, hoodwinked and deserted, thinking of how much she'd been rescued from the barrenness of her own disbelief by the religion she'd joined and now is nurtured by, how much she'd come to love her father-in-law for the belief she shared with him, how much she's missed him since his death five years ago. When you don't resolve things with your father, you live with his shadow until you die too, she wants to lecture Francis. It makes you crazy. She doesn't say that either.

AT THE FRONT DOOR of Marjorie's house, Francis hesitates. "This is Marjorie's house," he says. He's walked through this door hundreds of times.

"It's the headmistress's house," she reminds him. Then corrects herself: "The headmaster's."

He turns to her then, gives her a look as if she has just slapped his face. "Sorry."

"I can't," he says. "No way. Not in her house."

She takes his hand, tugs it. "Come on, Fran, let's go."

He resists.

"Grow up!" she says, tugging at his hand. "It's time."

When he still resists, she drops his hand, turns from him, goes through the door.

He hesitates, then, surrendering, follows her. He's always stayed close to her at parties, using her vivacity as a cover for his shyness, but this time they move to separate rooms in Marjorie's big house, which is loud with people talking.

Francis moves through the people in the foyer into the living room. It seems bigger somehow, empty of something he can't put his finger on. He stops walking. A surprising fear of the new largeness of Marjorie's living room rises in him. While anxiety takes hold of him, Marcia Holmes, his young friend in the History Department, moves across the rug to him.

Smiling, she tells him how much she liked hearing what he said about the girls he graduated. "You tell such wonderful stories," she tells him and goes on to say how much she wishes more girls liked her enough to invite *her* to graduate them and suddenly, while part of him tells her not to worry because next year will be easier, the second year always is, and another part of him watches her face, still another part watches the scene that suddenly appears inside his head for the second or third time that week while he begins to sweat and goes on talking to this lovely young woman in her sexy summer dress as if everything were normal: the stern of a ship is moving away, he sees the froth by the propeller, going away from him, no one's seen him fall overboard, no one hears his shouts. Marjorie's big sofa's missing, he realizes, coming back, fully, to his young friend, and the top three shelves of her bookcase are empty, and that's what he points out to her, as if it were a discovery of some amazing new scientific fact, interrupting her as she tells him of her summer plans, and there's a funny look on her face—part worry and part a question, as if she were hoping that he's telling her a joke she doesn't understand. "She's started to move out already," he says in a very matter-of-fact way.

"Yes," she says. She's waiting for a punch line, but he can't think of anything more to say. She pats his arm—he can't tell if it's sympathy or just her way of excusing herself—and moves away.

FRED KINDLER, the new headmaster, is standing by the fireplace in the center of Marjorie's living room. Marjorie stands next to him, a good six inches taller. They are talking calmly together—as if nothing has happened, as if everything's the same, and Francis remembers Marjorie telling him of her resolve to hide her bitterness. "These people, who wouldn't even have a school to be on the board of if it weren't for me, want me to pretend I yearn for retirement," she told him "Well, I'd rather yearn for death. But all this is for your ears only," she went on after a pause. "The last bitter statement I'm going to make. I'll take their advice. I'll say I want the time to take up— what: golf? My grandsons? You know, the truth of the matter is I'm not remotely interested in my grandsons," she murmured, speaking half to herself and half to Francis as if she'd just discovered this about herself. "This school is what interests me."

Francis is surprised again at the new head's red hair, the big red mustache, and the short, stocky, powerful body. For an instant, Francis, in his mind's eye, sees his own short, almost pudgy body, as if in a mirror, his round mild unobtrusive face. He can't resist staring across the room at

Kindler. He's so *male!* Francis thinks, and then registers what he had seen instantly when he first saw Kindler standing next to Marjorie: that he's wearing the same brown polyester suit that he wore during his interviews. Polyester! he thinks, shocked at himself that he even notices. He's always been proud that in the world of preppydom of which it is a part, Miss Oliver's School for Girls is studiously *un*preppy, so why does he care what the man wears?

Kindler and Marjorie both notice him. He sees Marjorie put her hand lightly on Kindler's wrist, and Kindler moves across the room toward him. He has an awkward gait; his feet point outward like Charley Chaplin's. For an instant, Francis feels sorry for him, imagines girls imitating that walk, every girl on campus walking like that everywhere they go, day after day, until the poor man has to leave.

Kindler's right hand is out. His left hand pats Francis on the shoulder. All Francis can see is the red of Kindler's hair and mustache. "Come see me tomorrow," Kindler says. "I'm here all day. Mrs. Boyd's lending me her office. I need all the advice I can get, and I want to start with the senior teacher. Want to collect the best ideas and get a running start when I come back."

Francis is appalled at the boyishness. He feels suddenly like a tutor. That's not what he wants—parenting his own boss. "I'm leaving for the summer dig project tomorrow. Six A.M.," he says.

A waiter from the caterer's comes by with a tray of drinks. Francis plucks a glass of white wine. Without taking his eyes off Francis, frowning slightly, Kindler murmurs to the waiter, "No, thank you," and then to Francis: "Oh? That so? You're going on that dig? Somebody told me that one of the teachers was going. I didn't realize it was *you.*"

"I signed up way back in February," Francis says. He almost adds: before you were appointed, but he doesn't feel like explaining himself.

"Well," says Kindler. "I could have used you around here this summer. But that's the way it has to be." His face brightens. "California, right?" Francis has the impression that the man has changed his expression on purpose to make him more comfortable.

Francis senses Peggy watching him from across the room. "Right, California." He takes a sip of his drink, notices that several people are watching him and Kindler. We're on stage, he thinks, it's a big scene, he sees himself now as some kind of fulcrum. Takes another sip, his hand is shaking, spills some wine on his shirt, feels its cold.

Kindler hands him a napkin. "Mount Alma, right?"

"Yes," says Francis. "Mount Alma." He sees himself driving out across the flat Midwest, lonely without Peggy in the car. Then he sees the mountains, feels a little surge of joy, but his hand's still shaking, and he spills some more.

"You all right?" Kindler asks.

For an instant, he thinks the question's sardonic, the new head's first spear thrust. Francis is relieved. Then looking at the man's too youthful face, he realizes the question's sincere, uncomplicated, devoid of subtlety, and he is panic stricken. "I'm all right," he manages. By now he is sure everybody's watching them.

"Look," Kindler says. "I understand." He's talking now very quietly so no one else can hear. "Why wouldn't you feel that way? You've served her for years. I've admired her too—just from a greater distance. Just the same, I'm sure we can work together."

"Well, as long as you don't change anything," Francis blurts. Then he realizes what he's said, how dumb it is. He manages a grin, a little chuckle, as if he'd been joking, as if he hadn't meant exactly what has come out of his mouth.

His camouflage seems to work. Fred Kindler smiles. Francis sees the red mustache move. "Good," says Kindler. "I look forward to working with you." Then he moves away to mix with the others.

THERE! FRANCIS THINKS, I've managed to get through it. Now I can go home! He looks for Peggy, sees her across the room, looks at her back until she turns. He signals her with his eyes that he wants to leave. But she turns her back to him to show she's engaged in the conversation. He feels empty, moves across the room to leave the house.

He figures if he can just get out the door . . .

But on the way, he overhears Milton Perkins telling one of his Polish jokes to a circle of uncomfortable-looking faculty members. Perkins, the recently retired president of one of the biggest insurance companies in the state, has been on the board a long time. Francis finds himself slowing down on his way to the door, listening to the joke. He's heard it before. Perkins is seldom able to resist baiting the faculty's liberalism and being politically incorrect in a loud voice, whenever he gets an audience of teachers. Francis has always forgiven the man, understanding that underneath, Perkins has a deep respect for the school and the people who teach in it— which he has shown by years of generosity. To Francis, who, if pressed, would admit he likes to make derogatory generalizations about businessmen, Perkins is merely a gambler in a fancy suit who is just smart enough to sense the inferiority of his vocation to that of teaching. So why should Francis be bothered by the old man's backwardness?

But now, listening to the story, knowing exactly how it will build to the punch line in rhythmic stupidities, Francis stops walking toward the door, turns, steps back toward Perkins and his group of embarrassed listeners. Francis knows what he's doing, knows he shouldn't, discovers that he's been holding back these feelings for years in order to make things work for Marjorie, realizes also that Perkins probably has been instrumental in Marjorie's dismissal. He takes another step toward Perkins and his group of listeners, and sees Rachel Bickham, the tall African American chair of Science and director of Athletics, whom he admires, looking at him hard. She shakes her head, an unobtrusive gesture meant just for him. Don't, she seems to warn. Just don't. But he loves the release he's about to get. The room is very bright to him now, all its colors vivid.

"Why don't you shut up?" he hears himself saying to Perkins. "Why don't you just clam it?"

That's exactly what Perkins does—for an instant. He turns to face Francis. He clearly doesn't know what to do. He's certainly not going to apologize! So he just turns his back on Francis and goes on telling his story. That's what enrages Francis so—the dismissal! After all these years! He taps Perkins on the shoulder, and when the man turns around, his face flaming, Francis tells the same story back to him, substituting *Republican* for *Polack*. The group of teachers to whom Perkins has been telling his story glides away, so it is just Perkins now, and Francis, in the center of the room. Francis is pronouncing the name *Perkins* with the same clowning sarcasm with which Perkins has emphasized the final syllable *ski* of the Polish person in the joke.

They are center stage. Francis glimpses Marjorie, who is still standing by her fireplace, staring across the room at him. Her expression is begging him to stop. Father Woodward, the local Episcopal priest and part-time chaplain who is one of Francis's and Peggy's best friends, is standing by the opposite wall making slicing motions at his throat.

Francis doesn't see Peggy. He goes on and on, building a vastly more complex story than Perkins's joke, a fantasy of ineptitude in which the absurdly Anglo-Saxon main character reaches mythical idiocy. When a few of the people in the room can't resist laughing, he is even more inspired, feels the lovely release, and goes on some more—until he realizes that Eudora Easter is standing at his right side and Father Woodward at his left.

Their hands are on his elbows. He shuts up.

"Jeeeezus!" says Perkins into the sudden silence. "What in hell was *that* all about?"

Nobody answers because Eudora and Father Woodward are escorting Francis from the scene of the crime.

TWO

THE INSTANT FRED KINDLER sees the look on his secretary's face when she comes into his office early on the morning of his first day as headmaster and catches him down on his knees giving thanks, he knows he's made a big mistake. If she found him working in his office in the nude she couldn't have looked more affronted.

Margaret Rice, a tall, large-boned, black-haired woman in her fifties, who to Fred's surprise is dressed in her summer-vacation clothes: jeans and a man's shirt, rather than the more professional clothes he expected and would prefer, stands in the doorway looking down on her new boss; and still on his knees in his coat and tie, he suddenly sees himself in her eyes: the bumpkin, country clod, ex–farm boy ascended. He is out of style, and, to boot, a man in a woman's place. "Oh, my God!" Mrs. Rice whispers, then quickly correcting herself: "Excuse me; I should have knocked." But the look is still on her face: feminists don't get down on their knees, it says. We've been there too much already.

Thank goodness he doesn't ask her to join him—which is his first reaction. Instead, already rising from where he'd been kneeling beside his desk, he hears the apology in his voice, hating the sound of it. "I didn't know you came in so early." She's looking past him, her eyes scanning the walls as if she were looking for something—which he knows she is: Marjorie's paintings, each painted by a Oliver girl. All gone, Marjorie's taken them with her, the walls are now bare and white. The office has a bright, clean, monastic look. He loves it, it energizes him, and seeing in his secretary's eyes her resistance to this new sparseness, he feels his own stubbornness rising and is glad for it. No more apologies. Just be yourself, his wife has reminded him, and so, in his awkward way, has his own proud dad who never even finished high school. "I'm a lucky man," he finds himself telling Mrs. Rice, his eyes focused on hers. But her eyes slide away, and he decides not to tell her how during his early morning run he was overcome with gratitude for his good fortune at being chosen as the headmaster of Miss Oliver's School for Girls.

"Marjorie always came in at eight o'clock," Mrs. Rice says. "I always came in at seven. It gave me time alone to get ready." Then she is out the door.

Alone now in the bright summer light pouring through the glass doors that look out on the campus, he realizes he's still standing in the exact spot beside his desk where he rose to after being caught on his knees by Mrs. Rice. His face is still burning. So it's not cool to pray! he thinks, suddenly angry. "Well, you've never lost a child," he whispers to the door. "How do you know what to be grateful for?" He moves to his desk and sits down, already feeling just a little childish, unheadmasterly, to have allowed the words. He recalls his wife's reminder not to let their old wound tempt him to take elevated positions—as if losing a child makes one wiser than all the people who haven't.

The day has already lost some of the luster it had when he walked into this office fifteen minutes ago at quarter to seven, two weeks before he was required. His contract calls for him to start on the first of July, but when Marjorie moved out of the head's house and cleaned out her office with surprising speed—"who wants to die slowly?" she asked—he was able to start earlier. He was too eager, too full of ideas, to sit around waiting. Now a piece of him wonders if he should have followed his wife's advice— or was it a request?—and taken two weeks' vacation. He shakes his head, like a dog coming out of water. He will get on with his day.

His desk is bare, save for a framed photograph of his wife and the file of papers he has requested from Carl Vincent, the school's elderly business manager. He opens the file, turning directly to the projected budget for the fiscal year, which is soon to begin on July 1, 1991. Attached to the first page is a note from Vincent, dated just two days ago, telling him that these are the latest projections "which the board has not seen because I'm presenting them to you first, according to protocol."

Fred feels a tickle of suspicion. Something's a little fishy about this note. But he puts this aside and turns to the numbers. For several minutes the figures are a blur because his mind insists on lingering over his awkward tête-à-tête with Mrs. Rice. Besides, he knows the gist of these numbers already; he's been over them many times during his interviews and since his appointment.

He already knows there's a projected deficit of $245,000. So he doesn't look at the bottom line. Instead he goes right to the revenue figures. That's where the problem lies: the school has been underenrolled for five years. And now there's a baby bust, a precipitous drop in the nation's teenage population. And even if that were not the case, the appeal of single-sex education for girls has been declining for reasons that only consultants pretend to understand. Large deficits have increased in each of those five years, culminating in this latest, biggest one. So now the accumulated operating deficit, on top of the capital deficit caused by the failure to raise enough money to fund the new theater, the last of Marjorie's pet projects, amounts to a total indebtedness of over two million dollars.

The way Carl Vincent has presented the numbers is hard to interpret. In fact, they are a mess. So it is a little while before Fred realizes that these numbers are not the same as those he studied so carefully just before he accepted the position, confident that the notion of single-sex education was so compelling to young women that all the school needed to fill again was a good marketing program. This budget he's studying now, he realizes, is keyed to nineteen *fewer* students than were predicted by the earlier version. Nineteen times the tuition of $18,600. That's $353,400! He finds himself averting his eyes from the bottom line. Then he notices that the line item for salaries is bigger than it was in the last version, by $77,000. Even though there are fewer students to teach! Either this number is wrong, or the previous number was wrong. So he pulls out the compensation charts for the upcoming year and confirms what his intuition is already loudly declaring: the latest is the correct number.

He can't keep his eye off the bottom line anymore, which he has already figured would show a deficit of $675,400, instead of only $245,000. He's right. If this rate of drain continues, the bank will surely call the loans, and there simply won't be enough cash to run the school. He thought he had four years to turn things around. Now, on his very first day in office, he discovers he will be lucky to have two.

When Fred accepted the board's offer, he did so on the basis of a very straightforward strategy that the board accepted: he would create an aggressive marketing campaign by which to rebuild the girls-only enrollment. He provided a schedule showing the targets for the addition of students each year. The board understood that failure to reach these targets even as soon as the first year was the signal to consider becoming coed, a strategy that some other single-sex schools and colleges were adopting. But it was best not to talk about this possibility, certainly not to write it into the formal plan. For this specter looming in the background would enrage the alumnae, many of whom would rather the school close down than admit boys. In his own mind, though, Fred wouldn't even think about the possibility of closing the school. He'd admit boys before he did that. He knew something about the grief that follows a school's dying. That wasn't going to happen to Miss Oliver's. *Not ever!*

Fred spends the next half hour reviewing budgets for the previous five years, noting once again the consistent gap between the optimistic predictions and the disappointing results, and a few more minutes thinking very carefully about how he's going to handle his conversation with Carl Vincent. Then he remembers that Vincent has left for vacation. That's the reason for his timing in presenting the corrected budget: he didn't want to be around when everyone got the bad news and learned how inaccurate his projections were. Fred feels sad for the old man.

All right, so the next thing to do is to talk with Nan White, the admissions director, to see what the chances are of making up some of the lost enrollment over the summer. So, at exactly nine o'clock he is about to get up from his desk and walk down the hall to Nan's office when Margaret Rice opens his office door (without knocking, he observes), steps a very small distance into his office, and announces that his eight-thirty appointment has arrived.

"Eight-thirty?" he says. "It's already nine!"

"Hey, it's summer time," she says.

"From now on, Mrs. Rice—"

"*Ms.* Rice."

"Ms. Rice. Right. Sorry. From now on, I need you to keep me informed about the appointments you've made for me. I'd like to know a day ahead of time if it's possible."

"All right," she says. "Fine. From now on."

"Who?" he asks.

"Who what?"

"Who is my appointment with? Whom, I mean."

"Three teachers."

"Mrs. Rice, please, who *are* the teachers? *Ms.* Rice, I mean."

"I bet they'll let you know when they get in here," she says, flushing.

He feels his face get hot, too. She looks surprised, maybe even a little chagrined. "We're going to have to talk," he says very quietly, very slowly. His sudden anger, always surprising to him, is a relief.

"There's just a way we do things around here, that's all." Ms. Rice's voice is almost conciliatory now, embarrassed. "Marjorie Boyd—"

"All right, Ms. Rice," he interrupts. "Later we'll talk. Right now, who are they?"

"Melissa and Samuel Andersen; she teaches French, he teaches history."

"I know what they teach," he says.

"They just got married last Christmas."

"Yes."

"Marjorie married them."

"Marjorie! Mrs. Boyd? *Married* them?"

"She performed the ceremony. It made some of the new trustees mad."

"Well, that's interesting. Who's the third teacher I'm about to see?"

But Ms. Rice goes right on, her tone of voice almost friendly now: "Marjorie got one of those Universalist Church preacher's licenses that were created for c.o.'s in the Vietnam War," she tells him. "Since the alumnae learned about it, Marjorie's been asked to perform quite a few marriages."

"The third person?" he interrupts.

"Oh. The third person." That's Fredericka Walters. She teaches German."

"I know," he replies, feeling a further surge of worry. He's made it a point, during his earlier study of the school, to know how many students each teacher instructs. Fredericka Walters is one of the highest-paid teachers on the faculty—with the fewest students. He's going to have to do something about that.

"Oh, that's right, you know what people teach," he hears Ms. Rice say, and immediately regrets cutting her off. It dawns on him that before doing anything else he should have had a long, relaxed talk with her.

"Some people call her Sam," Ms. Rice goes on. "She likes men's names; and others call her Fred, of course." Then after a pause: "But don't worry. It won't be confusing. It will be a while before anybody's going to call *you* by your first name." Her face floods with red again.

He forces himself to let that go, trying to believe she doesn't even know that she's insulting him; she's just describing his situation. "Show them in please, Ms. Rice," he says as gently as he can.

Margaret Rice goes out the door. In an instant, she returns. "They're not there," she says.

"They're not there!"

"Right. They must have gone over to the faculty room to get some coffee. While you and I were talking."

"We only talked for a minute! The faculty room's clear on the other side of the campus."

Ms. Rice shrugs her shoulders again. "They'll be back."

"When's my *next* appointment?"

"Nine-fifteen. Mavis Ericksen and Charlotte Reynolds. Two of the new board members," she adds, rolling her eyes.

I know; I met them during the hiring process, remember? Fred almost says. So did my wife. But he remembers what happened last time he told her he knew something.

"It's already five after nine," he says instead. "That only leaves ten minutes. So when the teachers get back from the faculty room, tell them I can't see them now," he tells her. "They can come back later."

Margaret Rice stands stock-still, staring at Fred for what seems a very long moment. "You're joking," she says.

"No," he says very quietly. "I'm not joking. Tell them."

"You can't just cancel an appointment like that. They're *teachers!*"

"Yes, I can."

"They're going to be mad!"

Now it's his turn to shrug. As Ms. Rice starts to leave, he says, "Let's leave the door open. I don't want anybody to think I'm hiding in here."

"WE HEARD THAT about making the teachers wait," Mavis Ericksen says. An alumna, she's a tall brunette, very pretty, in a red dress, stockings, high heels. She turns to Charlotte Reynolds for affirmation. Charlotte, also an alumna, and mother of an eighth, ninth, and tenth grader, is a stocky, thick-legged athlete in a short tennis dress. She nods back at her friend. "Good for you, Fred," Mavis says. Both women sit down in the chairs he offers. He comes from behind his desk and sits in a third chair facing them.

"Yes, good for you," says Charlotte, whom Fred finds it more comfortable to look at; that way he can keep his eyes off Mavis's heartbreaking legs.

"We're very glad you're here," says Mavis. "As a matter of fact, we are delighted! Welcome."

"*Delighted* is the perfect word," Charlotte pronounces. "How's everything going?"

"Fine," Fred fibs, thinking of Carl Vincent's numbers filed right behind him in his desk.

"Really?" Mavis asks, her eyes probing.

"Just diving in," Fred says, feeling suddenly guarded. He tries to make his voice sound enthusiastic. "There are a lot of things I need to learn about."

"One of the things you have probably already learned," Mavis says, "is that Charlotte and I are among the more recent appointments to the board. The result, I would say, of some. . . ." She hesitates, turning to her friend.

"Persistence," Charlotte supplies

"Yes. Persistence," Mavis agrees.

"The school was getting pretty close to shutting down, you know," Charlotte says.

"I know. We will all work together to make what Marjorie built here permanent." He imagines himself apologizing to Marjorie for such a lame statement.

Mavis's eyes focus intently on his. "You're right," she says. "Respect for Mrs. Boyd. That's how we need to approach everything. But I refuse to let anyone make *me* feel guilty."

"I'm sure *that's* not what you meant," Charlotte murmurs to Fred. Then more loudly: "How's Gail adjusting?"

"Quite well. Everybody has been very kind," he says, pushing out of his mind the fact that Peggy Plummer and Eudora Easter and Rachel Bickham, head of the Science Department, are the only teachers who have dropped in to say hello to his wife. "She's finishing hanging our pictures as we speak."

"Well," Mavis says, "we're sure you're busy, so we should get right to the point and tell you why we're here."

"Definitely," Charlotte murmurs. "Time to get down to business."

"We're here to stand firmly behind you when you get rid of Joan Saffire," Mavis announces, looking straight into Fred's eyes. Joan Saffire is the assistant director of Development.

"Absolutely," Charlotte nods her head. "We're right behind you."

"Uh . . . I'm afraid I don't understand," Fred says.

"There will be a rebellion, of course," Charlotte says, looking hard at Fred. "A huge fuss. Lots of the alumnae, virtually *all* of the faculty, and many of the board—all the trustees who voted for Mrs. Boyd to stay, as a matter of fact. That's almost 50 percent."

"Charlotte!" Mavis exclaims.

"Oh, come on!" Charlotte murmurs, not taking her eyes off Fred's. "He knows."

Fred feels little drops of sweat running down from his armpits inside his shirt. No, I don't, he wants to say—for that's the truth.

"Don't you?" Charlotte asks him.

He still doesn't answer. Because *now*, of course, he does know.

"If I remember correctly, we *were* talking about getting rid of Joan Saffire," Mavis says.

Charlotte shrugs. "So we were."

"Well?" says Mavis to Fred.

"I don't want to appear not to be listening," he says, trying to keep the tentativeness out of his voice. "Or reluctant to accept advice, but I, uh, I think I need to remind you that it is the head who makes these decisions."

"She's Marjorie's niece," says Charlotte. "You didn't know that?"

"Yes, I knew that."

"Charlotte, please." Mavis looks sternly at her friend. "That's not the reason. She's incompetent, that's why." Then turning to Fred: "The main thing is that she's always saying the wrong thing. She insults people."

"People like Joan Saffire need to keep their politics to themselves!" Charlotte blurts.

"Why don't you tell Fred about when your husband asked Aldous Enright if he would accelerate his pledge," Mavis says softly to Charlotte.

"Ladies," Fred asserts. "This isn't an appropriate way to evaluate—"

"You need to listen to this!" Mavis says.

Fred puts both hands up, a double stop sign, but Charlotte is already talking. "When Gerald called for the appointment, Mr. Enright just exploded!"

"It seems that Marjorie's niece had already talked with him," Mavis interrupts. "She called on him to ask him to make a *bigger* pledge and to restrict it to financial aid."

"Financial aid!" Charlotte exclaims. "From *Aldous Enright?* Everybody knows he doesn't believe in financial aid!"

"And when she talked with him, she talked about poor people in a way that made it look as if anybody with money is a *fascist,*" Mavis says. "This woman, who everybody knows wouldn't even be here if she weren't Marjorie's niece, is lecturing Aldous Enright about financial aid!"

"So, not only did Mr. Enright not accelerate his gift, he *canceled* it," Charlotte announces.

There's a moment of silence while Fred thinks of what to say. He hasn't been in office for a morning yet, and already this! "Maybe Mr. Enright would have canceled it anyway," he tries.

"He would not!" Charlotte says. "I already said: people like her need to keep their political opinions to themselves."

"It's only one incident, though," says Fred. Then he cuts himself off. That tack won't work either.

"Of *course* one incident isn't enough!" Mavis is insulted. "We're only telling you one incident as an *example.* I don't believe in firing someone for one mistake any more than *you* do."

"I appreciate your concern," Fred says, desperate for an end to the conversation. "Very much. I will bring it up right away with Dorothy Strang."

"Dorothy is an excellent director of Development," Mavis says. "But what difference does it make what Dorothy Strang thinks of Joan Saffire? The *board* has no faith in Joan Saffire. That's what counts here. That is, the part of the board who raises money doesn't. The rest just love everybody. So why are you trying to sell us on her?"

"I'm not selling, Mrs. Ericksen, I am insisting on ethical process." Fred hates the sanctimonious sound of his voice.

"This is no time for delicacy," Mavis warns.

"It certainly isn't," Charlotte says.

"And I resent being painted as the villain," Mavis says.

"Look, why don't we call on Aldous Enright again—give it another try," Fred says, "and in the meantime I guarantee you that I will evaluate Mrs. Saffire. I could do more harm than good by appearing to fire people arbitrarily before anybody trusts me."

"If you want to earn *my* trust, Mr. Kindler, just do what you have to do, and do it right away."

"When is it going to happen?" Charlotte asks.

"I can't tell you that," Fred says.

"I tell you, you don't have the time to be so delicate!" Mavis's voice is quavering now. "Because if you don't get this place in order they're going to let boys in here, and if that happens I don't care if the place *does* shut down!"

"I'm not even going to *think* about that," Charlotte murmurs.

Mavis turns on Charlotte. "Maybe *you're* not," she says. "But I am. Because all of a sudden, it feels like Marjorie Boyd all over again around here." Mavis's shoulders start to shake. "Oh, damn, just what I need, a crying jag!" She stands up, turns quickly around, and moves very fast out the door, slamming it behind her.

"She loves this school," Charlotte says, standing up. "And she's awfully frustrated, you know. It's been a long struggle."

"I know it has," he says.

"Good," Charlotte says. She turns away from him and moves toward the door. With her hand on the knob, she turns back to him "It wouldn't be smart if you didn't," she says. Then she opens the door and leaves him.

IMMEDIATELY AFTER CHARLOTTE leaves, Margaret Rice takes exactly one step into his office. "Karen Benjamin's here for her ten o'clock appointment," she says. "She's the editor of the school newspaper."

"Good. Show her in." Fred's spirits rise. It will be fun to talk with a student after all these adults. He's glad that summer school will begin this week. When there are no students present, schools are dreary places.

"Uh-oh," Margaret says. "The three teachers are back. As a matter of fact, they got back right after those two ladies showed up. They've been waiting."

He says nothing.

"Well, don't you want to see them now?"

"How can I? It's ten o'clock. Karen's right on time. All the way from Boston."

Ms. Rice just stands there.

"Show her in, Ms. Rice."

"All right, if that's what you want." Ms. Rice steps back out of the office. "Go on in, dear," he hears her say.

Karen Benjamin doesn't walk into the room; she darts. Moving with quick, birdlike motions, she closes the door to the office and turns to shake Fred's hand. "I *hate* it when grown-ups call me dear," she announces. She's short, very slight, dressed in a white T-shirt with the front page of the *Clarion* printed on it, her thin legs in cutoff jeans. Her black hair's cropped, almost shaved, so that her head appears as round as a ball on her thin neck. Her brown eyes seem to flit all over the office, noticing everything, as she sits down in the chair. Fred sits facing her.

"My *mother* calls me dear," she says. "That's what mothers are for." She peers into her briefcase. "Where are you, Notebook?" she says. "You're in here someplace." Then looking up at Fred, her intense eyes catching his: "But when other grown-ups do—"

Fred nods, grinning. He's enjoying this.

She stirs around in her briefcase some more: "Here it is!" pulling out a notebook. "You're going to be featured on the front page of the *Clarion* in September. The first new headmaster in thirty-five years. Ta da ta da!"

"Something tells me there are some people who aren't happy about that," he blurts, surprised at himself.

"Something tells me you're right," she agrees brightly.

"Well," he says, grinning again, "nothing's perfect."

"Anyway, I've got some warm-up questions. You ready for that?" When he doesn't answer immediately she says, "Tell me about your family. You've got children?" She poises her pencil over the notebook.

He hesitates, moving his eyes away from her face to the wall behind and above her head.

"Oh! I'm sorry. Did I ask—"

"It's all right. We have one child. Had one, rather. Sarah. She was killed in a car accident two years ago."

"I'm so sorry!" her voice is soft now. "I should have known."

"No, you shouldn't. We asked that it not be part of the information about us. We didn't want people's first reaction to us to be feeling sorry for us. Of course there are people here who know. News travels. But there are still lots who don't, at least not yet."

Karen puts her pencil down.

Naturally, Fred doesn't mention that he and Gail have been trying to have another child. That's much too private—though it would be a whole lot easier to tell this kid than anyone else who's been in his office this morning, and he likes her so much already. "Sarah'd be a ninth grader," he says instead.

"Here?"

"Yes. Definitely. Right here!"

"Maybe that's the answer to that other question," she says quietly. "Why a male head for a girls' school? That you chose a school where your daughter would have thrived." And, after a pause in which that comment registers on him, she adds: "I understand. It sort of makes up for her loss, doesn't it?—being with so many other girls the same age she would be."

He still doesn't answer.

"So now I know what to say in the article."

"Please don't."

"Still too early?"

"Still too early."

"But it would help."

"Not the way I want help."

"Maybe you should take it any way you can get it," she says.

"I'm not in that tough a spot."

She looks intently at his face and doesn't answer.

"Evidently you don't agree," he says.

"You're right. I don't. The students loved Marjorie. The only way they're going to know how to be loyal to her is not to like you. So she screwed up the money part. Who wants an accountant for a headmistress?"

"Yeah," Fred says. "Who does?"

Karen's face brightens now. "Time to change the subject," she announces. "Something light. Like why you wear such funny clothes."

Fred laughs. "You're kidding."

"Actually, now that I think about it, I'm serious," Karen says. "It's an important question."

"Not something light after all?"

Karen makes a quick dismissive gesture with her hand. "Whatever."

"What's wrong with my clothes?"

"Your pants are shiny. And those shoes are weird."

"I'm just a farm boy, you know," he says, struggling not to appear taken aback. "Shiny pants are de rigueur on the farm."

"Yeah, but this is a prep school, not a farm. You'll get crucified!"

"I thought at Miss Oliver's we didn't place value on such things—how people dress. I thought we rose above that kind of judgment."

"We do for women. This is a *girls'* school, remember? Men we judge very harshly around here. My father says that Miss Oliver's is the most sexist environment he knows of."

"I hope not."

"Actually, I hope so. It's about time we had some sexism in the *other* direction."

"We are going to have to argue about that, you and I."

"Of course. I'd be disappointed if we didn't. You *are* the headmaster."

"Head of School."

"No way. Marjorie Boyd was the headmistress, so you are the headmaster. You think you're going to hide your gender behind a PC name? Nobody's ever been able to hide anything at this school."

"All right," he says. "Headmaster."

"You really mean that?"

"Probably not. I dislike the term. But I like your point."

Karen bends over her notebook; he sees her mouth the words *head of school* as she writes. Then with that quick motion, she lifts her eyes and smiles. "So back to your clothes. Tell me. I'll write it down and win the Pulitzer."

"Cotton farming wrecks the land," he explains. "Sheep farming's not much better."

"But—"

"Everybody always says *but*. I'm getting a little tired of the word."

"Hey! All *right!*" She takes another note.

"After all, we have very advanced technology and a sophisticated financial system to support it. Why not use that to make more and more unnatural"—he makes quotation marks with his fingers—"things so we can let nature alone? That's why I wear polyester."

"That's why? That's really why?"

"Either that or bad taste," he says. "Probably both."

"Well," Karen murmurs, "that's different. Really different. Now we're getting somewhere!"

"Good!" says Fred. "Glad I'm not wasting your time."

"OK," she says, ignoring his little joke. "So much for that. On to other topics. What happened at Mt. Gilead School?"

"It closed down."

"When you were head?"

"Yes."

"It's another thing people are chalking up against you."

"Well, I was assistant head for six years there, and I fell in love with the place," he tells her, very aware that Karen is writing now. "The head was a wonderful educator and I loved him, but he didn't pay attention to certain things."

"Like Marjorie?"

"Three things: marketing, finance, and asking people who were mediocre to go away."

"*Teachers?*"

"Yes, teachers."

"Oh, my God!"

"So, when things looked desperate, the board asked *him* to go and asked me to take over and see if I could turn things around."

"What happened?"

"I got started too late. That's my answer, anyway. I suppose some could say I screwed up, as you would put it."

"That's what a lot of people around here are saying."

"There a little bit of truth in that. I've learned some things. But mostly, and the board of Mt. Gilead believes this too, I got started too late. Things had already deteriorated so much that there was just too much hill to climb."

"Hill to climb," Karen repeats, writing fast. "I hope it sells. Now, one other question. Do you believe in censoring?"

"Censoring?"

"Marjorie didn't. She refused."

"You talking the *New York Times* or the *Clarion?*"

"I'm not dumb enough to talk about either of them separately. If I did, I would lose my argument."

"Which is? As if I didn't know."

Karen moves her head, up and down, slowly, several times. "Of course you know. Last year we had a full edition—all four pages—about drugs on campus, and before that we did a poll of the students to find out how many of their parents were alcoholics. Marjorie let us print them."

"I know. I read them all. They were very good articles."

"So you *don't* believe in censoring?"

"It all depends," he says.

"So? What if I wanted to do a poll on our students' sex lives and write it up?"

"Well, your job is to make the *Clarion* as interesting as you can," Fred says. "And I'm sure that would be interesting."

"Yeah. So I'm still waiting for the punch line."

"And mine is to make sure that the public trusts this school enough to send their daughters to us."

"And to give us money," she adds. "So who wins, as if I didn't know?"

"When, in my judgment, the two interests collide, I do, but in most cases I'm sure we could work it out."

"Work it out? Working it out's not the point, and you know it. The point's the principle."

"That's right," he says. "You're absolutely right. It's the principle."

"Well, this isn't going to help you at all," she says. "Not with the students, anyway. This is another issue everybody's talking about. We all know it's one of the reasons Marjorie got blown away. The *Clarion's* going to go right on trying to put the truth out, whatever it is."

"Good for you. I think you should."

"Yeah, good for me. But it's going to make your life all the harder. And that's too bad." While he thinks about how to respond to that remark, she surprises him by suddenly standing up. "Anyway, I've got to run," she announces. "Those teachers out there are going to go ballistic." Her eyes focus on his face even more intently. "I've enjoyed this," she says. "I'm surprised. I was prepared to think you were a jerk."

"Really? Then why is it that I liked you the minute you walked in the door?"

"And it took me until—?" Her thin shoulders go up and down. "Until whatever."

"That's right. Until whatever."

"Because you're a professional. You're a *teacher*. And I go to school here. My father says the same thing. He's a rabbi. He says he automatically starts to love anybody who joins his temple—the minute they join. He says if he couldn't do that, he couldn't be a rabbi."

"I'd like to meet your dad someday."

"You will," she promises. "You guys would like each other. But not till graduation, OK? This is my turf, not his." Then she's out the door.

"WE'VE BEEN WAITING for hours!" Melissa Andersen, the French teacher, complains, plopping her tall, thin body down in the chair Karen Benjamin has just been sitting in. Melissa's face is pale, drawn, and there are strands of gray in her blond hair. Fredericka Walters, her hair as red as Fred's, stands behind Melissa's chair. She's a tall, bulky woman wearing dark glasses, which obscure a lot of her face. Neither Melissa nor Fredericka make any gesture to shake Fred's hand.

"Take it easy, Hon," Sam Andersen murmurs. He's a burly man in his early thirties, with huge arms, bald already. He wears a red T-shirt and khaki pants. Then, turning to Fred, he puts his hand out. "Welcome to our little world," he says. "How's it goin'?"

"Fine. Thanks."

Sam and Fredericka sit down on either side of Melissa, while Fred pulls his desk chair out from behind his desk so he can sit with them.

"We've come to find our what your agenda is," Melissa says.

"Hey, Hon, slow down," Sam says.

"Well?" Melissa asks.

"My agenda?" says Fred. "Maybe you could clarify—"

"Melissa believes in conspiracies," Sam says. "The Gulf War was started by Chevron. Seventeen reincarnated members of the gestapo killed Kennedy." He's leaning back in his chair, grinning.

Melissa turns on her husband. "If you can't take this seriously, why don't you go home?"

Sam looks directly at Fred, arching his eyebrows so that the skin of his bald pate moves up and down. "We take things very seriously around here," he says. "Everybody knows this is the center of the universe."

Melissa's still staring at Sam. "I already asked once: if everything's such a big joke, why are you here with us?"

"To find out if he plays tennis. Isn't that why *you* came? It's summer vacation, Hon, for crying out loud!" Then turning to Fred: "I hope you do!"

"I do," Fred murmurs. "I love to play tennis."

"That's a relief! I'm tired of playing with all these *females!* I need some competition." Sam's grin is bigger than ever. Fredericka takes off her dark glasses and glowers at him.

Melissa ignores her husband's remark. She's staring straight at Fred, leaning slightly forward, her body very tense. "Are you going to let boys in here?" she asks.

Fred feels his face flush.

"Whoops, that's a biggie!" says Sam. Fredericka puts her dark glasses on again.

"Because it's better to let the school die than to have it be what it isn't," Melissa adds.

Fred still doesn't answer.

"Well, are you or aren't you?" Melissa insists.

"I didn't come here to do that," Fred says.

Nobody responds. All three, even Sam, are staring at Fred.

"It's not my plan," Fred offers.

"You haven't answered the question," Melissa says.

"You know how to make God laugh?" Sam asks. "Tell Him your plans." When nobody even smiles, he shrugs his shoulders.

"I fervently believe in single-sex education for girls," Fred says.

"That's not my question," Melissa says.

"I think I've probably done as much research as anybody," Fred persists, "more than anybody I know, as a matter of fact. I've read everything there is to read on the subject." Melissa starts to say something, but he puts his hand up. "How teachers call on boys more, how boys get in trouble more, disrupt more, disagree more so they get the attention. How most schools support the stereotype that girls can't do math or science and always try to think the way the teacher thinks. How in English curricula most of the authors are men and how history departments obsess on kings and generals. I could go on and on. Because I've worked in coed schools, you know, all my life."

"That's *exactly* my point," Melissa says.

"Well, it's not mine," he says, feeling the anger coming. *"I'm* the one who's seen how people show up to watch the boys play football and stay away in droves when the girls play softball, and I've watched the girls grow up much faster than the boys." Fred stops suddenly, sensing he's talking too much. For an instant he sees the image of his daughter in his head, and feels the old despair.

Sam turns to Melissa. "Honey, isn't that enough?" he asks.

"No, it isn't enough," Melissa says, and Sam turns his face away from her. He raises his eyebrows again to Fred.

"No, it isn't," Melissa repeats. "He's said what he believes in, not what he's going to *do."*

"Not fair," Sam murmurs.

"Why isn't it fair?" Melissa persists. "It's the question everybody is asking. It's the ultimate question: What will the new headmaster do if he thinks the only way to save the school is to let boys in? Why isn't that a fair question—since it's the one that everyone wants to know the answer to?"

"And you? What would you do if you thought the only way to keep the school from closing down was to make it into a coed school?" Fred asks her.

"I'd never think that," Melissa says. "I'd refuse to think that."

"Hon, now *you're* ducking the question," Sam says softly.

"I'm telling you, I'd never think that! How could anyone who's been here more than twenty minutes?" Melissa's close to yelling now. "The only point, the *whole* point, the only reason for Miss Olivers', is that it is for *girls*. That's what the school *is!*"

"Let me tell *you* something," Fred blurts. "The one thing I'm *not* going to do is let this school be closed down!" He's leaning way forward. He can feel the veins throbbing in his neck.

There's a silence. Sam and Melissa glance at each other; Fred's sure he catches a told-you-so look on Melissa's face. Fredericka leans forward, her face still inscrutable behind her dark glasses. "Well," says Melissa, standing up. "I've finally got my answer!" She moves toward the door. Sam stands but stays near his chair, and Fredericka's, motionless.

Near the door, Melissa turns and stares at Fred. "Don't you dare!" she says. "Don't you fucking *dare* let boys in here." Then she opens the door and disappears, and Fred can hear her footsteps, almost running, as she crosses Ms. Rice's room to leave the building.

"Like I said, welcome to our little world," Sam says after a long pause. "Hang in there. I'll call you Sunday to see about tennis."

"Thanks," says Fred.

"Coming, Fredericka?" asks Sam.

"No," Fredericka replies, taking off her dark glasses. "I have one more question to ask."

Fred already knows what that question is.

"Hello," Fred says to Fredericka after Sam has left. As always, his anger disappears as fast as it arrived. "You didn't say a word."

"It wasn't necessary," Fredericka says. "It never is when Melissa's part of the conversation."

Fredericka is fidgety, clearly nervous, so he gets right to the point. "I think I know what's on your mind," he tells her.

"I'm sure you do."

"I really was going to address it, you know. I wasn't going to keep you on the hook. It just seemed a bit abrupt on my first day."

She looks as if she might start to cry.

"I thought we should get to know each other a little first."

She shakes her head.

"And I wanted to see if we could find something else for you to do."

"Something else! Do you know how humiliating that would be?"

"Not necessarily," he urges.

"I'm a *German* teacher! Twenty-seven years I've been here."

"Yes. And a good one, too. I know your reputation," he says. For all she has after all these years is that good reputation. She certainly didn't get rich.

"Marjorie promised me that I could stay until I retired. That's what she told me when everybody started taking Spanish instead of German. She *promised.*"

"We have a huge deficit—"

"That's not my fault."

"No. It's not your fault," he says. Not mine either, he thinks. Out loud, he says, speaking as gently as he knows how: "There are only nineteen students in the whole German program—all four levels—for a full-time teacher with one of the biggest salaries, and a huge deficit. We have to make some changes. Maybe you can be a dorm parent."

"I did that when I started! I'm not going to do that. I'm sixty years old."

"All right," he says, nodding his head, and the room goes quiet while she looks at him, waiting for him to say something more. But he knows if he does, this will go on and on and make it worse for her. So he steels himself and says nothing, and then she starts to cry.

"I'm sorry," he murmurs. She has her head bent down and waves her hand in front, as if to establish privacy. "I wish there were—"

"How old are you?" she interrupts, abruptly looking up at him.

The question catches him by surprise. "I'm thirty-seven," he answers. "Why?"

"You were ten years old when I started here!" she tells him. "A little boy! How do you think that makes me feel?" Then she turns her face away from him.

"Look," he says, standing up. "You need a chance to be alone. I won't need my office for a while." He stands up. "You stay as long as you need."

She waves her hand again and turns her shoulders so that her face is turned even further away, so that she would be facing completely away from him if the chair back would allow. Her shoulders are shaking very hard. He leaves her, closing the door of his office behind himself as quietly as he can.

HE USES THE TIME away from his office to consult with Nan White, director of Admissions. He's sure there must be some way to recruit more students over the summer.

Nan greets him warmly. They sit across from each other at a small table in the center of her office. She's a small woman, the single mother of three

Oliver alumnae, in her late forties, brown hair gone slightly gray. He thinks of her as calm, solid, honest. He has trusted her since their first interviews.

"Maybe we can get four or five new students before the end of summer," Nan tells him.

"Four or five's nowhere near enough," he says.

"The ones we get in the summer are the ones we tend to have to let go," she says.

"I know. It was the same at Mt. Gilead."

"Of course you know! You really are a risk taker, aren't you?" she says, thinking: First he took on Mt. Gilead. Now here too.

"That's what my wife says."

"Well, I'm glad," she says.

"Thanks."

"But." She hesitates. "These numbers aren't very accurate."

"Not accurate? Don't tell me they're worse! We're already nineteen fewer that I was told we'd be"

"They're worse, all right," she says. "Much worse."

"Jesus! Sorry."

Nan smiles. "You should hear some of the language *I* use when I look at these numbers."

"How much worse?"

"Maybe twice as many fewer than predicted. These are Marjorie's numbers, not mine."

"Vincent's," he corrects.

"*Marjorie* was the head," she replies softly.

He doesn't respond to that.

"The truth is we'll be anywhere from thirty to forty kids down when we open in September. Guaranteed."

"Forty!"

"Fred," she says, "some of the board blames this on me. They think I must not be working hard enough. If having me around gives you a problem—"

"No way. "Let's just figure out—"

"I don't have the slightest suspicion that it's my fault," she says. "That's not the point. The point is that if the board doesn't trust me, and you don't make me go away, they stop trusting you."

"I'm not about to start firing the *good* people," he says. "Let's just look together at your whole plan, all the ideas, where we can recruit, what alumnae are helping us, let's do that, and maybe we can come up with some ideas."

"God, I'd love to! When?"

"Right now."

"Wonderful! Somebody else besides me looking at this stuff."

"BOSTON, NEW YORK, PHILADELPHIA, the D.C. area, Baltimore," Nan says, taking several folders out of a file. Neither of them is aware they've skipped lunch. "That's one sector. In both New York and Baltimore I have families lined up who have promised to host receptions for potential students."

"Great!" says Fred. "So you and I go down there, we get a few current students and their parents to attend, and we talk about the school."

"Exactly. I've got some dates ready."

"What about the other cities—Boston, Philly, and D.C.?"

"I had offers in each, but they reneged. Maybe if—"

"When?" he interrupts.

Nan hesitates.

"When they learned the new head wasn't a woman?"

"I'm afraid so," Nan murmurs, and he likes her even more for not letting her eyes slide away. "But," she adds, brightening, "maybe they just need some time to adjust. If you call them, I bet they'll change their mind."

"I'll call them. You bet I will!"

"And in the southern sector, we have Richmond, Charleston, Atlanta, Fort Lauderdale. In the midwestern we have Cleveland. We've already got one family there, the Maynards, who've agreed to host a gathering, and then we have Chicago and Detroit. In the West we have Denver and San Francisco."

"San Francisco!" Fred interrupts. "Francis Plummer's out that way for the summer. Maybe he could join us—or maybe even save us the travel expense by speaking for us."

"I think not."

"Why not? Surely he'd be a draw for the alumnae."

"I just don't think we should," Nan says firmly.

"He's one of the ones who haven't adjusted yet?" he asks, remembering Plummer's little joke about not changing anything. He'd sensed the senior teacher's discomfort when they had interviewed each other during the search process and had received some subtle warnings from others about his resentment over Marjorie's dismissal. But he'd assumed that so intelligent a man, so celebrated a teacher, would have placed no blame for this on her successor.

"One of the ones," Nan answers.

"All right. I understand. When he gets back, though, and we get going in the new academic year—"

"I hope so," Nan says. "It's harder for some than for others."

They spend the rest of the day working on the plan and thinking of everything else they can do to improve the enrollment before school starts again in September. When they're through, they figure that if everything goes right, they can pick up ten or eleven new students instead of the five Nan has predicted. "That's all there is, there ain't no more," he announces. "But it's better than nothing."

"That's right," Nan agrees. "Better than nothing."

WHEN FRED GETS BACK to his office at five minutes to six, Ms. Rice is gone. Five minutes later, right at six o'clock as planned, Alan Travelers, the board chair, shows up. He's in his fifties, slightly taller than Fred, spare in body, pale skinned, with short gray hair. He wears a dark business suit that even now, at the end of the day, is as unwrinkled as if he'd just put it on.

He won't let Fred begin until he's had his say. "Fred, I was about to call you this morning until my secretary told me we were going to meet instead. Just to welcome you. On your first day. No agenda. Just to say once again that I am delighted that you are our new head. Well, this is much better, face-to-face."

"Alan, thanks," Fred responds. He already feels better.

"You're the kind of guy that will give it all he's got. That's why we're so delighted."

"Thanks. You can count on that." Fred points to the chair where Karen Benjamin sat this morning—it seems like days ago!—and takes the chair facing Alan.

"By the way, Fred, Mavis Ericksen dropped in today," Alan begins.

"She did?"

"She's really concerned about that Saffire woman, you know."

"I know. She dropped in to my office too."

"I know she did. What did you tell her?"

"I told her I'd look into it."

Alan nods his head.

"This is my call, Alan."

"I know it is. I just wanted you to know there's a lot of heat involved in this one."

"There's a lot more in what I'm about to tell you," Fred says. Then he gives Alan the news.

After Fred finishes, Alan sits very still, his face even paler. "Six hundred and seventy-five?" he asks at last. "You absolutely sure?"

"Positive." Fred starts to hand Travelers the papers: Vincent's numbers, and his own.

Travelers puts his hands up, shakes his head. He doesn't need to *read* them. "How in the world could we have fouled up so badly?" he murmurs. He's not asking Fred; he's looking at the ceiling.

"He was the business manager," Fred offers, but Travelers shakes his head, refusing the excuse. Now Fred likes him even more. "I believed him too," Fred goes on.

"Of course you did! Why wouldn't you? You weren't even *here* yet," Travelers exclaims. Then after a pause he adds, "The deal's off if you want it to be."

"I don't understand," Fred says. He sees Travelers looking hard at him, searching his face, and then it dawns on him what his board chair is getting at.

"You signed a contract thinking the situation was very different from what it is," Travelers says mildly. "I'm not dishonorable enough to hold you to it."

"But I want this!" Fred blurts.

"Think about it," Travelers insists. "You owe it to yourself. You can tell me in the morning," and Fred is taken by surprise. Out of nowhere comes this turning point! Now he's suddenly imagining himself backing out the door of this office, Travelers's eyes still on him. He can feel the relief; he's floating, breathing easy in an enormous space. But the feeling only lasts an instant, and then he is overwhelmed by huge regret at throwing away his treasure. He imagines begging to be allowed to change his mind and come back.

"I'm here," he says. "No way I'm going away."

"I thought that's what you'd say," Travelers says. He's smiling now.

"If there comes a reason I should quit, I'll recognize it," Fred says.

But Travelers pays no attention to that remark. Instead he's making plans. "OK, here's what we're going to do," he announces. "Executive committee meeting tomorrow. Noon sharp. We'll hold it at Milton Perkins's club, as usual, and he can buy us lunch, as usual. I'll call each of them tonight and tell them to be there, no matter what."

"You going to tell them what it's about?" Fred asks.

"Nope. Why ruin their sleep? They'll find out when you tell them, and we'll go from there."

"Yeah," says Fred, managing a grin, "why ruin their sleep."

Travelers is standing now, shaking Fred's hand. "We'll be all right," he says. "We've got the right guy at the helm." Then he's out the door.

BY THE TIME Fred arrives at the head's house he realizes he's had a booming headache for hours. He goes through the house to the back, where he knows that Gail will be gardening in the evening's softening light.

"Hi," she says, getting up from her kneeling to greet him. She takes her gardening gloves off and reaches a hand to him.

He kisses her cheek.

"How was your day?" she says.

"Don't ask," he says.

THREE

WHEN FRANCIS CALLS Peggy from just east of the Mississippi River the day after Fred Kindler's first day in office, she doesn't even ask where he is.

He's called to tell her how excited he is to be at the huge river, how much he wishes she were with him so they could see it together, but she starts right off before Francis hardly says a word. "He's already here!" she exclaims. "He showed up *yesterday*. What do you think about that?"

"Who?" Francis asks. "Who's already there?"—as if he didn't know.

Peggy leaves a freighted silence. Then, wearily: "Come on, Francis. You know who," and now Francis wishes he had traveled faster instead of spending four whole days at his college reunion in Ohio, and two more at a friend's house in Indiana, and then a whole week in Chicago easing his conscience at a math teachers' conference. It doesn't occur to him that maybe he's been keeping himself on a short leash by stopping so often so he could turn around and go back to the school before it's too late. Nor does it occur to him that the reason for his taking his school clothes with him, his blue button-down shirt, striped tie, sports coat, and slacks, isn't just the college reunion or the dinner at the end of the math conference; it's that these are his uniform, his identity. Instead, he thinks that if he had escaped across the big divide of the Mississippi right away, he'd now be much further into the West and he wouldn't care *where* Fred Kindler was. He'd have room to breathe.

"Marjorie left early," he hears Peggy say. "She cleared out."

"Oh," he says. "So soon?" Then he realizes he's not surprised. That's exactly what Marjorie would do.

But Peggy's not talking about Marjorie now; she's talking about the new guy. "Two whole weeks before he even needed to be here!" Peggy says. He knows what she leaves unsaid for him to think about: the new headmaster shows up early for his responsibilities—while *you* run away from yours. But that's not what he's thinking about. What fills his brain instead is the picture of Fred Kindler actually ensconced in Marjorie's office, enthroned behind her desk, surrounded by the pictures her students made for her. The wrongness of the fit, its *impropriety,* astounds him. It's Marjorie's office!

"Well, what *do* you think of that?" Peggy asks again.

"Maybe he can't read a calendar," he says.

"Very funny, Francis."

"I didn't call you up to talk about *him!*"

"Oh, you didn't?" Peggy mocks. "All right, then. So forget about it."

He lets a long silence go by, desperate for a way to rescue them from this. "Peg," he finally begs, "let's not fight."

That's right, she thinks, let's not.

"How are you, Peg?"

I'm confused, she wants to say, and I'm scared we've lost each other, but she's too angry to plead for sympathy. "I'm OK," she tells him.

"Only OK, Peg?"

She shrugs her shoulders as if he were there to see. There's a long silence, while he waits for her to speak. "Where are you?" she finally asks.

"Just east of the Mississippi."

"That's nice," she says, and fails to keep the sarcasm out of her voice. But she really does think it's nice that he's seeing the country and wishes she were seeing it with him. And then it dawns on her that neither of them ever considered her joining him. The reasons for his trip were too foreign to her for that.

"All right, Peg," he sighs, hearing only the sarcasm. "I'll call you later."

"All right."

"I miss you, Peg."

"I miss you too," she admits, "but if you were here we wouldn't have to miss each other."

Neither of them can think of what else to say. Francis hangs up first, and walks back to his old yellow Chevy and starts to drive again. In Denver, he will pick up Lila Smythe, next year's president of the Student Council, and give her a ride the rest of the way to California. Lila, one of Francis's and Peggy's favorite students, lives in the dorm they parent, and though Francis was delighted when she decided to join the dig, he now regrets his promise. She'll want to talk to him, as faculty advisor to the Student Council, about the Council's agenda for the coming year. He's much too preoccupied for that.

And Peggy lingers by the phone, willing Francis to call again. She'd speak more gently this time, she tells herself. But he doesn't call, and now she knows he's on the other side of the Mississippi, much farther away from her than he's ever been. She's never been in that part of the country and can only see it in her imagination as endless, empty space. And her husband's lost in it.

PEGGY LOOKS AT her watch. It's ten-thirty in the morning, and she has a meeting with Fred Kindler at quarter to eleven. She wants to get there a little early because he's told her that he has to leave at eleven-fifteen for a meeting downtown at noon. She's a little worried about how he'll react when, on only his second day in office, she tells him about a problem that's going to make the budget crisis even worse. So she leaves the phone, steps out of her house and across the thick green lawns of the campus toward the administration building. In the little distance, at the campus edge, she sees her own river gleaming in the sun.

The first thing she notices about Fred Kindler's office is the big clock on the wall behind his desk. It's an imitation of a Mickey Mouse wrist-watch, complete with huge leather wrist straps that reach from ceiling to floor. It wasn't there yesterday when she glanced through the door. She smiles, gets his message right away, wonders if Eudora Easter had a hand in this. Maybe people will start getting places on time now.

He smiles too, an easy greeting, and steps from behind his desk with that ducklike, toes-out gait she knows she would never have noticed if Francis hadn't pointed it out to her. When Kindler puts out his hand to shake hers, she realizes again how formal and old-fashioned he seems. They sit down in front of his desk, facing each other.

"How's Francis's trip going?" Fred asks her.

"He'll be in California by the end of the week."

"I hope he's having a great time."

"I hope so too," she says before she has time to think what this remark might reveal. She sees him look away from her for just an instant and knows that he's not hiding his surprise—there's no dissimulation in that not very handsome face—but being kind. Whatever else he is, he is a good person, she decides. One of the things she's proud of is her ability to size people up.

Fred isn't sure whether it is surprise flashing across her face as Peggy's eyes meet his and stay longer than most people's—maybe that's why he already likes her so much—or whether she is about to ask him a question. If so, he knows what the question will be: Are you considering allowing boys into this school? He wishes she would ask it. He guesses she's the kind of person you can think aloud in front of.

But of course she won't ask. Not yet. She's too kind to ask so early. That she's just admitted a hint of trouble between herself and Francis gives him a rush of sadness for her—and anxiety for himself. I need your husband too, he wants to say. He's the senior teacher. The most gifted on the faculty. Teaches both math *and* English beautifully. That makes him powerful. If he's against me, I'm dead.

"We need more air-conditioning in the Pequot Indian area," he hears Peggy say. "We had a consultant tell us that the displays would deteriorate."

"How much?"

"It's a lot. The estimate's for fifteen thousand." If he says yes, then she knows he understands how important the display is; it will mean he "gets" Miss Oliver's School for Girls—and Francis will be wrong.

"Fifteen thousand!" Fred exclaims; then to himself: What the heck. What's another fifteen thousand to a deficit like ours?

"I know it's not in the budget," Peggy says. "It's a lot to ask."

He makes a little motion with his hand in front of his face as if to brush her comment away. "When we get the budget to where it should be, you won't have to ask."

"Won't have to ask?"

"Department heads'll have their own budgets. They'll have discretion," he explains, discovering how easy it is for him to share his ideas with her. He wishes he could tell her about the emergency meeting with the board's executive committee that starts in just over an hour, where he's going to drop the bomb about the budget. He'd get her advice.

"Really? Discretion?" Peggy is surprised. "We always went to Marjorie for—"

"Well, anyway," he interrupts, "you've got it. Fifteen thousand."

"Really?" she says. "Wonderful!" He sees relief flooding her face, feels her eyes on his. Then a worried frown. "Where will we get the money?" she asks.

"I have no idea, but I do know what's indispensable and what is not."

Peggy sits very still, taking his comment in. See, Francis, you're wrong, she thinks—while it dawns on her how different this is from her meetings with Marjorie, how tired she was of sitting side by side with her head-mistress on a sofa having her arm patted every time Marjorie made a point. For that's how it always went: Marjorie making the point, not the other way around—and now she realizes she has something else to say, she's going to make a point—because she knows *he'll* listen. "Just one more thing," she says. "I know you're busy."

"I've got time."

"Don't you bring it up," Peggy tells him. "You'll get crucified if you do. Let the board do it."

"*It?*" he says. "You're being mysterious."

"No, I'm not. You know what I'm talking about. If we have to let boys in here, let it be the board's decision. Fight it. Even if you think it's right. Fight it anyway. For a while at least. Otherwise—"

"I've thought about that," he says, hearing again Melissa Anderson's *Don't you fucking dare*. "Still, it doesn't quite feel right."

"Of course it doesn't. Do it anyway!"

"You're a smart lady," he says. "I'll think about it."

"Good," she replies, standing up. He rises too and reaches to shake her hand. "I'm glad you're here," she says, realizing she's just done what Francis should be here to do: give advice. Show where the land mines are.

"Thanks," he says, tempted now to put his other hand out too, take her hands in both of his. But that's too forward; he hardly knows her.

RIGHT AFTER PEGGY leaves, Fred makes the call to Mavis Ericksen that he's been dreading.

"Hello, this is Mavis." Her voice is cheerful.

"Good morning, Mavis, this is Fred Kindler."

Silence.

"How are you this morning?" he tries.

She still doesn't answer. It comes to him that maybe she thinks his question is sarcastic, as if to say, Are you still crying? "I called to follow through on our conversation about Miss Saffire," he says.

"I've been waiting," she says, making it clear she doesn't like to wait.

Yes, for only twenty-four hours, Fred thinks. "Earlier this morning I talked to Dorothy Strang—"

"I don't care what Dorothy—"

"Miss Saffire *reports* to Dorothy Strang," he says. "Dorothy evaluated Miss Saffire last November near the end of her first year as having done quite well," he tells her. "Like everyone else, she's been given some goals and will be evaluated again this November." He doesn't tell her that one of the goals assigned to Joan Saffire was learning how to handle certain kinds of people, and that when he asked Dorothy, "What kind of people?" she whispered, "Assholes," and then got red in the face and started to giggle. And then admitted that she shouldn't have sent a beginner to see Aldous Enright. She would have gone herself, but she was on vacation.

"November!" Mavis's voice is quivering. "It's only July!"

"Yes. November. It's an annual evaluation."

There's another silence. Fred feels sweat running down the inside of his shirt. "You and I need to talk," he says. Maybe if he takes her to lunch and they get to know each other, she will understand why it's important that the board not intrude on the head's domain. "Let's make an appointment," he begins. Then he hears her hanging up.

How much safer he would be if Joan Saffire were incompetent and he *could* fire her, he thinks—and immediately regrets the thought.

AN HOUR AND a half later in a private dining room of the River Club in downtown Hartford, Alan Travelers gets right to the point. "Our new head-master's had a very busy first day," he tells the executive committee. "Among other accomplishments, he discovered that we have a larger deficit than we thought we did." Impeccable in his blue suit, Travelers is standing at the head of the table. His tone sounds surprisingly cheerful to Fred.

"Yeah?" Milton Perkins growls. "So what else is new?"

"You're about to learn," Travelers says. "I think it'll get your attention." He sits down.

"Oh?" Perkins says. "How much?"

"Six hundred and seventy-five thousand," Travelers answers.

Perkins sits back in his chair as if he'd been shoved in the chest. He stares at Travelers. Then he turns to Fred. "Tell me I didn't hear that right," he says.

"You heard it right," Fred says, and from their frames along the oak-paneled wall opposite the tall windows overlooking the river, an array of nineteenth-century patriarchs, masters of New England thrift, look sternly down at the room.

Now Fred hands round the papers he has prepared and proceeds to explain the difference between Carl Vincent's figures and his own, going slowly, line by line. While he talks, no one touches the raw oysters that Perkins, who has lived at the River Club ever since his wife died five years earlier, has ordered for the lunch, and when he finishes, the members continue to stare down at their papers. They can't bring themselves to look at each other. Perkins gets up from the table, goes to one of the windows, and stares at the river, his back to everybody.

"So much for the bad news," Travelers says dismissively, breaking the silence. He knows he needs to get these people past their disappointment, and worse, their humiliation, at having been so gulled by Vincent's num-bers. "There's good news too. We've got a head who before he does anything else—on his very first day!—gets us to the truth. That's huge."

"Yes," says beautiful alumna Sonja McGarvey. "Finally some reality around here!" She turns to Fred, sends him a grateful—maybe even an admiring—look. Only ten years out, Sonja's already rich. Marjorie has often pointed to her derring-do, entrepreneuring in software, as proof of the empowering effect of single-sex education on women, and Fred is already planning to ask her for the lead gift from the board this year.

"Exactly!" Travelers says. He has to admit: he likes this challenge, since it gives him something to sink his teeth into, puts some spice in his life. He's won battles like this before. "We'll just go faster," he urges. "We'll just rebuild the enrollment in two years instead of four. We've got the right head finally. We'll just do it!"

But now Sonja is shaking her head in disagreement. She has black hair, blue eyes, pale skin, and her lipstick's very red. She's leaning forward across the table toward Travelers, pent up, waiting to speak.

"Because that's exactly what we're going to do!" Travelers goes on. "Revise the plan and move on."

"That's unrealistic," Sonja snaps. "It's a pipe dream."

All eyes come off Travelers and move to Sonja, then back to Travelers, who is obviously surprised. He's not used to being contradicted, especially by a woman who's not yet thirty. He starts to say something, but from the window, Perkins beats him to it.

"So it's unrealistic," Perkins says. His back is still to the group, and he's still staring out the window, as if he were addressing the river. "When you don't have a choice, who cares?"

"What's *he* been smoking?" Sonja asks the group. And when Perkins turns to face her, she asks him, "Can I have some too?"

Perkins leaves the window and taking his seat again, leans to Sonja across the polished mahogany. "You *could* be right," he growls. "Bean counters are every once in a century. But maybe you aren't. Maybe we'll pull something out of a hat." He's grinning now, egging her on.

"Oh, for Christ's sake, here we go again!" Sonja says.

"And if we don't," Perkins says, "the one thing we *aren't* going to do is let boys in here." He's not grinning anymore.

The room goes silent once again. Everyone stares at Perkins, who's plunging a fork into an oyster now.

"Fred didn't say anything about letting boys in," Travelers says. His voice is tight. "Neither did I. Neither did anyone. That's not even on the table."

"Good," Perkins says, waving the fork with the oyster still on it. "We got that settled."

"Jesus!" from Sonja. "Welcome to fantasyland!"

Now Perkins turns again to study her. He's miming mild scientific interest at the source of such a strange remark. He extends the fork, the oyster he was about to eat still dripping on its tines, across the table to her. He raises his eyebrows, keeps the oyster before her. It's a test: if she takes it, then she is normal after all.

Sonja, of course, is much too smart to rise to this. She hardly looks at the oyster—or at Perkins, turning instead to Travelers as if chastising the chairman for letting the meeting get out of hand. So Perkins shrugs, plops the oyster into his mouth, nods up and down, then breaks into a grin and aims it around the room.

On Sonja's right, the elderly Miss Richardson, who hasn't said a word, is too ladylike to acknowledge the animus that's just drenched the room. She nods her birdlike head at Milton Perkins. "For once you and I agree," she murmurs. Miss Richardson, the former academic dean at one of New England's most prestigious women's colleges, stares intently across the table at Perkins, her tiny body very erect. "It would be a tragedy," she says. "An abandonment of the reason we exist."

Milton Perkins is grinning again. "You and I agreeing, that's a sign things are *completely* out of control," he tells her. For Perkins even to appear to agree with the likes of Miss Richardson, a worshipful biographer of FDR, is more than he can stand.

"I'll say it again," Travelers says. "Nobody said anything about letting boys in."

"Not yet," Sonja says.

"My dear, you aren't suggesting—?" Miss Richardson's tremolo trails off, while Sonja puts her blue eyes on Miss Richardson's face and stares. Miss Richardson tries again: "We have a vision to uphold!"

"It's not a *vision*. It's a hallucination!" Sonja hisses. "We're supposed to know the difference." Miss Richardson's face goes pale, and Sonja, who is trying to learn diplomacy and regrets her harshness, softens her voice. "Miss Richardson, girls-only just doesn't sell anymore," she says.

"Sell! My dear, this isn't a store!"

So much for Sonja's mildness. She reaches across the table, taps her bright, red-nailed forefinger on Miss Richardson's copy of the papers Fred has distributed. "See where the number is below the bottom line on Carl Vincent's budget?" she asks.

Miss Richardson takes the bait. "Yes," she says. "I see."

"The one in *parentheses?*"

Miss Richardson doesn't answer.

"Now look at Fred's numbers; the figure in parentheses is *bigger.*"

"Sonja McGarvey," says Miss Richardson. "I can read."

"By almost three quarters of a million dollars."

"Six hundred and seventy-five," says Miss Richardson.

"I can read too," says Sonja. "I just like to round things off."

"Six hundred and seventy-five," Miss Richardson insists. "My dear, six hundred and seventy-five is not three quarters of a million; it is six hundred and seventy-five."

"People!" Travelers raps his knuckles on the table. He's clearly irritated. Sonja and Miss Richardson stop.

This is the opening Fred's been waiting for. "Even if it were three quarters of a million—a full million—it wouldn't make any difference to *me*," he tells them. "I came here to help turn this thing around in four years. So now that we've only got two, we'll do it in two." Everyone's eyes are on him as he speaks, for the hunger for leadership is palpable among this board which, until the unseating of Marjorie, was so dominated by her that they never developed the will, or the sophistication, to do their job. And he's doing what he came here to do—he's leading. He's giving them a solution to their problem in the cash flow projections he's put in front of them, which demonstrate that the addition of twenty-six girls, recruited during each of the next two academic years through aggressive marketing of the school's excellence and the efficacy of its single-sex mission, puts him on the same pace to a balanced budget as the original plan, which called for thirteen additional enrollments each year.

It's a good plan, he tells himself, his confidence blossoming, because it provides him a fighting chance to save the school as single-sex, while leaving the option of admitting boys as a last resort if it becomes apparent the enrollment targets aren't being reached. Because the one thing he *won't* do is close the school! Nor will he offer himself as sacrificial lamb by being the one to suggest bringing boys in. He remembers Peggy Plummer's advice.

"I've given you new numbers," he says aloud. "They're challenging, but if we get the message out, we can do it."

"Good for you!" Perkins exclaims. Then: "Whose numbers? Not *Vincent's* I hope."

"No," Fred answers. "They're mine."

"Fred tells me he's going to let Mr. Vincent go as soon as he comes back from vacation," Travelers says very quietly.

"Carl! Gone?" Miss Richardson asks, staring at Fred.

"Well, good for you," Sonja murmurs.

"Yeah," says Perkins. "Good for you. Poor old guy. Didn't know a number from a road sign."

"Well, anyway," says Travelers, "we're in trouble, and Fred's recommended a solution."

"We are not in so much trouble that we can let loyal longtime employees go just like that." Miss Richardson snaps her fingers.

"Jeez, he couldn't even *count!*" says Perkins. "As soon as he finishes getting Alzheimer's his IQ's going to double."

"That's enough, Milton!" Travelers says.

Miss Richardson is still staring at Fred. "You mean you're *firing* him?"

"Oh, *please!*" says Sonja.

"There's a principle here," Miss Richardson says. "Mr. Vincent has been allowed to perform for years in this way, and suddenly he's dismissed? We don't interact that way at Miss Oliver's. I'm surprised at you, Mr. Kindler."

"Alan, for God's sake, we have an *emergency!*" Sonja exclaims before Fred can respond. "Can we deal with it?"

"We've already dealt with it," Perkins barks. "We're going with Fred's new plan."

"And if that doesn't work? What then?" Sonja asks.

"We're going to close the school. That's what. Because if its not going to be a girls' school, the hell with it. You think I'd let myself be bored to death in board meetings for a school where boys get all the attention so they can run the world while girls stay home and cook? I've got three daughters, and I know what they learned here. You might as well think it's going to snow in Florida in the middle of summer to think that boys are ever going to come in here. So why talk about it?"

"We're going to talk about it," Sonja says. "I promise. Because the one thing I'm *not* going to let happen is closing the school. So if you people won't bring it up at the September board meeting, I will. I'll force the issue."

Once again the room goes silent while everyone stares at her. "Why in the world would you do that?" Travelers asks at last.

"To save the school, that's why."

"It's a terrible idea," Travelers says.

"It's being whispered everywhere," Sonja persists. Travelers leans toward her shaking his head, but Sonja holds her ground and tells him, "I'm going to put it to the board. Where it counts And get some clarity."

"You put letting boys into the school on the table like that, how're you going to keep it quiet?" Perkins asks. He shoves his plate of oysters aside. Cracked ice spills onto the table. "The board'll decide not to do it," he says. "They're not *that* crazy. But the story that'll come out in the first three seconds after the meeting anyhow is that right away we're going to admit seven hundred boys—all of them nine feet tall—and with extra big dicks. Fred here will have a crazy house on his hands."

The instant Perkins is finished with his harangue, Sonja turns back to the chairman. It is as if to her Perkins isn't even in the room. "Alan," she asks, "are you going to try to tell me I can't speak my mind at a board meeting?"

"No, Sonja, I'm not saying that. I don't have the right. But I wish you wouldn't."

"Good," says Sonja. "Because if you were, I'd do it anyway."

"So that's what firing Mrs. Boyd was *really* about!" Miss Richardson exclaims.

Now it's Miss Richardson's turn to be stared at.

"Where did *that* come from?" Travelers asks.

"You are very clever, Mr. Travelers," Miss Richardson says. "Far more clever than I. But even I can see how this meeting has been contrived." She turns her stare on Perkins. "First Milton Perkins opens the door for all the posturing by saying the one thing we aren't going to do is admit boys," then, turning to Sonja, "which of course gives Miss McGarvey the opportunity to propose that we should admit boys and that she will recommend admitting boys to the board of Miss Oliver's School for Girls. And *you,*" she says, aiming her glare at Travelers again, "pretend that you can't stop her."

"You're out of line, Miss Richardson," Travelers finally says. "You need to take that back."

But Miss Richardson actually believes she has discovered the truth and isn't about to take anything back. "All along I suspected," she says. "But I put my suspicions aside. I kept *my* faith." Her voice is a quaver, she's on the verge of weeping. "Now I see how naive I was. All along. A plot: prey on the school's misfortune, use it to pry Marjorie Boyd out of her office so we can bring in this *man* and open the doors to boys!"

"You couldn't be more wrong," Travelers says, clearly amazed.

"Oh, please, don't go on with this." Miss Richardson's tiny shoulders are shaking. "It's out now! In the open! Why else would you fire the finest educator this school has ever had? I could never answer that question. Why fire the person who has made the school what it is?"

"And *you!*" she turns on Fred when no one answers. "You have just confirmed my original suspicion, which I put aside because you seemed a gentleman and so sincere. Well, now I know. First, we get a male chairman of the board. Then a cabal under his direction gets rid of Mrs. Boyd to make room for you; then you, on your very first day, get rid of one of her most faithful colleagues, and then on the very *next* day it is proposed at the executive committee that the board of trustees contemplate the admission of boys. It's plain what's coming next. I won't be part of it. I'll resign."

"Miss Richardson, you've misinterpreted everything," Fred says softly. He's devoid of anger. Instead, he's fascinated. For an instant he thinks maybe he can unravel this for her.

"Oh? You deny it!" he hears her say, mocking surprise. "Then let me ask a question. Which one do *you* favor, Mr. Kindler?" She's not on the verge of weeping anymore. Her face has gone hard.

Fred sees the mine she's planting. Now he *is* irritated.

Travelers is standing up. "Harriet, stop!" For he sees what's coming—and he doesn't trust Fred to lie. "Just stop!"

But Miss Richardson calmly goes right on. "We did have two philosophies proposed this morning," she says, like a teacher reviewing the lesson for the dumbest student. "One that we should admit boys in order to keep the school in operation. The other that it would be better to close the school than to admit boys."

Fred's face flames, his chest constricts; he feels everyone watching, and for an instant he can hardly see.

"Don't be *angry*," Miss Richardson says. "Just answer the question."

"I'd close the school before I admitted boys," he says, lying deliberately and looking Miss Richardson right in the eye.

It's very quiet in the room while she returns his stare. Then she says, "You don't lie as skillfully as you need to yet, Mr. Kindler, but I'm sure your performance will improve with time."

Travelers cuts in. "Miss Richardson—"

But she isn't finished yet. She's still facing Fred, her back to Travelers. "The truth is, Mr. Kindler, even if you were an honorable person, you shouldn't be here."

"Harriet, you offered your resignation a minute ago," Travelers says.

"No I didn't. I only threatened."

"Yes, you did, and it's accepted." He looks at Sonja McGarvey and Milton Perkins.

"Yup," says Perkins. "I heard her resign."

"Me too," says Sonja. "Plain as day."

"It will be in the minutes," Travelers announces. "We'll take a short recess now. It will give you time to gather your things, Miss Richardson."

She stays in her chair. The frown on her pale face shows she's making a decision. Travelers has no legal right to remove her. She turns to Fred. "It was over for me as soon as Marjorie left," she says. "I could have saved you your little charade." She starts to collect her copy of the financial papers.

"Not those," says Travelers. He reaches to take them. "They're confidential. For board members only."

Harriet Richardson takes a sudden breath, stares at Travelers, and holds the papers in her tiny hand. Travelers wears a little smile, gives a tug;

Miss Richardson lets out her breath, and now Travelers holds the papers.

Miss Richardson sits very still for an instant. "You won't get away with this," she whispers, then gets up, walks across the room. The big oaken doors don't open for her, she's so little. Fred wonders if he should get up and open them. She pushes again, and the doors open just enough, and then she's gone.

DURING THE RECESS Perkins murmurs to Fred, "Just in case you're worried, I've told a few lies myself in my day. I'm kinda proud of them. They did more good than harm."

Then he hands Fred a note. It says, "Let's give old Vincent a little going-away present. I'll take care of it. Two years' salary. Anonymous. He obviously doesn't have any money."

After they reconvene, Travelers tries to persuade Sonja not to bring her proposal to the board. She refuses. "I have to do what I think right," she says. "Besides, the biggest problem isn't going to be the *board*. It's going to be the *faculty*. As soon as they find out the board's even toying with the idea of going coed, they'll be rabid. And the biggest problem on the faculty will be Francis Plummer. You think that little old lady who just resigned feels strongly?" she asks. "Wait'll you see how our senior teacher reacts to the idea!"

"Whaddya expect?" Perkins grumbles. "He's loyal."

"He's loyal to *Marjorie*," Sonja says. "You think he's going to be loyal to Fred here? And he's everybody's hero. The girls call him Clark Kent, you know—from before I was there. He's a loose canon with a great big bang, and he's cracking up."

"He might be," Travelers says. "Look at the way he took you on, Milton—right in the middle of the reception for Fred."

"So I told a story and he told a better one." Perkins says. "Who cares? We were both playing games."

"Completely out of control," Sonja says, and Fred remembers that Gregory van Buren, in one of his insistent appointments during the search process mentioned, sotto voce, that he thought people who are cracking up are the most difficult to control because you don't know what they are going to do next. He also remembers hearing that Francis had taken to referring to Sonja McGarvey as Sonja Testosterone. He laughed when he heard that. Now he has to be careful that the name won't slip off his own tongue.

Goodness knows, he is worried about Plummer. When he interviewed with him last January just before being appointed, he could tell how distraught the senior teacher was at Marjorie's dismissal. It was one of the many warning notes that would have told a more detached, analytical person how great a risk it was hitching his wagon to Miss Oliver's star. On Fred the warnings had the opposite effect; he was inspired by the challenge. And Karen Benjamin was right: Miss Oliver's was the school he would have loved his daughter to attend. Why wouldn't he want to rescue it? So he persuaded himself he could win Francis Plummer's loyalty. Surely a man so in love with his school as Plummer would control himself, tamp down his anger, and join the new head in keeping the school alive. Now he wonders if the man really is out of control, really cracking up? What better way to get back at a board member who helped get rid of the headmistress he loved than by taking him on in front of the faculty? Sometimes pretending to be out of control is a very good strategy. All he knows is that he needs Francis Plummer.

"You better reel him in, Fred," Travelers is saying. "Or else you'll have to get rid of him. I hate to say that. He's been a loyal teacher."

"There you go with *loyal* again!" Sonja turns to Travelers. "He's loyal to what *was*. We are responsible for the future. If it were me, I'd reel him right out the door."

"You guys sound like Congress," Perkins growls. "I could get sick." He turns to Fred: "So, you want to know all this crap about Plummer or not?"

"Let me handle him," Fred says. "That's my job."

"I hope that's possible," Sonja murmurs.

THAT NIGHT AFTER DINNER, Gail and Fred sit on the back porch, and Gail knows something bad happened at the meeting, something he doesn't want to talk about, or else he would surely have told her at dinner, but he was so distracted it was as if she were not even in the room with him, and she waited and waited for him to tell her what was bothering him. Whatever it is, it must be worse than the budget fiasco he told her about last night. "Don't ask," he said. Which of course meant exactly the opposite, and even before they'd gone inside, he told her that the underenrollment was exactly twice as large as he had thought and that he had only two years instead of four to save the school. So what's going on now, only a day later, that he's hiding from her?

"You're not telling me something," she says, sitting beside him in the twilight. "It's all over your face.

He prevaricates by telling her everything about the meeting, describing it blow by blow, except the part where Miss Richardson turned on him. He doesn't tell her that part. That's what's been bothering him. That's what he doesn't want to talk about.

She sees right through this. "Come on, tell me," she urges when he's finished. "What's really bothering you?" She knows the board bringing up the prospect of admitting boys, instead of him, isn't bad. It's good. It takes the heat off him, it's what he wants.

He gives in finally and tells her how Miss Richardson made him tell a lie. "How suddenly it all happened!" he exclaims. "First she's a kind, elderly woman, then she's Machiavelli."

"You were right to lie to her, Fred," Gail says. "You're a realist. A grown-up. It's nice to be married to a grown-up."

They sit side by side in the squeaky wicker chairs. June bugs bang on the screen door, hungry for the light. Gail picks up Fred's hand and kisses it, holds it to her cheek, then returns it to his knee. Neither of them speaks. After a while Gail stands up. "It's ten o'clock, I'm going to bed," she says, bending down to kiss his forehead. "Come on up when you think you can sleep."

He takes her hand, holds her back. He's still mulling over what she said. "A realist? You usually say idealist."

"That too. You're both. You're Don Quixote with a brain."

He laughs and lets go of her hand.

She wants to add, You could have chosen a school that doesn't need to be rescued. That would have been just fine with me. But she keeps the thought to herself, bends to kiss him again, and goes upstairs to bed.

He sits for a while, nowhere near ready to sleep, remembering the hollow sound of their voices in their house at Mt. Gilead after the furniture was taken out and put in the moving van. It is a relief that Gail's profession is portable. A graphic artist as good as she can be successful anywhere, make as much money here in Fieldington as she ever did—more than he does—and maybe, when she's ready, after she gets her roots down, and he gets things at school a little more squared away, whatever's keeping them from getting pregnant will stop happening, and they'll be parents again. "We're going to stay right here," he says to the empty porch. "This is the place for us."

After a while he goes into the house, tries to read; when that doesn't work, he turns on the TV, soothes himself with late-night blather, finally dozes in the chair. Near dawn when he goes upstairs and gets in the bed beside Gail, he finds she is awake. He puts his hand on her shoulder. That's when she starts to cry.

"Hey!" he says. He puts his arm around her, cradles her head. "You said yourself it's not so bad. And anyway, it isn't going to happen. They'll never let boys in here."

"That's not what I'm crying about," she says. "Besides, I'm stopping."

"I know," he whispers, kissing her cheek. "I know, I know." How safe things used to be, that's why she's crying. For that. Before he decided to be a head. Before they learned that a car accident could actually kill their daughter. If I were a great teacher, a Francis Plummer, he thinks, maybe I wouldn't be a head.

"It's like you're out in space," Gail says. "All alone."

"But I'm not," he says. "I'm right here in bed. With you."

AND, FAR WEST of the Mississippi now, in the same dawn, Francis can't sleep either. In this huge landscape where there are no woods, no little hills to wall him in, he feels released, but unanchored too, much too restless to sleep. So he drives instead, goes faster and faster. It's four-thirty in the morning, fifteen hours after his phone call to Peggy, and there's no other car in sight. Just a big semi up ahead getting bigger and bigger.

He's promised Peggy he wouldn't eat greasy breakfasts at roadside restaurants, so he's fasting , three cups of black coffee, that's all, and the caffeine's throbbing in his temples. He zooms by the truck and waves to the fat guy, pasty faced, loaded on speed, NoDoze, everything but sleep, who from miles above waves back, then blasts the air horn, a crazed hello in the early morning.

Now Francis is going almost a hundred, the car's beginning to quiver, he starts to laugh. Once when he was a little kid crossing the living room, past the black-robed glowering of his ancestor's portrait above the mantel, and tripping on the rug, he heard his father mildly explain to a visitor: "Francis lacks coordination. And he's so dreamy, he doesn't always know where he's going." Francis, who at age fifty-five is still small, unathletic, and absentminded, remembers that now, so he pushes harder on the accelerator: risk is the best revenge. When the car's shuddering increases, he laughs again, surprised that he's laughing, that he isn't crying, wonders why he's speeding; he never knows anymore how he is going to feel in the next moment. He thinks maybe he's finally living up to the romance the girls have built up around him, living a secret life they insist on believing in.

Signs, telephone poles, fence posts blur by, and after a while he finds himself wondering how it would be to steer for one of them, smash his car and himself, and go to sleep. The image frightens him more than the midnight ocean into which he's fallen overboard and is drowning all alone. So he slows his car way down, gains control of it, and of himself.

Now he has only several hundred miles to go until Denver, where he'll pick up Lila Smythe. He feels less regretful now about his promise to give her a ride; he's had enough of loneliness. And there's something comforting about keeping a promise to a student, something solid and practical and helpful, about saving her the money it would cost her to fly. He hangs on to that.

Three hours later, he sees the front range of the Rockies up ahead. Soon he'll be in Denver.

FOUR

With Francis farther and farther away and Siddy wandering in Europe, Peggy is remembering what it is to be alone. She's thirteen again.

The pale winter light slides through the window, it shows the grease lingering on the tiles behind the stove. The kitchen smells of the old linoleum her mother hated, that wouldn't be there anymore if her mother hadn't died giving birth to the stillborn baby who would have been Peggy's little sister. Peggy peels potatoes, alone, it's four o'clock, school's out, her father won't come home till seven.

They'll eat together, he'll ask her questions about her schoolwork, he'll wash the dishes, thanking her for making dinner, for being such a good daughter, then she'll go upstairs to her homework: gray geometry, Caesar dividing Gaul, a history text heavy with graffiti left to her by an anonymous predecessor: misshapen human forms, huge heads, penises that look like guns. Her father's downstairs in the armchair across the fireplace from the matching empty one. Soon she'll hear his tread on the stairs, he'll come into her room, shyly kiss her on her cheek—she knows he wishes he weren't so distant. Before she goes to bed, she'll hear him crying in his room.

Then she's twenty-two, newly married, standing on a warm thick carpet, the color of roses. The walls of the big room are a bright clean white, and Francis's father in a blue suit stands by the fireplace. He's smiling at her, he's standing under the portrait of John Plummer, Puritan Divine, black robe, white bib, round cheeks, stern, stable man, proud roots! The smell of roast lamb wafts from the kitchen. Francis's mother's in there with the black lady who helps, who calls them by their last name while they call her by her first— all except Francis, who puts a Mrs. before her last name, while his father rolls his eyes.

They've just come from church. Peggy still feels bathed in the light from the rose window over the altar. Francis's father turns to her, he knows *she'll* listen, he's talking about the sermon. "Unless I believe as a child believes," he says, she doesn't hear the rest, it's not the words she wants, she doesn't need to understand. It's what's in his eyes. More than belief. More than confidence. More than knowledge. A vast beneficence has been granted! He smiles at her. He's tall, he's wearing a vest, there's a gold watch chain across the front. His blue eyes shine with his belief. She loves those blue eyes!

More than ever lately, Peggy finds herself talking to her father-in-law. She can't see him, has no idea what the heaven she's sure he lives in looks like, but she knows all she has to do is open her mind to him. Their conversation is more intimate now than when he lived in a real body on the edge of Long Island Sound in the house that Peggy loved so much. She is sure he knows now that the only reason Francis begged her to join his family's Episcopal faith when they were married was to please him. "I didn't see that then," she tells her father-in-law—"maybe because Francis didn't either. Or if he did understand, maybe it was kindness, he didn't want to hurt your feelings. What I really think, though, is how in the world could he have stood up to you?"

"Because when Francis thinks of God he thinks of *bears,*" she explains, and *turtles,* and *fish.* "How's he supposed to tell you that? He told me once. I just laughed. He was joking then—before he knew it was true."

PEGGY FINALLY GETS so lonely on the night after Francis called her just before he crossed the Mississippi, that she invites their dog, Levi, into their bed with her. Levi's a big brown mongrel who drools a lot. His other name is Spit; he's lonely too. He stands by the bed as Peggy gets ready, his rear end wagging with his tail, and when Peggy gets in on one side, he leaps up onto the bed on the other, offering to lick Peggy's face, while Peggy pushes him away, and then he snuggles down beside her, groaning with satisfaction like an old man in a steam bath.

Levi is afflicted with fleas in the summer time, and so when his scratching reaches an apogee in the small hours of the dark, the bed shakes, and Peggy wakes up thinking for an instant that she's in California with Francis and there is an earthquake and they're both dying.

"But my dear," her friend Father Woodward says to her that afternoon when she goes to his cluttered little office to tell him about her vivid earthquakes, "Francis will be living in a reconstructed Indian village on Mount Alma. Nothing's there to fall on him." Father Woodward speaks in the faintly affected upper-class British accent he jokes that he learned by mistake in theological school. "Francis is going to live forever," he predicts.

The little priest sits opposite her in a chair to one side of his desk, his feet barely touching the floor, while the light from the window shines on his bald head. Before coming to Fieldington, he'd been a curate in a big New York City parish, and though she'd miss him terribly, Peggy thinks he should return to the city's more eclectic scene. He told her once that the bishop urged him to take the Fieldington parish ten years ago when the position opened. "He said living in suburbia would test my faith. He obviously suspected it wasn't very strong." But now the thought comes to Peggy that maybe the bishop just wanted him out of the way.

"Don't worry, my dear," he murmurs now, "Francis will be fine. He's exploring." She watches his little sandy mustache move up and down above his lip, which she finds herself comparing to Fred Kindler's red one, and the thought strikes her that she'd do better to go to Fred with her grief. She's sure *his* faith is not so damn supple as to allow the idea that what Francis is up to is *exploring*. She shakes the treacherous thought away. How does she know what Kindler believes? Besides, he's her boss, not her priest.

She knows Woodward misses the point on purpose, so she presses on. "Coming to Miss Oliver's was the best thing that could have happened to Francis and me. We found our calling. And now he risks it all," she says—and goes on to remind him that the only thing Francis knew about what he wanted to do with the rest of his life before Marjorie hired them was that he *didn't* want to be a businessman. "Though he didn't have the foggiest idea what a businessman does," she says. "It was just what his father did."

"He knew you had to wear a suit," Father Woodward smiles. He's dwarfed by his chair, his tiny hands motionless in his lap. His knitting sits on the pile of papers on his desk in his dark little office, and she knows he's itching to get his hands on the needles. She's advised him lots of times not to let his parishioners know he knits. "If it were fly tying or something, it would be OK," she says. "But *knitting!* You give your parishioners too much credit. This isn't San Francisco. It's New England. We're even less broadminded than you think."

Father Woodward's eyes flit to his knitting, but he doesn't move his hands. His eyes, behind the owlish glasses, focus on her. He doesn't say anything. He's taking courses on how to counsel, Peggy thinks. How to be like a shrink. But she doesn't want his advice, let alone his therapy. She wants his *prayer*.

She has no idea how hard her friend is working not to tell her what he thinks she should discover for herself. It's not just panic that's driving Francis, he wants to say. It's also courage. Francis shouldn't have to defend his spiritual quest to anyone. It's his escaping, his running away, that's indefensible. He's going to have to figure out for himself that he can't do both at once. But Peggy's not ready to hear this yet. So he waits.

"Francis has been having dreams too, all year," she tells him. "I wonder if he's still having them way out there in the West, and if he is," she adds, "I probably wouldn't understand them."

"That's not surprising," Father Woodward says. "If you could understand them, you would have gone with him."

"That's not fair," Peggy says, and Father Woodward shrugs his little shoulders.

"And it's beside the point," she adds.

"All right, then, my dear, what *is* the point?"

"You tell me," she demands. It's his last chance. Silently she's begging him: don't tell me he's *questing*. Tell me he's *straying*. Say *let us pray!*

Father Woodward looks out the window to the bright sunshine on the lawn. "It's easier to explain than to understand," he murmurs. "You could *explain* it. A Sioux medicine man could tell him what's really going on. But where are we going to find a Sioux?" Father Woodward turns his face from the window and adds, "One could claim they're the same. What Francis wants and what you believe."

Oh, please! Don't be so damn liberal! she wants to yell. I don't need a priest who believes in Everything. Instead, she keeps her face as expressionless as possible. He has enough problems without knowing how much he's failed her.

Father Woodward shrugs. "Don't you two grow apart," he begs. "I couldn't bear it."

"It's time to go," she says, stretching the truth. She has plenty of time, and so does he. She stands, moves to his desk, leans over it, and kisses him tenderly on his forehead like a sister—her forgiveness. His bald pate gleams beneath her eyes. He keeps his hands flat on the desk as if keeping it from flying away. His face is slightly flushed.

"I'll pray for you both," he murmurs, and she goes out into the bright summer light.

STRAIGHT TO EUDORA'S STUDIO. If Father Woodward can't help her, surely Eudora can.

Peggy loves the smell of the studio: turpentine, clay, oil paints, dust. Her spirits lift as soon as she's through the door. Ever since Marjorie hired Eudora, a young artist, newly widowed and still thin, thirty-two years ago, just one year after she hired Peggy and Francis, Eudora's been the colleague whom Peggy trusts the most.

"I've lost him," Peggy begins. And stops when Eudora shakes her head. "All right, an exaggeration," she admits. "But it's how I feel."

"You don't lose them until they die. That's when they go away." Eudora tosses this off, a bright encouraging matter of fact. She's not speaking from grief—her husband died years ago, two weeks after their honeymoon, drowned absurdly in a swamp on a reserve Marine Corps training exercise—but from memory of grief. She sits motionless in her red work smock in her chair across from Peggy's, more of a presence even than the mammoth wooden chairs she has inspired her students to create. Kinesthetic sculptures she calls them, her latest enthusiasm, and they dominate the space. And demonstrate Miss Oliver's at its best. For here is one of the several areas in which the school has freed itself from the ant mentality that craves to departmentalize the curriculum of almost every school. As if life came in boxes! These creations surrounding Peggy now in her colleague's studio are at once furniture and works of art and machines. And also jokes—as if to prove that, in the right atmosphere, teenagers can be counted on not to take themselves too seriously. The piece nearest Peggy's a red-white-and-blue throne, bright and arresting in the cracked and crazed enamel of its varnished paint, that plays "The Star Spangled Banner" as soon as you sit in it—so that you have to stand up—and that of course stops playing as soon as you do. It's the sixth version; the first five were not sufficient and were destroyed.

"Francis is doing what he needs to do," Eudora says.

"No, he's not. He's running away."

Eudora shakes her head again. "Let's not talk about Francis. Let's talk about you and what you need to do."

"Like what?" Peggy asks.

"See? I knew this wouldn't take long," Eudora smiles.

"Like what?" Peggy repeats.

"Like helping this new guy save the school. That's what *you* need to do."

"Of course. But what has that got to do—?"

"We save the school, we save everything."

"I already gave him some advice," Peggy murmurs.

"And that's all you're going to do?" Eudora asks.

Now Peggy's too restless to sit. She gets up, moves around the room, stops next to a larger-than-life sculpture, the one she loves best. It's Humpty Dumpty sitting on a wall, and in the center of his round, white stomach is a door that lets you inside to sit on a bench where, when you pull a lever, Humpty falls off the wall and comes apart into exactly fifteen pieces. The students who thought it up, designed it, and built it have named the piece *Undefeated* because they, unlike the king's men, can put Humpty back together again—in a jiffy.

Peggy rubs her hand over Humpty's smooth surface. She thinks she knows what Eudora's going to say; it brings a little surge of joy.

"You can help him recruit," Eudora says. "Travel round the country selling the school with him and Gail and Nan. You'll be good at it. You'll be wonderful."

Peggy has no doubt that she can speak for the school, and she wants to. But that's not what she needs to hear. For on the heels of her excitement about it comes her anger. "That's what *Francis* should do!" she exclaims. "It's his job."

"So *you* do it," Eudora says. "You're just as senior as Francis is. You be the head's right hand."

"Me?" Peggy says to stall for time.

"Oh, baby!" Eudora murmurs. "I've been counting on it." It's true; she saw this coming, as soon as she learned that Marjorie was fired.

Peggy sees how striking this exchange of roles would be. "What place will Francis have when he comes back?" she wonders aloud.

Eudora studies her and smiles. "You're catching on," she says.

"I don't want to catch on," Peggy answers. "I'm no politician."

"Yes, you are. Everybody is."

"It will create an even bigger separation between me and Francis," Peggy persists.

"And this is the way to heal it," Eudora also persists. "How else? Run after him and drag him back? Go out there with him and pretend to be an Indian?"

This is too much for Peggy all at once. She doesn't say anything. She needs to be alone now. She needs time to think. She stands to leave.

And besides, here comes Mary Bradford, a tall blond kid with coltish legs, a summer student, into the studio. Mary was so eager to get away from her family in San Francisco, where she'd been for only a week since the school year ended, that here she is back on campus two days before summer school begins. She's carrying a big black portfolio case. In spite of the bounce in her step, she has the drawn look teenagers get when they are tired and won't admit it. After flying in from the West Coast yesterday, she stayed up most of the night to finish her drawings and can't wait to show them to Eudora.

"Hello, Mary," Peggy says, then turns to Eudora, smiles her good-bye, and starts to move away. Mary is Eudora's business, not hers. Besides, she can't wait to be alone.

"No," Eudora urges. "Stay here with us." She wants Peggy to see the drawings.

Eudora reveres Mary's talent, which she knows is greater than her own; she's using all her skill and passion in nurturing it. That's what Miss

Oliver's is all about. She wants to confront Peggy with the result of her teaching, so clear in the blossoming of Mary's work. Maybe that will stir Peggy to acknowledge that if they save the school they save everything she cares about, including her marriage. After all, the Plummers are as much married to the school as they are to each other—and what's wrong with that? She turns to Mary. "Let's show your work to Mrs. Plummer too."

Mary hesitates.

"Mary, Mrs. Plummer is my friend."

That's all Eudora needs to say. For Eudora's claim to an adult affection, to loyalty and trust, names exactly what is absent in Mary's family—and the original reason for her being sent away from home. "I'd love to have you see them," Mary says to Peggy, and now Peggy has no choice. Later, she will realize how clever Eudora was.

Mary takes her drawings out of the case and lays them side by side on a big table. Eudora studies them. A year ago, she would praise all of Mary's work. But now, a year of hard work later, the stakes are up; she'll award no easy praise. She says nothing for the longest time, merely looks.

"It's a joke," Mary tells Peggy, breaking the silence—and Eudora's rule: *Never explain. If it's not clear on the paper, do it again.* But she can't help it, she loves her idea too much to chance Peggy's not getting it. "It's a double computer," she says. "The place you put your feet is one keyboard, we'll use organ pedals with the letters painted on them, and the other's a wrap-around, so you can type with your feet and your hands at the same time, write two different books. And that's not all. We'll start with a hairdresser's chair. It'll have one of those weird old-fashioned hair dryer hoods so you can write two books and get a shampoo all at once!"

Eudora's still looking at the drawings, frowning now. It is as if she hasn't heard a word. "I'm sorry," Mary says to Eudora's back. "I broke the rule. But my parents are always bragging about how busy they are. Multitasking," she adds. "How's that for a stupid word?"

Eudora ignores Mary's excuse and keeps her back to her, still staring down at the drawings. She points with her left hand to the first picture in the sequence. "This one's good," she says. "Very good. These are even better," pointing with her right hand now to the next three in the sequence.

"Thanks," Mary says.

"Don't thank *me,* dear," Eudora answers. Then abruptly picking up the fifth drawing, holding it with both arms extended in front of her, "What about this one?"

Mary hesitates.

"What about this one?" Eudora insists.

"I was in a hurry," Mary says.

"Do it again," Eudora says.

Mary doesn't speak. A tiny smile appears on her face. Peggy thinks she looks relieved.

"Tomorrow?" Eudora asks.

"All right. Tomorrow," Mary responds. Then, pointing to the sixth drawing, "What about this one?"

Now it is Eudora who is smiling. She shakes her head back and forth and doesn't answer. She knows that Mary understands: we'll look at the sixth when the fifth one's as good as it can get.

"That's what I thought," Mary says. She gathers her drawing into her case, slowly, deliberately, while Peggy and Eudora watch. Then she smiles at Peggy. "Thanks," she says and turns to Eudora. "Same time tomorrow?"

Eudora nods. "I'll be right here," she says, and Peggy thinks, yes, and the next day too and the next and the next and the one after that, and knows—as if there were ever a time when she didn't!—how right Eudora is: we save the school, we save everything!

She follows Mary out the door and heads for Fred Kindler's office to tell him he needs *her* on his recruiting trips.

TWO THOUSAND MILES away on the outskirts of Denver, Lila Smythe and her mother, Tylor, wait at Tylor's house for Francis to pick up Lila for the trip to California and the dig. He's been expected for an hour.

Mother and daughter are drinking their morning coffee at a little table on the patio. They are very much alike: tall, sturdy, their blond hair cut short. Tylor's is fading. She wears dark glasses against the glare. She glances at her watch. "Where do you think he is?" she asks, hoping that Francis is still miles away so that she can extend this time with her daughter.

"He'll be here," Lila answers. She feels a rush of tenderness for her mother, knowing how lonely she'll be. She keeps her voice casual to hide her eagerness to get going. "He's absentminded. He's probably lost the directions."

"What do you think *he'll* do if—?" Tylor starts to ask, and then stops. She knows this worry irritates her daughter, but she can't leave it alone.

It's true. Lila's been home for two weeks, and almost every day her mother's brought up her worry that Miss Oliver's will abandon its single-sex mission. She's never thought of her mother as a worrier before, and it's making her impatient. "Don't worry, Mom, we'd never let the school go coed," she has insisted each time. This time she doesn't. She's tired of the subject, so she changes it. "Look, Mom." She moves her chair around the table, puts her hands on her mother's shoulders, and turns her. Now they both stare at the side of the house. It catches the fierce light of the morning sun. The stucco glows. "Light's so different out here!" she says. "You taught me that. "Back East it's—"

"Pastel," her mother supplies the word. She turns her head back to Lila, grazing her daughter's cheek with her lips. "Thinner. Watery and vague. It's the first thing I noticed when I escaped out here."

That word: *escape*. Sometimes Lila envisions her mother as if she were emblazoned with a sign: *I escaped. That's who I am*. Her mother's refrain: that she divorced her husband fifteen years ago when she realized he would never think of her painting as anything more than a nice weekend hobby for a wife, and then picked Denver off the map as the place to live because she didn't have any family there to criticize her, especially not her father, who had refused to send her to college. He paid her tuition to Katherine Gibbs instead so she could be a secretary. "Yes, I know," Lila would say. "But you refused to go. You got yourself a full scholarship at Smith instead. And now you're a painter. A *professional*." What she doesn't say anymore to her mother—now that she knows how much it hurts—is that she wishes she had a father.

Lila's grateful to her mother for sending her to a school where there are no males to paint over the picture of what she chooses to become. Now she knows that when you can choose what to do with your life, *then what you do is who you are*. It scares her to know that. And makes her happy. It's why she sucks up all the biographies of women that Gregory van Buren keeps giving her to read, one after another. How does he know this is exactly what she needs?

And here's Francis Plummer coming around the corner of the house. He must have heard their voices. "Hello," he says. "Sorry I'm late. I got a little lost." Tylor is surprised to see how tired he looks.

He joins them at the table and tells them what he's seen on his journey, how flat the middle of the country is, how stunning his first sight of the Rockies—but nothing of what he's been thinking about.

Then there's a little silence, and Tylor says, "We were just wondering what you would do if Miss Oliver's went coed."

"*You* were, Mother. I wasn't," Lila says. "I wasn't even thinking about it."

"All right," Tylor acknowledges. "I was. And I pay the tuition." She's looking intently at Francis, waiting for his answer.

"Well?" Tylor persists, and Francis still doesn't answer.

"Evidently, I've hit a hot spot," Tylor says.

"Mother, please, it's not going to happen," Lila says, but Tylor's eyes are still on Francis.

"It's not a hot spot for me," Francis finally says. "Because Lila's right. It won't happen."

"A school can't change its mission?"

"It's not a mission; it's what we *are,*" Francis says. "The alumnae wouldn't let it happen." What's going to happen already has: Marjorie's been thrown out. The rest he can't imagine.

Tylor shakes her head. She's not convinced.

"The students wouldn't either," Lila says. She's looking at Francis now, not her mother, chastising him with her eyes for not including the students in the saving of the school.

"Don't be naive," her mother warns.

Lila smiles. Naive is what I'm not, she wants to say, feeling a slight resentment that her mother can't see how much she's changed. She wouldn't have to explain it to anyone at school. "I mean it, Mom, we'd burn the school down first."

Tylor's not going to answer hyperbole. Instead, she turns to Francis and asks her other question. "Why didn't they make *you* the headmaster?"

"Mother!" Lila exclaims. "For God's sake!"

Francis is too surprised to speak. The idea of his being the head has never crossed his mind. Tylor Smythe leans slightly forward, waiting for an answer. Her dark glasses mask her eyes.

"Mother, he's a *teacher!*" Lila says.

Tylor keeps her eyes on Francis. "Is that the answer?" she asks him.

"I've never thought of myself as a head," he answers, stunned to realize it.

"Shouldn't the best, most experienced teacher be the head? The one who understands the school the best?" Tylor's question is perfectly logical—for one who doesn't understand how proud many teachers are to think of themselves as *labor,* and how preferable the act of teaching than sitting, removed from students, and the subject that you love, in an office worrying about diplomacy, budgets, trustees, and strategic planning. As if a school were merely a business!

Francis is still too stunned to answer. Tyler leans back in her chair. "All right, I won't go there," she says. "I didn't mean to pry. I'm sorry."

"It's all right, Mother," Lila says. "It's just not who he is, that's all. It's hard to explain." Then she looks at her watch, glances at Francis. "I've had enough coffee," she tells him, getting up to leave. "I'm going to put my back-pack in the car."

Tylor watches her daughter walk away. Francis sees the longing in her face. Then Lila disappears inside the house, and Tylor turns her eyes back to Francis. "Did you notice how she said that?"

"What?" he asks, jolted by the sudden change of subject. He needs to linger over her question, why he isn't the headmaster of Miss Oliver's School for Girls. It seems that everything is happening much too fast.

"*The* car. If it were my car she would have said *your* car."

"Oh, I don't know—"

Tylor takes off her dark glasses, studies his face. Now he can see her eyes. They are gray, little lines around them. "She never sees her father," Tylor says.

"I know. She told me."

"Sometimes I think she fantasizes that *you're* her dad."

"Oh, no! She wouldn't do that."

"Why wouldn't she? You and your wife—married for years!—make a home for her where everything that's important to her happens. My home is just where she visits. It makes me sad."

Francis wants to avert his eyes. He feels much too vulnerable to be getting into this.

She reaches across the table, takes his hand as if she's known him for years. "I'm grateful. To you *and* your wife. In loco parentis. That's the phrase, isn't it? Can't do that and also find time to be the head. Maybe that's what Lila meant."

"Thank you," Francis murmurs. He doesn't know how to tell her it's not what Lila meant.

"Well, give me a minute to say good-bye to my daughter." She lets go of his hand, and stands and puts her dark glasses on again. "Then join us in the driveway, and I'll wave good-bye to both of you."

She goes out to the driveway to help her daughter put her things in the car. Lila's already finished when she gets there. She closes the trunk of Francis's car and turns to hug her mother. "Thanks, Mom," she says. "Thanks for everything." She means thanks for escaping. And thanks for letting me go.

Francis is coming down the driveway now. He says, "I guess we'd better say good-bye," and he and Lila get in the car and close the doors, and her mother leans in through the window and says good-bye again. Francis backs the car out of the driveway, and Lila waves to her mother, who lingers in the driveway. She knows her mother will go straight to her studio—and smother her loneliness with her work.

HOURS AND HOURS LATER, Lila barrels the dented yellow Chevy down Route 80 in Nevada, and Francis sits in the shotgun seat watching her out of the corner of his eye. Her two sturdy arms reach forward, her hands grip the steering wheel, she stares straight down the road. She drives just like Marjorie Boyd drives, he thinks: everything gets out of the way. She's going someplace, this kid, blasting forward toward some passion that she'll ride for a lifetime. He thinks of Siddy, his son, so different, wandering in Europe, tasting everything, circling, and lonely suddenly, he riffs on the fantasy that Lila's mother planted: that he and Peggy have adopted Lila too, Siddy's younger sister by five years, and the two kids are telepathic, they don't need words to understand each other at the core.

He wonders if Lila remembers how much she disapproved of herself when she arrived at the school three years ago—for her tallness, her thick legs, her braces. Now she likes her tallness, she thinks her sturdy legs are just fine, and her braces are gone. In a coed school Lila would be one of the girls whom the boys don't want to date. At Miss Oliver's she's president-elect of the Student Council; she'll have more influence than many of the faculty.

"It's weird how things happen," Lila finally says without turning her head. Neither of them has said a word for miles. "If some little man, an archeologist with a funny name, doesn't show up at school in February and give a speech, I'm still in Denver now with my mom, instead of here."

"I didn't think it was a funny name," Francis says. "Livingstone Mendoza, what's so funny about that?"

Lila smiles at his joke. "I knew the minute he started to talk that I was going to sign up," she says.

"Me too," Francis murmurs, remembering the little man, almost as small as Father Woodward, standing at the lip of the stage, promising that they would find the remains of the village that was there on the side of the mountain for thousands of years before the Europeans came. "So they could see what the Ohlones saw," he said, "maybe even dream their dreams." Blue work shirt, dark tie, brown corduroy pants, and hiking boots. Mendoza's intensity made up for his small size, and his voice filled the auditorium.

"How could I have spent three years at our school and passed up this chance?" Lila asks. "Three years thinking *about,* and then pass up this chance to *be.*"

"I guessed that you would sign up," Francis says. "It didn't surprise me. Though quite a few of the people on the faculty thought he was a phony. Or a lunatic," he adds, remembering Mendoza's telling them that the Ohlones were not just outnumbered by the animals but by every species of animal, and claiming in a kind of chant that "if we put one of you and one of them side by side in their world, you would see emptiness and would despair. They would see the majesty of First Things, the nearness of God."

For the first time, Lila takes her eyes off the road, glances at Francis. "But not you?" she asks. "You didn't think he was a phony?"

"No, not me."

"Why not? I mean he *was* kind of intense. Sort of overboard."

Francis hesitates. He'll concede Mendoza's funny name, but he doesn't think he was overboard at all.

"Like, you'll be three thousand miles away from home for two months, away from your wife and the school."

"Yeah, it's a long way."

"So why'd you come if it's so far away?"

"I'm only gone for the summer," he says, thinking of his conversation with her mother. "You're away from home from September to June."

Lila frowns, takes one hand off the wheel to push her blond hair away from her forehead. "Now you're acting just like my mother," she says. "Whenever she doesn't want to tell me something I want to know, she changes the subject."

"All right," he says, giving in. "It's like this: once when I was a little kid, I was fishing with my dad." He begins to speak very fast now that he's discovered he's going to tell her this amazing thing. "In a canoe. And a huge turtle swam up to the surface of the lake. Came right up beside me where I was in the bow of the canoe. He looked right at me, looked me right in the eyes." He stops talking suddenly, aware of how foolish he sounds.

"And you looked back at him," Lila finishes.

"Yes."

"And then he went away?" Lila's voice is very quiet.

"Yes. And then he went away."

"You recognized each other," she announces, and now he's surprised at how matter-of-fact her voice is. "He chose you," she says. "He's your totem. From out of the time when the earth was here and human beings were not," and all Francis can think about is how different this kid's reaction is from Peggy's when he tries to tell her what this moment means to him.

"Thanks for telling me. I know you better now," Lila says. "I've always wanted to know you. Now I do. Thanks."

Later, in a campground near Winnemucca, Lila waits for sleep to come. She'd rather be out under the stars, but Francis has insisted she put up her tent and sleep in it. Afraid some crazy rapist would come through. "Who knows who comes to public places like this?" he asked. Speaking like a dad! He's in his tent too, not far from hers. She imagines she can hear his breathing over the noise of the big trucks on Route 80 half a mile away. She shivers with her happiness, and hugs herself, and then she falls asleep.

FIVE

IN FRED KINDLER'S OFFICE Peggy is saying, "I think I can help you" and wondering if he can hear the shyness in her voice. She still feels she's usurping Francis's place. "I think I'd be a good recruiter."

Fred doesn't respond for several seconds that seem like forever. Forget it, she wants to say. It was just an idea.

In fact, he loves it. He's embarrassed that he hesitated, caught assuming that Francis should be the one, not her. But he's sure she's right. "I should have thought of it myself," he says. "You've been here longer and know the school better than anyone."

"Except my husband," Peggy murmurs. She needs to let Fred know he's forgiven.

"Yes. Well, he's busy. He'd help if he could," Fred says, and Peggy thinks, Thanks. Thanks for saying that, wondering if her new friend would be this diplomatic if he weren't the headmaster.

TWO DAYS LATER, the plane that Fred and Gail Kindler, Nan White, and Peggy take from Bradley Field to Hopkins Airport in Cleveland is two hours late; by the time they get across the airport and into their rented car for the drive to Shaker Heights, they know the audience of potential students and their parents has already been gathered for half an hour in Steven and Sharon Maynard's house. They arrive at the Maynard's front porch at eight-thirty, feeling harried and rushed—an hour and fifteen minutes tardy, just as the summer sun is setting. Above them, draped from a second-story window, is a big American flag to celebrate the Fourth of July weekend, which starts in just two days.

Sharon Maynard greets them in the spill of light from the front door of the big brick house, a tall, angular woman in her late forties, dressed in a white blouse and floor-length blue skirt. Her faded blond hair is pulled severely back, her face is pale, she wears no makeup; Peggy remembers a rounder face. But she feels warmly greeted when Sharon takes her hand and smiles, then does the same with Nan. "It's lovely to see you again," Sharon says; "I'm glad *you're* still at the school." Nan lets the comment go, and while Sharon is still holding her hand, Nan turns to the Kindlers, who are standing to her right, and introduces them. Very slowly, Sharon releases Nan's hand and then proffers her own, only partway, and limply, and just the end of her fingers, first to Gail, then to Fred, while looking at a space above their heads. The Kindlers pretend they don't notice the slight.

Then they are in the house, and they hear the noise of conversation stop, and Steven Maynard is greeting them in the front hall. He's still in his brown business suit, a big man, gone comfortably to roundness who wears a fifties crew cut. He takes Gail's hand, and holds on. "Gail! Welcome to our house. Thanks for dropping your own work and coming all the way out here to be with us." Then he turns to Fred. "And Fred! We're glad you're here!" When he bends down to put his huge hand on Fred's shoulder, Peggy and Nan exchange quick glances of gratitude, and Peg feels the impulse to hug this big, round bear. Behind Steven, through the archway into the living room, the guests are watching.

Steven puts his long arms out as if to corral the four of them, and shepherds them into the living room, leaving his wife in the doorway, and Peggy sees the surprise appear on Sharon's face. She watches the expression glide into a pout. Steven's not going to let her make the introductions! He saw the way she greeted Fred and Gail. Peggy feels another rush of gratitude.

The furniture has been pulled to the sides of the Maynard's airy living room to make room for the folding chairs, where at least forty people sit. The walls are a stark white; an Oriental rug covers the center of the polished hardwood floor, and abstract paintings hang on the walls. Peggy thinks they're ugly. It flashes through her mind that maybe Steven doesn't like them either.

The four recruiters sit down in folding chairs at the front of the room facing the audience. Peggy scans the room. She looks at every face. There is no one here she doesn't recognize. She knows everyone here! Can't remember everyone's name, but recognizes every face. So everyone here is either a parent of a present Oliver student, or an alumna, or a parent of an alumna. Wait! she thinks. There's been some mistake. *Not one potential new family is present! Not a single girl of high school age is here!* She glances across the room at Sharon Maynard, who is standing in the archway to the living room, watching Peggy discover this. It dawns on Peggy then that maybe this isn't a mistake. She stares at Sharon's eyes, burning in, until Sharon has to look away, and then she knows: it *isn't* a mistake.

She hears Steven introduce her first. But she doesn't hear much of what he says because, along with her surprise at such treachery, she is aware that everyone in the audience is looking at her, not at Steven, while he talks. Their eyes pin her to the wall, as if to ask, Who's side are you on?

His, she wants to answer, her anger flooding her. That's right, *his* side. I'm loyal to *him, this new guy, the man—and you better be too.* She wants to jump up in the middle of Steven's little speech and explain to these people all the reasons why Marjorie had to go. Instead—for she will keep her cool—she forces herself to smile and nods her head in acknowledgment of the warm applause for her that she knows Fred won't get when he is introduced.

She needs to lean across Nan and Gail and whisper the news to Fred—make sure he understands no potential families are here to recruit, so he won't make a fool of himself. Nan can't be sure; she hasn't been with the school long enough to know everyone in the room. But Steven has already begun his introduction, and Fred is already standing up. "I'm proud and delighted to introduce our new head," Steven says to the audience, doing his best to whip up enthusiasm. "We are fortunate to have a person of such high caliber." Peggy searches the crowd to see if others noticed *person* instead of *man.* Faces are stony, expressionless. The clapping is halfhearted, so minimally polite as to be insulting, and Peggy is amazed at the fierceness of the feelings in the room, which burn even fiercer now as Fred Kindler stands to make himself their target. It isn't until these last few months since Marjorie was fired that Peggy has truly begun to learn, deep in her gut, not merely in her brain, just how volatile school communities are, how charged with emotion. She's getting another lesson right now, and wondering where she's been. The answer, of course, is that she's never been at the head's right hand, let alone at this new one's, who has to follow in Marjorie Boyd's footsteps and do all the things she wouldn't do, and isn't even the right gender. She wouldn't have Fred Kindler's job for a million dollars.

"Thank you for coming to hear about our school," Fred begins, and Peggy's heart sinks. "And thanks also to you alumnae and parents who have brought friends so they can learn about our school," Fred goes on, for he isn't cynical enough—not yet—to believe this absence of school-age girls is the result of a dirty trick. In fact, the idea doesn't even occur to him. He assumes instead that these parents want to check out the school—and him—on their own, before their daughters get interested. He would have preferred a less cautious approach, but he takes what he can get and soldiers on. "And if what my colleagues and I say tonight inspires you enough, as I believe it will, to persuade your daughters and the daughters of your friends to hear more, we would be delighted to return and talk with them." But now, someone in the back row is laughing. And a surprised, embarrassed expression appears on many of the faces, and Fred hesitates, and Peggy sees a look of confusion on his face.

Then she watches him guess the real reason why there are no Oliver-age girls in the audience. Steven Maynard, who has just taken his own seat in the front row, stands up again.

"I'm sorry, Fred" he says. "I assumed we had sent you the lists of who was coming and who wasn't." He glances, appalled, at his wife, who is still standing in the archway.

Fred nods an acknowledgment to Steven, turns back to his audience, doesn't miss a beat. "Well, then," he offers, "since you obviously know the school, let's get to know each other," and Peggy is awed at her new head's quick-footedness.

No response from the audience. Stony faces still, staring at Fred. They leave him hanging.

Peggy watches Fred as he figures out what to say next. He's not quick enough. "Oh, it's all so slick!" a red-haired woman in the second row exclaims. Peggy can't remember her name, who her daughter is. Next to her, her husband nods his head in vehement assent. "A very professional spin job, your coming here," the woman continues. She wears a red dress as if to match her hair. "But we didn't come here to hear you talk. We came to ask you questions."

"That's right," from the back row. "We have questions." It's Mrs. Johnstone. Peggy knows her well. She's the mother of Karen Johnstone, a terrific kid who lives in Peggy and Francis's dorm. "Lots of them," Mrs. Johnstone's voice is brass. "We have lots of questions."

"We're *angry!*" the woman in the red dress exclaims, looking as if she were about to cry, and Mr. Loyal Spouse next to her makes a show of holding her hand, while Peggy's disgust blossoms. Let your wife be angry all by herself, idiot! she thinks.

Now Carl Beecher stands up in the back row. He's short, very round, and bald. Peggy knows him well, he's the father of two alumnae and a present senior. Her spirits rise; she knows *he'll* say the right things.

She's right. Carl looks directly at Fred: "Yes, there's lots of anger," he admits in a gentle voice. "But it's certainly not your fault. *You* didn't fire Marjorie. We need to move on."

Thank you, Fred wants to say, for he's certainly grateful, but decides he won't. For that would make Carl's statement of fact look like sop to a weak leader. So he merely nods his head at Carl.

"That's exactly right, we need to move on!" Steven Maynard says. He smiles at Carl, then stares at the woman in the red dress to shut her up. Then he turns to Fred: "So Fred, let's hear your thoughts."

"First *I* have question," Carl announces before Fred has a chance to begin. Still standing in the back, he faces the archway and stares at Sharon. "It's not for Mr. *Kindler,*" Carl adds, and Sharon blanches, knowing what's coming. "Why didn't you tell us this was a *recruiting* gathering?" Carl asks, speaking very slowly. Sharon's tall frame stiffens, and she doesn't answer. "Instead of just a chance to meet the new head," Carl continues. In the front, Steven turns now to stare across the room at his wife. "You set him up," Carl says to Sharon. "Didn't you? You called us up, but you didn't ask us to bring anyone. I bet you didn't even call the list of families the school sent you." Everyone's eyes swing from Carl to Sharon, like people watching a tennis match.

"I'm right, aren't I?" Carl persists. "Aren't I, Sharon. You set him up." Steven Maynard's still staring at his wife. It's all over his face that he knows the answer.

Now Fred knows exactly what to do to be the leader. He will take them down a better track. "I don't think we need to pursue this," he says. "Let's not go down that road," and Peggy is amazed again.

Carl turns away from Sharon, puts his eyes on Fred. Sharon does too. Steven has to face completely around, putting his back to his wife. His face is very pale as he sits down. In the back, Carl sits too. Sharon remains standing.

"I understand how people feel," Fred says into the silence. He moves his eyes around the room, seeking individual faces. "I'm glad you've put it on the table."

Hooray for you! Peggy thinks. You're running this thing, you're the boss!

"I know the size of the shoes I have to fill," she hears Fred say next. "With your help, I'll fill them," and suddenly she is very angry. Oh, don't be so damn humble! Peggy wants to yell, and the next thing she knows she's on her feet, and she's the one who's making a speech. "Marjorie resigned of her own free will," she lies. "You need to know that. She decided on her own to quit," she hears herself saying. "She was tired. She knew the school needed new ideas." She looks into people's eyes, stares them down. "All right, I shouldn't have interrupted. But he"—nodding at Fred—"is too gracious to say it, and it needed to be said." So get over it! she wants to add, just get over it! She feels Fred's eyes and turns from the audience to meet them, and sits down. Her knees are shaking; she feels empty, as if she'd been holding her breath.

In the silence that Peggy has created, Fred feels a surge of joy. He begins to talk. He lists the traits that make Miss Oliver's so special. The tension in the room begins to melt. In everyone but the lady in red, who whispers something to her husband. Fred goes on, tells the audience what they need to know—that he loves what they love about the school. He's proving me right, Peggy thinks. He knows what he's doing, understands what *works*. She scans the audience again. They're listening, at least. Give this man a chance, she wants to say.

An half hour later, Fred's finished and invites discussion. It's near the end of the meeting. He thinks he's going to win this game. Steven Maynard stands, and everybody knows he's going to ask an easy question, throw a softball. But Steven doesn't get a chance because the woman in red stands again. "You've been avoiding the subject all evening," she says. "Do you plan to admit boys, or don't you?"

"Why shouldn't I avoid it?" Fred snaps back. "Since it never crossed my mind." He feels another rush of joy: that he can lie so quickly!

"So?" her voice rises. "You're telling us there is absolutely no circumstance—none whatsoever—under which you would consider admitting boys?"

Fred hesitates for just an instant, and Peggy waits, and Fred hesitates another instant to draw breath—for he's going to blast this woman—but Peggy's not waiting any longer, she's on her feet again. "You heard him," she says, focusing on the woman as if there were no one else in the room. "You heard what he said. No boys. Ever. That's what he said. And he's the *headmaster*. Why do you even bring it up?"

Steven is looking at Fred. "Exactly!" Fred says. "Exactly why I didn't bring it up." He stares at the woman until she sits down. And then he realizes: this has to end right now.

As if reading Fred's mind, Steven turns to the audience. "That's a good place to end this meeting," he announces. The audience is obviously surprised. There's a restless shuffling.

"Wait!" says Sharon from the archway. "We're not finished."

But Steven turns his back on his wife. His gesture is blatant, his disgust obvious. Then he steps across to the front of the room and takes Fred's hand in both of his and pumps it. "We're so glad you're here!" he booms. "You're just what the school needs." Then, turning back to his guests: "Thanks so much for coming, everyone. Drive safely."

Still, the audience is in their seats. They turn to look at Sharon—like basketball players waiting for the second referee to reverse the call of the first. To no avail: she's not looking at the audience, she's clenching her fists, and trying not to cry, and staring at her husband, who's turned his back to her again. The guests want no part of this. They move quickly to the door and out of the house.

Then Steven stands in the doorway—conspicuously without his wife—and says good-bye to the four recruiters. He puts his big hand lightly on Peggy's shoulder and says to Fred: "You've got some damn good people around you, don't you, Fred!"

"You bet," says Fred.

On the way back to the airport Gail drives; Fred sits next to her in the front.

"I'm coming back someday," Nan announces from her seat in the back next to Peggy. "Mark my words, I'm coming back to exterminate Mrs. Sharon Maynard."

"I'll help," Gail says. "I'll bring the poison."

Neither Peggy nor Fred can bring themselves to speak. Peggy thinks it's time to keep her mouth shut. She fears she made Fred look weak when she butted in and spoke up for him that second time, saying, "You heard what he said." As if he couldn't speak for himself.

And Fred is marveling at how quickly his lie flew out of his mouth. He's not the slightest bit ashamed. He wants to turn to Peggy and explain that he really didn't need her to stand up and save the day for him. But that would seem defensive and ungrateful, so he doesn't. And then it dawns on him that his new friend *did* save him, not from his reluctance to persevere in an untruth, but from his temper. He was drawing breath to blast the woman when Peggy stood up and blasted her for him, much more temperately than he would have. He would have told the red-headed woman to sit down and shut up and asked her who the hell she thought she was to argue with *him*. That would have made a great impression! he tells himself.

"I'll check up next time," Nan says. "I promise. I'll check the guest list myself. I won't give anybody another chance to be so treacherous."

"Please don't apologize," Fred says. "There's no way you could know that anyone would be like that."

"I do now," Nan says, and Peggy is struck again by how fascinating the lesson she is getting about the leadership of schools is. From now on when she thinks of school politics she'll think of red cans of gasoline—and lit matches.

Thirty minutes later as Peggy and Gail get out of the same side of the car at the rent-return, Gail lays her hand on Peggy's arm. "Thanks," she murmurs. "When he has to tell a fib, he needs lots of help." She doesn't know how far her husband has progressed in the art of diplomacy since becoming the headmaster of Miss Oliver's School for Girls.

Peggy doesn't answer right away. Here's Gail, she thinks, right here with her husband, while Francis and I are miles apart. She's been remembering

Steven Maynard turning his back on his wife, and the parallel between what the trauma of Miss Oliver's is doing to the Maynards' marriage and her own does not escape her. "Do you think they believed me?" she asks at last.

"Some of them. Maybe. Just a little. Anyway, it saved the day."

"That's good," Peggy says out loud. To herself she thinks: If Francis had been there—if *he'd* said it—they would have believed.

MILES AND MILES AWAY, and three time zones earlier, Francis is eating a paltry supper just outside the boundary of Mount Alma State Park, where Livingstone Mendoza's ardent little band is in the second week of its search for the Ohlone village. Francis, Lila, and the nine other students in his team sit in the long shadow of one of the huge oaks in the dry smell of oat grass that Mendoza has carefully explained didn't exist in the Indian days; it came with the oats the Spaniards fed their horses, which then shat the seeds over the hills, the horse food as new to the country as the horses were, as invasive, Mendoza accuses, as their pale-skinned riders.

Francis and his companions refuse to look east to where the tops of the hills are being scraped away, and south where already the exuberant vulgarity of a thousand steroid mansions spreads like a rash to the horizon. Instead they look only westward, down over the lion-colored hills toward an area where there are still no houses, where they seek the mounded earth that covers the thousand-year accumulation of ashes, bones, shells. Francis has been keeping to himself his growing conviction that the allotted time to find the village, between now and the end of August, is nowhere near enough. He's beginning to feel slightly absurd, embarrassed as if caught believing a gnat could conquer an elephant, to think that in all this space they could find the little village in so little time.

Now, just as the little band stands up from their supper to return to work, they see Mendoza trudging up the hill toward them. He has an angry expression on his face.

"Greed!" exclaims Mendoza, panting and waving his arms as he arrives. "Greed, irreverence, and intransigence. I've never seen so much!"

"What?" Francis interrupts.

"They just don't care!" Mendoza says.

"What?" Francis asks again. "Who doesn't care about what?" The last thing he wants is listening to Mendoza rant. There's only a little time before it's too dark to work, and they need every minute they can get.

"A thousand years!" Mendoza points his arm down the hill. "A thousand years they lived there."

The students study Mendoza, warily. This distraught little person isn't the same charismatic leader who recruited them. Francis wonders if they are coming to the same conclusion he's reluctantly been coming to: that Francis's colleagues were right. Mendoza *is* a phony and a screwup. How else to explain the man's inability to understand that much more time is needed?

Lila is the first of the students to recover from the shock of their leader's disarray. She puts her hand out to touch Mendoza's, and Mendoza appears to grow a little calmer. "It will be all right," Lila says softly. "You can tell us."

"We've only got till August first," Mendoza announces. "Not the end of August. August *first!*"

Nobody says a word.

"They just told me," Mendoza says after a long pause. He seems to be shrinking to an even smaller size; the students tower over him.

"They can't do that!" a tall girl says. "No one can give people orders like that!" and Lila looks at her as if she were three years old.

Mendoza doesn't get a chance to answer the kid, because suddenly Francis is in his face. "Why in the world didn't you find out how much time we had *before* we came all the way out here?" he blurts. "How could you possibly not do that?"

"Officialdom! Rules, permits, lawyers!" Mendoza cries. Francis's question hasn't made a dent. "They don't give a damn what we're trying to do. All they think about is money!" he goes on, and Francis realizes it doesn't occur to Mendoza that this disaster is *his* mistake. He thinks it is caused by what he's trying to cure. He's not a phony at all; he's a total screwup.

Even if, in spite of the little archeologist's awesome incompetence, they do find the Ohlone village, it will be the result of mere demeaning luck, Francis realizes, win or lose, the whole venture a dreamer's folly. He hears again his colleagues' jeering and realizes that he's not surprised—if not this disaster, then some other—and asks himself why didn't he check up on Mendoza—at least ask for a résumé and talk with his references—and knows the answer: he didn't want to; he needed the cover. And this was good cover. For he really did need to do this spiritual exploring. Without that cover, he would have had to stay home and help the new head. It shames him to realize he could be so sneaky, even with himself.

"That's when the developer comes in?" Lila asks Mendoza. "August first?" There's no indignation in her voice, no panic. She just wants to know.

Mendoza nods. He takes a red kerchief out of his pocket and wipes his face.

Lila rests a calming hand on Mendoza's tiny shoulder while she turns her head to Francis. "So, Mr. P.," she asks him, "how do we fix this?"

"We could go to the developer and ask for an extension," he tells her. He holds back from saying, It won't work but we might as well give it a try. These kids need his faith to seem as strong as Lila's.

"Good idea!" says Mendoza, optimism flooding right back in. "I'm sure he'll agree!" Francis has to look away.

Lila's studying Francis, not Mendoza. "Whatever we have to do we'll do," she says. Her voice is firm. She turns away and goes down the hill to the site, the first to return to work.

When it's finally too dark to work, they return to the huts they have made out of the tulle grass that Mendoza has somehow arranged to have gathered for them. Their replicated Ohlone village even has a sweat house, though they haven't used it yet. There's an argument, proposed by Lila, that though only male Ohlones did, the women should also participate. As he tries to fall asleep in Mendoza's ersatz little village, Francis wonders at the purity of Lila's youthful heart.

The next day, a Saturday afternoon—less than a month before their time is up—Francis, Mendoza, and Lila (whom the students have elected as their representative) go together to the president of Mount Alma Improvement Company, Conrad Bullington, to ask for an extension. Bullington greets them in his office, his obese body clad in a sky-blue warm-up suit.

All during the meeting, Francis wonders at Bullington's unfailing courtesy. He is far more respectful, less strident, Francis thinks, than people who disagree with each other on the Oliver faculty, who are quite given in their tweedy attire to offer polysyllabic insults to one another, while this gigantically unattractive man in his funny warm-up suit and greased hair remembers each of their names, offers them cool drinks, and explains very gently—but firmly—that it would drive up his costs prohibitively to leave the bulldozers and other heavy equipment idle beyond the agreed-on time.

As if to alleviate their disappointment, Bullington offers to build a model of an Ohlone village. He would have it prefabricated and set up and prominently displayed once a year for the edification of the thousands of homeowners.

"Where would you *put* it, for crying out loud?" Lila exclaims, leaning forward in her chair. Bullington leans back in his, as if pushed. Francis thinks maybe after the meeting he will advise Lila not to come on so strong.

But Bullington recovers immediately. "Why, I'd put it on this very commodious lawn in the center," he responds, pushing his huge body up out of his chair. He lumbers across the office to a map on the wall. The sun coming in through the window glistens on his shiny hair. "Right here. A very expansive lawn that fronts the central golf course, near the lake with the fountain."

"On a *lawn?*" asks Mendoza.

"Right here. We'll put it up every year at the same time we have the Concourse d'Elegance."

"But the Ohlones didn't have lawns," Mendoza objects.

Inspired by his idea, Bullington ignores Mendoza. "Thousands of people come to the Concourse," he says. Francis begins to giggle. He turns his face away so Bullington can't see. He finds that he doesn't want to be impolite to this man. The giggling feels a little crazy. Scary—like maybe it will turn into something else.

"What in the world is a Concourse D'Elegance?" Lila imitates the developer's wooden French.

"Antique cars," Bullington answers. His voice takes on a fatherly tone. "Very elegant automobiles: Rolls Royces, Pierce Arrows . . ."

"Next to a *lake?*" asks Mendoza.

"Daimlers, wonderful old Mercedes . . . "

"With a *fountain?*" Mendoza squeaks.

"A Stanley Steamer too. People will come for miles, pay a very significant entrance fee. The opportunity to view an authentic representation of how the Indians once lived here would be an extra draw. White Eagle would be delighted to place a commensurate portion of the proceeds with any archaeological project you identify."

"But surely we don't want to give the impression that we believe the Ohlones had *lawns!*" Mendoza exclaims. He leans so far forward he is almost out of his chair.

"Not for a minute, sir," Bullington says, easing his body back toward his desk. Francis can feel the meeting coming to an end. "But I do think we could suggest that they would have enjoyed them," Bullington continues, and now Francis can't tell whether he is serious or just playing with them. "Why wouldn't they have enjoyed them? After all, people are people. If they could have mastered the technique of transporting water, as we have, who knows, maybe they would have had lawns, instead of ashes and old clam shells to put their dwellings on."

Mendoza is back in his seat. His mouth is open, but he isn't saying anything.

"Why not put it in the area you're not going to develop?" Francis finds himself suggesting. "The part designated for open land." Maybe that would make Mendoza feel better, he thinks.

"By the chaparral?"

"Yes."

"Because nobody would go there to see it," says Conrad Bullington, standing up.

THAT AFTERNOON, as if to put a capstone on Francis's sense of absurdity, two mammoth tractors, each dragging a trailer, labor up the hill to the replicated village. On each of the trailers are three well-used Portapotties, which a band of workmen who have followed in a jeep remove from the trailers and place in a ring around the little cluster of tulle huts like the walls of a medieval town. The Portapotties stand prominent under the ethereal California sky, a plastic Gothic; as they warm in the yellow sunshine, they begin to radiate a stink. Almaville's city manager, who would of course prefer to sprinkle these fields with huge houses and hot tubs and lawns, explains to the enraged Mendoza, "You can't just go defecate in the fields like a bunch of Indians." Francis is sure that it is Bullington who informed the city government that this was exactly what was happening and suggested the Portapotties—and wonders if the gesture was an act of friendship or an insult. In either case, Francis disobeys the city manager's edict, getting up at first light the next morning to climb further up the mountain, as he thinks an Indian would. But when he returns, the ring of Portapotties makes him laugh, a disillusioned giggle. His sense of the absurd is now complete.

THAT AFTERNOON, Francis gets a message that Peggy has called. He hurries down the hill to Mendoza's tiny office in a trailer to phone her back. He's happy that Peggy's called him, and not the other way around; but he has no idea why she's calling, and by the time he's halfway there, he's begun to worry that she's sick, or that Siddy's had an accident in Europe.

"You went to Cleveland!" he exclaims after Peggy tells him about her helping Fred Kindler with the recruiting. "With *him?*"

She doesn't answer. Why should she? She's already said it.

"Really?" he asks.

"Yes, and as a matter of fact, we're coming to recruit in San Francisco the last Monday of the month," she tells him "About three weeks from now. You can offer to join us there and help. That's why I called you." She doesn't tell him—why rub it in?—that she's sure the only reason Nan and Fred haven't asked him to help at the meeting even though he's right next door is that they don't trust him. The only reason she hasn't brought this up with them is that it is too embarrassing. That's why, just this morning, she decided to call him on her own and ask him to call Fred Kindler and offer his help.

"Francis, we can both help him," she says. "We can get together and help make things work for our new boss. So will you come or not?"

"Yeah, I'll be there." In fact, he's delighted to have this chance to redeem himself. Before he even leaves California!

"Good!" she says. "I knew you'd say that."

"You're coming out here! We can spend the night together."

"We're leaving right after the meeting," she says. "Night owl to Bradley. We have another recruiting gathering on campus that night."

"Peg! Go in the early morning."

"I'll think about it. I'll ask Fred."

"Ask Fred!"

"Of course. Who else would I ask, Francis? He's the headmaster, remember?"

He hears her resentment rising again, so holds himself in check—as if he were counting to ten. "We've been away from each other for weeks," he says at last.

"And who's fault is that?" she asks. Then, "I'm sorry. I shouldn't have gone back to that." She's so tired of being resentful! "Just join us in San Francisco, Francis," she pleads. "Just come and help him. Just do the *work*, all right?"

"Of course I'll come," he says. "I already said I would."

"Fine," Peggy says, her voice softening. "Call him and tell him."

"I'll call Nan White," he says.

"I think you should call *him*. He's the headmaster."

"I'll call Nan," he insists. "She's the admissions director. I'm not going over her head."

She knows this isn't the real reason. He's never cared much for such niceties. Now she's resentful again.

He waits for her to respond; he's ready to relent. What the hell, he'll just grit his teeth and call Fred Kindler. He knows perfectly well he doesn't have to like the guy, doesn't even have to approve of him; all he has to do is work for him. But when Peggy doesn't say anything, he drops the idea and changes the subject. He wants to make love to her, is what he wants. "How are you, Peg?" he begins.

"You know what? Let's wait until you're home to tell each other how we are. Over the phone it just makes me angry."

"All right, but I still miss you."

"Me too," she confesses.

"Maybe after San Francisco you won't be angry anymore."

"That would be nice, Francis."

"Then we'll spend that night together. There's no way I'll let you fly away that night."

"Maybe," she says. "Anyway, I'll see you in three weeks." Then she hangs up. Right away she regrets this ending. "Of course I'll stay the night," she whispers, to see how the words would sound, and thinks of calling him back—she knows he's waiting for just that. But she keeps hearing him refuse to call Fred Kindler. How childish! He could square things with Kindler with one simple call. She loves Francis one minute and is furious the next. How tired she is of going up and down with all these feelings!

Francis stands by the phone, hoping. After a while he knows Peggy isn't going to call. So he picks up the phone again and puts in a call to Nan White. It's Saturday. Back East it's three hours later, and even Nan has gone home. Unless she comes in on Sunday too, she won't get the message until Monday morning. Nevertheless, he leaves the message on her tape that he will attend the San Francisco recruiting meeting and asks her to call back with details. Then he hurries up the hill to the dig and gets back to work. They still have a few hours before it gets dark. Tonight, thinking of his chance to redeem himself, he'll sleep better than he has since leaving Connecticut.

When Nan White comes to work on Monday morning to hear Francis's message on her voice mail, she has no idea that Peggy has called him and urged him to attend the recruiting event. She assumes instead that Francis knew about it all along. Who more than the senior teacher to know such things? She forgets that the plan was made after Francis left. So she sticks to the original decision that Fred made on her advice not to include Francis Plummer. She's not going to ask Fred to make the same decision twice. If Francis Plummer is angry about this, let him be angry at her.

So she picks up her phone and leaves a message for Francis on Mendoza's tape. If she had waited a little longer she would have realized her mistake. But she has a rule: whenever you have something unpleasant to do, do it right away. "Thank you, but our plans are all set," she records at seven-thirty in the morning in Connecticut, while in California Francis is still asleep. "We have a very specific design," she adds to make the message less insulting. Then she puts Francis out of mind. She has a million things to do.

At breakfast, Mendoza hands Francis the note in which he has transcribed the message that Nan left on his tape. *"Thank you, but our plans are all set,"* Francis reads.

Mendoza sees the shock on Francis's face. "Anything wrong?" he asks. His voice is kindly, worried.

Still looking down at the note, Francis shakes his head. *"We have a very specific design."* He has no idea, of course, that these words aren't Kindler's and were added by Nan White to alleviate the insult. They have exactly the opposite effect. For who else but the head of school makes such decisions? *Specific* means without him. Kindler's slapped his face.

"I sure hope everything's all right at home," he hears Mendoza say.

"I have to go make a phone call," Francis says. "I'll be back in half an hour." He's going to call Kindler, interrupt whatever he's doing—he'd call even if it were the middle of the fucking night, he's so mad. What do you think, I'm not going to help get kids into the school? he wants to yell. But as he walks down the hill, he begins to change his mind, and by the time he's in the office he's decided: he won't stoop to argue with Kindler about his worthiness to represent the school—after all these years! It's humiliating enough already without his begging. And the insult to Peggy—after she's already invited him. Let Kindler do his own recruiting.

Mendoza is surprised to see him returning so soon. He sends Francis another worried look. "Everything's fine," Francis lies. He's tempted to tell Mendoza what is happening, and everything that has led up to it. After all, Mendoza's a kind of priest, a medicine man. He rejects the idea as just as crazy as Mendoza is. He keeps his mouth shut and goes to work.

By the middle of her day, Nan wakes up to what a dumb mistake she's made. Of course Francis will tell Peggy that he offered to come to the meeting and was refused. She's not about to let this insult to Peggy happen. She'll just have to call Francis right away before he tells Peggy and invite him after all. She'll make up something about how excited they were about that specific design, but now that they've had time to think about it. . . . And she'll make sure Francis understands the whole thing was her mistake, not Fred's. So she picks up the phone and leaves her new message.

But this message, which Francis listens to on Mendoza's office tape during the lunch break, doesn't assuage his feelings even a little. Instead, it makes him even angrier. And though he's been thinking that maybe he would show up at the event after all—what right has Kindler to tell him he can't participate?—now he's ten times more resolved not to attend. For he doesn't believe for a minute that the original refusal of his offer came from Nan. Why would she do that? They've known each other for years. He knows damn well she's the kind of person who doesn't pass the buck. So she's taking the heat for Kindler because he won't take it for himself. And what enrages him further is his assumption that the only reason for this recanting is Peggy's going to Kindler. Begging! She, a favored subject kneeling to the king on behalf of her unworthy husband. How do you think that makes me feel? he wants to ask her. But he's so deeply insulted he knows he won't ever be able to bring it up with her. There are some things between husband and wife best not talked about, and this is one of them. And another thing he knows: he's not even going to respond to Nan's recanted disinvitation; it doesn't deserve an answer.

MENDOZA'S CREW WORKS fervently for the next two weeks to find the Ohlone village. Francis commits entirely to the cause, discarding as much as he can his sense of absurdity and disbelief, and working harder than anyone except Lila, whose energy and passion he can't begin to equal. If the dig succeeds, his western adventure will not have been merely an escape.

Two Sundays later, with only six days left before their August first deadline, they've still found nothing. Mendoza stays up all night searching for an idea to rescue them, and at dawn, confusing desperation with inspiration, decides that impurity of resolve is the reason for the failure to find the village: "We haven't truly walked in the shoes of the Ohlones," he explains, and so he resolves the argument about whether only males should use the sweat house by declaring that they all will imitate the Ohlone purification ritual. They will stay most of the night in the sweat house, scraping the sweat off their bodies with willow sticks, building the heat to the fainting point, then building it more, until the present melts and they see visions. They will make themselves worthy by sweating out of their bodies the evil that causes them their blindness. While Mendoza urges fervently, Francis starts to giggle again as he did in Bullington's office. But when Lila reaches out from where she sits across the circle to touch his hand, he realizes that she's not doing so to join him in his laughter but to calm him down, and when he turns back toward Mendoza's voice, the little professor gives him such a pleading look that Francis agrees to the ritual.

Francis joins the others in helping Mendoza prepare the sweat house. He works hard, trying not to admit that every once in a while in the last few days he's found himself wondering if he really wants to find the village. The relentless searching has made him begin to feel it would be an invasion of the privacy of defenseless strangers to probe around in what they've left behind—especially if they find the burial ground. And now it's not much of a jump for him to understand that he will feel the same way when he gets home and stands in front of the Pequot display in Peggy's library. Maybe, deep down, he's always felt this way. He doesn't even want to think about that.

He tries also, unsuccessfully, to keep his mind from the fact that a crucial recruiting event for Miss Oliver's School for Girls will take place without him tomorrow night just across the Bay. As the afternoon goes by, he senses Mendoza's spirits lifting. "We won't let them sweep everything away, we'll protect their village, we'll protect their bones," Mendoza urges in his mesmerizing chant. "They are in the ground because they were the lesser-ranking members of the tribe and they didn't rank the honor of a funeral pyre," he adds—as if to prove that the meek shall inherit the earth.

That evening, twenty-four hours before the recruiting event in San Francisco that Francis has decided to spurn, the group assembles in the sweat house after the sun goes down.

They sit, male and female, in a tight circle, in their underwear, a completely asexual near-nakedness. Mendoza pushed for complete nakedness. "To be like Indians," he said. But Francis talked him out of it, over Lila's objections. "We don't have to go *that* far," he said. Now in the fading light, he sees Lila's face across from him, her eyes closed, sweat faintly glistening on her shoulders. He and she both know that Mendoza hasn't even got this right: the fire to heat the rocks still burns, and there's a hole in the domed roof to let the smoke out, but the Indians used rocks heated earlier by a fire and there was no hole above. Nevertheless, Lila's given herself, completely, unselfconsciously, to the ritual, entirely serious, and Francis is envious of youth, regretful of his common sense.

His almost naked butt itches where it presses against the scraped earth; he suspects there are bugs down there exploring; it gets hotter in the little hut; he's already wondering if he'll make it. To his left, one of the male students groans. "Shut up!" the girl next to him whispers, and from his right another girl: "Are you sure we're doing this right?" "Hush!" Says Mendoza. His face is uplifted. Sweat's running down his neck toward the black hairs on his puny chest. Francis looks longingly at the tiny closed doorway, imagining the spacious night outside, the cool evening air. Mendoza starts to chant.

It grows hotter. Without stopping his chant, Mendoza leans, stirs the fire. The lodge is full of smoke. Above through the hole in the roof blurs a single star. The rocks in the center gleam red in the coals.

The guttural syllables of Mendoza's chant rise in volume. Several of the students have joined him. Francis can't bring himself to join the chanting, though after a while it begins to sound more authentic. Different from the psalms that Peggy loves. He's glad Peggy can't see what he's doing. He sees two Francis Plummers simultaneously; one is dressed in sports coat and gray flannels and is talking convincingly to a group of teenage girls and their parents about Miss Oliver's School for Girls; the other sits almost naked, on the ground in a fake Indian hut, listening to Mendoza's chant while an army of bugs crawls up his ass.

As an antidote, he tries to keep his promise to Mendoza—and to himself—to see with Indian eyes. But no vision arrives. He sees only his little group of students and Mendoza in the blazing weather of the tiny hut. He is much further away from an Indian consciousness than he ever is back home—where the Oliver campus overlies an ancient Pequot village from which, sometimes, some hint seeps up into his brain—and where he knows he is needed.

Nevertheless, he starts to chant, forcing himself to get into it. In the red glow of the rocks, he sees Mendoza glancing at him in thanks. Mendoza stirs the coals with a long stick. The rocks grow redder. The end of the stick flames, lighting the hut. Shadows flicker. Lila's pouring sweat. Francis is dizzy, short of breath.

The chant seems strangely beautiful suddenly, the rhythm more accentuated. He feels the heavy frightening beating of his heart. It's much hotter now. The girl next to him moans softly. Mendoza stirs the fire again. Francis's heart's a loud drum. He starts to faint, feels himself falling away.

Then, in the acme of the heat, Mendoza makes a little motion with his hand, stops chanting. A syllable later, so does everyone else. Francis hears moaning, and one of the boy students, giving up, scoots out through the doorway. Lila leans, puts the tulle mat the boy kicked aside back over the doorway.

"Another hour," says Mendoza. "One more hour."

"Whatever it takes," Lila whispers. "A day, a week, a year, whatever it takes."

Half swooning in this furnace, his brain melting, Francis despairs: still no new visions arrive; instead he hears himself babbling to Peggy about church, stale territory, he's trying to make her laugh. "When the priest says 'lift up your hearts,' he tells her, "I see this huge red giblet I'm holding above me and it's dripping on my head," but she's not laughing. "Hotter," he hears Lila saying. "Make it hotter!" He can hardly see her across the little space, vague figure, disembodied, she hangs in air. Mendoza's airy body leans forward, he stirs the fire. "And when he says 'it is meet and right so to do,' Francis goes on in his unreadiness, "I always imagine 'it's meat and rice, LUUNCH TIME!' because by that time I'm so hungry! But the service goes on and on." Peggy's looking at him as if he were a little kid.

And then, as if he were outside himself, he listens, horrified, to his brain decide to try one more thing. He'll tell a joke to *this* congregation. That'll take the heat off, you can't fail if it's only a joke. "What's the difference between a BMW and a porcupine?" he asks. Mendoza looks across the fire at him, disgust written all over his face, Lila looks away, and no one else seems to hear. "With a porcupine the pricks are on the outside," Francis announces.

"All right, enough!" Mendoza shouts, giving up. He starts to get up on his knees to crawl out the little door, faints. Lila reaches to support him. Francis does too, but Lila pushes his hand away. Mendoza stirs, gets back onto his knees, pushes aside the tulle mat, and crawls out. Everyone follows. Outside the little hut in the cool of the starry night, Francis is as embarrassed as he has ever been. He can't wait to escape to his hut.

"There's one more thing," says Mendoza, looking straight at Francis. "We'll give you one more chance." Mendoza, Lila, and Francis are standing now by the entrance to Mendoza's hut. The others have drifted off to bed. They've just finished hosing themselves down, in the stink of the Portapotties, from the water truck, parked between two of the them. "Because there are no creeks left," Mendoza explains, after they are back near his hut, away from the stink. "In those days, before the white man destroyed the water table, these hills were traced with creeks, the country was actually wet." He sweeps his hand. The windless night is domed with stars. Behind them, Mount Alma's dark shape looms. Smell of dew on dry adobe ground.

"One more thing," Mendoza says again, then disappears into his hut. "For those who dare," he says, reappearing and looking again straight at Francis. He's carrying a canvas bag.

He pulls out a plastic tarp, spreads it on the ground. Then an Atlas jar, with something white inside. "Lime," he says. "I made it myself; ground up seashells." Then a canvas pouch. "Tobacco. The final step in the purification process was this." He dumps a little pile of lime on the tarp, mixes in the tobacco. "The Ohlones grew tobacco on these hillsides," he explains.

"You can't smoke lime," Francis says. Lila gives him another funny look.

"Wasn't going to," Mendoza says. He's dividing the mess into three parts. "Going to eat it." He stands, one pile cupped in his two hands; holds them out to Lila. "Ladies first," he says. Lila puts her hands out, cupped like Mendoza's, and receives.

"Eat it?" Francis hears the squeak in his voice.

"That's right. We eat it."

"What for?" he says as if he were curious and wanted to understand.

"It's an emetic," says Mendoza, holding his cupped hands out to Francis.

"Emetic?"

"A cleanser."

"Do we do it here?" Lila asks.

"You take it to someplace you want to be alone," Mendoza answers. "It's a very private experience."

"How do you know, you ever done it?" Francis asks. His hands are down by his sides. Mendoza's hands are still held out to him, offering.

"I read about it," Mendoza says. "Makes you clean. Empty like after fasting."

"You mean you *puke?*" asks Francis.

"Well, if you want to talk about it that way."

"I don't like to puke." Then trying to be funny again: "It comes out my nose." He glances at Lila. She's looking hard at him. Not smiling.

"It's different," he hears Mendoza saying. "You get convulsions, go in and out of consciousness. You don't get sick and then get well. You go in one place and come out another."

Francis's hands are still down at his sides. Mendoza looks hard at his eyes, drops his outstretched arms, shrugs, turns, walks away, taking the offering for himself. He leaves the third portion on the tarp by Francis's feet. Francis stares down at it. When he looks up, he can see Lila walking away through the dark. He knows where she's going: a ridgetop on which he has watched her sitting in the early morning waiting for the sun. He leaves the powder on the tarp and goes to his hut.

But, of course, he doesn't sleep.

He lies on his cot hearing the wind that rises now, riffling the walls of his hut. In his head he watches again as Lila walks away toward her ridgetop, and sees himself spurning Mendoza's offering hands, and it comes to him, now that they know the dig will fail, that it will be his fault, not Mendoza's. He knows the thought doesn't make any sense—it was Mendoza's bungling that doomed the venture—but it won't go away, and he spends the few hours remaining in the night tortured by it. In the morning as the group returns dispiritedly to work, the students avoid his eyes.

At the lunch break he sits down next to Lila; he wants to apologize and explain to her that he is not as free as she is to be like an Indian, he has too much history in another role. Before he can even begin, she gets up and moves away.

It's not hard to understand how insulted Lila is, how abandoned she feels, by what she can only interpret as Francis's irreverence, the apogee of which was his dumb joke in the sweat house. For it was Lila who listened to the story his wife never wants to hear, and gravely explained its meaning. It was she who legitimized his spiritual hunger, who said, "He's your totem," speaking with no hesitation of the turtle who chose to appear to Francis, "from out of the time when the world was here and human beings were not." A few years hence, Lila will lighten her disappointment with a helpful dose of irony. Right now she and her passion are too young; and, after all, she thought she'd found in Francis an adult soul mate, something very rare, and a surrogate dad—and now she thinks he's neither.

And on Francis's part, he can't see the legitimacy of his spiritual hunger anymore—though it is just as legitimate as it always was. Not after this summer's chain of events, he can't, for all he can see is the farce of his western adventure: the Portapotties, Mendoza's bungling, Bullington's greasy infallibility, his own sacrilegious delirium in the sweat house. That and the embarrassing fact that he's been running away from his responsibilities. And so, right here and now, he declares to himself that he is through with all that: all spiritual questing from now on will be in tune with Peggy's, he tells himself, forgetting that he tried that for years and was always hungry.

And he'll return to his responsibilities, his legitimate role at the head's right hand. On this, at least, he's on solid ground. For there *is* a school to save. And he *is* the senior teacher.

The first step he'll take is to show up tomorrow night at the San Francisco recruiting event. So what if he's not wanted? Fred Kindler, mere upstart, has no right to keep him away.

SO, LATE IN THE afternoon of the next day, he walks down the hill to where his yellow Chevy is parked, opens the trunk, pulls out his suitcase, extricates his gray flannels, his tweed sports coat, his blue button-down shirt and striped tie. He puts them on in the shade of an oak tree, and now he's in uniform again. Then he gets in the car and combs his hair in the rearview mirror. Francis starts to drive.

Sylvia Jackson, a spinster, class of 1958 (the first year of the reign of Marjorie Boyd) is hosting the event. Francis gets to her big Victorian in Pacific Heights too early. He wants to arrive after most of the guests have assembled so he can enter unobtrusively and take a seat in the back after Kindler has begun to talk. Less of a scene that way. Then, after the talk, he'll mingle with the guests and say the things about his beloved school that bring the families in. He doesn't even think about what he'll say to Kindler and Peggy after the meeting's over.

To kill time, he drives the several blocks to Divisadero to find a place to park. Then he sits in the car, listening to the news. George H. Bush is giving a news conference. Usually whenever Bush says anything, Francis talks back to the radio or TV screen, loudly explaining all the ways he's sure the president is wrong; but tonight he's so keyed up he barely listens. At eight-fifteen he gets out of the car and starts to walk. From high up on Divisadero hill, he can see the water in the Bay shading to purple in the sunset. The air is cold and sharp. In this, the most beautiful city in the world, Francis is hungry for the smell of his New England woods, the sight of his river.

Fifteen minutes later, he climbs the steps, crosses the porch, and stops at the door. For an instant he thinks he'll turn around, he's never gone anywhere he's not wanted before. Then he pushes on the heavy door, and now he's standing in the foyer and to his left through the opening to the living room he sees the backs of about eighteen people, three of whom, he notices immediately, are teenage girls. Some of the guests are sitting on sofas, some in folding chairs, and Fred Kindler is standing facing them. Fred sees him first as he tries to tiptoe in. Their eyes meet and hold, and Kindler stops talking.

And everyone turns around to see who's coming in the door.

In the front row, Gail and Nan and Peggy turn too. At first, all he can see is Peggy. Her face is lit with relief. "Hello," she mouths to him, and Fred Kindler smiles and says aloud, disguising his surprise, "Here's Mr. Plummer, everybody, our senior teacher. I'm so glad he's here."

All the alumnae and parents of present students know Francis, of course. They stand up to greet him, so that only the three families who are being recruited remain in their seats; and in the back row of folding chairs nearest him, Marcia Bradford, whom he's known since she entered the school twenty-one years ago and whose daughter, Mary, is Eudora's kinesthetic furniture student, reaches for his hands and holds them while her husband slaps his shoulders. "Why, it's Francis Plummer," she loudly exclaims. "My favorite teacher! It's so good to see you!"

"I didn't mean to interrupt," Francis says to the room, speaking the truth and stepping gently back from the Bradfords. This glaring entrance is exactly what he didn't want.

"That's all right, I've finished," Kindler says. But he really hasn't. He has a few more things to say—that now he can't say because it would be too awkward to start again.

And anyway, nobody's even looking at him anymore.

"Mr. Plummer, give us your thoughts. Come on up here and tell us what *you* think makes this school so special" Fred urges, forcing himself to smile. What else can he do in front of all these people? He's wary, thinking of how little Nan trusts this guy, and remembering Cleveland, Sharon Maynard's treachery, and the woman in the red dress. Just the same, Plummer's here, he must have come to help, he tells himself and glances at his teammates. Gail is frowning. Nan looks worried. But Peggy's smiling at Francis. She wants her husband to come up front and stand beside me, Fred thinks. So maybe it's going to be all right. He beckons to Francis.

"No. Really, I didn't mean to interrupt," Francis insists.

But that's just what you did! Fred thinks. You came in late and made a showy entrance. Now he feels small for even thinking this way. Just the same, he'd never do what Plummer just did if it were the other way around. He beckons again. Peggy's nodding across the chairs to Francis, urging him.

"Come on, Clark, talk to us!" Marcia Bradford says.

"All right, I'll just say a few words from here," Francis says, relenting— he knows how churlish it would appear for him to keep on refusing. But he's not about to go up front and be even more obtrusive. And besides, he isn't going to stand beside Kindler and help the man pretend he's glad to see him. When he had to be forced to invite him!

But Francis's attempt not to draw attention to himself has the opposite effect. All the guests turn completely around in their chairs to face him. Some, in the folding chairs, even turn the chairs themselves around. Now all their backs are to Fred. He might as well not be in the room. Nan watches Gail's face. Do you see what I see? she wants to ask her. He's sucking the power right out of the room and to himself, the egotistical little bastard! He's cutting your husband's legs right out from under him.

Francis is only going to say a few things, for he feels like the bull in the china shop. He roves his eyes around the room, thinking what to say. He looks at each of the three potential students. Affluenza, he thinks, the symptoms printed on their faces: entitlement warring with the unacknowledged hunger to have their desires resisted, and starts to talk directly to them—as if they were the only ones in the room. "I'd think carefully before I signed up for Miss Oliver's School for Girls," he starts. "You need to be sure that's what you really want to do. Don't say we didn't warn you." And then he tells them why: "Because there's never enough time at Miss Oliver's School for Girls."

"Something in the air of Oliver's demands that limits be pushed," he tells them. "It's just the way we are, it's a crazy kind of place. When you write a paper for an Oliver teacher you'll always get it back, it won't be good enough, you'll *always* do it again. Are you ready for that? If you think you're weak in math or science, don't worry: we'll pile on the math and science until you know you aren't. Same with history. Same with art. Nobody gets enough sleep at Miss Oliver's School for Girls." He goes on like this, much longer than he intended, strewing hyperbole to make his point. He never shows them the top of the mountain he's inviting them to climb, only how hard the climb. That's what grabs *these* kids' attention, focuses their minds, changes what they want. If they needed to see something else about the school he loves, he'd show them that.

He knows only great teachers can bore into someone else's mind like this—only they have this kind of power. Maybe that's why teachers are paid so little: what they earn has more power than money.

When he stops, there's silence. And then there's applause and Fred Kindler announces that the formal part of the evening is over—for anything more would be anticlimax—and the guests get up from their seats, and the next thing Francis knows is that at least ten of the guests are moving to him. They surround him, virtually backing him against the wall, thanking him for his talk, telling him stories about when they were in school, asking questions, and Marcia Bradford is hugging him. Over her shoulder he sees Fred and Gail talking with exactly one guest. The three potential students are gathered around Nan and Peggy. Francis extricates himself as soon as he can, pretending to be dying for a glass of white wine, moves to the table that serves as a bar, pours himself a glass, and then, as soon as he sees that Nan and the three girls have drifted away from her, he moves to Peggy, and stands beside her. He senses her body stiffen. "Hello," he says under his breath.

She doesn't turn to him, stares straight ahead.

"Hello," he says again. She still doesn't answer. He sees Kindler glance at them from the other side of the room, then look away. "Hey," he murmurs to Peggy, "this *is* a recruiting session, isn't it? Well, I recruited." He points with his chin to where, on the other side of the room, Nan is handing folders to each of the three girls. "That's the application packet," he says. "How much you want to bet they sign up?"

"We'll talk later," she says, and moves away from him.

He starts to follow, putting his hand out to hers to hold her back. Then he changes his mind and lets her go, watching her as she moves across the room to where Gail and Nan are talking to some parents.

A few minutes later, the guests begin to leave. Fred Kindler and Sylvia Jackson stand at the front door to say good-bye. Nan, Gail, Peggy, and Francis stay in the living room. Soon most of the guests are gone, but the conversation drifts in through the open door from the front porch where people are lingering. Just as the last guest goes out the door, Francis hears an angry voice. It's clearly Mr. Bradford's, Marcia's husband, Mary's father, and it's loud enough to for everyone inside the house to hear: "Why didn't they make *him* the head, Francis Plummer, for Christ's sake, can anybody answer that?"

After a little moment, Fred moves from the foyer where he's been standing with Sylvia by the door, toward the living room. He stops in the archway and looks right at Francis.

"Look," Francis begins. "I didn't mean—"

"I know you didn't," Fred cuts him off. It's true: he can see what happened. The guy has gifts, that's all. Just the same, he's furious.

Francis tries again. "Really, I came to help," he says.

"Fine. Thanks," Kindler says. He's not going to talk about it. Not in front of all these people. Maybe never. Gail moves across the room and stands beside him.

"I think you people could use a drink," Sylvia offers. "How about it? Anyone want to join me?" She moves toward the bar.

"Thanks, but we have to get back to the airport," Nan says.

They all move toward the front door now where Sylvia stands saying good-bye. Then out on the porch, Fred turns to Peggy. "Good-bye, Peg," he says. "I'll see you tomorrow." He gives her a hug. "Thanks for all you do," he adds. "You're wonderful." Then he turns to Francis and shakes his hand. "I'm glad you came," he says, and forces himself to add, "We probably will enroll those three girls. It was your speech that did it." What else can he do in this situation but hide his resentment and blossoming mistrust—and be gracious? He knows he'll be hearing that Bradford person asking his question over and over, probably for the rest of his life.

"We all did it, not just me," Francis says, and Kindler gives him a look of contempt and Francis knows that Kindler knows he's lying—for it *was* his speech that nailed those kids—and now he feels his own anger rising. Everyone is blaming this on him! Learn how to make your own fucking speeches, he wants to say. He keeps his gaze on Kindler's eyes. Maybe the guy will read his mind. Then Gail and Nan hug Peggy too, and nod coldly to Francis, and Gail puts her hand through her husband's crooked arm, and the three walk down the steps, leaving Peggy and Francis alone on the porch.

"So?" he says, "you're staying."

Peggy sighs. "I made a reservation at the Hilton. I changed my flight to tomorrow morning."

"Good." That's all he's going to say. He's wary. It's her move. When Peggy doesn't respond, he says, "Wait here, I'll bring the car around so you don't have to carry your bag." Then he goes down the steps and heads for Divisadero.

"I wouldn't have if I'd known what you were going to do," she murmurs. He pretends he doesn't hear.

On the way to the hotel they keep their distance, hardly talk at all. Francis is sure that when he's alone with her in their hotel she'll admit she understands that what happened at Sylvia's house was the farthest thing in the world from what he'd intended. And he'll confess that, yes, maybe whether or not he approves of the new headmaster, he should have stayed home to help him. I'm through with all that, he's going to say. I'm going to put that quest aside, beat those feelings down, and rush home as soon as the dig is over at the end of the week, do my job. My head's on straight again, he's going to promise her. And there's a school to save.

Fifteen minutes later, alone with her in their hotel room, he starts by trying for a hug.

"I'm tired," she says. She puts her hand on his chest, holding him off, then steps back from him.

"It's only eleven o'clock," he says.

"It's two o'clock my time, and I got up at six."

He turns his back, goes to the mirror over the bureau, and starts to take off his tie. "What was I supposed to do?" he asks. "Give a lousy talk? Bore 'em to death?"

"Don't be funny, Francis"

"What then?"

She doesn't answer.

"What, Peggy?"

"I don't want to talk about it," she says.

"Maybe he just doesn't have it, Peg," he says. He knows he shouldn't—especially right after making up his mind to help the guy—but he feels hurt that she pushed him away, and now *he* wants to hurt. "Is that why you don't want to talk about it? Maybe your hero's the wrong guy for the job."

That gets her. She comes up behind him. He can see her face in the mirror, to the right of his. "How would you know?" she asks. "You've talked with him for exactly ten minutes at a cocktail party, for goodness sake!"

"Yeah, the first two minutes were enough."

"Just before you made an ass of yourself by insulting Milton Perkins."

"I wasn't making an ass of myself, Peg," he goads. "I'm *supposed* to insult him. He's a *Republican!* That's what they're for."

"And then you run away and come sauntering back a month later, and barge right in in the middle of his speech, and make him look bad."

"Yeah," he says. "It was so easy I couldn't resist."

Peggy doesn't say anything now. He watches her face in the mirror. She stares back over his shoulder. He thinks he sees her expression slide from anger to contempt—and then to sadness. "Make all the jokes you want," she finally says. "He's worth six of you!"

"Oh, he is?" he says. "Then marry him!"

"You bastard," she says. Then she crosses to her suitcase, gets her pajamas and her kit with her toothbrush in it, and goes into the bathroom and shuts the door. When she comes out, she gets into bed. He gets ready in the bathroom too, then comes out and gets in the other side. They lie miles apart, listening to each other breathe, each waiting for the other to take the words back. They wouldn't hurt so much if they were true. Neither of them speaks, and finally they fall asleep. Early in the morning, when Peggy leaves for the airport and Francis leaves for Mount Alma, they barely say goodbye, and don't touch each other.

Four days later at noon, when there is only one afternoon remaining to Mendoza's allotted time, and it's absolute that the dig will fail, Lila looks Francis steadily in the eye, not trying very hard to hide her disillusionment, and tells him she won't be going home with him, she'll go by air instead, and he pretends he really does believe she wants to get home in a hurry. The next morning the bulldozers come, and Francis starts his long ride home, alone.

SIX

FRANCIS IS ON Route 80, zooming eastward. Still in California, he already feels the homeward end of the long cement, a string on which he's gladly nowhere, here and there at the same time. He drives on and on, planning not to stop. Climbs the Sierra, cranks the windows shut, turns on the air conditioning so he can't smell the world. He's in a tunnel shooting home.

But when he comes down the steep eastern slope where the evening light washes the Nevada desert, he gives up because he can't resist what's outside his car any longer. He opens the window, kills the air conditioning, swims in the rushing air—and gets off Route 80 west of Winnemucca onto a thin, pocked, blacktop road so he can be closer to the land.

The road follows the shape of the earth, up rounded brown hills and down, while the sky grows red, then fades to the deepest blue, then dies and through the windshield he can see the stars. The space between him and the bright pinpricks in the black, and this space on the solid, is the same.

Francis stops the car, gets out into the caressing night, walks down the side bank. When he looks back over his shoulder, nervous about getting lost, he sees the car silhouetted above him; so he walks farther away, up over a hill, until when he looks back, his car is gone. He sits down on the ground, wrapped in the cooling air, the smells of dry earth, cactus, sage. He hears a scrabbling behind him: maybe a gopher, he thinks, maybe a fox?

No people, no buildings. No churches, no schools. No meetings, no books. No theories. If he stays here long enough, refrains from thinking, casts off his memories, fasting, he will become part of this, he tells Siddy in his mind, feeling a little crazy, and longing for the presence of his son. Maybe Mendoza was wrong: his offered potion wasn't Francis's last chance after all, maybe this potential hermitage is yet another.

"Jeez, Dad, get a life!" says Siddy, red-faced with embarrassment, and then melts, and now Francis is wondering if he'll find his car, remembering stories about people dying in the desert. He waits, recalling what Peggy would say about being open to the grace that comes, for isn't that what happens in the desert, the spirit's livening as the body struggles not to die? But grace doesn't come and all he feels is agitation. He can't sit still. He gives up, rises, trudges, finds the side bank immediately, discovers the disappointment of the lost fear, the car looming above him in the dark. As he nears it he can hear the ticking of the cooling metal.

In an hour, Francis is in Winnemucca: red neon, smell of frying meat, yellow glow that tries to dim the stars, straight streets that end. He's falling asleep, can't drive anymore. So he gives up.

The motel room is pink. The double bed is reflected in a mirror that covers one wall, there's a condom machine in the bathroom, it takes him forever to peel the plastic wrap from the plastic glass so he can have a drink, the taste of chlorine mixes with the smell of the disinfectant they've cleaned the room with, the air conditioner hums full blast, and it's freezing in the room. It's not in him to understand that he can adjust the temperature on the air conditioner, so he gets on the bed with all his clothes on, pulls the polyester blankets up to his chin, noticing the tiny sparks they give off when they rub against his hands, and falls asleep.

And dreams: his ancestor, semifamous Divine, the founder of a town, the beginning of a line—whose portrait Francis's father loved, and stood below to lecture him—has come weirdly down out of his frame above the mantelpiece from where his eyes followed wherever you went and stands now glowering over his bed in this pink motel room in Nevada. His pudgy, sanctimonious hands, one on a Bible, the other lying open on the rounded stomach, he wants to know what Francis was doing acting like a naked redskin savage in a sweat house miles from home and wife and work.

Francis opens one eye and winks, "If you have to ask, you'll never know," he says, quoting Louis Armstrong, and wakes up laughing.

Bolt upright on the bed, he's amazed at his answer—and stunned by the lightness he feels. He's made the right decision: he's rushing home to heal his marriage, protect his reputation, and save the school. He doesn't have to defend himself to anyone! In the very early morning he starts driving again.

THREE NIGHTS LATER, past midnight, Peggy opens the door to Francis's knock. He's standing in the doorway, a suitcase in each hand. Levi's standing on his hind legs, trying to lick his face.

Peggy grabs Levi's collar, tugs him back into the house. "Hi," she says. "Come in." Like welcoming a neighbor who's come across the lawn to borrow a cup of sugar.

He's in the house now. She can see the two suitcases side by side where he's left them on the welcome mat. "Peg," he says and reaches out. But his arms are tentative and she stays back.

"Have you eaten?" she asks.

"Not hungry."

"Sure you are," she says. "It's the middle of the night. You have to be." If she can be busy making a sandwich, and he can be busy eating it, it'll make this easier. She goes into the kitchen, and he follows. He almost trips over Levi, who is banging against his legs.

Peggy opens the refrigerator door, bends down, looks in. "I'm really not hungry," he insists. She stands up, holding a plate of cold cuts in one hand and faces him. He steps across the little space between them, touches her face and hugs her. She puts her arm around his shoulder, but keeps her other arm stiff, still holding the plate.

"Half a hug is all I get?"

She doesn't answer. She doesn't put the plate down either. For now, she thinks. It isn't just that's she's angry; it isn't just that she's sad. I don't know what I'm supposed to do, she wants to say. I don't know how to act when I feel like this.

She's relieved when Levi doesn't follow them into the bedroom. She doesn't want Francis to know where their dog's been sleeping. They turn their backs to each other when they undress. Then Francis lies down stiffly next to her on the bed. She turns the light out. He doesn't move, and neither does she. "Peg," he says into the dark. "I'm sorry."

She doesn't answer. He hasn't turned to her; he's said the words straight up at the ceiling.

"I'm home, Peg. It's all right now. And tomorrow, I'll go see Fred Kindler. I'll work it out with him."

She hears him draw a breath, is sure he is going to explain. "Good," she says. "I'm glad of that. And I'm glad you're home, I really am. But don't ever try to tell me why you went away. What you were looking for. I'd rather have my head in the sand," then waits in the silence hoping he'll insist on explaining anyway.

"I wasn't going to try," he says at last.

She knows he doesn't want to turn his back to her, and neither does she to him. So they both lie on their backs, not touching, and after a while she drifts off to sleep.

SEVEN

THE FIRST THING Francis does early the next morning is call Fred Kindler's office and ask for a meeting. He's surprised when Kindler answers instead of Margaret Rice. He doesn't know yet that now the head-master gets in before the secretary.

"Wait a sec," Kindler says, "you don't mean *today*. You're in California!"

"No, I'm not. I'm home."

"Really! You're home? What happened?"

Francis doesn't answer for a second.

"You all right?"

"Yes, I'm all right."

Now it is Kindler who doesn't say anything.

"Really, I'm fine," Francis says.

"And you want to *talk?*"

"Yes."

"Good!" Kindler exclaims.

"I mean it," Francis perseveres, assuming that Kindler's being sarcastic. "I want to talk."

"So do I." Kindler responds. Francis is taken aback. He was wrong: there's no sarcasm in Kindler's tone.

"Mr. Plummer?" Fred says softly. For he's had time since San Francisco to think about what happened there. He's explained to himself that Francis Plummer's just a better speaker than he is, that's all. And he wasn't late because he wanted to show the new headmaster up, he was late because he's been at Miss Oliver's all his life, where everybody's always late, and then he stayed in the back of the room because he was embarrassed. Fred's resentment still boils when he hears inside his head Mr. Bradford's loud question: Why didn't they make *him* the head, for Christ's sake? But Fred s a grown-up; he understands these things. He's tamped his resentment down so he can receive the message: *if people think Francis Plummer should be the headmaster, then make Francis Plummer his partner.* "Mr. Plummer, you there?" he asks again.

"I'll be right over," Francis tells him.

With Fred Kindler's surprisingly friendly tone ringing in his head, Francis is full of hope as he crosses the campus toward Kindler's office.

Francis Plummer, aka Clark Kent, is home again where he belongs, and where he's always known exactly what to do.

But the first thing he sees as he enters the headmaster's office is a huge Mickey Mouse wristwatch on the wall behind Fred Kindler's desk. Its fake straps extend all the way from the ceiling to the big round figure of Mickey in the middle and then down to the floor. And next to this dipsy timepiece is a floor-to-ceiling computer printout of an exclamation point.

For all his good intentions, Francis is appalled. He can't remember a time before he started to hate this cornball little rodent, and all his cutesy friends, romance stealers of his youth. In his boyhood he'd been a Phantom freak, a Batman worshiper. Who could want a *mouse?* He knows it's silly to be so put off by a mere office decoration, but there *is* a certain style at Miss Oliver's, a certain way of being that says who we are in ways that words can never say. And this just isn't it!

Fred Kindler stands up quickly, comes around his desk toward Francis, sticks his hand out. "Welcome back, Mr. Plummer. It's good to see you."

They shake. Kindler's hand is very firm. "I really appreciate your wanting to talk," he says, and they sit down, facing each other in the two chairs in front of Fred's desk. Francis squelches the urge to make the space between himself and Kindler bigger.

"I'd like to get something off my chest right away," Kindler says.

Francis is sure that Kindler's going to tell him it was wrong of him to go to California when he was needed here. I'll agree, Francis thinks. I won't defend myself.

"That was a great speech you made," Fred Kindler says.

Francis is too surprised to answer.

"Thanks to that speech, we got the three girls who attended."

"We did?" Francis says, pretending surprise.

"Yes, we did. We didn't get any in Chicago, and we didn't get any in St. Louis. Philadelphia netted exactly one, and Boston two, and I'm sure Peggy's told you what happened in Cleveland."

Francis keeps his face blank. Kindler's the last person in the world he wants to know how little he and Peg are talking. He doesn't have the foggiest idea what happened in Cleveland.

"She did tell you what happened?"

"Not yet. I just got home."

Fred nods to cover his surprise, then realizes he's *not* surprised. But he is embarrassed: he didn't mean to look as if he were prying. As briefly as he can, he tells Francis what happened in the Maynard's house in Shaker

Heights. He skips the part about how Peggy got up and told everyone that Marjorie left of her own free will. That would just make Francis angry. But he does want to warm Francis up by telling him how much he admires his wife. So he makes it very clear how thoroughly Peggy blew the lady in the red dress right out of the water when she asked if he were going to let boys in. "She saved the day," Fred says. "She was wonderful."

What Francis hears is miles away from Fred Kindler's intent. He thinks Kindler is rubbing it in how much more admirably Peggy has been acting than he has. Francis is ready to admit he should have stayed home. But he isn't ready to hear Kindler go on and on about it. Now the humiliation of Peggy's having to beg Kindler to let him participate in San Francisco rankles more than ever. Just thinking about it makes him angry all over again.

"I wish we had some more recruiting events to do," Kindler goes on. "If I'd known you were coming home so early, I would have scheduled at least two of them for later."

"Now that you know I'm not a traitor?" Francis blurts.

Kindler is surprised. Where did *that* come from? "No," he murmurs. "Now that I know how good a recruiter you are."

Francis waits for Kindler to say more. He wants to hear Kindler apologize for making Peggy beg.

"I never thought you were a traitor," Fred says.

Francis is still waiting.

But Fred, who doesn't have even an inkling that Francis assumes Peggy had to beg for him, isn't about to let Francis know that the person he should be angry with is Nan White, not him, first for advising him not to invite Francis, then for standing by the decision, then for changing her mind. Fred Kindler is the head. He doesn't pass the buck. "*Traitor's* not the word," he says. "I could get a little irritated for your suggesting that I thought it was."

All right, Francis thinks. He's not going to do it, he just doesn't have the guts to clear the air.

"As a matter of fact, I could get more than a little irritated," Fred Kindler says, because clearing the air is exactly what he is trying to do. "It was perfectly reasonable for me to assume that having been here for thirty-three years, intensely loyal to Mrs. Boyd and her right-hand person, you might well have been a little too uncomfortable with the change."

"To be a good recruiter," Francis finishes bitterly.

"That's right," Fred Kindler agrees. His tone is mild and matter-of-fact. "That's what I thought. I'm glad I changed my mind."

Francis hears the generosity of that remark and forces himself to accept it. "Well, I'm home now. I'm here." He needs this meeting to succeed as much as Kindler does.

"I'm glad you are," Fred says, and then adds, "I hope everything's all right." For he doesn't know that one of the reasons Francis is home so far ahead of time is to get back to work for the school right away.

"It is and it isn't. I'm glad to be home. But the dig failed," Francis says, sharing his news to nurture this friendly tone—though he doesn't share that he's beginning to feel relieved that they didn't find the village—especially the burial ground. What would they have done with the bodies? "We ran out of time," he says.

"So soon!"

So Francis tells the story of what happened. He says nothing about his spiritual quest that he's abandoned for his marriage's sake; and he down-plays Mendoza's incompetence as much as he can. He feels a surprising loyalty to Mendoza, wants to protect him.

Fred sees right through Francis's defense of Mendoza—and likes him for it. "Poor Mendoza," he says. "Such an interesting man. All he needed was a little administrative help."

Once again, Francis has been slapped in the face. He assumes that Kindler's telling him that not only did he fail as the head's right-hand man but as Mendoza's too.

Kindler has no idea that he's insulted Francis. It never even crossed his mind to think of Francis as an *administrator*. "Well, anyway, I hope you had an interesting time," he says.

"It was a good experience," Francis lies.

"That's one of the things I miss from when I was a teacher," Kindler says, "the long summer."

Francis nods again.

"But by the time the summer was half over, I was always itchy to get back."

"Yes, that happens," Francis murmurs.

"I had a nice talk with your wife about that just that a week or so ago," Fred says, still trying hard. God, this guy's hard to talk to! he thinks.

Francis nods again. "That's nice," is all he can think of to say. He tries hard to focus, but he soon loses track of what Kindler is saying because he's still burning about Kindler's administrator remark. And besides, he's *still* waiting for the chance to say what he came here to say: that he knows it was a mistake to go away; that he really is back on track, ready to go, he can be counted on. If he can get that off his chest, he'll be fine again. He sees

Kindler's lips move under the red mustache, hears his voice, but the shape of the words is indistinct and distant. Like the far-off quacking of ducks.

"Of course, we weren't really talking about her because *she* was quite busy here all summer," Kindler says, and immediately regrets it. Plummer will take it as a dig. Maybe it *is* a dig, he thinks. Maybe I can't help it.

"Who?" ask Francis. When he sees the surprise on Kindler's face, he catches on. He knows now, but it's too late.

"Why, your wife," Kindler says. "Peggy. That's who we were talking about."

"Oh! Of course," Francis mumbles. *Whom,* he wants to say. *Whom* we were talking about. "Yes, she was very busy," he says out loud.

"May I get you a cup of coffee?" Kindler asks, drifting now from irritation to worry. Maybe Plummer *is* cracking up. Francis shakes his head. "Tea? Water? Anything?"

"No, thanks. I'm fine."

There's a silence, and then Kindler resumes: "Well you certainly weren't bored either. Can't wait to hear you talk to the students about it. You and Lila Smythe."

"She did better than I," Francis confesses. "She threw herself into it."

"Oh?" Fred Kindler leans forward in his chair. Now their knees are almost touching. "It must have been tough not to find the village. Especially for Lila." Kindler is genuinely interested. He's finally gotten this conversation rolling!

"For her it was," Francis says. "She never doubted until the end. While I just felt silly a lot of the time."

Fred leans even further forward; he's frowning slightly, intently interested. "I *think* I understand," he says. He senses the hunger in Francis, how unassuaged it is, and discovers a deepening respect. It's a good surprise.

On the verge of intimacy, Francis hesitates. He wants to spill his feelings, get them outside himself, find their validation—the way he can with Father Woodward, and could with Lila who, before he lost her, understood him instantly. But he's not ready to share with Kindler what he can't even explain to Peggy. He shrugs his shoulders and looks away.

Fred leans back in his chair. He's disappointed. "Some other time, maybe," he murmurs. "I'd really be very interested." He looks at his watch. "Right now let's talk."

"All right. Let's," Francis agrees. The moment for sharing's gone. He already regrets that.

"Now that Mrs. Boyd is gone, you are the embodiment of this school,"

Fred begins. "You symbolize it for everybody, the alumnae, the students. More than anybody. Surely more than me—the newcomer."

Francis looks past Kindler to the monstrous watch on the wall. More than *I*, he thinks. Not *me*. *I.*

"I need your help. We need to work together, it's as plain as that."

"Listen," Francis interrupts. "That's what I came in here to say. I want to work with you—and you didn't have to ask. That's why I came home so fast—that and to be with my wife. I will do anything you want except—" Francis wants to say it: *except help you bring in boys,* but he hesitates, and Kindler cuts him off.

"Let's not get to the exceptions," he says. "Not now. Because if we do this right, there won't be any."

"All right," Francis says.

"Good," Fred says. Then, softening his voice: "I think I understand how difficult this change must be for you. I really do."

"That's not the point," Francis declares. He doesn't want excuses for himself.

"It's one of them. You've been here for thirty-three years. I'm only thirty-seven years old, for goodness sake!"

"I can handle it," Francis says.

"All those years serving one person! I know how much you depended on each other."

"I can *handle* it," Francis repeats.

"Well, I'm not sure *I* could," Kindler says even more softly. "Not without some help."

Francis stares. "Help? What do you mean, *help?*"

Kindler is looking him right in the eye. "I simply mean there's a lot of stress. A huge amount in a change situation like this."

Francis turns his head ninety degrees away from Kindler's gaze.

"All right, I've overstepped," Kindler says. "All I meant is that if you, or anyone else on the faculty, wanted some counseling, some advice about dealing with the kind of strong emotions that come with this kind of change, I want it known that over the summer I got the board to extend the insurance to cover it. But I intruded on your privacy. I should have waited. I'm sorry."

Francis isn't hearing Kindler talking about the predictable, normal stress that organizational change engenders; he's hearing his new boss, Marjorie's usurper, telling him he's sick. He starts to stand up.

"Please, Mr. Kent. I apologize."

Francis is standing now, staring down at Fred Kindler.

"Could you sit down? Please. I really want us to talk."

"Mr. *Kent?* My name is *Plummer!*"

"Slip of the tongue," Kindler murmurs, touching the fingers of his left hand to his forehead. "I seem to be really fouling up this meeting." He pauses, then shrugs. "It happens," he says. "You'll have to forgive me. When I hear that the girls call you by that name—Clark Kent—it puts the name into my head. It makes me happy that I have a teacher on my faculty who the girls admire so much he becomes a myth." Kindler is almost smiling now. "So, please sit down. You should be very proud."

Francis makes no move to sit down. "It's a tradition that the adults in this school never mention the secret names," he says, voice quivering. The guy thinks I need a shrink! And he mocks my name! "Only the girls ever mention those names," he preaches, forgetting that Marjorie had been the one exception. *"That's* the tradition."

"Oh? Then forgive me," Kindler says very quietly. He's silent for a moment, frowning; then he says: "I'm still learning. I'll not make *that* mistake again."

Francis starts to say, "Just the same, you shouldn't," then realizing how foolish he sounds, he stops.

"Just the same I shouldn't *what?"*

"I was just going to explain," Francis murmurs. How did he let himself get into this? He really does want to explain the traditions that Kindler needs to know.

Now Kindler is standing too. It's very sudden. Francis sees again how small the man's body is—just as small as his own. The anger on his face is clear, a kind of hardness. "Well now, I'm suddenly not in the mood for explanations." Kindler's voice is quiet, the words come slowly. In the back of his mind he's aware he should be controlling this sudden rage. But he can't—or won't—he doesn't care which. "In our next meeting, *I* will do the explaining," he announces. "I'm sure it will be more productive than this one—which is over."

"Wait a sec!" Francis says. "I didn't mean—"

"You heard me, Mr. Plummer. Our meeting's over."

Francis still stands there. "You're actually kicking me out of your office?"

Kindler doesn't answer.

"All right. But I'll be back," Francis promises.

"WELL, HOW DID your nice little talk with our new headmaster go?" Margaret Rice asks as Francis walks through her office on his way out of the administration building. She came in while he and Kindler were talking.

"Fine."

"I bet!"

Suddenly Francis wants to talk to his old friend. He sits down on the love seat, where visiting parents always sat when waiting to see the headmistress. Now, before walking through Ms. Rice's office, they wait in a special room that is full of shiny school brochures that appeared over the summer. When, at breakfast this morning, he looked through one of the brochures, which Peggy had brought home, Francis had a strange feeling that he was reading about a school he'd never seen.

"Well, what was so fine about it?" Margaret asks belligerently.

"It ended quickly."

Margaret laughs. She sits very still behind her desk, a large woman in a yellow sweater the same color as the leaves on the aspen trees in the Rockies he's still seeing inside his head. She and her ex-husband, Bob Rice, whom Francis remembers as maybe the only male he has ever loved the way one might love a twin, used to invite Peggy and him and Siddy, every Thanksgiving, to their place in New Hampshire near Mount Chocorua. He remembers the five of them walking down abandoned roads through the leaves that lay deep as their ankles on the frosted ground.

But one day Bob told Francis, "I just can't stand it here anymore." Francis knew that Bob meant he couldn't tolerate the idea that only a few of his students would become full-time professional artists. His fine teaching made them see themselves as artists, but Bob had learned that in many parents' view, one of the unspoken aims of so expensive an education was to insulate their children from such disturbing adventures of the spirit. Bob Rice had received more than one call from an agitated parent suggesting that he be not too inspiring, that perhaps being a lawyer was a sounder goal for a student. Or a stockbroker. Even an old-fashioned full-time mother. But an artist? Only on weekends. "I've awakened to reality," he told Francis on the day he went away. "I've finally faced it, and I can't stand it anymore."

Margaret followed him to their place near Chocorua, where he still ekes out his living as a sculptor, but after several years she came back. She didn't like living all alone, the wife of a man so obsessed he didn't have any needs other than his work. Francis marveled at his friend's courage to have discovered, at so much cost, who he really was. Discovery and grief are the same thing, he thought to himself, smiling that faraway smile that inspired the girls to imagine he was reliving his exploits as Superman.

Peggy saw Bob Rice's departure in a different light. "He just gave up," she said. "Why should every parent immediately agree with him? Besides, if he really were obsessed as a sculptor, he'd be in New York City—not hiding out on a farm he inherited."

Margaret breaks into his thoughts. "How old are you now, Fran?"

"You know my age as well as you know your own. I'll be fifty-six in January."

"Plenty of time left. Nine years, at the very least. You'll outlast him."

"Maybe. And maybe not," he says. "And besides, that's not the point."

"Oh, yes it is, Fran. Very much the point. And don't worry. We'll both be here long after he's gone."

"What makes you so sure?"

"Because his mustache looks funny," Margaret says with a straight face. "That's the one thing they didn't teach him at the New Heads' Workshop: when your mustache looks like it should be under your armpit you need to shave it off." Margaret grins.

Just then the door to the new headmaster's office opens, and Fred Kindler's red hair appears. He looks surprised when he notices Francis sitting on the sofa. Francis forces himself to meet Kindler's eyes. Then Kindler turns to Ms. Rice. "I need you for a moment, Ms. Rice," he says. "Please bring the calendar." He closes the door and disappears.

Margaret turns back to Francis as he stands up. She's smiling again. "Good thing he can't hear through that door," she says. It's obvious she wants some reaction to her armpit joke. He fails to respond, doesn't return her grin. That's not how he wants to defend the school, making jokes about the new guy's funny mustache; he wants some higher ground than that. If Kindler tried to bring boys in, he wouldn't owe him any support. But he does owe him support.

He sees a worried look in Margaret's eyes. "You'll be all right," she murmurs. "Say hello to Peg."

CROSSING THE CAMPUS back to his apartment, Francis remembers how happy he always used to be this time in the summer when the grass on the school lawns smells like hay and the leaves on the big oak tree in front of Fergueson Hall are already shimmering with faint traces of red, and the new school year is going to begin in just a couple of weeks. Marjorie used to remind him all the time that he was in love with the school. That's why she trusted him. He knew she meant in love the way a man loves a woman. "Schools are just like people," she would say. "They go through stages and are even more complicated." He used to wonder if Marjorie thought that Peggy loved the school the way a woman loves a man.

Peggy's still home when he arrives. She's usually in her library by this time in the morning. "How did your meeting with Fred Kindler go just now?" she asks.

"Who?"

"Don't be funny, Francis. Fred Kindler. Your new boss."

"He told me I need a shrink."

She waits for Francis to say more. She so wants Francis and Fred Kindler to be friends!

But Francis doesn't want her to know how badly the meeting went. "That's what he told me: I need a shrink," he repeats, trying to make it seem like a joke.

She sees right through this. Her heart sinks. And she's angry again. "Well, maybe he's right," she says, as she leaves for her library.

EIGHT

WHEN THE PHONE RINGS in her Cambridge apartment at supper time on August 18, two weeks before the September board meeting, and just a few days before the opening of the new school year, Miss Harriet Richardson, late of the Oliver board of trustees, knows who's calling. She sighs, disappointed with herself for her procrastination. It will be Sandra Petrie, an Oliver board member. Sandra always calls two Tuesdays before the board meetings to offer Miss Richardson a ride. It seems strange to Harriet that so volatile a personality could be so rigidly organized.

If she had just written a note right after the summer executive committee meeting to tell Sandra that she wouldn't be needing a ride to the September board meeting in Sandra's Mercedes, Sandra would have forgotten to call and ask why. But now she will probe, Harriet thinks, reaching for the phone. If she figures it out before the board meeting . . .

"Hello, Sandra," she says. She hopes knowing who's on the phone before Sandra even says a word will shock Sandra into forgetting to ask why she doesn't need a ride.

It doesn't work. "You don't?" says Sandra, sounding disappointed. It takes her less than a minute to tease out of Miss Richardson that the reason she doesn't need a ride is that she has resigned. She wants to know why.

"The reasons are personal, Sandra," Miss Richardson says.

"Personal?"

"I'm getting on, you know. I will be seventy-seven years old in November. It's time for younger blood."

"I don't believe a word you're saying."

"Really," Miss Richardson insists. "Seventy-seven is getting on."

"They're letting boys in, aren't they? That's what happening. They're letting boys in!"

"No, we are not." Then remembering: "I mean *they* are not. You're on the board Sandra; they wouldn't make such a decision without you."

"Oh, my goodness! They're letting boys in!"

"Sandra, they've made no such decision."

"I knew it! I just knew this would happen!"

"Sandra! Listen to me! Please! They have *not* made that decision."

Silence again; then softly: "Oh? What decision *did* they make?"

"They merely agreed to let one of the members bring it up at the board meeting."

"*Merely!* No wonder you quit!"

"Sandra. Please. Keep this to yourself. Deal with it at the meeting. But don't tell anyone. Let the board deal with the issue."

"Let the board deal with the issue," Sandra mocks. "Are you crazy? You think it's just an *issue?* You sound like Alan Travelers. Or Sonja whatshername. *I'm* going to deal with the issue!"

"Sandra, be careful."

"I'll be careful, all right. Very careful! Careful to do whatever I feel like doing. That's what *you* should have done. You should have stayed on the board to vote against it."

"I thought if I threatened to quit it would change their minds," Miss Richardson says very quietly. "I thought it would shock them to see how I felt about it."

"Well it didn't work, did it!"

After Sandra hangs up, Harriet tries to guess what Sandra is going to do. Whatever it is, it will cause trouble. She has to admit she's glad. But she decides not to put off calling Alan Travelers and warning him that the cat is out of the bag. She owes him that much. Let *him* try to guess where Sandra is going to strike!

By the time she has moved to the sideboard to pour herself a sherry—just one glass to calm her nerves—she has changed her mind. Why should she help that *man*—and his new headmaster—ruin the school? Whatever Sandra's going to do will make it harder to bring boys in. "No," she says aloud to herself, "I'll keep mum. That's the least I can do." This is a first for her, she's always been known for her integrity. She takes a sip of sherry, feels its warmth. "But this is different; they're the enemy, and I don't owe them anything. Not after what they did to Marjorie."

BOOK TWO

FALL TERM

NINE

ON AUGUST 20, the second anniversary of her daughter's death, Gail Kindler wakes up crying and turns to reach for her husband and finds the bed empty. So she turns her back, away from the place he's left, and cries all by herself.

Fred is up, dressed, and in his office. Today is the day the faculty reconvenes to prepare for the new school year, which will start in several days.

Gail, though, with no new job to run to, stays in their bed and again sees herself standing on the front porch of their house on the Mt. Gilead campus while her husband runs across the campus to her to get the news. She had phoned him to come home so she could tell him face-to-face. "I need to tell you something," she said. "Something bad has happened." She still didn't believe it when she said it over the phone—and didn't believe it until she saw his face as he came up the porch steps and understood that he had guessed. "Sarah's dead," she said.

She'd never dreamed she would ever see a face so crushed as Fred's, so melted, a perfect stranger's face, and they didn't dare touch each other, not a hand clasp or an embrace to share their pain, for all the hours and hours it took to call their relatives and tell them; they knew that if they gave in to their need to comfort each other, they would break down completely and never finish the phoning. She's read in lots of places since then that for many marriages the loss of a child is the end. But not for us, she thinks, we wouldn't either of us do that to the other, or to Sarah. Our bond's too strong for that.

She stands up, takes off her nightgown. She might as well get dressed and go to work. She's almost glad that he's forgotten, the grief spread out to every day, for what difference does it make which day she died on, she's dead every day, and today's a special day in a very different way. Nevertheless, she hates this place, this house that belongs to someone else, it's like living on an iceberg.

She turns now to get to the chair where her clothes await her and sees him standing in the doorway. "You forgot," she says.

"I only started to." And then he's across the room and hugging her, and she's crying again, harder than she's ever cried, as if the last pieces in the hollow insides of her were shattering again to even smaller shards, and he picks her up, right off her feet, and puts her in the bed and gets in beside her in his sports coat, his tie, and his flannel trousers. His shoes, muddy from running to her across the garden, make a smear on the sheets, and now he's crying too. "Oh, it hurts!" she says. "It hurts. It hurts." And after a while they go to sleep.

They don't wake up until five minutes to nine—and he has to run to the meeting.

BUT PEGGY PLUMMER'S walking across the campus toward the meeting with a springy step. Under her new headmaster, the new school year really is a tabula rasa, a brand-new chance to do things right and save the school. Next to her, Francis, who's relived his disastrous meeting with Fred Kindler a thousand times, is more subdued. He's promised himself that in future meetings he'll try to see through Kindler's eyes—and be alert to Kindler's sudden storms of temper.

They are headed to the exact center of the campus, to the library where the full faculty has always met in the big central room. Sometimes it makes Francis just a little jealous that so much of the school's life is centered in the library.

In the library, Peggy and Francis sit next to each other at the same place at the same table where they've always sat. He's calm enough. He touches Peggy's hand beneath the table, where no one else can see, to show her he's going to make this work.

Fred Kindler stands to open the meeting, and Francis sees again how much shorter than Marjorie this new guy is. He doesn't fill the space around him the way Marjorie did. There's something subdued in the man— except when he's angry!—some hint of sadness that Francis hasn't noticed before and doesn't seem right in someone so young.

The first thing Kindler does is point out that the meeting has started ten minutes late.

"At nine o'clock, our starting time, I took a head count," Kindler announces. "And discovered that about a dozen of us hadn't arrived yet or were just coming in the door." He pauses for an instant and then resumes: "So I waited to start the meeting because I wanted all of us to be together." Kindler's voice is calm, the only person in the room who's not embarrassed.

"I won't wait again to start a meeting," Kindler goes on. He lets his eyes rest on Francis's face, and waits. It's clear to everyone that Fred Kindler is waiting for the senior teacher to say something in support of the new emphasis on punctuality; but there is something Francis wants to add. He wants to explain that Oliver lateness is a function not of carelessness but of intensity: the need to say one more thing in class, to finish up a conversation with a student. We're here all day, he wants to say, we're not on a treadmill. Oliver people aren't going to be dominated by *anything,* let alone a schedule. What he doesn't understand, of course, is that he's not defending the faculty's bad habit with this flimsy argument. He's defending Marjorie. He can't help feeling that every change the new head makes insults his predecessor and demeans the past.

His hesitation lasts too long. With a barely perceptible shrug of the shoulders, Fred Kindler moves his eyes away from Francis. "Let's start making Oliver Time mean On Time," he says. The man's voice is pleasant, and he is smiling, but Francis hears his stubbornness.

Then Fred gives a little talk to start the year. He tells the faculty how honored he is to be the headmaster of Miss Oliver's School for Girls, how much he admires the school and how strongly he believes that, working together, they can regain for the school its historical position as the premier all-girls school in the nation. It is an appropriate talk, Francis is ready to admit, measured, respectful, and not self-centered. But, for Francis, there's an ebullience missing that he's trained to expect, and there's that trace of sadness again, as if a little piece of Kindler's mind were someplace else. It makes Francis feel sad too, in a vague way he can't account for.

If Francis knew of the Kindlers' loss, he'd understand. But only a small part of the Oliver community has learned of the Kindlers' tragedy. Among those who think of Fred as Marjorie's usurper, those who possess this knowledge are keeping it to themselves so sympathy won't develop for him. Among his friends those who know don't tell because he asked them not to.

Next Kindler gives the faculty the bad news about the budget. Having been so shocked himself when he perceived this news at the beginning of the summer, he's hardly surprised when he sees how shocked the faculty is. What he doesn't know is that part of what stuns the teachers is they are actually being told, and he's using specific numbers. Marjorie never shared financial realities in any specificity with the faculty. For she and they were *educators,* and in her mind educators don't involve themselves with such mundane matters as budgets. These are to be relegated to the lower orders: the business manager and bookkeeper and the members of the finance committee.

But the truth of the matter is that even the board's finance committee had little to say about the finances of Miss Oliver's School for Girls. For Marjorie actually ran the board. She ran *everything*—until the revolution, initiated sadly and as kindly as possible by Milton Perkins, and less kindly by Sonja McGarvey, which brought in new board members, including Alan Travelers, to save the school from the very person who had made it so worth saving. How many times and in how many different kinds of organizations has *this* story been played out!

Fred is careful to disguise how badly Carl Vincent fouled up, and he is glad he's being truthful when he makes it clear that Vincent retired of his own free will. For it's true that as soon as the ancient business manager learned of Milton Perkins's anonymous gift to his retirement fund, he couldn't wait to quit.

Fred knows better than to linger on the bad news. So he moves quickly to his plan for recouping the enrollment. Admittedly, there are no strategies unknown to other schools in his plan. There are only so many ways a school can be marketed. What is new and what lifts his spirits as he talks is the energy, the care, the discipline, and attention to detail the school will invest. Near the end, he passes around the new brochure, designed pro bono by his wife, which emphasizes the school's academic rigor and de-emphasizes its idiosyncratic culture (one of the reasons Francis feels it describes some other school) and which, in Fred's and Nan White's opinion, is better written, printed on better stock, and more graphically sophisticated than its predecessor. He ends by inviting the faculty not to think of enrollment as exclusively Nan White's province but as theirs too, urging them to reach out to every visitor to campus.

The faculty listens intently to Fred's talk. All are aware that his entire emphasis has been on the recruitment of *girls*. Thus the specter of boys invading the school has faded—at least for now. Looking around the room, as he finishes, Fred feels satisfied with this beginning.

Near adjournment time, he says, "At one of our next meetings, I'd like you to come prepared to think about the way our students dress. I would have put it on the agenda for today if there had been time for it."

No response.

Kindler looks around the room, rests his eyes on Francis's face again. Then he looks away, much sooner than he did before. "I think if the students look more presentable it will be easier to sell the school," he says.

Several teachers are nodding their heads in agreement. Francis turns, as if by instinct, to see how Gregory van Buren is reacting. Gregory is looking around the room to see how *others* are reacting. The son of a bitch is counting votes! Francis watches while Gregory's eyes go all around the room. Then Gregory puts his hand up.

Most of the time, Marjorie would try to ignore Gregory's upraised hand. But Kindler calls on him right away.

"You don't actually intend us to incur the students' *wrath?*" Gregory asks, looking directly at Kindler. "You don't really think that we should actually invade the sacred teenage right to emulate the appearance of sexual perverts, freaks, and criminals?" and Francis realizes this isn't going to be the usual windy sermon. For Gregory's not putting his hands together as if in prayer, just beneath his nose, as he usually does, and he's not pursing his lips between sentences, and he's not nodding his head in assent to his own wisdom, and he's not speaking very slowly to allow his listeners time to comprehend the elegant thoughts he is assembling in his ponderous syntax. He's not doing any of these things! He's waving his hands! And being sarcastic! And speaking very fast. He's been pent up for years on this subject. Kindler's uncorked the bottle.

"You are not daring, sir, I *hope,* to ask us to ignore the increasingly alarming fact that no one outside this hermetic little enclave understands our misbegotten allegiance to the concept that it is a good idea—a meritorious educational *strategy,* in fact—to allow girls studiously to take on the appearance of female garbage collectors, or drunken agriculturists—when they don't manage instead to look like strippers nearing the climax of their dance. Surely you don't actually believe that it is difficult to explain to parents that our allegiance to this arcane concept is one we hold on *purpose,* that it is a considered choice among other options—such as occasionally requiring our students to look like normal persons."

While Gregory pauses to refill his lungs, Fred Kindler tries to cut him off. Marjorie used to say: "Never mind, Greg, we already know how you feel on this subject." But Kindler's too polite, or not quick enough, and Gregory rushes on: "Failing to understand our strange philosophy, these outsiders who, I take this opportunity to remind us, constitute our market," Gregory adds, "that's correct, our *market*—a blasphemous word in these elevated precincts—think we don't give a damn about how our students look. Or perhaps they think we can't *see* the children who have been committed to our care, that one of the important filters through which candidates must pass in order to be awarded the privilege of teaching here is that they be *blind*. How else could they explain such self-destructive eccentricity?"

"You make your point quite clearly," Fred finally manages, with just a hint of irony. "Thank you, Gregory."

"My point is that we are underenrolled, sir. We are dying!"

Fred looks around the room to see if anyone else wants to speak.

But Gregory still isn't finished. "Thank you, sir, for bringing the subject of student attire up," he says, his tone gliding now from passion to his customary unction. After all the years with Marjorie, he can be forgiven for not understanding that with this new head he doesn't need to act as if addressing royalty. "Mrs. Boyd—who couldn't bring herself to censor the students' writing in the school newspaper—wouldn't allow the *faculty* to discuss how students dress. I am delighted that we finally have a leader who—"

"Marjorie Boyd was right," Francis hears himself blurting. Gregory shuts up, and everyone stares at Francis and then turns to Fred to see his reaction. He's clearly surprised. But Francis isn't even thinking about the new head's opinion; he's just saying, automatically, what he deeply believes. And besides, he's not going to let anyone criticize Marjorie, especially not Gregory van Buren. "She never would have put it on the agenda," he says; then he realizes that didn't come out right, he doesn't want to say the new head can't bring up what he wants to bring up, and he goes on because he really does want to explain, he really does have a reasonable point to make. "Marjorie and I figured out a long time ago that you can't talk to a teenage kid about how she should dress without sounding like an idiot to her."

"Really?" Kindler asks, and Francis has no idea whether or not he is being sarcastic.

"So then you can't talk to her about the really important things," Francis explains. "You have to choose how you're going to use your ammunition. You only have so much."

Gregory takes his eyes off Francis's face and looks across the room at Kindler, and waits. The room is silent. Peggy slides her chair a few inches further away from Francis. "Well, I certainly don't want any of us to sound like an *idiot,*" Kindler finally says. His face is blank. Everybody, except Peggy, who is looking down at her hands in her lap, is glancing back and forth between Francis and Kindler. Suddenly Kindler's face isn't blank anymore. He's smiling. Everybody understands: *he's decided to smile.* "It's noon," Kindler announces. "The time I promised this meeting would end. We will start meetings on time. And we will end them when we say we will end them. So we'll bring this up another time. The meeting's adjourned." No one stirs. "We *will* bring the subject up again," Kindler adds. "I assure you. In the meantime, have a productive afternoon." Then he stands up to end the meeting.

A WEEK LATER, on the last day of new-student orientation before classes begin, one of the six new upper-class students, a junior, Sylvia Lapham, from Norwich, Vermont, walks, by herself, back to her dorm after the evening meal. She's too unhappy to feel like company. She already knows it was a big mistake to persuade her parents to let her enroll at Miss Oliver's School for Girls.

Closer to the dorm, she notices an old beat-up Subaru just like her brother's in the dorm parking lot and feels even lonelier. She wishes it really were her brother's car. But Charley's a sophomore at Trinity College in Hartford, an hour away, and he's very busy and has his own life to lead, and she's only been away from home a few days. So why would he come see her?

Just two months ago in July, Sylvia's parents told Charley and her that after Charley was born, they'd spent three years trying to have another child, and when they realized they couldn't, they'd adopted Sylvia. Right up to that instant, neither Sylvia nor Charley had had any idea that she wasn't their parents' biological daughter. "We waited to tell you till we thought you were both old enough to know and we could tell you both together," their father said. And then their mother turned to Charley and said, "We thought you'd like a sister." As if he was the one who needed comforting!

Sylvia's first reaction was that she needed to go away to find a place where she could have a family of her own. She chose Miss Oliver's because Sylvia's best friend's mother, who graduated from Miss Oliver's in 1965, always said the school was like a family. Well, it hasn't felt like a family to Sylvia. She misses her real family and would give anything to be helping her parents in their construction business in the afternoons after high school gets out, instead of being stuck here. But she can't go home. Her parents, who at first had refused to enroll her at Miss Oliver's, finally relented under the proviso that she promise to stick it out whether she liked it or not, through her junior and senior years, and graduate from Miss Oliver's. Sylvia made that promise eagerly at the time, and now she'd rather die than come crawling home, begging to be released from it, admitting she was wrong. It's a mantra in her family that you finish what you start.

A few yards closer to the dorm, she realizes it *is* Charley. She sees his blond head. He sees her too and blows the horn. She quickens her pace. He leans and opens the passenger door for her. He's in jeans and moccasins with no socks; the sleeves of his T-shirt are tight around his arms. His summer work with their parents has provided him with enough money to pay for his college expenses and his car, and has made him strong. Sylvia is almost as tall, but as if to advertise their different genes, she's much thinner than he, and her hair is brown.

"I just thought I'd come by and see how you're doing," he says. They're shy with each other, and don't hug. They've not always been the best of friends.

"Thanks." She doesn't want to give away how happy she is that he's taken this trouble.

"Well, how are you?" He makes it sound like a challenge. He doesn't want her getting sentimental.

"I'm OK."

"That's what I thought," he says. "What's wrong?"

She doesn't answer.

"You don't like it here?"

She shakes her head.

"Give it time. It's only been a few days."

But she knows that's not what he really thinks. He's not surprised she's unhappy here. He argued with her when she told her mother and father—right after she learned they weren't her mother and father—that she wanted to go away to school. Charley knew better. "You'll feel even more lost," he said. "Stay home and get used to the idea." But he didn't know how it feels when the people who are your mother and father all of a sudden tell you that they're not.

"Thanks for not saying, 'I told you so,'" she tells him now.

"I just wish they'd kept it a secret," Charley says.

She shakes her head. They've been over this before. She thinks it would be wrong not to know and wants to defend her parents. "It's not like them to hide the truth," she says. "That's not Mom and Dad."

"Hey, I hope you heard the words you just used? I hope I didn't hear them wrong?" He looks away. That shyness again! It's new between them, and surprising. As if he were embarrassed to have it confirmed that he has a different status in the family than she does.

"Well, what *should* I call them? Mr. and Mrs. Lapham?"

"Don't talk like that," he says.

"Maybe they should charge me rent," she says, "since I'm really only a guest."

"Come on," he says. "Cut it out. You know they love you just as much as me." There. He'd said it. They've avoided this subject for years, since long before they learned that Sylvia was adopted.

"That's what you're worried about, isn't it?" he says. "Well, it's crazy. We're still brother and sister."

"We're not brother and sister, we're not even related," she says. "If I were eighteen, we could fuck and it wouldn't even be illegal."

He's stares at her, not saying anything. There she goes again, he thinks. Saying outrageous things to get attention. It's not his fault she doesn't take the pains to make life easy for herself by acting the way Mother and Father expect. That's why they're always on her case and not on his. He remembers how, even when she was still in middle school, Sylvia loved to eat the greasy hamburgers in the school cafeteria because her parents, dedicated vegetarians, were heavy into animal rights, and she's always sworn a lot because her parents hate profanity, and he knows the reason that she worked so hard to win the high school rhetoric prize when she was still a sophomore with an essay "proving" the rightness of the Vietnam War is that their parents are pacifists.

Charley understands too that, until a year or so ago, her orneriness didn't disturb their parents. They understood it as her way of establishing her identity, finding it amusing, sometimes even endearing. But now as she approaches adulthood, she really does have an identity, which her father especially finds less than endearing, because he suspects that she smokes and drinks and does drugs with her friends and is maybe even getting sexually involved. (All of which, in fact, she's so far abstained from, mostly to be different.) And, maybe even more irritating to her father, she can now best him in their arguments—which he thinks she starts and she thinks he starts—successfully demolishing what she describes as his thoroughly unstudied liberal positions with facts and statistics Charley suspects she makes up as she needs them. Charley knows damn well that if their father were a conservative, Sylvia would be a liberal, rather than the other way around. "You're too smart for your own good," he tells her now, "and you're a pain in the ass."

Just the same, he wonders how he'd feel if he were the one to learn what Sylvia learned just a few weeks ago, and he remembers he came here to see how she was doing. "Let's go for a ride," he says. "Maybe that'll cheer you up."

"I can't," she says, looking at her watch. "I'm supposed to be in the dorm by eight o'clock. It's five of. They check you in." She's learned how carefully Mr. Van Buren, her dorm parent, takes attendance.

"What is this, a school or a prison?" he asks.

"Both," she says, but they both know it's not Miss Oliver's that's the prison, it's her pledge to stick it out here.

"But on weekends it's different. I can check out," she tells Charley. She's already heard the stories about how tricky some of the girls are in convincing the teachers on weekend duty that they're invited to somebody's parents' house where adults will take responsibility: forged letters of invitation, friends pretending to be a parent over the phone. And sometimes they just sneak out after the final check-in at eleven.

"Yeah, we have some big-time parties you could come to, " Charley says, his voice brightening at this reminder of his release from the strictures of home. It's not partying, the booze and the drugs, so much more accessible than they were at home, that excite him. He's already felt a tinge of boredom at the parties, which all seem exactly the same. It's that he doesn't have to lie to his parents when he gets home.

"Promise?" she asks. "You'll invite me?" She knows he means at his fraternity. She's heard those stories too.

He shrugs and makes a gesture that says of course he will, she doesn't have to ask, and she leans to hug him. Her resentment's flown away.

But as soon as she's out of the car, waving good-bye to him as he drives off, she feels depressed again.

When Sylvia gets to her dorm, Gregory van Buren is already coming down the hall, checking the girls in. Clarissa Longstreet, Sylvia's roommate, from Riverdale, just north of Manhattan, is sitting at her desk when Sylvia enters their room. She looks up from her book and says to Sylvia, "Where've you been? I was worried." Clarissa's an African American, very small with a round face and dyed blond hair and glasses, whom Sylvia, who towers over her, has decided that she likes. "You don't want to get on the wrong side of Mr. Van Buren," Clarissa warns.

Sylvia shrugs. Maybe that's exactly what she wants to do. She lies down on her bed.

Clarissa shakes her head. "Really," she says. "You don't." Clarissa writes for the *Clarion,* to which Gregory van Buren is faculty advisor. She knows how sharp his tongue can get when you don't do things on time, and do them well.

The door opens then, and Mr. Van Buren is standing in it. It's eight o'clock at night and he's still wearing a blue blazer, white shirt, dark tie, and flannel trousers. He glances quickly at Clarissa and nods his head. "Reading ahead," he says. "Very smart."

Then he turns to Sylvia lying on the bed and stares. Clearly, he doesn't like that's she's lying down. "You were almost late," he says mildly. She can't read the tone of his voice or the slight smile on his face, has no idea whether he's angry or simply stating a fact. "It would be advisable, I think, not to be almost late again," Gregory van Buren says. Then, turning to leave, he looks back over his shoulder and raises his eyebrows at Sylvia as if to show how seriously she should take his advice. Then he closes the door and is gone.

"Pretty weird, huh?" Clarissa says. "But wait 'til you have him in class. He's the best English teacher in the world."

Sylvia's only been at Miss Oliver's for a few days, and already she's heard how some students argue, as Clarissa does, that Mr. Van Buren is the best and others that nobody could be better than Francis Plummer, aka Clark Kent. Right now, if she cared enough to have an opinion, Sylvia would agree with Clarissa. She liked it that Mr. Van Buren didn't harangue her about lying down while he was talking to her, the way her father would have. She would have sat up, if he'd not left so soon. And she admires the ironic way he used the word *almost.*

But he's a *teacher,* and she's still in his presence at eight o' clock at night and will be again in half an hour when he presides over a dorm meeting "to get properly organized for the year." For Sylvia, school has always been a scene she is released from to a larger world at three o'clock in the afternoon.

Now she's sealed in twenty-four hours a day, and there's no relief. She can hardly breathe.

ON THE FIRST DAY of classes, the students entering the dining hall for breakfast find a stack of the *Clarion* on each table, two pages of which are filled with Karen's article on the new headmaster. To be greeted early in the morning of their first day of classes by a feature about the new headmaster makes them even more resentful of Marjorie's dismissal. They want to be greeted by Marjorie. For all their intelligence and good education, what many of the students take away from the article is that the new headmaster has ripped down all the pictures that students gave to Marjorie and that he's going to take away the freedom of press that Marjorie championed.

Only her close friends will learn that Karen, who has had an hour with Fred Kindler, is well disposed to him. If Karen wanted to express her personal opinion in the *Clarion,* she'd write an editorial supporting the new headmaster, instead of an objective report of an interview. But she won't do that; it would look to the students as if the new headmaster had manipulated her and make him even more contemptible in their eyes. There's nothing she can do to make Fred Kindler popular. He's on his own.

THIS FIRST MORNING OF CLASSES, Francis gets to his classroom long before his students. He teaches both his math and English classes here, where he also has his office; lighted by big windows that look out on the campus, it's his seat of power, a little kingdom, for it is one of the perks of his seniority that no other teacher uses it. The front wall and the wall opposite the windows are covered by blackboards, and today the back wall, behind the big model of the Globe Theater created by a student years ago, is covered by a collection of black-and-white photographs of comely New England farmhouses that Bob Rice has sent to him because he knows that Francis teaches a lot of Robert Frost. The floor is covered by a thick rug. The tables in the classroom have been put together to form a three-sided square whose open side faces the front, where Francis's desk is placed. He never sits at it when he is teaching.

This morning, as he enters the empty classroom, the first thing Francis sees is A FIRST DAY OF SCHOOL GIFT FOR MR. P! emblazoned on the blackboard. Under this greeting, the big slate is covered with a math problem that goes on and on, over the front blackboard and around the corner onto the one on the adjoining wall. He sees that the problem is worked two ways with two different answers. AND THEY'RE BOTH RIGHT!!! CAN YOU PROVE THEY'RE NOT? HUH, CLARK, HUH, I BET YOU CAN'T! Whoever has snuck out of the dorm in the middle of the night and spent hours in here doing this has used her non-dominant hand. The figures are a little child's; she wants him to guess who she is.

Francis smiles, his spirits lifting. He decides to leave the problem up there on the board for the advanced calculus class that will troop in here in a half an hour. That's the way to start a day! Math's a game, play is the mind at work, and he's going to get the bagels and coffee ready.

But he only gets a minute or two to himself, because there's a knock on the door, and he opens it, and there stands Lila Smythe. His heart skips a little beat. Next to Lila, but shyly standing half a step behind, one of the new ninth graders faces him.

"This is Sara Warrior," Lila says. "She's a ninth grader. She wants to talk with you." Lila stands stiffly, unsmiling, in the doorway.

She didn't even say hello, Francis thinks. "All right," he says. "Come in."

Sara hesitates. Lila turns and smiles to her. "He won't bite," she says. He can't tell if she's being sarcastic, and now the two are in the room, and he is motioning them to seats at one of the tables and takes a third, facing them.

"Sara's an Indian," Lila announces. "A Pequot. That's why she wants to talk to you."

"Native American," he corrects. He's read the admissions folder. Sara, who can trace her Pequot ancestry all the way back to the 1870 census, lives in Stonington.

"All right, say it the PC way." Lila shrugs. "Who cares?" And for an instant Francis thinks he'll ask Sara to excuse herself and have a talk with Lila. But he changes his mind. That wouldn't be fair to Sara.

Sara's a small girl, dressed more formally than the Oliver custom in a simple green skirt, a white long-sleeved blouse. She's looking at him, studying his eyes. He can't read her face. But he does know she's the first Pequot citizen to be enrolled at Miss Oliver's School for Girls. He finds himself wanting to apologize for that. "Welcome, Sara. We're very glad to have you," he says.

"Thank you." The first words she's said.

"Are you glad to be here?"

"I don't know," Sara says. For she really doesn't. She remembers how glad she was at first, and how kind Mr. and Mrs. Kindler were at the reception for new students and their parents. Her mother and dad had driven her to school and were going to leave right after the reception, and she was already homesick, but the little red-headed man with the funny walk who she was surprised to learn was the headmaster crossed the room to greet them. Her father and he seemed to like each other right away as they shook hands. They were the only two men in the room who were wearing suits, the headmaster in a funny brown one, her father in his pinstripe blue. That made her glad. She knew the headmaster wore a suit for the same reason her dad did: to show respect.

But now, after what she's discovered in the school library yesterday, she feels like a stranger. And she knows why the student who toured her around when she was visiting as a candidate skipped over the library, claiming she had a class to get to.

Sara also remembers how excited she was when her English teacher, a tall, thin, black man with dreadlocks in his first year of teaching, who she sensed felt just as out of place as she did—and on whom she had a crush—persuaded her to think seriously about attending Miss Oliver's. "They make you work," he said. "They actually want you to think for yourself." He'd heard about the school when had he reached out to the Mashantucket Pequot Reservation, just a few miles away, to see if he could arrange some interaction between the tribe and his class in order to broaden his students' view of the world, which, to his disillusionment, he found to be exceedingly narrow. He was soon chastised for including in his curriculum material so incapable of being reduced to a standardized test—but that's another story.

"Sara's been to the library," Lila says.

"Good!" he says brightly. Lila turns her head away, stares out the window, and then it dawns on him what Sara is going to say. Her eyes are full on his.

"It's wrong!" Sara says.

He doesn't want to think about this. He doesn't need it between him and Peggy.

"Sara's right, isn't, she? If it were *white* people's bones, they'd be in a graveyard, wouldn't they?" Lila says. "Not in a display in a private school library."

"Yes, I suppose so," he murmurs.

Lila just watches him.

"But it's mostly artifacts: clothing and tools and weapons," he says half-heartedly. "There's only a small piece of one femur." Sara Warrior is still studying him.

"Is that what we would have done if we had found the Ohlone village?" Lila asks.

"I've been thinking about that," he admits.

"I never thought about it at all," Lila says, "but then Sara came to me."

"I asked her how you got them," Sara says. "I asked if they were given to you."

"But of course she already knew the answer," Lila says.

"I was hoping they were gifts," Sara says. "That you hadn't taken them."

"I see," says Francis.

"It was my new school," Sara says. "That's why I was hoping."

"There *are* two ways to look at this," Francis begins. He owes it to Peggy to defend what she believes: that the display is a presence that students don't just read about but *see*. It puts the understanding in their gut, not just their brain, of how many ways there are to be human.

But Sara cuts him off. "Not if they weren't given to you," she says. "Not if you *took* them. Then there's only one way."

We didn't take them, he wants to say. We found them. But he knows that's lame, because they weren't *given,* and he can't think of anything else to say. Let Peggy try, he thinks.

"What do you think?" Lila asks. "You're the advisor." He can hear the accusation in her tone: that he's going to back off this time too.

He hesitates again.

"All right, I'll decide," Lila says. "We'll bring it to the school. The Student Council. In Morning Meeting."

"Won't we, Mr. Plummer?" Lila prods. And now they're both silent, because he's thinking about how this issue, if it gets in the papers, could hurt the school, and she's thinking here's another time when he can't take the heat.

"All right," he says at last. It's the Oliver tradition when an issue comes up: Student Council airs it in an open discussion in Morning Meeting. It is one of the things he loves about the school.

"You don't have to sit on stage. We can break that tradition," Lila says.

"You think I'm going to hide?"

"You think I came in here to embarrass you? You've already said they're two ways to look at it. Suppose Mrs. Plummer wants to defend the other way?"

"I'll be on stage," he says. "I'm not about to break the tradition. Besides, my wife is a reasonable person. And I'll let her know what's going to happen so she won't be surprised."

"Good for you," Lila says. There's no bitterness in her voice. Maybe he's earned back a glimmer of her respect.

"I'll introduce the issue," Lila says. "Then we'll put Sara on, and she'll make her proposal."

"Proposal? I thought it was going to be a discussion."

"Tell him, Sara," Lila says.

"To give it back to its rightful owners," Sara says. "Of course. To get it off this campus right away."

"Otherwise it might be hard for her to stay here, don't you think?" Lila says. Though her tone is mild, he's a little irritated. He knows what her rhetorical question means: if you're going to be inclusive, you have to adjust to the ways the people you include see the world. Well, he doesn't need a lecture. You're so much nicer when you're not being sanctimonious, he wants to say. But of course he doesn't. He's lost the chance to be her guide.

The bell for first period rings. Francis's advanced calculus class, waiting outside the classroom door, knows his closed door means he's having a private talk. They won't come in until he opens it. "Thank you for listening," Sara says, and Lila nods and both girls stand up and leave. Then his students troop in. They talk quietly, sleepy in the early morning; their chairs scrape against the floor as they take their seats, and Francis makes a mental note to go to Fred Kindler's office first thing after classes. He needs to know this issue is coming up. Right after that, he'll tell Peggy.

What Francis doesn't know is that Sam Anderson, the history teacher whose sense of humor Francis likes so much and whom he has seen playing tennis with Fred Kindler, is designing a new course that he will teach later in the year in the spring term. It fits right in with the Oliver emphasis on experiential education: an archeological dig right here on the campus, where there must be many artifacts still to be found. Sam wonders why in the world no one's thought of this before. He's shared his idea with Peggy Plummer—who thinks it's wonderful.

TEN

IN THE SAME MORNING that Lila and Sara confront Francis about the Pequot display, Fred arrives at the River Club parking lot a few minutes before his first full board meeting. All during the drive from Fieldington he heard, over and over again, Miss Richardson say, "You won't get away with this," and now he wishes Alan Travelers hadn't persuaded him that Miss Richardson would never stoop so low as to tell people that Sonja McGarvey was going to propose the admission of boys at the board meeting. "Miss Richardson would never break a confidence, I don't care how angry she is, and if I'm wrong the worst part for me won't be holding the meeting in public," Alan said. "It will be my disappointment in a friend" and went on to say he'd be damned if he were going to sneak around and hold the meeting at a secret time and in a secret place. "We'll just handle it, if it happens," he said to Fred. "You and I. We'll take it as an interesting challenge."

Through the windshield, Fred stares at the river, just yards from the edge of the parking lot. How peaceful it would be just to sit here all morning watching the unresisting water flow! He shakes his head to jettison the thought, gets out of the car, and enters the building. As he approaches the oak doors he hears the sound of angry voices, and when he enters the room, he sees right away that most of the people sitting at the table aren't board members—he recognizes very few of them—while the legitimate members, their places usurped, stand with embarrassed and angry looks on their faces among the crowd that surrounds the table, taking up all the space between the table and the walls. It's obvious to him that these invaders made sure they arrived very early, before the board members, and have commandeered the seats.

The room goes silent as he stops in the doorway, and everyone turns to look at him. *We* have the power, not you, the invaders' expressions say. You can't do anything we don't want you to do. He sees this on their faces: that they can riot to get what they want, and his nervousness flies away. He's suddenly calmer than he'd ever be staring at the river. And even more surprising, he's *happy*. This is exactly what he wants: a fight! Oh, yes, I can! he thinks, I will do exactly what I want.

"Good morning," he says.

No response.

No matter: waiting for an answer provides an instant in which to think. He is grateful also to discover that Alan Travelers is one of the few board members who are at the table; he's sitting at the chairman's place at the end of the table opposite where Fred is standing. His eyes meet Fred's.

Milton Perkins is also at the table, next to Travelers. Fred knows right away he will be the first to speak. He's right. Perkins's voice is a whisper, intended only for Fred, but it is nevertheless loud: *"We've got a traitor in our midst!"* Fred hears irony and chagrin in Perkins's voice, but the crowd does not, and there are boos and hisses. *"Well, damn it, we do!"* Perkins says, this time not in a whisper, and now there's laughter. Fred's gorge rises even more: that these people would ridicule the old man! The students would never be so unkind.

Fred keeps his face perfectly calm, almost expressionless—as if he were about to go to sleep. He puts his hands up to the people who stand to his right and left along the wall. The laughter stops. He gazes around the room, looking into people's eyes while he lets his anger flood him. He doesn't see the oak walls behind the people, is oblivious to the array of Hartford's patriarchs in their golden frames, and doesn't notice that the sun, breaking through the clouds and sparkling on the river just outside the windows, has lit up the room. He only sees each face, and stares, and sends his message: now you have to deal with *me!* So don't you ever mock a human being again!—wondering all the while: Where the hell did I learn to do this? The room goes very quiet.

He turns his gaze steadily on Alan Travelers, who instantly stands up. Now Fred and Alan, at opposite ends of the table, are the only ones at the table who are standing.

"It seems that all of a sudden there is a lot of interest in what goes on at board meetings," Travelers says, speaking as if no one other than Fred were in the room with him.

"Clearly," says Fred.

"It's about time!" someone yells from the crowd to Fred's left. He doesn't want to take his eyes off Travelers to find her. *"We should have been watching you all along!"*

Now another young woman is waving her arms. She's in the crowd near the other end of the table, directly behind Travelers. *"What are these men doing on the board? is what I want to know,"* she shouts. *"We never had men before. This is a girls' school!"*

Suddenly everyone—except the board members—is talking at once. Fred waits for Travelers to get control. It's wrong for the head of school to presume to do so. This is a *board* meeting. So he's relieved when Travelers puts both hands up above his head. When the noise level descends just barely enough for him to be heard, Travelers speaks in a loud voice: *"Your attention, everybody. Please. Your attention."*

Above the noise Travelers shouts—though, to Fred's admiration, he keeps his calm. *"Would the members of the board who are standing please take seats at the table, and will those guests who are at the table please give their places to board members."* Several board members step forward from the crowd along the walls. But no one at the table moves. The noise level rises even higher. The standing board members hesitate, clearly embarrassed, then step back. Someone in the crowd yells *"No men!"* It quickly becomes a chant: *"No men! No men! No men!"* Fred looks around the room to see who's *not* chanting. Many are refraining. He can see their embarrassment; several are trying to help Travelers get order. Across the room Mavis Ericksen stares at Fred with an expression that seems to say: "See what you've done?" The chant continues. The noise bounces off the walls. Fred thinks of standing on a chair and shouting for order.

Instead, Milton Perkins stands up. His hands are shaking. The noise subsides, and into the relative silence he yells: *"Shut up! Just shut up and get away from the damn table!"* There's an immediate silence, a kind of gasp.

"Sit down, Mr. Perkins," Travelers says very calmly into that silence. Perkins sits down. It grows even quieter.

When a woman on Fred's left steps forward into that silence, Fred knows instinctively that she's going to grab the power back, if Travelers gives her time. *"Oh!"* she wails. *"I am so outraged!"* She stamps her foot, and Fred's heart sinks: Travelers isn't going to be quick enough. The man hasn't been to enough faculty meetings. *"Not for me!"* the woman wails. *"It's not for me that I am outraged. I'm used to abasement,"* and Fred knows she's the perfect person to play this part. He hates himself for noticing how unattractive she is, a tiny woman in mud-brown slacks, a blouse that looks as if it should be worn by a third grader, oily brown hair, and wire-rimmed glasses. Behind her, Charlotte Reynolds is nodding her head encouragingly. *"But for all the women in the world!"* The mousy lady writhes her hips and shoulders as if somehow the motion will pump even more volume out. *"All of them who have been slaves to men from the beginning of time! All of them in every country, in every century, who have labored while men have rested, who have nurtured the children whom men have ignored, who have stayed home while their brothers went to school."*

"Hear, hear," someone yells.

"Jesus, all of a sudden we're in *England!*" Sonja McGarvey says.

"*And now it will happen again. Men will enter our sanctuary and take the spoils. So I am especially outraged. I am violated. I am raped by the thought that our young women of Miss Oliver's School for Girls, our hope of victory, of transcendence, will once again—*" Here she hesitates, overcome; she looks around the room, her mouth opening and closing as if she were still speaking, but no words are coming out. Now the majority of people in the room are clearly embarrassed. "Once again," she's finally able to say. "Once again." Then she stops.

"So whadda we do now?" Milton Perkins asks in a loud voice, "Hold hands and sing 'We Shall Overcome'?"

In the silence that follows, a few titters. Then more.

"At a *board* meeting, for cryin' out loud!" Perkins says. Travelers reaches his hand out to Perkins's shoulder. Perkins pushes it away. "Who's got a violin?" he asks.

That's when the mousy lady begins to cry. Fred knows instantly it's a mistake. She's taking it much too far, he thinks, much relieved. She hasn't been in faculty meetings either! While the woman sobs, some watch, some look away. But one very young alumna comes all the way around the table with her arms outstretched so far in front of herself she looks as if she might fall down, and puts them around the weeping woman. The two of them sway together for what seems an eternity. Perkins wears an expression as if he were watching a freak show. Fred prays he will keep his mouth shut.

When the weeping subsides, and the hug ends, Travelers speaks and Fred marvels at his grace. "Thank you, Ms. Aguire," Travelers says very gently. "We deeply appreciate your great concern." Fred watches the woman's face lose it staginess. "Thank *you,*" she murmurs, her hand flying up to her mouth in her surprise that her feelings have been affirmed and her name known.

"Now," Travelers says in the same gentle tone, "I do hope that we can make places for every board member at this table." As he speaks, he moves to a place just behind the nearest chair occupied by a non–board member, and places his hand at the top of the chair back. The woman sitting in it glances up at him and rises, as Alan Travelers, with a graceful gesture, pulls her chair back to ease her standing up. Then he turns to the nearest board member who stands next the wall and invites her to the empty chair with an equally graceful gesture of his open hand. The woman takes the chair, and Travelers moves toward the next chair in which a non–board member sits. But he doesn't have to. Simultaneously each of the usurpers gives up their seats. The last board member to sit down is Mavis Ericksen.

When all are seated, Travelers says, "Now we'll begin. May I have a motion that the minutes of our last meeting be approved?"

"Just a minute," Fred says.

Travelers stares down the table.

"We're missing one of our members." Fred announces. He's staring now at Sandra Petrie, who has remained with the crowd against the wall.

"So we are," says Travelers. His tone of voice makes it clear that he too has suddenly figured out who has broken the confidence and started this riot. Harriet Richardson must have told her what Sonja was going to propose today. Why else would she remain standing at the wall?

Sandra's face is pale. "I'm resigning," she whispers.

"There's a process for that," Travelers says. "Not appropriate in the middle of a board meeting. I insist that you join us."

Sandra shakes her head, remains standing. Travelers stares and waits, and Sandra finally sits down, just to get out of the limelight. She averts her eyes from the other board members.

"The motion to accept the minutes, please," Travelers says.

"How about you, Mrs. Petrie," Fred says. "Wouldn't you like to make the motion to accept the minutes?"

Sandra Petrie flashes him a confused look. Now that she's sitting down, she seems much shorter than when she stood by the wall; all her height must be in her legs. Her face is thin, very pale—almost pretty, Fred thinks— if it weren't for the frown.

"Ms. Petrie?" Fred says.

"All right, I move the minutes be approved." Her voice is tentative.

"What about the misspellings?" Fred asks.

"I don't understand," says Sandra.

"The misspellings."

"Where?" she says.

"I don't know," he says. "You're the one who's approving the minutes."

"Fred, please," Travelers says.

"Don't you think we should spell things right at Miss Oliver's School for Girls?" Fred asks, looking directly at Sandra.

Her face is very pale.

"Well?" Fred insists.

Sandra looks down at the table, hunching her shoulders. Clearly she isn't going to speak.

"She only talks when she's standing up," Fred announces across the table to Travelers, who's looking at him as if he's never met him before.

"I move the minutes be accepted," say Reginald Griffin, a new board member. He's struggling not to laugh.

"Second," Sonja McGarvey says.

Travelers chairs the rest of the meeting through every committee report, none of which has anything to do with the subject that brought the intruders. After a while, some of them leave. Those who stay grow increasingly restless. "When are you going to get to the *real* question?" asks a tall woman in a green dress from where she stands by the wall.

"Madame, we've been dealing with real questions all morning," Travelers responds innocently.

Fifteen minutes later when the old business is finished, Travelers opens the meeting to new business. Sonja McGarvey is the first to raise her hand. Travelers recognizes her.

"We have a fiscal crisis," Sonja says. "Everybody knows it. We are going to go under unless we make a change." She stops here. Everyone in the room is staring at her. "Therefore, in order to ensure the continuing existence of our school, I move that we accept boys."

There's a silence in the room. Then "bitch traitor!" from a woman standing by the wall. A murmur starts to rise.

Travelers is fast: "Is there a second?" he asks. The room goes quiet again. No one at the table raises a hand.

"The motion fails," Travelers announces, and the tension leaves the room, like air through a window.

"All right, I'll make another motion, then," Sonja says.

"No more, bitch!" the same woman hisses. Travelers calls on Sonja.

"I move the admission of boys as an alternate strategy to closing down when we reach a point where it is obvious that the goals in the headmaster's schedule for rebuilding the girls-only enrollment cannot be reached." The board members stay quiet. The angry murmur rises again among the standees.

"Will you accept a change from *when* to *if?*" Travelers asks. The room goes quiet again.

"Oh, all right," Sonja says, and repeats word-for-word her previous motion except that she changes *when* to *if*. She turns away from Travelers then, puts her eyes on Fred. He thinks he sees a hint of a smile on her determined face. Thank you, he wants to say. *If* is exactly what he needs!

"We need a second," Travelers says.

No one puts up a hand.

"The motion fails," Travelers says.

"Well, I've done my best," Sonja says. "Let the school commit suicide if it wants to."

"So we've just decided we'd close the school down before we let boys in?" Reginald Griffin asks. "We've painted ourselves into a corner?"

"We haven't decided anything," Travelers says. "The motions weren't seconded. We didn't vote."

"All right then, I move that *if* the school gets into financial extremis, we *consider* the option of admitting boys," Reginald Griffin declares.

"Second!" Sonja McGarvey says. Then under her breath, "Chicken shit's better than nothing."

Travelers stands up. "Any discussion?" He frowns. It's clear that if anyone raises a hand, he'll kill. And anyway, the members can't wait to get out of here, off this stage. "Good," he says. "We'll vote by secret ballot," and hands a tablet of paper down the table.

The room is quiet while the board members write either *yes* or *no* on their ballots and hand them back to Travelers. Fred is not a board member, so he doesn't have a vote. Travelers makes two piles on the table in front of him. Then he counts each of them. Twice. "There are twelve *ayes* and eleven *nays* and two abstentions," he announces calmly, and Fred knows right away that if the members had been asked to raise their hands in front of their audience, there would be only two ayes, one of them Sonja McGarvey's, and the other, he is fairly sure, Travelers's, though Alan hates the idea of going coed.

"So you've voted to let boys in!" one of the invading alumnae declares. In her forties, blond hair gone mostly to gray, the woman is clearly trying to keep her voice calm in spite of her agitation. She has been glancing at her watch for the last hour.

"We have not," Travelers responds. "We've simply included it among the options to consider if we're in extremis. And in the meantime, we are going to do everything possible, under the leadership of our new head of school, Fred Kindler here, to rebuild our all-girls' enrollment."

"I wish I could believe it won't happen," the alumna says.

"Trust us to try," Travelers says, standing up. Then turning back to the table: "A motion to adjourn, please."

"So move," says Reginald Griffin.

"Second," says Sonja, standing up.

"One more question, please," says the gray-haired alumna.

"Madame, we have an adjournment motion."

"For Mr. Kindler," the alumna says.

Travelers knows that she's up to something, so he ignores her. "All in favor of the motion to adjourn," he says to the table, and all the board members raise hands. "This meeting is adjourned," he declares. The board members rise quickly from the table, and so does Fred.

But he doesn't escape. The woman and about ten others surround him as soon as he steps away from the table. "Surely, you're not going to refuse to talk to us," she says.

"No, of course I'm not." Fred glances at Travelers, who has seen what is happening and is listening hard.

"Mr. Kindler, my name is Elizabeth Preston, class of '61."

"How do you do, Mrs. Preston," Fred says gravely.

"I have a daughter in the class of '93. I don't suppose you've had time to get to know her yet," she adds sarcastically. Her implication is clear: he's been so busy plotting to let boys in that he's had no time to get to know the students.

"I'm looking forward to getting acquainted with every student, Mrs. Preston."

Mrs. Preston nods, leaving a loaded silence. Then she says: "My question is where do *you* stand on this issue?"

Now Travelers is by Fred's side. "Mrs. Preston, in the first place, it was a secret ballot, and in the second he doesn't have a vote."

"I'm not talking about a *vote,* Mr. Travelers. I know he doesn't have a *vote,* and I know why: so you can protect him. But that won't work, will it? I mean we're grown-ups here, and he *is* the leader, isn't he?"

"Madame, it's a *board* position."

"Oh, please, Mr. Travelers. He's the *headmaster.*"

"Mrs. Preston," Fred interrupts. "Believe me—" Then he sees the trap she's laying and stops. He has to support whatever position the board takes—or resign.

"I'll do my best," Mrs. Preston murmurs.

Fred takes a breath. He stares at her.

Mrs. Preston shrugs her shoulders, doesn't flinch. "Just as I thought, she says. "You'll do whatever you're told to do. The board's little patsy."

"Let's go, Fred," Travelers says, tugging at Fred's elbow. "There's no point in this."

"We would have preferred someone with *conviction!*" Mrs. Preston says.

Fred resists Alan's tugging. "I'm not going to lower myself to respond to that," he says.

"I wouldn't care if you did," Mrs. Preston says. Then she turns her back and walks away, and her supporters dutifully follow.

"She's smart," Alan says to Fred after the room is empty. "She's crazy, but she's smart. You say you're against letting boys in and the board votes to do that, you have to leave. I could have killed her."

"How do they get so good at smelling blood?" Fred wonders aloud. "Instinct? Or a plan?"

"We'll never know," Travelers says. "She probably doesn't either."

ELEVEN

NOW FRED KINDLER'S in a rush. He needs to get back to campus as fast as he can and be the bearer of this news: *the board is willing to consider admitting boys;* otherwise someone else will bear it. If he doesn't get there first, and do things right, Milton's prediction will come true: he'll have a crazy house on his hands. His walk across the parking lot to his car becomes a jog, and then a run.

First tell the faculty, he decides. That's protocol, that's courtesy. That puts them on his team. He'll call a meeting right away and tell them, sculpting the news, keeping it to its truthful context: *only* if the only other choice is to close the school. Then together, they'll call a meeting of the school and he'll tell the students. And he'll call Travelers and ask him to write a letter, today, from the board to all the parents and alumnae. It's a matter of getting the news out first, calmly, from the people in charge— before the crazy people do.

Then, brilliant thought, the way to do this thing *exactly* right: tell Francis Plummer first, the senior teacher. *That's* the protocol. *Then* go to the faculty. Plummer will appreciate that. So will the faculty. He'll take five minutes, do that first, make it clear to Plummer that for all their problems he's still the senior teacher. Honor that, and he'll be honored back. Stick to protocol. In a crisis do everything right.

That plan made, Fred has room in his mind to think over what happened as he rushes back to school. He has to admit he's irritated at Alan Travelers for trusting that Miss Richardson would honor the principle of confidentiality, and then being so careful of his own integrity that he wouldn't consider moving the meeting to a secret place and another date just in case she did break the principle, which now it's clear she did. That was Travelers's first mistake. His second was not pulling Sonja McGarvey aside before he started the meeting and telling her to hold her proposal to admit boys for another time when the board would meet in private and have the time to figure out how to let the community know what was being considered and how to manage the reaction. Maybe Travelers assumed Sonja would make her proposal anyway, being the kind of person she is. Sonja would scorn any approach that seemed round-about, convinced that the only road to salvation is the quickest and most direct. Maybe she didn't trust her colleagues ever to muster the courage, at least not until after it was too late, if she didn't force the issue.

By the time Fred arrives on campus, his irritation's melted. Who is he to judge this board, still virgin in the heated politics of school after having been so long a rubber stamp, vassal to a royal head, for making his job even harder? He could have turned the job down, it's not as if he didn't know the risks. He knows how bored he'd be tamely managing the status quo. Besides, he knew he could fall in love with Miss Oliver's School for Girls; and there was the subliminal push from his dead daughter. He still wants to lead the school that he's sure she would have loved.

Francis gets the message in the middle of a class. He can tell it makes the students as nervous as it makes him. Teachers being summoned to the head's office in the middle of a class? That's never happened before. The only reason he can think of for Kindler's wanting so urgently to see him is that he's gotten wind of the Student Council's plan and needs to talk with the faculty advisor about it. For that issue would make even Marjorie nervous. Maybe Lila paid Kindler the courtesy of telling him what she and Sara Warrior and the advisor to the Student Council decided this morning. Good for her if she did, he thinks, but he wanted to be the one to tell Kindler. He was going to go to Kindler's office right after classes, not only because Kindler really needs to know, but also so it wouldn't look as if he were withholding information to catch him unawares. He wishes he told Lila that *he* would bring the information to the new headmaster.

He's forgotten—maybe he didn't even know—that Kindler's been off campus at a board meeting all morning and so no one could have warned him about this delicate issue that's going to complicate both their lives.

When Francis steps through the door to the head's office, he can see the tension on Kindler's face. Kindler stands up, reaches across his desk to shake Francis's hand, then sits down behind his desk. This time he isn't going to come around his desk and sit near Francis. "Sit down, please, Mr. Plummer," Kindler says, motioning to one of the chairs in front of his desk. Francis sits. Behind Kindler the crazy wristwatch looms.

Francis doesn't wait for Kindler to start the conversation. "I'm sorry that I didn't get to you earlier with this news," he says. "But I had classes."

Fred stares at this little man sitting across the desk from him. "What?" he says. "You knew?" He starts to stand up.

"Only since this morning," Francis answers. He tries to keep the defensiveness out of his voice.

"This morning was early enough. The meeting didn't start till nine o'clock." Fred's standing up now. He's so angry he can hardly see. It doesn't occur to him that there wasn't much he could have done if Francis had told him as late as this morning that people were going to invade the meeting and actually sit in board members' places. Actually take their places! All he knows is just how little he trusts this bastard. Conniving with Sandra Petrie! And I was going to tell him *first?*

"Wait a second!" Francis says. "So Lila got to you by nine o'clock? Good for her. I had classes. I'll be goddamned if I'm going to skip classes to tell you something you don't need to know right away. The Student Council isn't going to do anything for a couple of days at least. What the hell are you standing up for, for Christ's sake?"

"Get out of here!" Fred Kindler says. "Just get out."

"No," says Francis very calmly. "No, I won't get out."

Kindler's still standing. He's gripping the edge of his desk with both hands. Francis can see how white the backs of Kindler's hands are.

"You called me in to talk about the Student Council proposal," Francis says. He's sure now this guy shouldn't be the head of Miss Oliver's School for Girls. He's out of control, you never know what's going to set him off. "So let's talk about that," he goes on. "Not about the fact that I didn't sprint across the campus to tell you in the first three seconds after *I* found out."

"What Student Council proposal?"

Francis doesn't answer for a second. "Oh?" he says. "That's not what I'm here about?"

"What Student Council proposal?" Fred Kindler asks again.

"To give the bones back," Francis says.

"The bones back," Fred repeats. He's still standing, and he's frowning, but the anger is beginning to leave his face.

"The bones and the whole display," Francis says. "They think it's blasphemous."

"Who thinks what's blasphemous, Mr. Plummer?"

"Sara Warrior. She's a Pequot."

"I know who Sara Warrior is, Mr. Plummer." Fred sits down.

Francis shrugs.

"All right," Fred says. "I shouldn't have told you to get out. I'm glad you resisted." But just the same, his mistrust lingers.

"Sara Warrior came to Lila, since she's president of the Student Council," Francis explains as Fred looks at his watch. "And Lila brought her to me."

"And then what happened?" Fred interrupts.

"The decision to bring the proposal to the students in Morning Meeting."

"To give the display away?"

Francis nods. "If you want to put it that way," he says.

"That's what you decided?"

"Hell, no, that's what *they* decided."

"They! Well, tell them no! We just spent fifteen thousand dollars we don't have on—"

"I can't tell them no," Francis interrupts. Don't you think I'd like to? he wants to ask. The librarian's my *wife*.

Fred stares at him. "You're the advisor, for goodness sake, tell them no."

"You don't really mean that," Francis says. "That the Student Council can't bring up an issue at Morning Meeting?" That Kindler can even think of the idea proves he isn't the right head.

"Let's drop this for now," Kindler says. He's looking at his watch again. "I've got something really important I want to talk to you about. I'm going to need your help."

"But *this* is important!" Francis says. "Discussing issues in Morning Meeting is a tradition."

Kindler's face goes red again. "Oh," he murmurs, "you're going to give me another lecture about tradition."

Margaret Rice steps into the office right then, without knocking. There's a new, satisfied look on her face.

"We're talking," Kindler says.

Margaret arches her eyebrows, shrugs her shoulder's. "OK," she says, and leaves.

"Let's start all over again," Fred sighs to Francis.

"All right," Francis says. "Good."

Kindler nods. He looks relieved. "This morning at the board meeting—" he begins.

Then Margaret is back in the office. "She says it's urgent."

"Who?" asks Kindler.

"Peggy Plummer," Margaret says, looking straight at Francis.

"Wait a second," Francis says. "I haven't talked to her about what the Student Council's going to do."

"You *haven't?*" says Kindler, looking at him even more sharply. Then turning to Margaret: "Urgent? Somebody hurt?"

Margaret doesn't have to answer because by then Peggy's in the office. She doesn't even look at Francis. "You need to be in the auditorium, Fred," she says.

"The auditorium?"

Peggy nods her head. "The whole school's gathering there right now. As we speak. A board member came on campus just a half hour ago. She went to every class. Announced in each one that the board has just voted to go coed. She's leading the meeting. I think you've got a riot on your hands."

"Who?" Kindler asks, standing up.

"Why, Sandra Petrie," Margaret Rice says gleefully. "Who else?"

TWELVE

FRED STANDS UP so fast he knocks his chair over. He takes two steps toward the door, trips over the edge of the rug, and almost falls into Francis's lap—which he prevents by throwing his hand out to brace himself against Francis's chair. He misses, hitting Francis in the shoulder instead, hard, as if he were punching him. Better if he'd hit him in the face! He's out the door and gone before Francis even stands up.

He sprints up the steps to the Marjorie E. Boyd Auditorium two at a time. On the big green front doors someone has posted a placard:

Estrogen Yes!

Testosterone No!

Inside, at the back of the auditorium, the first thing he sees is Sandra Petrie up on stage, standing at a podium. He's noticed the podium before, stored offstage. She must have moved it onstage to make herself seem authoritative. Sandra sees him right away. He stops in his tracks to stare at her. She stares back. He feels her anger as if it were a weight pushing him back, right out the doors he's just come through. This isn't the same woman who was so embarrassed by what she'd done that she obeyed Travelers's command to join the board at the table just to get out of the limelight. And for her this isn't just about letting boys in anymore; it's about Fred Kindler too—for keeping that limelight on her, for showing his contempt for her with that business about the minutes. If he hadn't stirred her anger so, she wouldn't be here, doing this.

Fred realizes that later when he has time to reflect. But he's not reflecting now—he's walking up the aisle toward the stage, and everyone in the audience is turning to see what Sandra is staring at. He walks very slowly toward Sandra, who stands at the podium, as if she were waiting for him at the altar, and, as if he were outside himself, watching, he finds himself whispering to a girl on the aisle, "Here comes the bride!" But his little joke is wasted on her. The only sound in the auditorium is the sound of his walking.

As he climbs the steps onto the stage, someone in the audience shouts: *"We don't want boys! We want Marjorie. Give us Marjorie back! Marjorie and no boys!"* By the time he reaches the podium, the chant has swelled: *"Boys no, Marjorie yes! Boys no! Marjorie yes!"*

Sandra doesn't budge from the podium. Inside his head Fred watches a movie of himself bodily picking her up—though she's taller than he is—lifting her off the stage floor, and dropping her over the edge.

Instead he stands next to her at the podium and looks out over the chanting crowd, keeping his face blank, as if he were watching an uninteresting phenomenon that has nothing to do with him. He will simply wait for them to stop. After a little while, after they have expressed their feelings, they'll catch on to how discourteous they're being. Without turning his face from the crowd, he says, just loud enough for Sandra to hear, "This is not your podium, Mrs. Petrie. You should sit down."

"It doesn't appear to be yours either," she hisses.

He doesn't answer, just keeps waiting. There is now a rhythmic stamping of feet to accompany the chant. But quite a few of the girls have stopped; maybe they never started. Sandra's daughter, Melissa, sits at the outer edge of the last row on his left, very close to a side exit door, her face averted from the front. He looks for the faculty, discovering that many of them are not there, and feels a rush of respect at their refusal to be a part of this. The rest are spread out through the audience. Rachel Bickham sits in the back row. He is surprised that she's there. She seems much too—well, noble—to participate in something like this. He looks into her dark, handsome face, and she looks right back. What bothers him the most is Gregory van Buren's presence in the front row. I thought you were *for* letting boys in, he wants to say, then realizes, as Gregory continues to avert his eyes, that maybe Van Buren is there in the front row to be supportive of him. It would be nice to know.

The noise slightly subsides. However angry they are, the girls are too sensitive not to get the message implied by his calm standing there, waiting. One of the girls in the front row stands up and faces the crowd, shouting *"Give me an M!"* she gets only a halfhearted reply from fewer than half the girls. *"Give me an A!"* the girl yells—to which even fewer students respond, one of whom adds with a disgusted shrug: "In all my subjects, so I can get into my daddy's college." That's when Rachel Bickham stands up in the back row.

Sandra Petrie points to Rachel, and Rachel starts to speak. "This is outrageous!" Rachel is very tall; her voice is quiet, but it fills the room. The chanting stops.

"Yeah, he wants to let boys in," someone says.

"Maybe he does," Rachel says.

"Maybe?" Sandra Petrie interrupts. "You know very well he does! That's why I called this meeting."

Rachel's beautiful, long-fingered hand is up, signaling silence. "Don't embarrass yourself anymore," she says to Sandra.

"But," says Sandra, "I—"

Rachel shakes her head back and forth, a subtle gesture, and Sandra says no more. When a student rises, starting to speak without raising her hand, it is Fred who points to Rachel. "I believe Ms. Bickham has the floor," he declares.

"When the other team shoots fouls shots, we don't make any noise," Rachel says. "That's the *Oliver* way. Fairness. This would be the worst time to abandon it." Then she sits down. The auditorium is suddenly much quieter.

So, thanks to Rachel, Fred has the floor. He steps forward toward the lip of the stage to explain what the board *really* decided. Then he notices Francis Plummer at the back of the auditorium, and he has a better idea.

"Good morning, Mr. Plummer," Fred calls loudly across the auditorium. "I assume you've come because you heard some noise and thought we might need your help." His voice is loaded with sarcasm. He doesn't care how much the girls like this sneaky little creep who—it's as plain as day—kept him in his office on purpose with another one of his lectures about tradition so there'd be time for a riot to get started behind his back. He's going to take him on right here, right now!

Francis says nothing.

"Mr. Plummer, you have no answers for us this morning," Fred says, and as soon as Francis opens his mouth to speak, Fred cuts him off. "Well, anyway, thanks for dropping by. You're just the right person to help us out." Ignoring the several girls four rows back who are silently mouthing an exaggerated imitation of his every word, he keeps on. "I think I'm right in saying that it's the Oliver custom"—*Oliver custom*, now a whole row is mouthing his words—"that the Student Council is the body that calls special all-school meetings."

Still no answer from Francis, who's trying to figure out what's happening.

"Well, then, maybe the president of the Student Council can tell us." Fred Kindler looks around the audience, peering, as if he doesn't know where Lila Smythe is sitting. "Lila?"

"That's right," says Lila, her voice tentative for once.

"Fine. It is also the head of school's prerogative." He can't keep his eyes away from the mute imitators, but he refuses to react. "So, since this meeting was called with neither *my* authority nor the Student Council's, I'm treating it as if it hasn't happened. It was a nonmeeting. So, Lila, would you like to call a *real* meeting for tomorrow morning so we can discuss our situation, or do you want me to call it?"

Lila hesitates.

"Lila?"

"I'll call it," says Lila.

"Good. What time?"

Lila turns toward Francis at the back of the auditorium.

"*Your* decision, Lila," Fred says.

"First period?" says Lila.

"Good," Fred says. "Will you run the meeting?"

"Yes," says Lila.

"Excellent. And since *this* is a nonmeeting, I'm canceling it as of now. We've missed a whole class period. Funny how something that doesn't happen can take up time. That's not a problem, though. Mr. Plummer here can figure out the best time for us to make it up." There are a few hisses from the audience at this, but Fred goes right on, riding his anger. "What do *you* think, Mr. Plummer, would this *Sunday* or the Sunday after be better?" Some more hisses. Francis starts to say something, but again Fred cuts him off: "Give yourself time to figure it out," he says. Then, obviously addressing the whole crowd: "Have a good morning, everybody. Mr. Plummer will let us know." He turns to Sandra, raises his eyebrows at her, steps away from the podium, and walks down the steps to the orchestra and up the aisle.

Behind him, he hears Sandra Petrie say: "All right. He's left. Now let's continue." He hears someone else say, "Tomorrow." By the time he nears the doors at the back of the auditorium, he can hear people getting up to leave. He's not surprised. He's always known that whether they like you or not, teenagers respond to the grown-up who's willing to risk, to put it all out there—to be a little crazy when it counts. As he passes Francis, who is still standing in the doorway, he says: "Be in my office in exactly five minutes."

FRANCIS ENTERS THE head's office, takes a chair.

"I didn't invite you to sit down," Kindler says.

Francis can't believe the man is serious, continues to sit.

"Stand up," Kindler says.

So, not knowing what else to do, how to act in the presence of this man who's so obviously out of control, Francis stands up.

"This won't take long. I've only got two things to say," Kindler announces. "Listen carefully to both of them."

Francis says nothing.

"The first—as you would have already learned from me without our little riot—is the board has decided that under extreme conditions it would consider whether or not it is in the school's best interest to become a coed school."

"Consider? Or actually decide?" Francis asks carefully. His own rage is rising now, a counter to Kindler's—if he can control it.

"What do you think, Mr. Plummer?"

"Just tell me," Francis says. "This isn't a quiz show."

"Consider, Mr. Plummer, merely consider. And I expect you to treat their consideration with respect. That's the second thing."

Francis starts to say how crazy it is even to think about this, how it will never happen, no matter who's running the school, but Kindler starts talking again before Francis gets a word out. "If you had behaved yourself, you wouldn't have had to ask. I would have told you," he says, staring at Francis.

Francis opens his mouth to speak, but Kindler puts his hand up and waves it back and forth in that gesture that drives Francis crazy. "Not now, Mr. Plummer. And not to me. I'm not interested in your opinion anymore. And won't be until you get your act together."

"My act together?" Francis repeats, realizing suddenly: *He thinks I knew! He thinks while he was talking with me in the office I knew there was a riot getting started. He thinks I set him up!* He's forgotten the coed issue. All he can think of is this.

"If you fail to do whatever you have to do to get yourself back on track, I'll fire you," Kindler says.

"Whatever I have to do? What does that mean?"

"I've suggested therapy already, Mr. Plummer, Fred says, aware that last time he called it counseling. "Do I have to again?"

Francis opens his mouth, but no words come out. If Kindler had stood up, reached across his desk, and punched him in the face it wouldn't feel any worse.

"Well, do I?" Kindler says.

Francis still can't speak. He's dizzy with anger; Kindler's face is a blur.

"I guess so," Kindler says.

"Don't you ever say that to me again," Francis says at last. "Do you hear? Ever."

Kindler just shrugs.

"Or you'll *fire* me? Who do you think you are?"

"Be careful, Mr. Plummer. Or I'll show you who I am."

"I'll resign then," Francis blurts, thinking, I'll be goddamned if I'm going to get down on my knees and tell him that I didn't even know what was happening! I was already in here when Sandra came on campus.

Kindler puts his hands on his desk, leans forward. "You think I'd let you resign? You even begin to, and I'll fire you. I won't give you that to hide in.

I'll fire you *publicly*. I'll announce it in the school newspaper. I'll write an article in the alumnae magazine. I don't care what kind of hornets' nest it stirs up. If it weren't for my respect for your wife, I could even enjoy such a fight. That's how you win fights, you know. The ones you get in just for the hell of it are the ones you always win."

"My wife's none of your business, Mr. Kindler."

"Except for the fact that she's the best damn librarian in the business, you're right."

"This fight's just between you and me."

Francis watches Kindler's body tense. He thinks for a moment he's won, the man's going to lose it completely, go totally out of control. He's wrong. Kindler speaks very slowly. "It doesn't have a damn thing to do with either you *or* me," he says. "It's about the *school*. Why don't you grow up?

"Think about that," Kindler adds. "This meeting's over."

THAT EVENING IMMEDIATELY after dinner, Peggy has an appointment with the ninth graders to teach them how to use the library. She goes straight there from the dining hall. The minute she's finished she'll hurry home. She needs to talk with Francis.

She's still hearing the bitterness in Fred Kindler's voice this morning as he mocked Francis in front of the whole school, telling him to pick the Sunday for making up the classes, and cutting him off when he tried to speak. There was something irredeemable in that very public insult, something much too reckless. How does he retreat from that, she wonders, how does Francis forgive him?

And she watched the stony expression on Fred's face as he walked down the aisle, stopped and said something to Francis, and then went out the door. Only minutes later, she saw Francis heading for the administration building, and she was sure he was going to Fred's office. She needs to know what happened there.

Francis goes home after dinner and waits for Peggy to finish with the ninth graders. As soon as she gets home, he'll tell her about the Student Council's proposal to give the Collection to the Pequots. He doesn't want her to be taken by surprise when it comes up in Morning Meeting. He wanted to tell her right after morning classes to be sure she'd hear it from him rather than someone else. But then there was the riot in the auditorium and Kindler attacking him in public and threatening to fire him in his office, and the Pequot issue went clean out of his mind, until he sat with Peggy just now at dinner, presiding over their table in the dining hall.

While he waits for her, he has two sets of compositions to comment on and grade—and a rule of his own to obey: every paper will be returned within forty-eight hours. Gregory van Buren almost never keeps papers longer than that, and Francis isn't about to be bested by *him*. But it isn't long before he finds that he's going to have to disobey his rule, because he can't keep his mind on the students' writing. He's too full of the pain of everything that happened that morning. All day he's been hearing the new headmaster say, "I'll fire you publicly. I'll write it up in the alumnae magazine." He'll have to tell Peggy about it someday, though right now that's too humiliating even to imagine. His new boss, half his age, leaning across his desk and asking him why he doesn't grow up!

He gives up and goes out into the dorm, pokes his head into each girl's room to say hello. His spirits lift, a little, when Lila Smythe asks for advice about an essay she's written for Gregory van Buren's celebrated course: "Tragedy from *Oedipus Rex* to *Death of a Salesman*." Gregory's told her to do the essay over, because there's a subtle flaw in the logic of her argument that she needs to find on her own, and that at first reading Francis can't see either. When he does catch on to Gregory's point, he asks her some leading questions to help her discover it on her own and watches her understanding dawn. "Thanks, Mr. P.," she tells him. "You've helped a lot." He's grateful for this warmth from Lila, and forgets for a moment his trouble with Kindler; but he understands that he never would have caught Lila's error; he would have given her an A. And just the other day, Rachel Bickham casually suggested to Gregory and Francis that they do what the teachers in her department do and visit each other's classes. Of course that's what they should have been doing all along: learning from each other, like grown-ups. . . .

Peggy finishes with the ninth graders quickly. After all, there are only nine of them. Then she hurries across the campus and finds Francis in the dorm just as he's finished helping Lila. "I need to talk to you," she says, motioning toward the door to their apartment.

Naturally, he thinks she's heard about the proposal through the grapevine and wants to know why he didn't tell her. He could kill himself.

He's wrong. She hasn't gotten wind of the proposal. The near-riot in the auditorium, the specter of boys at Miss Oliver's, have shoved all thoughts of the Collection out of everyone's mind. The Council members aren't thinking about it right now, and they aren't telling anybody about it, and if they were, no one would pay attention.

In their apartment, Levi comes across the room to welcome them, wagging his tail, his toenails clicking on the floor. They ignore him. "What happened?" she asks before they even sit down.

"I'm sorry," he says. "I meant to tell you before anyone else did."

She shakes her head to tell him no. Of course Fred Kindler didn't tell her what happened between him and Francis in his office. How could Francis think he would?

He thinks she means no, forgetting's no excuse. "Well, I think you would have forgotten too," he says, a little angry now.

"Francis, please," she says. "What happened? Between you and Fred Kindler today." Both of them are still standing up.

"Oh, that's what we're talking about!"

"Francis!"

He's stunned and realizes that maybe he wasn't ever going to tell her what Kindler said to him today. So now he feels guilty about that too. "Which time? I had two meetings with him," he says. Anything to postpone having to admit to this disgrace.

"After the auditorium. I saw you heading for his office."

"Yeah," he says. "You did. That's where I went."

She waits.

"He threatened to fire me," he says at last, and adds. "That's all, nothing important," as if it were a joke.

"That's what I thought," she says, discovering that it's true, though until he said it, she didn't dare think it. She looks away. She can't bear to look at him, he's so chagrined.

"He thinks I set him up. He thinks I knew Sandra was on campus."

"Oh, come on. He wouldn't think that."

"Yes, he does, I could tell. He thinks I kept him in his office to give her time to get the meeting started without him."

"You?" she asks. "How could he?" Even if Francis were devious enough, he doesn't have that kind of cunning.

Because he goes out of control at the drop of a hat, Francis wants to answer her. Because he gets angry and acts before he thinks. But he won't say that. She would just leap to Kindler's defense.

He's right; she would. But she did see Fred Kindler attack the school's most beloved teacher this morning, right in front of everyone, and then, another reckless act, just leave the auditorium, just walk away. How did he know Sandra Petrie wouldn't get the power back?

"Peggy, I'm going to keep my promise. I'm going to do my job and help him, whatever he does."

"Don't say that, Francis."

"What?"

"Whatever he does. As if he were an idiot."

"That's not what I meant, Peg. I think you know it."

"All right," she sighs, "it's not how you meant it."

"Good," he says. He's dying to change this subject. And he wants to tell her about the Student Council proposal before ten o 'clock, the time to go through the dorm checking the girls in and saying goodnight. "Lila Smythe came to me this morning—" he begins.

She interrupts him, "Francis, why can't you and Fred be friends?" As soon as the words are out of her mouth, she knows how naive they sound.

That stops him. It never occurred to him that he and Kindler could be *friends.*

"It would save everything," Peggy says. Naive or not, it's true. Not just our school, but our marriage too, she thinks, remembering Eudora's "we save the school, we save everything." She tries to imagine Francis getting fired and teaching at another school and can't. But she wonders nevertheless if she would stay at Miss Oliver's or go with him. It amazes her that she can't answer the question.

"I don't have to be his friend to work for him," Francis says.

"Maybe not, but you better explain to him, Francis. You need to go back and tell him you had no idea that Sandra was on campus. He'll never trust you otherwise."

"Maybe," Francis says. "I'll try" and knows he won't. He's not going to watch Fred Kindler decide that he's a liar as well as a sneak. Peggy's watching him. His answer is not enough for her. But before he can think of the words to convince her he's going to be loyal to Fred Kindler whatever Fred Kindler thinks, the clock in the library's steeple rings ten times.

It's a relief. They can retreat from this problem between them into the routine that's been there for them to escape to all the years of their marriage. They go through their dorm, chatting with the girls, checking them in. When they get back to their apartment at eleven o'clock, Francis sees the uncorrected papers on his desk. He thinks he'll get up at five in the morning to get them done, then rejects the idea. He's knows how tired he will be. So he sits down at his desk and goes to work. Peggy goes to bed.

When he finishes the papers at two o'clock in the morning and gets in bed beside her, she stirs in her sleep. He turns to her and kisses her cheek. She doesn't awaken, and anyway, he doesn't know what he'd say to her. Maybe if it were not for the pile of papers he still had to correct in the middle of the night he would have remembered to warn her about the proposal to give away the Collection. And yet there's nothing unusual about his staying up until early morning correcting papers. It's more likely that if Fred Kindler hadn't threatened to fire him that morning, he would have remembered. And if Peggy had woken when he kissed her again in her sleep, he might have remembered. They would talk about it then and go in the morning to Fred's office with their ideas about how to respond. But she doesn't wake up, and then *he* goes to sleep.

BY TEN MINUTES after eight the next morning, five minutes before the beginning of first period, all 345 students are seated in the auditorium. Fred sits at the right-hand end of the first row, near the same steps he climbed up onto the stage yesterday to the deafening chant of Marjorie and no boys! Today the auditorium is tomblike. The twelve members of the Student Council—three from each class—sit in chairs on stage. As tradition dictates, Francis Plummer sits with them, looking uncomfortable.

President Lila Smythe rises from her chair, next to Francis, and slowly walks downstage to the podium. She stands there for a moment, prolonging the silence, much more poised than Sandra Petrie was the day before.

Lila's voice is clear. "The Student Council has called this meeting." She pushes the microphone, still off, to one side of the podium. She doesn't need a mike; she's a presence; her voice carries. "Our head of school has an announcement."

The steps squeak as Fred climbs onstage. The girls study his awkward gait as he crosses to the podium. By the time he gets there, Lila is sitting down. "Thank you, Lila," Fred says as he steps behind the podium.

The thing comes almost up past his shoulders, dwarfing him. It was built for Marjorie! Why didn't he notice that and stay away from the damn thing? Yesterday when Sandra stood behind the podium she was plenty tall enough, but now that he's behind it, it's obvious he isn't. It dawns on him what the girls are seeing: only his head. A titter rises somewhere in the silence, begins to grow, and for a crazy instant he has the idea that he will play with this absurdity. He'll bend his knees to make himself even shorter, disappear completely, clown around. That's how some people he knows could handle this: join the laughter, relieve the tension, win the war. But that's not who he is, he knows—a fleeting regret—he couldn't pull it off. So he steps around the podium, moves downstage, and stands at the lip of the platform. The laughter stops.

"It is a little more than an announcement," he says. He's silent again. He wants them to know that for him this is heavy too, he isn't trying to slide it by.

Then, careful not to speak down to the students, he lays out the whole situation: the baby bust, the national trends that began several years before away both from boarding schools and from single-sex schools for girls. "In spite of our school's excellence," he goes on to say, "the result has been a serious underenrollment, and the result of that has been a very disturbing deficit. We have less money in revenues than in expenses. When that happens several years in a row, schools get into serious trouble." He stops here, hoping for some reaction, some questions he can answer. To get them involved is to enlist their help in saving the school.

No one raises her hand; no one says a word. He's speaking to a sea of stony faces.

He soldiers on, speaks passionately about his commitment to rebuilding the girls-only enrollment, describes the efforts made over the summer, and turns the disappointment of the meager result—only six new students, other than the ninth grade—into positive news by exclaiming how wonderful all the new students are, what excellence he expects of them. For this, but for nothing else, he receives a mild applause.

He doesn't realize how foreign a territory he is describing. How could he? Francis Plummer could have helped him understand that Marjorie was even less inclined to share the realities of the financial situation with the students than she was with the faculty. But Francis Plummer and Fred Kindler aren't talking to each other; and even if they were, Francis is probably not ready yet to recognize this characteristic of Marjorie's leadership as a weakness. Instead, he would explain it—maybe even proudly—as "just how we do things at Miss Oliver's." So now, when Fred invokes such terms as *deficit, revenue,* and *budget* rather than the school's glory, because he assumes that especially at Miss Oliver's, financial realities, the way things *actually* work, should be part of the curriculum, he becomes for the students even more the interloper, the man who doesn't belong.

Sitting on the stage behind Fred and staring at his back, Francis can hear in his tone how passionately he wants to build the girls-only enrollment, and for all his anger and his conviction that Kindler's the wrong person for this job, he is relieved. It is then that he realizes that his meeting with the new headmaster yesterday had almost nothing to do with admitting boys. They were so angry with each other, they went by the issue. Their fight was merely personal, he's ashamed to realize. Neither of them was doing his job.

Finally, near the end of his talk, Fred actually has to say it, to put it out there: "Therefore the board of directors, at its last meeting, decided that it was its responsibility to the school to consider admitting boys if our effort to build girls-only enrollment doesn't produce enough revenue." He almost says, *instead of shutting down.* He catches himself just in time. Those words, released to the air, would be too much reality all at once.

"Please understand: the board hasn't decided to admit boys: only to consider it under certain circumstances, which I believe will never develop." He hesitates again. "And of course, if that did happen, they would have to look at the fundamental question: Is there any point in being Miss Oliver's if we are not for girls only."

Silence.

"I'd like to hear your thoughts," he says. For he's still hoping to entice them, get them involved, make them part of the rescue.

No one raises a hand.

"This school is known for facing problems square on. We can discuss this."

Still no response. Everyone in the audience is watching him. No one says a word.

After what seems forever, he hears Lila's voice behind him. "Here is our answer." Then she's standing next to him, handing him a sheaf of papers. The heading of the top page is DECLARATION. He reads: *We, the undersigned members of the student body, declare our undivided loyalty to Miss Oliver's School for Girls, and are adamant that this school remain for girls only. We also declare that we will not attend any school that admits male students, and that if Miss Oliver's School for Girls decides to admit boys, each one of us will leave this campus permanently.* Underneath, and on to the next three pages, are the signatures.

"There are three hundred and forty-five students," Lila tells Fred in a clear voice, which everyone can hear, "and three hundred and twenty-eight signatures. I understand there is a similar declaration going around the faculty."

Fred stands, holding the sheaf of papers in his hand, saying nothing. He makes no effort to disguise the fact that he is stunned. "Oh! Well, thank you, Lila," he finally manages. "I'll pass this on to the board."

"Good," says Lila. "So this meeting's over, right?"

"Seems to be," Fred says, though now that he's over his surprise, it's dawning on him that he's proud of these kids for their resistance. Later, he will realize that he should have turned back to the audience then and told the students so, praised them for their conviction and their faith, and thanked them. But he's too stunned and doesn't think fast enough.

If Lila had known what was going through Fred's mind she would have waited to adjourn the meeting so Fred could express his thoughts, tell the students how proud of them he is. It could save the day for him. But Lila can't know, and she is already at the lip of the platform. "This meeting is adjourned," she declares. "Time for classes." In silence, the girls stand, their faces impassive. As they leave, Fred joins them, walking down the aisle.

No one looks at him.

THIRTEEN

THE LAST THING either Francis Plummer or Fred Kindler needs is to be face-to-face with each other. But that is exactly what is about to happen a day later as Francis hurries across campus to his classroom and Fred Kindler walks on the same path in the opposite direction to his office. They both consider stepping off the path to avoid one another. But of course they reject the idea. They are grown men, after all.

Francis forces himself not to look away from Kindler's face as they approach each other. Fred Kindler does the same: he keeps his eyes up, full on his senior teacher's face. Let *him* cringe, he thinks. He's already crossed Francis off his list. He's hurrying to a meeting with Rachel Bickham. He can trust *her* advice. And Peggy Plummer's too. And there are others, maybe, to help him steer the course.

Nevertheless, it makes him sad to think how good it would have been if this Plummer were a different kind of guy and he could have had him for a partner. When Fred visited Francis's English and math classes during his visits as a candidate, he saw the demands Francis was able to make of his students, the standard to which he raised them. It was a revelation for Fred. He's sure that if he and Plummer were working hand in hand, they'd be able to turn the Declaration Lila presented to him yesterday into a victory for both of them and the school. The four of us, he thinks. Gail and I and the Plummers. That would have made a home.

"Good morning." Francis tries to say it first, but they both say it together—a kind of unison. The irony will occur to Francis later. Right now, all he is aware of is that every interaction he's had with Kindler has been a disaster.

And then they're are past each other, and he wonders if he should have stopped, put his hand on Kindler's elbow, said something to give them both a chance to start again. But he doesn't know what it is he could have said to make that happen. He could be a mentor to Fred Kindler if Kindler needed some advice as to how to run some *other* school. But here? Following *Marjorie?* How could *that* be! He doesn't look like the head of this school, he doesn't talk like the head of this school. And he doesn't think like the head of this school. How could he not see how wrong he is for us?

Nevertheless, he'll keep his opinion to himself, let others have their own.

ON THE OTHER SIDE of campus, Fred's spirits lift. He's looking forward to this meeting with Rachel Bickham. The high standards to which she holds herself intimidate some of her colleagues. But they delight him.

Chair of the Science Department, teacher of physics, head of athletics, and coach of the varsity basketball team, Rachel Bickham is six feet tall, thirty-four years old. Her stately African American presence draws one's gaze when she enters a room. Her face is more handsome than beautiful, her voice quiet enough so you have to pay close attention to hear what she is saying, and when she teaches, she moves her graceful hands through the air to express her passion for her subject. "The study of science reveals how elegantly the world works," she tells her students. "What could be more inspiring than that?"

Five years earlier, Marjorie Boyd recruited Rachel by pointing out that a major goal was the annihilation of the female stereotype as weak in math and science. One of the first things Rachel did as chair of the Science Department was to announce to Marjorie, who almost never could bring herself to fire anyone, that the teachers who had been teaching science at the school for years were good—but not good enough. She didn't wait for Marjorie to get up the nerve; instead, against ancient protocol, she took it on herself to inform the least effective teacher that she no longer had a job as of the end of the winter term, and gave the rest of the department one academic year to find other schools at which to teach. Then, by making it clear that her standards would be extraordinarily high, and her demands on them relentless, she succeeded in luring away from other schools three gifted teachers, each of whom had graduated from a single-sex college for women. And she did all this with enough directness and courtesy that the dismissed teachers left causing much less furor than Marjorie had predicted, their self-esteem reasonably intact.

"I think you may have chosen a consequence that doesn't quite work," Rachel tells Fred, her long legs taking up much of the space between their chairs. "Taking their Sunday for a class. It doesn't feel right."

"Well, now, it doesn't feel right to me either," Fred agrees. "Besides, the girls could refuse. Just stay in their dorms, and then where would we be? It was much too arbitrary, but you know, I was just riding with whatever came to mind."

"I could see that," Rachel smiles. "So could everyone else! Riding hard, too. No one was going to get in the way."

"And that's what came to mind: Sunday class. Dumb idea."

"Clearly off the cuff. But thanks for not getting steamrolled. I would have hated to see that."

"I might have," Fred admits, "without your remark about foul shots. Thanks."

"No way. You were doing fine. Besides, if it weren't me, it would have been somebody else."

"I hope."

"Anyway, our kids just needed a little reminder. They know how to behave."

"Signing that Declaration is behaving right, you think?"

"For the students? Yes, I do."

"So do I," Fred says. "It's what I would have done too."

Rachel studies Fred's face, doesn't say anything.

"What about you?" Fred asks. "If we went coed, what would you do?"

"I'd leave."

Fred nods in agreement. "That's how you signed the faculty Declaration?"

"You don't know? You didn't read it?"

"I did not. I wasn't about to pretend that the *faculty's* Declaration had any weight. It's not that I don't care; it's just that it doesn't make any difference. We're either broke or solvent."

"That's why *I* didn't sign it," Rachel says, very quietly.

"You didn't?"

"Hell, no."

"Sorry. I shouldn't have assumed."

"Some other teachers didn't sign it either."

Fred nods. "Speaking of grown-ups."

"Yes. Some are. Some aren't. What about the board, did they read it?"

"Don't know yet. I sent it to the chair with a strong note suggesting he send it back, unread."

"You did?"

"I did."

"My goodness!"

Fred waits.

"I kind of hope he doesn't take your advice," she says.

"I kind of hope so too," Fred says. "Now that I've had time to think about it."

"Well, anyway," Rachel continues after a little silence. "Back to that Sunday. I have an idea."

"First I have a different question," Fred says, realizing how much he wants her advice.

Rachel looks surprised. She waits.

"What is your opinion of the appropriateness of our Indian display?"

"Oh," says Rachel. "That."

"Yes. That."

"I wouldn't go there if I were you."

"Suppose I don't have a choice? Suppose the Student Council brings it up and says it's wrong?"

"Yes, I hear rumors that will happen."

"It *is* going to happen."

Rachel nods. "Well, when it does, I'd say they're right."

"You would? Really?"

Rachel shakes her head. "No, I guess I wouldn't. It's what I believe, but it would be wrong to say it."

"Wrong? If you believe it?"

"Not for me. For you. The head. We've had the display for years. It would sound disrespectful of the past."

"Including Marjorie?"

Rachel nods. "When you speak, yes. *Especially* Marjorie."

"Just what I need right now," he says and wishes right away he could have those words back; they sound too much like whining.

But Rachel doesn't seem to notice. "The idea has come up before," she tells him. "Five years ago in my first year. It didn't have much heat around it. Nobody was using words like *blasphemy* and *racism,* so Peggy Plummer wasn't offended. And Marjorie just let the controversy die. She liked the Collection right where it was, and besides, it would have taken a fair amount of work to reach out and make the arrangements with the Pequot authorities, whom, I regret to say, we've never had anything to do with; and maybe she was afraid that when the Pequots realized we've had these things for years, they'd accuse us of racism and disrespect, which, of course, would be all over the news."

"All right," he says. "I'll just let the discussion happen. I won't take sides, at least not at first." He doesn't say—because he's already sounded like a whiner—that sometimes the person with the most responsibility is the one with the least power. Instead, he murmurs out loud: "It's going to be tricky."

"Very," Rachel says. Then after a little pause: "Sometime I wonder if I could do your job."

"Sometimes I wonder if *I* can do it," Fred says, smiling.

Rachel smiles too. "You're doing fine," she says again. "Just keep at it. Anyway, back to my idea."

"I could use one!"

"Yes, you could," Rachel grins. "And here it is. Instead of classes on a Sunday, we do a service project. That way you still make your point."

"What about my just calling the whole thing off, just admit I was off base?"

"Don't you dare!"

"That's what I thought you'd say."

"They'll feel useful," Rachel points out. "You don't want to use classes for punishment. Besides, it will be good publicity."

"It's a fine idea," Fred declares. "Let's get the Student Council to choose the project."

"Good idea."

"Why in the world didn't *I* think of this?" Fred asks himself out loud.

Rachel reaches out, pats his hand. "Maybe because you're human," she says. "I'll tell Francis."

"That will help," says Fred, not quite succeeding in keeping the sarcasm out of his voice.

Rachel stands up to leave. He can see she's heard the sarcasm, but, good politician that she is, she ignores it. "Just one more thing," she says, "an afterthought. I'm sure you've thought of it already."

"Don't count on it," he grins.

She smiles. One of the things she likes about this guy is his self-depreciation. "Bring Francis and Peggy Plummer in together to discuss the Council's idea," she advises. "So they can work it out between themselves and you before it's dropped on her in public."

"I will," he says. "Of course."

AND, ON THE OTHER side of campus, in the classroom that has been his for thirty-three years, Francis's spirits also begin to lift. He's about to do what he does best.

The bell's just rung. The students in his ninth-grade English class troop in and take seats along the outer edges of the three-sided square of tables. Francis stands at the front of the classroom, just inside the square, like an actor in a theater whose stage projects out into the audience. "Home Burial," he says, "by Robert Frost." It's one of the poems he assigned for them to read last night. The girls open their books to the page and follow him as he recites this poem from memory about the young New England husband who from the bottom of the stairs catches his wife staring from the landing above him, out the window at the little graveyard behind the house, where their firstborn lies.

He doesn't try to hide how much he loves this poem he's been teaching for years, how it really is by *heart*. For Francis (who doesn't know the Kindlers' secret) there could be no greater draw on his compassion than a parent who's lost a child.

It's a long poem. It takes him several minutes to recite, and when he finishes there is silence, which he allows to linger. He knows that many of these kids, whose programmed childhoods have been thicketed with expensive lessons in tennis, soccer, yoga, piano, gymnastics, martial arts—and the skills of outdoing less affluent people in the taking of standardized tests—seldom hear poems recited from memory. For who among their parents has the time or the inclination to memorize a poem? He wonders if Sara Warrior, who has been watching him intently from the back of the room, is an exception. Her head's not been down in her book like the other girls. Is that because she doesn't need to follow with her eyes, she can listen? Maybe her people don't hold their stories at arm's length as if borrowing them for only a little while. Maybe they take them into memory, drawing them up inside themselves, and owning them.

But next to Sara, what Amy Leveret is intent on is showing how *dis*engaged she is. She's slouching as far back from the table as she can get at the rear of the room without knocking the Globe Theater off its table. Black pants, black leather jacket on this hot September day, black hair dyed even blacker spiked straight up. Still intent on improving the students' attire, Fred Kindler told Amy to take the ring out of her nose on her first day of school. She's been looking for revenge ever since.

"Well, Amy, what do you think of the poem?" Francis asks her. He usually stays away from such open-ended questions for their tendency to engender uncritical, self-reflective answers. But if he doesn't smoke Amy's distemper out into the open, it will subvert the class for the rest of the period.

Amy slouches still further. "I think it's boring," she says.

"Why do you say that?" As if he didn't know the answer: because he's yet another adult who professes to know what's good for her, what clothes she should wear, what poetry she should love as much as he does. If she is seduced by this poem, the anger she's been nurturing for months will begin to melt, and then who will she be?

"Because you asked," Amy says.

"Boring?" he repeats.

"Yeah. Boring."

"How do you know, Amy?" There's no challenge to the question. He just wants to know.

"Because I was bored," Amy says. "How else would I know?"

"Well, Amy, that's one way to find out," he says. He's smiling, relaxed. He's not going to blame her, but the entitled upbringing that makes her answer by talking about herself. Besides, he likes her nervy quickness. He's glad the low enrollment gave Nan White an excuse to accept this kid.

Because he won't fight, she doesn't know how to respond to him. She looks around. Her classmates aren't looking at her; they're looking at Francis.

"But it's the one I like the best!" Francesca Burke objects. She sits up very straight to the left of Francis, her back to the blackboard, her red hair lighted by the windows across the room. She leans forward, her arms on the table, her feet wiggling nervously beneath it. Francis knows she's going to explain why she likes the poem. That's exactly what he doesn't want. He puts his hand up to Francesca, smiling gently. "Wait," he says. Francesca returns his smile, thinking he's asked her to hold up long enough for the others to understand what he and she already do.

"Do any of you live in a house like the one in the poem?" he asks the class.

No one raises her hand. "No one?" he repeats. Usually there are several.

"I do," Joanna Perrine finally admits. Her voice is tentative and shy. He knows from reading Nan White's notes to the faculty about incoming students that Joanna lost her brother in a skiing accident a few years ago. "We live in New Hampshire too," she adds. She sits to Francis's right, by the windows, across from Francesca. Under the table, her long legs reach out toward the empty space in the center of the room; she's almost as tall as Rachel Bickham. Everybody knows she's from New Hampshire; it's not what she's trying to say. "The front door is at the foot of the stairs in our house too," Joanna murmurs.

He needs to keep this safe for her, he better be careful. But if she didn't want to engage with this poem about a loss so like her own, from a house just like the one she lives in, she wouldn't have raised her hand to answer his question. Maybe she's found some solace in the poem, which she wants to secure more deeply. At any rate, his heart goes out to her. He'll help her engage. He'll bring her up here to the front to help him teach. "Can you draw it for us, Joanna?" he asks.

Joanna hesitates. She's not sure what he wants.

"The way the scene in the poem is laid out," he explains. He turns, steps to the blackboard behind him, takes a piece of chalk from the tray beneath it, and holds it up, inviting her, and she gets up from her place at the table, moves across the space to him, takes the chalk, turns her back to the class, and starts to draw. She makes a perpendicular line on the board and labels it *front door*— as far away from the graveyard as she can get, Francis thinks. Then, just to the right, a side view of a staircase ascending to the right. She labels the top step *landing*. Then to the right of that, another perpendicular line, with a break in it, which she labels *window*. To the right and below that window, she draws four gravestones, and next to them a little mound of earth—a child's new grave without a headstone yet. She doesn't label those. Then she puts the chalk into the tray beneath the blackboard and turns to him.

"Exactly!" Francis says, and recites again:

He saw her from the bottom of the stairs
Before she saw him. She was starting down,
Looking back over her shoulder at some fear.

Joanna takes a little step away from the front, from all these eyes watching her, toward her seat at the side of the room. He puts his hand lightly on her elbow, "So, Joanna. Does the young husband stay at the bottom of the stairs?" he asks.

"No, he goes up the stairs to her."

"To find out what she's looking at?"

"Yes."

"And does he find out?"

"Yes: the grave where their child is buried in the family graveyard."

"Their only child, you think?"

She nods her head.

"What makes you think so?" he asks her.

"Because it's so sad."

"All right." Ordinarily he wouldn't accept this answer; he'd make her go to the text, where the facts are. He'd make her find the words *baby* and *first child* as evidence that the young couple's loss is complete. But she's brought her own grief to the poem. So he says, "Yes, it's very sad. They only have each other now." He hopes she takes some comfort that though she no longer has her brother, she has her parents and her parents have her.

"And does she stay at the top of the stairs?" he asks.

"For a while, that's all."

"Just for a while, yes, and then what?"

"She ducks beneath his arm and goes downstairs."

"Where he was at the beginning?"

"More than that," Joanna says. "She goes right out the house."

"Hey, Joanna!" he says. "You're a good reader." He lets go of her elbow.

"Thanks." She smiles shyly, and moves back to her seat. She's glad he gave her a second chance to raise her hand.

He turns to the class now and asks, "What's the husband's reaction when he discovers what his wife's been looking at?"

Angela Nash has her hand up before he's finished asking the question. She has black curly hair and pale skin and looks younger than her fourteen years. "Angela," he says, "you're going to tell us?"

"He's kind of amazed," Angela answers.

"Amazed, yes, you're right. It's in the way he speaks, isn't it? It's in the tone of his words," he says, rewarding her for leaping in, taking a chance with half an answer—the way a boy would. Angela smiles and nods, proud of her success.

"Amazed at what?" he pursues. "What is he amazed *at?* Surely he knew the graveyard was out back and his child was in it."

Angela hesitates.

"Read the words," Francis tells her. Angela looks down at her book. She scans the poem, looking for the passage, doesn't find it right away. Now a lot of hands are up. One of them is Sara Warrior's. He calls on her.

> *The wonder is I didn't see at once.*

Sara reads. Her voice is quiet.

> *I never noticed it from here before.*
> *I must be wonted to it—that's the reason.*
> *The little graveyard where my people are!*
> *So small the window frames the whole of it.*
> *There are three stones of slate and one of marble,*
> *Broad-shouldered little slabs there in the sunlight*
> *On the sidehill. We haven't to mind those.*
> *But I understand: it's not the stones,*
> *But the child's mound.*

Sara stops reading, looks up from the book. He can't read the expression on her face, has no idea what's she's thinking.

He's tempted to read the passage over aloud, because Sara's read it so quietly. But he won't risk her taking that as a put-down, for she's fragile, too, a stranger in a foreign place. Instead, he says, "Thank you, Sara" and asks the question again, this time of the whole class. "What is it exactly that he is amazed at?"

Several hands go up. One of them is Amy's, though she only puts it up halfway—and takes it down as soon as she remembers how bored she is.

"Amy!" he says. "Tell us."

Amy sighs.

"You don't know?" he says, laying his little trap: if she doesn't answer she won't appear above this; she'll just look dumb.

"He's amazed that he had to look out the window to find out, that he didn't know all along what his wife keeps looking at," she finally answers.

Francis waits for more.

"He wonders why he didn't look out the window too every time he went by it."

"Your evidence?" he asks. "The line?"

"I must be wonted to it," Amy quotes, quick as a flash, without looking at her book.

"And how does his wife feel?"

"That he shouldn't be amazed. I mean, his kid is dead," Amy says, and almost adds "for Christ's sake" to get back to being negative, but she doesn't dare.

Francis doesn't answer, just stands there and waits as if she hasn't answered yet. Now she's thinking hard in spite of herself. He looks away from her to ask someone else, and then, just in time, it comes to her, the precision he's demanding. "Oh, all right," she says, as if he were just quibbling. "Her point's not that he shouldn't be amazed. Her point is he shouldn't get used to his kid being dead."

"Good catch, Amy," Francis says.

"Well, it's obvious," she says, and checks out again, returning to her slouch.

Francis scans the room and asks another question: "What does the wife do now, the woman named Amy?"

Sara answers. "His wife, Amy, tells him to stop talking, and then she ducks under his arm and goes down to the bottom of the stairs." Francis nods and recites aloud to confirm her answer:

> *"Don't, don't, don't, don't," she cried*
> *She withdrew, shrinking from beneath his arm*
> *That rested on the banister, and slid downstairs;*

And turned on him with such a daunting look,
He said twice over before he knew himself:
"Can't a man speak of his own child he's lost."

As he recites, he moves across the space in the center of the room to where Mary Younger sits at the right-hand row of tables, blond head down, taking notes. She's written pages of notes in the classes they've had so far but hardly said a word. He reaches across the table and points to the lines in Mary's book in which the husband answers his own question: *"God what a woman! And it's come to this! / A man can't speak of his own child that's dead."* He says the lines out loud while he keeps his finger on them. Now Mary can't write in her notebook because his arm's across it. "Mary," he asks, "can you read her answer?"

Mary looks up at him. He can see how anxious she is, how afraid of failing, and knows she hasn't even begun to know the pain of the young couple in the poem; all she knows is that if she writes down everything her teacher says, she'll be safe. And all he knows is that he wants to give her poetry, the skill of reading it that engenders the love of it that will last the whole of her life. "Give it a try, Mary."

You can't because you don't know how to speak, Mary reads.

"Right!" he says and her face brightens just a little, some of the anxiety melting. "So go on."

Mary reads:

You could sit there with the stains on your shoes
Of the fresh earth from your own baby's grave
And talk about your everyday concerns.
You had stood the spade against the wall
Outside there in the entry, for I saw it.

Francis interrupts her here and says the husband's lines:

I shall laugh the worst laugh I ever laughed.
I'm cursed. God, if I don't believe I'm cursed.

Mary looks up at Francis, encouraged. She resumes:

I can repeat the very words you were saying.
"Three foggy mornings and one rainy day

Will rot the best birch fence a man can build."
Think of it, talk like that at such a time!
What had how long it takes a birch to rot
To do with what was in the darkened parlor.
You couldn't care!

He stops her there. "Good work, Mary," he says. Then, "So what is it exactly that Amy find indefensible in her husband's behavior?" he asks her, throwing her this softball to build her confidence.

Lots of hands go up. But not Mary's. Her hand is holding her pen above her notebook, poised to write down whichever of her classmates' answers Francis approves. "Mary?" he says.

Mary looks up at him but doesn't answer, and now Francesca's waving her hand, dying to answer. "*Mary* will answer," Francis says. He reaches across the table, puts his fingers around Mary's pen, gently removes it from her hand. He holds it in his own and waits. He repeats the question: "What does she object to, Mary?"

"That he can think of things like birch rotting when his child's just dead?" She's still eyeing her pen in Francis's hand.

"You tell me," he says.

"All right. That's what she doesn't like."

"You're absolutely right," he says, and Mary smiles. He puts the pen down on the table in front of her. But when she reaches for it, he puts his hand over it until she takes her hand away, and leaves the pen alone. Then he turns to the class. "Let's see how it comes out," he says. "We'll act it out." He wants them to see how dynamic the poem is, the action, the movement up and down the stairs, the changing of places. "Yes, we'll act it out," he says. He's looking straight at Amy.

She shakes her head; she knows what's coming next.

"Amy?"

Amy doesn't answer.

"We need you to play the young mother's part," he says. "You've got the same name as she does."

Amy puts the collar of her jacket up. "Not me," she says.

He waits.

Amy shakes her head again, scrunches her chin even further down in her collar.

He moves his gaze to Joanna.

"You want me to be the wife?" Joanna asks. She thinks he's given up on Amy.

He shakes his head. "I want you to be the husband."

"No, you," Joanna answers. "You're the only *man* in the room."

"That's immaterial," he says. "You can take another's part."

"I'll be the narrator," Francesca says. Her hand's way up, waving again.

"Good, Francesca!" For he won't refuse her again. He's delighted that she understands how different this is from many poems in which the poet does all the talking. He'll get them to think about that tomorrow. "You can read the narration from your chair," he goes on. "But I'll not be the husband," he adds, hoping that Joanna will relent. To give her time, he tells the class how he loves to walk in New England woods, where a hundred years ago there was pasture, and find the little graveyards behind the cellar holes.

"Can we do the poem now?" Francesca interrupts.

"Oh, all right, I'll do it!" Amy announces, relenting, as if she were doing the class a favor, and stands from her chair, moves around the square of tables to the front of the room.

"All right, Amy!" Francis says. "Joanna?"

But Francesca can't wait any longer. She clears her throat. "Home Burial," she announces.

"Wait a minute, we need the husband," Amy says. She's looking at Joanna. Francesca stops.

"OK, I'll be the husband," Joanna says.

Francesca's so eager she starts again before Joanna gets to the front of the room:

> *He saw her from the bottom of the stairs*
> *Before she saw him. She was starting down,*
> *Looking back over her shoulder at some fear.*

"So where's the window I'm looking out of?" Amy interrupts.

Francis doesn't answer. He just raises his eyebrows, and then leaves the front of the room, moves to the seat that Joanna occupied, and sits down.

"Behind you," Joanna says, standing next to Amy. She takes Amy's hand, and turns her so that her back is to the windows of the classroom. "You're on the landing now," she says. "And here's the window you are looking through back over your shoulder to the graveyard." She points to the classroom windows. Then she backs away from Amy, facing her, toward the other side of the room. "Here's the foot of the stairs," she says, "and the door is right behind me." Her staging mirrors her drawing on the blackboard. She reaches behind herself to touch an imaginary doorknob. Francis allows himself a smile as Francesca begins to read:

> *She took a doubtful step and then undid it,*
> *To raise herself and look again. He spoke*
> *Advancing toward her:*

Then Joanna reads the husband's question:

> *What is it you see*
> *From up there always—for I want to know.*

And Joanna, the young husband now, takes her hand off the latch of the door behind her, tilting her head up toward Amy on the stairs, and everyone sees the young husband moving up the stairs to his wife, then climb past her to the window and discover the grave she's been staring at.

The three students ride the poem until, near the end, Amy's hand is on the latch. She reads the wife's concluding lines:

> *Friends make pretense of following to the grave,*
> *But before one is in it, their minds are turned*
> *And making the best of their way back to life*
> *And living people and things they understand.*
> *But the world's evil. I won't have grief so*
> *If I can change it. Oh I won't, I won't!*

Then Amy mimes pushing the door wider open, stepping backward, away from her husband and out of the house, and Joanna reads the last line:

> *I'll follow and bring you back by force. I will!*

And then it's over. The stairs melt away, the front door disappears. The two stand, looking at each other, surprised to be who they used to be again, and sensing they are not.

After a while someone asks, "Do you think she ever comes back?"

The students look to Francis, waiting for him to answer. But of course he doesn't. He's still in Joanna's seat, as if he were one of the students. Joanna and Amy still stand up front. It's their class now, more than his.

"Naturally she comes back," Joanna says. "You think he's going to just let her walk away?" She's very sure. After all, she ought to know, she just played the part. "It says right here: he's making the best of his way back to life and living people and things they understand."

"And that's good, you think?" Francis asks. "That's what he should do?"

"Oh, yes," Joanna says.

"I do too!" he says.

Nevertheless, an argument ensues about whether Amy comes back. Some of the girls insist the poem's too sad for a happy ending. Finally one of them asks Amy: "How'd you feel just now, when you played Amy in the poem?"

"I don't know," Amy says, shrugging to show she doesn't give a damn, wants to get back to her disengagement. None of her classmates believes her. They stare and wait.

"Answer the question, Amy," Francis says from Joanna's seat.

Amy turns to Francis, keeps her mouth shut. She's not used to being ordered around.

"Your opinion, Amy," Francis demands again. He'll keep her there forever if he has to, to make her answer.

"She comes home," Amy says, giving in.

"Why?"

"Because she has no other place to go," Amy says, thinking quickly. For she's damned if she's going to admit she thinks the bereaved young mother comes back to her husband out of love. "The woman needs a house like everybody else," she says. "She has to eat." Amy knows damn well marriage as an economic contract and a trap isn't what Frost was getting at, but it's a smart answer. She can tell by the look on her classmates' faces she's the only one who has thought of it. Now she has her persona back to go with her black clothes and spiked hair. Francis has to admit: he likes her answer, it shows how smart she is.

Nevertheless, he won't let her get away with this. "I don't think that's what you think at all," he says.

"How do you know?"

"It's not in the poem," he tells her. "There's not one word to suggest it is. You're too smart to think there is."

She doesn't answer.

"And besides, it's not how you read the part," he says.

That stops her. She has no answer now. Everyone in the room saw how much of herself she put into the other Amy. She looks out the window, and he lets her go. They've made enough inroads for one day.

A few minutes later, in the middle of a discussion—in which he hardly says a word—of all the meanings of *home* that shimmer in the poem, the time runs out. When the bell rings to end the period, the conversation goes on. He has to order the students to leave.

There are bad days when no matter what you try, nothing works; and there are good days when everything you try is magic. This has been one of the good days. No one in this class will ever be the same again.

FRANCIS DOESN'T HAVE MUCH time to savor his satisfaction. The phone rings on his desk before the last ninth grader is out of his classroom. It's Margaret Rice telling him the new headmaster wants to see him right away. "I know it's just exactly how you want to spend your free period," she says.

"Oh, really?" he asks, matching her sarcasm. "What does he want this time?" She doesn't half know how much he doesn't want this.

"How would I know?" Margaret answers. "We don't talk a lot, remember?"

But by the time Francis is halfway across campus he has guessed. It's the business about the Pequot Collection.

And he hasn't told Peggy yet!

So now Peggy will have heard through the grapevine, rather than from him, that the Student Council he advises will give the Collection away to some people who have never asked for it and probably don't even know it exists. He needs to apologize to her.

He needs to bring this subject up with her before she brings it up with him—and certainly before Kindler brings it up with her. Even Kindler's sensitive enough not to want to do that. So he'll explain the issue fully to Kindler now, and then right afterward, he'll talk with Peggy. He'll even skip a class if he has to. Then he and Peggy together will plan with Fred Kindler for how they should react to the Council's proposal.

"Go right on in," Margaret tells him a minute later, waving him to Fred Kindler's office. "They've already begun to talk."

"They?" He's relieved he won't be alone with Kindler. Margaret doesn't answer. Just looks at him as if he ought to know. He guesses it's Rachel Bickham. At least that's one of the people *he'd* go to for advice if he were the head.

He opens the door to Fred Kindler's office on that meager burst of optimism, and it takes an instant for him to realize who's sitting, her back to him, in the chair in front of Kindler's desk. It isn't Rachel. He stops dumbfounded, staring at Peggy's back. She's facing Fred Kindler, who's staring past her at Francis.

She turns around in her chair to face him. "Hello," she says. He can't read what's in her voice, and Kindler doesn't say a word, just points to a third chair. Francis enters the office and sits. They're in a circle, Kindler to his left, Peggy to his right. Their three pairs of knees are almost touching.

"We're talking about what the Student Council wants to do," Peggy says to Francis. He can't tell if she's chastising him, or just letting him know that the meeting's about a subject delicate for both of them.

"Peggy, I'm sorry," he says. "I just forgot to tell you." He's about to go on and tell her why he forgot: because everything that happened yesterday pushed it right out of his mind. But Kindler's watching him, and he can't make the words come out. He wouldn't apologize to his wife in this office in front of *Marjorie,* for Christ's sake, let alone Fred Kindler.

"It's all right, Francis," Peggy says. "I understand." She doesn't want to have this apology here in front of Fred Kindler any more than he does. And she does understand how Kindler's threat to fire him would make him forget.

But the damage is done: he's already apologized to her in front of Kindler. Francis feels naked under Kindler's eye, as if the man had caught him in some perverted act. He turns on Kindler. "You should have talked with me first about this," he says.

"Well, I'm glad I didn't," Fred Kindler says. "She might never have found out."

Francis is stunned. "Say that again," he says.

"I think you heard me," Fred Kindler says.

"You mean *you* told her? She didn't know when she came in here?"

"Francis," Peggy says softly. "Please. What difference does it make?"

It makes so much difference to Francis he can't speak. Kindler doing what he should have done. How intrusive can this bastard get?

"*I* didn't want her to be kept out of the loop," Kindler says. He doesn't even try to keep the contempt out of his voice. He was shocked to have figured out from the way Peggy reacted in their conversation just now before Francis entered that Francis hadn't even mentioned this to her. "Or perhaps you don't think the person in charge of the Collection should be the first to know it might disappear," Kindler adds. Then regrets his bitter words. Here he is taking sides between a husband and a wife, butting into a private place. And he's the head, for goodness sake!

Peggy watches as these two men look at each other, then away, and she sees nothing but potential disaster: the dissolution of her marriage, the school's succumbing, Fred Kindler's defeat. Worse than this, and more surprising, she feels a sudden disgust for both of them. That scares her more than anything. She'll do whatever has to be done to erase that feeling. "Let's get on with this meeting," she says. "What are we trying to get done?"

Fred sends her a look of thanks. He'll answer her question and be a pro again—instead of just an angry man. "I brought us together so that there would be no surprises for any one of the three of us tomorrow when the Student Council makes its proposal," Fred says. He's already feeling a little calmer. "I want you to know how I intend to react and why. And give you a chance to do the same."

"Fine," Peggy says. "Thank you." Francis, feeling wary, says nothing.

Then Fred finishes. "I'm aware there could be some difficult feelings, some tough emotions around this situation. I thought we could put them on the table here in this privacy so they would be easier to deal with in public tomorrow." He's looking straight at Peg.

Francis is appalled. Oh, Jesus! he thinks. It's touchy-feely time. He feels the same as when Kindler told him he should go to a shrink. He's always cringed when the younger teachers wanted to "share their feelings"—in faculty meetings, for Christ's sake!—and was always grateful to Marjorie for cutting them off. He turns to Peggy. He knows how she'll react. She's always felt the same way. She isn't about to share *her* feelings. She'd rather get undressed in public.

"All right, I'll start," Peggy says.

"You'll *what?*" Francis asks.

She turns to him. "I'll clear the air," she explains.

Now he wonders if she's going to change her mind and chew him out for forgetting to tell her. Right here in public. If she says one fucking word, he'll leave the room.

"I know you weren't trying to surprise me," she says. What else can she do but change her mind and talk about this now? She can't turn to Fred Kindler and talk about Francis as if he weren't in the room. But Fred *has* to know that Francis wouldn't ever try to pull a fast one. "I know you just forgot to tell me," she says. "I know you didn't want me to walk into the auditorium tomorrow and see you up on stage and learn that the—"

Francis looks out the window. He has to struggle not to flee, and Peggy sees how deeply she's insulted him.

"I'm sorry," she says. "I shouldn't have said that you would think—"

"Don't even say it!" Francis interrupts.

"All right, I won't," Peggy says, but really, she's already said it.

"Fair enough," Fred Kindler says, keeping his eyes on Peggy. He doesn't want her to know how much he distrusts her husband.

He needs to change the subject and get the focus onto tomorrow. "I'm going to be neutral," he says. "I'm not going to be for or against. I'm going to let the discussion happen. You need to know that." He's looking straight at Peggy. "I hope you're OK with that."

"I'm not, I hate it." Peggy says.

Fred's taken aback.

"You asked," she says.

"All right," he says, and turns to Francis. "And you?"

You think I'm going to disagree with my wife in front of *you?* Francis thinks. Out loud, he lies, "I hate it too."

"Well, we've got a problem," Kindler says.

Peggy leans back in her chair, she's not sure why—to distance herself from both of them? Let them figure it out, she thinks. Why should I? The silence goes on until she hears herself say, "No, we don't. Not much of a problem, anyway. I'm not crazy. I can see both sides." For she really can, and besides, she's here to save the day.

Fred is too relieved to think of what to say. Francis isn't sure he believes her.

"But if anybody even begins to spout PC theology, if anyone even utters the words *blasphemy* or *sacrilege* I'm going to fight back," Peggy says. "And if we don't find the right Pequot authorities and they don't guarantee they'll take care of it, I won't let it out of my sight."

"Me too," Francis says. He's feeling a little better now.

"Believe me, we won't give it away to just anybody—if we give it away at all," Fred says.

Now there's a silence. No one knows what to say.

"Is there anything else we need to bring up?" Kindler asks.

Francis shakes his head. Later, when it's too late, he'll understand what a big mistake he's made, but right now all he wants is for this meeting to end.

"Just this ironic fact," Peggy says. "That it's the Collection in our midst that inspired the moral development in the girls to make them not want to keep it in our midst."

"Will you say that tomorrow?" Kindler asks.

"If no one else does," Peggy answers.

"Good," Kindler says, and Peggy waits for him to say more, some recognition of how much she's surrendered, but he keeps his mouth shut. He'd love to tell her how much he agrees with her, how he loves the paradox she's named, but he's damned if he will engage in a philosophical conversation with Francis Plummer in the room. "Anything else?" he asks.

"I can't think of anything," Peggy says.

"Well, that didn't take so long," Kindler says.

Francis can see Kindler's trying to end the meeting on a strong note. He isn't going to hang around for that. He stands up and turns his back on Kindler. "Let's go, Peggy," he says, and moves to the door.

Peggy hesitates. Kindler says nothing. He'll not rise to the insult.

Peggy watches Fred make that decision. Francis waits for her by the door. They'll leave together, side by side. But she makes a little gesture with her hand, refusing him. He understands: right now she's more Fred Kindler's right-hand person than Francis Plummer's wife! She doesn't move from her chair until Francis leaves.

When she gets back to her library, she'll stop in front of the Collection and look at it as if maybe she'll never have another chance.

THE NEXT MORNING, the Marjorie E. Boyd Auditorium is loud with conversation as the students troop in and Francis and the Student Council take seats on the stage. Peggy takes a seat near the front right behind Sam Anderson.

Lila stands up, moves to the front of the stage. The room grows quiet. "Some of you already know Sara Warrior, our new ninth grader," Lila says. She gestures to where Sara sits in the front row of the audience. "As you know, Sara's an Indian, a Pequot," Lila goes on. "She wants to talk to you."

Sara stands up and moves toward the stage and climbs the same steps that Fred Kindler climbed the other day. She looks small and frightened.

"Listen carefully," Lila says. "Sara is going to make a proposal," and steps away from the mike, goes back to her seat. The students applaud. It's the Oliver custom to make new students feel at home.

But Peggy's not applauding. Francis didn't tell her *Sara* was going to make the proposal. He didn't even tell her that Sara was the one who brought the issue up. The Student Council is bringing up this issue, and Sara's not on the Student Council. Peggy stares past Sara to where Francis sits right next to Lila Smythe at the back of the stage. How could he do this to this kid? How could he use her so? A fourteen-year-old child, a Native American to boot, who is homesick and lonely and needs to be nurtured. Put *her* up there on stage and see who dares present the other side. Francis, you bastard! Peggy thinks. We said there'd be no surprises!

The microphone is much too tall for Sara. She looks for the screw that she can turn to telescope it down, and for the longest time can't find it, then finally does and starts to talk. But her voice doesn't carry; it's hard to hear her. Peggy wants to rush up there and mother the kid, put her arms around her and take her offstage where she'll be safe. Lila gets up from her seat and rescues Sara. She puts one hand on Sara's shoulder, with the other turns the switch to activate the mike, then smiles at Sara and goes back to her seat.

"It kind of bothers me that I'm the one who has to tell you this," Sara says. Her voice quavers, and she looks as if she might start to cry. She looks back at Lila, who nods her head. "Go ahead," Lila whispers. "You're the one to do this."

"All right," Sara says, and begins. "There were twenty-six villages along the Connecticut and Rhode Island shore and up and down the river. In 1630 the captain of a white man's merchant ship kidnapped the chief and demanded six thousand feet of wampumpeag for ransom, and when they got it, they killed him and put his body into a canoe and floated it into the harbor where now New London is." Sara speaks with more assurance now as she recites this history she knows so well and that enrages her. "They killed the warriors and burned the villages and murdered the mothers and the children, and then they stole the land."

Some of the older students are restless in their seats. They resent this talk. They have studied this history, and they feel guilty and have no power to undo the injustice. If it had been the other way around, you would have done it too, they want to say.

"And you shouldn't act like them," Sara says, and immediately understands she's made a mistake, and pauses. She's flustered now. She knows these kids don't murder people, don't invade and kill women and children.

"I didn't mean it like that," she says, "I didn't mean that you would do it," and tries to find the words to say what she does mean. But her mind's all a jumble now, and she can't find the words, because she's only fourteen and she's up there all alone with all these people looking at her, and she's never made a speech before.

Then she sees the headmaster standing in the back of the room. He's the one who should be doing this. And he's the one who can help her, she thinks. The students turn to see where Sara's looking. There's a lot of silence. Everyone in the auditorium can see that Sara wants Fred Kindler to say something so she can be a ninth grader, not a prophet, and everybody's waiting to see how he'll respond. But he's already decided he won't take sides. He restrains himself, and the moment passes. Sara, more alone and disillusioned, tries to speak.

She's supposed to make the proposal. Then she can sit down. She draws a breath. "We should give it back," she says, not the words she was going to say, the elaborate ones Lila helped her with. She soldiers on. "It's not right to put the things of people who your ancestors murdered in a case just so you can study them. And pieces of a person's body in a case too so you can stare and stare and stare." Then she remembers what Lila said. "That's sacrilege," she says. "That's blasphemous."

Now Peggy's on her feet. Sara looks her way and stops talking.

"I think you misunderstand," Peggy says. "Let's talk, Sara. Please. Later." Sara stares at her, and Sam Anderson turns around in his seat in front of Peggy. He finds her eyes, and shakes his head, a gesture he hopes only she can notice. She understands and wishes she could have the last ten seconds back. "I'm sorry, Sara," she murmurs, and sits down, even more furious now at Francis for what she thinks is his part in putting Sara onstage.

Sara's crying. How could she not be? First her fear of public speaking, then her outrage, and then the headmaster not pitching in for her, and finally this woman challenges her. This woman who pretends to be a mother in the dorm and is the guardian of the bones, stands up in front of everybody and says Sara doesn't understand. What is there not to understand?

Lila comes downstage and puts an arm around Sara, kisses her cheek. That's all the signal needed: the students stand and clap for Sara's bravery, her fierce conviction. Shaken, Sara leaves the stage and takes a seat in the audience.

Then Lila makes the announcement that Sara was going to make. "On your behalf, the Student Council will petition the headmaster and the board of trustees for the immediate return of the Collection to the rightful owners, the Pequot people," she says. "We'll make the petition in our next meeting and send it around. You can decide for yourselves whether to sign it. I hope you will."

There's a long silence now in the audience. Everyone's eyes move up front and go back and forth between Peggy in the second row and Francis up on the stage. Everyone's waiting for Peggy to speak. But she won't. She's not going to say anything about her opinion that there are two sides to this issue, or mention the paradox she named yesterday in Fred Kindler's office. She won't even defend the Collection from the accusation of sacrilege and blasphemy. Not with Sara in the room. Because Sara is the one who uttered those words, and she's the one who needs protection.

Fred Kindler watches Peggy. He guesses why she's not talking. Nevertheless an idea comes to him, bringing a surge of excitement. As one more strategy to save the school, he'll reach out to the Pequot Nation, recruit their children (and wonders why that hasn't been done before) invite several of their parents to join the board, and instead of returning the Collection, thus looking guilty and suspiciously correct, persuade the Pequot Nation to create an even more significant Collection to honor their tradition right here at Miss Oliver's School for Girls—of *every hue*—where once a Pequot village thrived. And the Pequots will participate in the dig that Sam Anderson will organize. Thus turn a potential public relations disaster into a victory. That's how to build a school: reach out, bring in, include, make layers, build strength.

Then the bell rings, and Lila adjourns the meeting. Feeling vaguely dissatisfied, for they still want to know what Mrs. Plummer thinks, the students move out of the auditorium and to their classes. Karen Benjamin, stringer for the *Hartford Courant's* weekly column that covers teenage concerns in Capital Area schools, skips her class to phone the story in.

THAT EVENING IT SEEMS to Francis that he waits for hours and hours for Peggy to come home from the library. He's not going to let one minute go by before he clears the air with her. He's not sure she really does forgive him for not telling her about the proposal before Fred Kindler did. And he's not sure she really can see both sides of the issue. Why should she after all these years? But it doesn't even cross his mind that she could think that the reason Sara was chosen to make the proposal was to shut Peggy up. Sara was chosen because she was the one to object to the Collection. What could be more obvious than that?

He is surprised when suddenly the door connecting their apartment to the dormitory opens, and there Peggy is, framed in the doorway, and frowning at him, instead of at their front door where he's been listening for her. He realizes she's been touring their dormitory before coming home, avoiding his company as long as she can. For thirty-three years they've made a point of visiting with the girls together in the evening. He feels a wisp of anger rising, stuffs it down beside the hurt, and stands up from the chair he's been sitting in. "Hello, Peg," he says.

She stops just through the doorway. She can tell from the way he's looking at her that he's been sitting there waiting for her, about to pounce on her with excuses and reasons before she even draws a breath. There's no way she's going to listen. "I need some tea," she announces and goes to the kitchen.

All right, I'll wait out here, he decides, and sits down again. She needs a little space. Besides, he's not going to follow her like some faithful puppy. He hears the water gush into the kettle, hears her crossing to the stove and putting the kettle on it, even hears the click of the handle for the gas. As the minutes pass his sadness blossoms.

"So now you're politically correct?" she says at last through the doorway, speaking the term as if describing vermin. "How stylish!" She's misinterpreted his staying in the living room, thinks he's going to act as if nothing's happened. No way. She needs to fight.

He keeps his mouth shut. He's not going to rise to crap like that.

"You sure you're name isn't Van Buren? Francis van Buren, politician?" She imagines his face getting red. He sits there. He's not going to say one word to this.

"No, I guess not. You're just twins. Two of a kind."

Now he stands up. But he's not headed for the kitchen. He's headed for the front door. Fuck this. He'll just leave. She can talk to air.

"You could kiss and make up," she says. "You and Gregory. He could be up on stage too. He could sit in your lap."

He whirls around. Now *he's* the one who needs to fight. He goes through the kitchen door. She's facing him, her back to the stove. "You need to watch your mouth," he says.

"Really? Like when you blurted out in the middle of the first faculty meeting of the year that the new headmaster shouldn't even talk about how the kids dress because *Marjorie* wouldn't?" she asks, grabbing at the opening he's given with his comment about watching her mouth. She doesn't care how crazy this is, how off the subject. The way he behaved in that meeting—in front of everybody! "Is that how you watch *your* mouth?" she asks him.

"Why are you talking about that?" he asks her. "Speaking of running at the mouth."

"Because he had to save your butt, that's why. He had to stop the meeting just so the senior teacher wouldn't go on acting like the biggest asshole in the world in front of everybody."

"What else, Peggy?" He takes a step forward, he's in her face. "What else?" He's close to yelling. "Think of everything. Make a big fucking list."

She stares at him. Then, very quietly she says: "We don't have much in common anymore, do we, Francis?"

She doesn't wait for his answer. Instead, she takes a step toward him, puts her hand on his chest, pushes past him and walks out of the kitchen, through their living room, toward the front door. He follows, passes her, reaches the door before she does, puts his hand on the knob. "Open the door," Francis," she commands. "I'm going to the library to work."

"That's a relief," he says. She reaches for the knob. He lets it go and steps back, makes a big sweeping gesture with his arm to usher her out. "Don't hurry back," he says. He's more hurt than he's ever been.

Outside, she turns back to him. "Using that little girl that way," she says. "Preying on her feelings. Putting her up on the stage like that so nobody could argue. How could you let that happen!"

"Oh!" he says.

"Don't act surprised, Francis. After we told each other there would be no surprises."

"Oh, my God, so that's what this is about!"

She stares at him. "Well, what did you think it was about?" she asks. Then she turns and walks away.

FOURTEEN

FRED IS RELIEVED a few days after Sara Warrior's talk to discover in the *Hartford Courant* that Karen Benjamin's report on the Student Council proposal is only one short paragraph in the Teen Section, buried in the middle of a series of reports from several schools. He's grateful for the Hartford editor's preference for banal stories featuring football stars and pretty cheerleaders. If Fred were the editor, he would feature the controversy over the Pequot Collection. It's exactly the kind of issue that students and their teachers should be weighing.

But Fred, who has almost never read a newspaper article about an independent school that didn't use the word *exclusive,* knows how inclined the public is to stereotype schools like Miss Oliver's as arrogant. Even a very objective article on this issue would feed the stereotype, exactly what he doesn't need.

He has reason to be worried: not only did the summer recruiting effort only manage to garner a mere six additional upper-class students, and the smallest ninth grade in the school's history, but so far, in September, there have only been three requests for information from families exploring schools for next school year, the second in Fred's programmed two-year race against the growing deficit. Nan White has told him that even in last year's dearth there were fifteen such requests by this time, the second week in September.

It won't occur to Fred until much later that maybe Karen had the same worry that he has and wrote a boring article on purpose.

However unimportant to the public, the proposal to give away the Collection is momentous to the school, and Gregory van Buren, faculty advisor to the *Clarion,* hopes that it will require enough of Karen's editorial attention for her to abandon her article on the sex lives of the seniors, a project he despises. There is huge opportunity in the Collection story. On the day her sparse report appears in the *Courant,* he calls her in to his classroom to ask her how she proposes to cover it in the *Clarion.*

"I've given it to Clarissa Longstreet," Karen tells him.

"Very amusing," he murmurs.

"Really. I have," she says, and now he's staring at her.

"Aren't you proud of me? I'm delegating. I'm giving away the plums instead of taking them for myself," she says, keeping a straight face. She knows what he's trying to do, and she's tired of his indirection.

"All of it?" he asks. "Karen, there are at least three features in this story."

"Let Clarissa decide how many features. She's probably going to be editor in chief next year."

"The scene in the auditorium with the Warrior girl's talk," Gregory says, interrupting to list the features. He counts them on his fingers. "The place of the Collection in the development of the school. An editorial on the rightness, or wrongness, of giving it away or keeping it." He knows that Karen understands all this. Clarissa too, he's taught them both. But he's trying so hard to lure Karen into this story and away from the article she wants to write! Just thinking about celebrating adolescent sex by writing about it in the school's newspaper offends him.

Perhaps one source of Gregory's feelings on this subject is simple envy—his own sex life seems to be finished. But Gregory, forty-five, divorced twenty years ago, sticks with a monkish life because he really does believe that sex without love and lifelong commitment degrades our humanity, and Gregory is too absorbed by Miss Oliver's intense, inward-looking scene to have the time to fall in love again. Maybe the reason Gregory seems so pompous and anachronistic is that, though surrounded by irony on every side, he takes himself seriously enough to believe he has an eternal, precious soul that can be stained by fornication. He knows, because he's felt that stain a few times when, during his summer travels in foreign places, he's fallen off the wagon, punctured his celibacy with some other lonely person, and then suffered weeks of remorse. At any rate, he takes his students just as seriously as he takes himself, give him credit for that. They have a soul too, just as eternal as his. That's really why he teaches. If he thought otherwise, he wouldn't bother.

And give him credit too for being one of the reasons Miss Oliver's goes against the tide. At Miss Oliver's, Gregory van Buren is cool precisely because he isn't.

"The whole subject?" he asks again. "Karen, you're still the chief!"

"I've got other fish to fry," Karen says.

"I know you do, and it's wrong!"

Well, why didn't you just say that at the beginning? she thinks. Out loud she says, "I'm sorry you feel that way." She really is. She's grateful for how tough he's been on her, making her revise everything over and over until she got it right. Now she does that for herself. She knows Gregory disapproves of her article on moral grounds and also because it will be bad publicity for the school. Well, the headmaster's already told her that if he thinks the article will harm the school, he won't let her publish it.

"I can't tell you not to do the interviews," he says, as if reading her mind. "You can talk about anything you want. But you know the new headmaster won't let you publish the article, so why do you persist in wasting your time? Mr. Kindler has more sense than his predecessor about such things," he adds, giving in to his sudden urge to goad her. Karen gets his goat. He's always been able to control his editors until this one came along. And she's the one he admires the most!

"Well, then," she asks, "if the new headmaster won't let me publish it, what are *you* so worried about?" It doesn't occur to either of them that Gregory would be the one to make the decision to ban the article. The school's been trained by Marjorie, who made all the decisions.

"Because it's wrong. It's perverse and degrading. That is what disturbs me, not the PR that the head worries about."

Karen wants to say that there's nothing degrading about telling the truth, but she knows him well enough to know he would say that there's no such thing as objectivity, that just writing about teenagers having sex with each other without saying it's wrong will make it seem to teenagers that it's right. Well, she doesn't agree. *She* doesn't think it's right, and she's a teenager.

"I'm sorry you don't agree with me that it's wrong," he murmurs, giving up. He stands to show the conversation's over.

Karen stays in her chair. She wants to say something more, but it doesn't come to her, and she stands up. "Clarissa will do fine," she says. "I promise."

He nods his head to affirm he knows that's true, and sits down again, and feeling very sad, he watches her walk out the door.

When she's halfway across campus heading to a class, she realizes that one reason she wants to write this article is to earn Gregory van Buren's praise. For once she wants to write a piece that's so good he can't find one thing to criticize. She's come close lots of times, but there's always been something. He's taught her how to *work,* and she wants to prove to him she's learned. Just trying to make him admit that this one, which will be harder to do well than all the others, and that he hates, is as good as it can get, is worth the risk that the headmaster won't allow it to be printed.

THAT AFTERNOON, Fred has an appointment with the officers of the Student Council.

Lila arrives at his office before the others, bringing a greeting that has nothing personal in it, neither of animosity nor of affection—a mere "hi" as she comes through the door. He senses that she hasn't written him off like most of the students.

"Good morning, Lila," he says warmly and gestures to one of the chairs in front of his desk. Sitting down, she never takes her eyes off his face.

"Well, I guess you know what this is about," she says.

"Well, I'd be pretty dumb if I didn't," he smiles.

But Lila, with too much on her mind to catch his playfulness, pushes on with her agenda. "I've asked Sara Warrior to come too," she tells him. "Even though she's not on the Council. Since it was her idea, I thought I should."

"That's fine," he says—though it isn't; it'll make the meeting more tense.

"Thank you."

"You OK?" he asks. He's worried about her now. He can see how pale she is, how tired, this eighteen-year-old who's the force behind the Declaration, the person who took responsibility for Sara's claim. She has more pressure on her than many of the faculty.

"I'm OK."

"Just OK?"

She doesn't know how to answer. If it were later in the year they would know each other better, and she could explain how Francis Plummer disappointed her, and he might observe that finding out her hero has clay feet shows she's outgrowing Miss Oliver's School for Girls, as she should in her senior year. But they're too unknown to each other for such a conversation, so she simply nods her head to insist she's feeling fine.

And besides, here come the other girls.

Angela Nash has been picked by lottery because nobody knows the ninth graders well enough yet to vote for one. She's so eager to get this job permanently when her classmates vote in January that she trips on the rug and almost falls down making sure she gets the chair nearest Fred. He has to turn away to hide his smile. Take it easy, he wants to say to her. I don't have a vote.

Sara sits down beside Angela, her eyes cast down so she doesn't have to look at Fred. Marie Safford, a junior, is taller than Lila and stately, a young black woman wearing dreadlocks and studious glasses. She stalks, as if entering dangerous territory, to a chair on the other side of Lila from Fred. She's clutching a manila folder.

"We have a proposal," Lila says.

"I figured you did," he smiles. "Let's hear it."

Lila nods to Marie. Marie looks at Angela and moves the folder toward her, offering it. "No, you," says Angela. "Go ahead." The quirky way she holds her head when she says this reminds Fred of his daughter, and now, suddenly more than ever, he doesn't want their proposal between him and them. He would give anything just to sit and chat with these kids, just pass the time of day.

Marie opens the folder. *"We, the Student Council of Miss Oliver's School for Girls . . ."*

"Please," says Fred. "Don't read it. Just talk it through with me."

Marie shakes her head. "Why not?" Angela asks. "We'll explain it as we go."

"No," Marie says. "I want to read it. This is not a conversation; it's a proposal."

Lila looks at Fred. "Go ahead, read," he says to Marie. So she does:

"We, the Student Council of Miss Oliver's School for Girls, require the administration and the board of trustees officially to return the artifacts, sacred to the memory of the Pequot culture, to their rightful owners, along with the human remains of a member of that tribe for burial in accordance with their sacred customs, and moreover, that the school now and forever relinquish all claims of ownership to these items, currently on display in the school library."

Jeepers! Fred thinks, trying hard not to giggle. How about some iambic pentameter to dress it up? Out loud he says softly, "Don't say *require*. Say *request*."

"Why?" Lila asks.

"Because you'll get further. That's the way the world works."

"I'm not sure I like the way the world works," Lila says.

Angela puts her hand on Lila's knee, but Marie just rolls her eyes. "Lila's been studying history again," she explains to the ceiling. "She's just now learning about racism." Sara, stiff with tension, hasn't said a word. Fred tries to catch her eyes, but she looks away.

"Well, I have an alternative proposal," Fred says and tells them of his idea of rendering the ownership of the Collection to the Pequots while keeping it on campus in the library. He grows even more enthusiastic as he sees Lila's expression brighten. Why shouldn't she like it since everyone wins? "We'll build another wing," he goes on. "It will be *their* Collection, honoring *their* history on ground where *their* village was situated, and we'll invite members of their nation to be on our board and recruit their children—"

"Oh!" Angela interrupts, smiling, and sitting up even straighter. "What a wonderful idea!"

"It stinks," says Marie

"Well, *I* don't think it stinks," Fred says.

"It stinks of compromise."

"Compromise is how the world works," Fred says, then wishes he hadn't.

"Oh, let's stop pretending!" Marie exclaims. "This isn't a Pequot village. It's a school for rich white girls."

Marie, please, what color are you? Fred thinks.

"That's right, *white*," Marie says, as if reading his mind. "We live in Greenwich, for God's sake! My father's a lawyer for Exxon; my mother belongs to the Junior League. They're whiter than you are."

"Well, why shouldn't they live in Greenwich if they want to?" Angela asks, and Marie looks at Angela as if she were three years old.

"Hey, Marie," Fred says softly, feeling a sudden flood of empathy for her parents, whom he hasn't even met. "We need to talk." He knows she wants to know why the school can be so proud of its diversity—all those skin colors living together—when hardly anyone comes from neighborhoods where kids get shot and the only stores are liquor stores. That bothers me too, he'll tell her. It's one of the things I want to fix.

"OK, we'll talk," Marie says, shrugging her shoulders. "Sometime. Maybe."

So now Fred turns to Lila. "Well, Lila, what do *you* think of my idea?" he asks, and then the room is very quiet and everyone's looking at Lila, and right away Fred realizes what a lousy thing he's done. Sara's staring at Lila's face, counting on her to answer. And he's the one who's worried about the pressure on Lila, and now he does this to her! Forget it, don't answer that, he wants to say.

He doesn't need to, because Marie's too heated by this issue to wait for Lila's answer. Or maybe she's trying to save Sara from the disillusion of Lila's deserting her. She's certainly not trying to take the pressure off Lila. "It doesn't make any difference what *you* think, or what *Lila* thinks or what *I* think," she says to Fred, and he can feel her anger, it fills the room. Marie's rage at injustice is inflamed by her thinking she's been cheated out of the hurt of it because her family's rich. She thinks she'll never have a chance to be as passionate as those other young people who before her time sat scared to death at white lunch counters to try to make the world the way it ought to be. "The only person in this room who has any right to an opinion about this is Sara," she says.

"That's not fair," Angela blurts.

Marie ignores her, keeps her eyes on Fred. "I ask you: who are you to decide what should be done with the Collection? The only jurisdiction you have is that it's in your *possession.*" And that you're white and male and the head*master,* she's tempted to add. But she's too smart to go that far. "We need to not be the owners anymore," she says instead. "We need to give the stuff back to the *rightful* owners. If they want to put it back here in our library, that's their decision."

"Oh, you're just splitting hairs!" Angela exclaims.

"No, she isn't," Fred says. "She's being precise. That's a good way to be." Then turning to Marie, "I like your approach. I like it a lot. But you have to know I like mine better."

"Why?" she wants to know.

"Because more good comes from it," Fred answers, and Marie shuts up. She senses how stubborn he is, how fixed in his plan. There's another way for her to win: collect a ton of signatures on the petition. Let him deal with those.

Sara still hasn't spoken. Lila feels the weight of her gaze. How to explain to Sara that she likes Fred's idea? And how to explain how much she wishes she didn't? She envies the purity of Marie's belief, the single-mindedness of it.

"Anyway, Marie," Fred says, "I think the proposal's fine, and I admire it. But I like mine better. So I'll deliver both to the board of trustees at the November meeting."

"Well, we already know which proposal they'll take, don't we," Marie says. "You're the headmaster."

Yup, you're right, Fred is tempted to say. That's the way the world works.

Instead he doesn't say anything, and that's all the signal that Sara needs. She stands up and flees the room.

Fred stands too, all his instincts pushing him to follow her. He wants to put his arm around her, he wants to explain, but he knows that won't work: he'll end up chasing her through the building, making her feel even worse, so he stands still behind his desk. Marie and Lila and Angela stand now too. All three are looking at the door.

"Yes," he says. "Take care of Sara." The girls move to the door.

"Right," Marie says bitterly, "We'll make sure she's learned her lesson."

"What lesson is that, Marie?" he challenges.

"How the world works," she answers over her shoulder as she goes through the door. "Isn't that how *you* put it?"

FIFTEEN

"THE LORD BLESS YOU and keep you," Father Michael Woodward says to his congregation as the service ends this first Sunday in October. "The Lord make his face to shine upon you and be gracious unto you." He makes the sign of the cross. "The Lord lift his countenance upon you and give you peace." As he says this benediction, he looks straight at Francis and Peggy, and sees Francis inching his way closer to the aisle so he can be the first to get out of there. Well, good for you, anyway, for trying to conform, Father Woodward wants to say to Francis, though the last thing he'll pray for when he prays for them both and for their marriage is that Francis will succeed in this pretense. Instead, Father Woodward (who annoyed the vestry at last month's meeting by suggesting only half in jest that the road to world peace was to give everyone who believes in a God a lobotomy to make them forget the differences in their beliefs—and then proceeded to go to sleep during the finance committee report) will pray for Peggy's belief to broaden to embrace her husband's too rather than just the other way around.

In fact, there is another reason, besides his alienation from the service, for Francis's haste to leave the church. This is the Sunday the Student Council chose for the service projects Rachel Bickham suggested to Fred Kindler instead of Sunday classes as a consequence of those missed during the Petrie invasion. So right after church, Francis hurries to join Rachel to lead a group of students in the cleanup of a salt marsh near the mouth of the river. When he gets to the bus that will take them to the marsh, Rachel and the students are already there, waiting for him.

On the way south to the marsh, Rachel reminds the students how wondrously complex an estuarine marsh is, how like blood is the mix of salt and fresh water that comes and goes over it, how the marsh itself is like a womb where many of the creatures that live in the ocean are born.

They spend the afternoon walking in line abreast back and forth across the marsh, picking up discarded tires, bottles, cans, plastic bags that, floating in the ocean, choke turtles to death because they think they're jellyfish. The students wonder at the many different kinds of crabs they see, the balls of matted fur and crushed bones shat out by birds of prey, the variety of birds, grasses, animal tracks.

When they are finished, they walk back to the bus in the slanted sunlight of the autumn afternoon, and just before they climb on, Rachel tells them that each acre of a healthy salt marsh delivers an average of sixty-two tons of foodstuffs to the food chain every year. "Without one hour of human labor," she tells them. "No farm in the world can match that, no human ingenuity needed. We could disappear off the earth, and it would still happen," Rachel says, echoing Lila's words last summer when she told Francis that his turtle appeared to him from out of the time when the world was here and human beings were not. Francis is struck by how similar Rachel's words are to those Livingstone Mendoza spoke when he came to the school last February and inspired Francis and Lila to follow him out West. Yes, in*spire,* Francis admits, for it really was about the breath of life that Mendoza was talking. It dawns on him that his efficient colleague, Rachel Bickham of the orderly mind, gifted teacher, able administrator, destined for the highest posts, would not have been as embarrassed as he, Francis, was to have been playing Indian for a child like Livingstone Mendoza. They would have recognized in each other that openness to the grace that comes, as Peggy puts it. For to be as a child—full of wonder—is to be full of grace.

Standing on the narrow black tar road just before he climbs back up into the bus, October's woods flaming behind him, Francis looks out over the brown grass and living mud of the salt marsh to the sea beyond it, and seeing, he hopes, with Indian eyes as Mendoza offered, he wonders if he will be able to keep his promise that from now on his spiritual yearnings will be in tune with Peggy's.

A WEEK LATER, just home from church, he's still in doubt, though the words of peace in his friend Michael's benediction echo in his head. He wonders if he should bring the subject up with Peggy—ease their pain by talking about it. But he doesn't get this chance, because the doorbell rings.

Peggy gets there first. She opens it, flooding the apartment with golden light, and framing a tall woman in the doorway who's smiling and reaching out for a hug.

Looking into the visitor's face from where he's standing behind Peg, Francis knows exactly who she is, who her friends were, what her mother and dad were like, the exact year she graduated—but he can't remember her name, and he's in his ocean again. He's always remembered the names before, it's the young teachers who forget. All this in an instant, a little spear of panic, and then Peggy says, "Why, Hannah! Hannah Fingerman!"

and Francis, rescued, can't even imagine the moment a second ago when her name didn't exist in his brain. "Come in!" Peg says. "It's wonderful to see you!"

Hannah's the same tall person she was twenty years ago, though now the blackness of her hair is fake and she's a little thicker in the middle. Francis remembers she wasn't one of the "smart" ones, couldn't get in to any of the colleges to which her friends were admitted. The faculty gave her the benefit of the doubt when they graded her final exams in her senior year so she could graduate. "And why shouldn't they?" Marjorie applauded. "Everyone knows that the kids who flounder in classrooms are the ones designed to shine later." That's what Marjorie was trying to say when she irritated the trustees year after year by refusing to publicize the invariably impressive list of the most competitive colleges to which the seniors had gained acceptance. "That's not how *we* measure success," Marjorie would say, while Francis's heart flamed with pride, and Gregory van Buren shook his head.

Hannah steps through the door, fends Levi off, who's trying to put his nose up under her dress. "You guys never change!" she says. "You had a dog like that twenty years ago!" Now she's in the middle of the room, and Francis is kissing her cheek. "God!" she says. "You don't look any different."

"Being around kids keeps you young," he says.

"Yeah, lucky you." Hannah tosses her hair—a familiar gesture, but it doesn't look the same, somehow, she's too old for it. "What was *that* dog's name?" she asks.

"Levi," says Peg, smiling.

"Levi? Oh, yes. I remember! What's *this* one's name?" reaching down now to pat Levi, whose whole rear end is wagging. "God, it's good to see you guys! It feels like ten minutes ago. Lots of water over the dam."

"And you're going to tell us all about it," says Peg.

"Levi," says Francis. "The dog's name is Levi."

Hannah looks up from her patting, searches Francis's face. "You're kidding."

"The one you knew was Levi One. This one's Levi Two," he says.

Hannah is grinning now. She sits down on the sofa.

"Really," says Peg.

Hannah plays along, a big grin on her face. "Is he Jewish?"

Peg looks at Francis. "Yup," says Francis. "He's Jewish."

"Now I really feel at home," Hannah says.

"Hannah," Peggy murmurs, "tell us where you've been."

Hannah shakes her head. "I love it when things don't change," she says.

"Well, we could talk about that!" Francis says.

"Hannah, catch us up," says Peg.

"I've made a bunch of money," Hannah announces. "Surprise! Surprise!"

"We're not surprised," says Francis.

Hannah tells them how she married a Canadian whose health club in Montreal was failing, and how, offering to help, she took it over bit by bit, discovering an instinctive talent. "It's the right brain," she informs them. "As long as I don't think too hard about things, I always get them right. My husband was just the opposite. He planned everything so much he never got around to doing anything. Too much business school, not enough guts. Well, we're divorced now. He couldn't stand it that his wife was better at something than he was, poor thing. Hell, I'm better at *everything* than he is, and now I have three clubs in Montreal, one in Toronto, and two in Vancouver. I'm *national!* Also, I'm a free woman. Being single is almost as much fun as being rich!"

"That's wonderful, Hannah!" Peggy says. "We're very happy for—"

"Yeah, and I hear you might go coed," Hannah interrupts. She leans forward, her voice suddenly harsh. She couldn't have done *that* to a conversation as a kid.

"If we hadn't been just girls when I was here I'd still be an assistant club manager and married to a wimp."

"Right!" says Francis.

"It's not definite," Peggy says. "A long way from being definite. The girls—"

"Yeah, yeah, I know, but I have a way to *guarantee* it won't happen."

"What's that?" Francis asks.

"Money!" Hannah, leans back, spreads her arms along the back of the sofa, taking up as much space as any man would.

"You're going to make a donation." Peg's tone is matter-of-fact.

"That's right." Hannah keeps her arms spread, her head tilted back, relaxed—as if she did this every day. "You bet! A big one."

"Hey! hey! hey!" says Francis. "Hannah baby!"

"How big?" Peggy asks.

"Two. Two big ones," Hannah grins.

Francis and Peg look at each other, disappointed. Two thousand? What good is that? Peg starts to get up to get Hannah some coffee.

"Two million," says Hannah. "How's that?"

"Two *million!*" says Francis.

"Two million," Peggy repeats, as if testing the sound.

"That's it!" Hannah leans forward again. "Two million to buy the deficit until the school builds the enrollment back up. And I mean the enrollment without any boys around. Just girls!" She leans further forward still, gesturing with her hands in front of her. She's projecting herself, filling the room.

"Just girls," Hannah repeats. "No boys. We keep the old school, just the way it always was. That's the whole point of the place, right? I make a deal: the school agrees to stay for girls only, and I cover the deficit while it builds the girls-only enrollment up again."

"We can do that," says Peg.

"We better!" Hannah says. "No compromises."

"Right," says Francis.

"Besides which, I go on the board," Hannah declares.

"Of course!" says Francis.

"When's this going to happen?" asks Peggy.

"Soon as my lawyers finish squashing my ex-husband's attempt to get some of this dough."

"Oh," says Peggy. Already she's lost heart. She starts to get up again.

Hannah gestures to Peg to stay seated, she didn't come for coffee. "Don't worry. I mean it. It's close to a done deal. Two months at most. I wouldn't have come to you about this until it was actually done, except the board needs to know about this before it goes and does something stupid."

"Really?" asks Peg.

"Count on it."

"OK," says Francis. "We're counting on it!" His mind is full of schemes. He takes this gift right now, it puts *him* in charge. Whose gun is going to make a bigger bang than this?

There's a little moment of silence while Francis thinks of this, and none of them speaks, and the Sunday morning dormitory sounds of showers running on and on, padding feet, sleepy voices drift into the apartment. "Ah, Sunday morning," Hannah says. "The only day we could sleep."

"Yeah, we keep 'em busy," Francis says.

"That was the hardest thing for me to get used to," Hannah remembers, "Saturday classes. You know, Mr. Van Buren would harp on that, quoting from Thoreau all the time: 'Simplify! Simplify! Simplify!' I loved the guy, but on this he was full of crap. That's not what this school is about."

"So, what is it about?" says Peg.

"Why, intensify, of course," Hannah says, spreading her hands. "Anybody can see that. Intensify! Intensify! Intensify!" And Francis thinks: you were never dumb. We just asked you the wrong questions.

"Well, Hannah," Peggy says, "I'm sure you're right. We can count on your gift. It's wonderful! How marvelous! I hope you'll march right over to Fred Kindler's house right now and tell him. It will make his day!"

"Fuck him!" Hannah says.

Peg moves back in her seat, as if she's been slapped.

"All right, then, screw him, is that a little better?" Hannah asks.

"No. It's not a little better," Peggy says.

"He's trying to ruin the school. He's a traitor."

"Peggy's never liked swearing," Francis offers.

"And you always have?" says Peggy turning to him.

Hannah's eyes go back and forth between them. She looks like someone trying to figure what the weather's going to do. Peggy's looking at Francis, waiting. "*Traitor's* not the right word," he tells Hannah, speaking softly. But *outsider* is, he wants to add.

Hannah's looking directly at him. "So? What is the right word?"

"Headmaster," Peg says.

"Head of school," says Francis. "For Christ's sake!"

"You *do* like to swear, don't you?" Peggy says.

"What's going on here?" Hannah's voice is alarmed.

Nothing, Francis would love to say. We're just the same.

"The guy's a traitor," Hannah says. Her voice is harsh again. "If he gets credit for this gift, he gets power. We want to get rid of him, not make him stronger."

Peg reaches out her hand to touch Hannah's. For a second, Hannah starts to pull her hand away, but changes her mind. "Hannah," says Peg softly, "your gift is going to save the school. We'll always be just for girls. That's what counts."

"So you'll take it?"

"No, Fred Kindler will. He's the head," Peggy says.

Hannah turns to Francis.

"That's right," Francis murmurs after a little hesitation. "He's the head."

Hannah pulls her hand gently away from Peg. "That's the deal?"

"That's the deal," Peggy murmurs, and when Hannah doesn't reply, Peggy adds: "You will go see him, won't you?" And after a little pause: "Won't you, Hannah?"

"All right," says Hannah. "With just a little added proviso."

"What?" Peggy asks warily.

"To honor you. He gets the gift, but you get the honor."

Peggy shakes her head; she doesn't understand.

"I'll specify," Hannah explains. "The two million bucks will be specifically to support the specialness of the curriculum. The whole anthropological thrust, or whatever it is. I'll get a lawyer to think up the words. The whole anthropological thrust that makes Miss Oliver's the best damn school in the world, the idea you started in your library. How about that?"

"I think it's just fine!" Francis says.

"Wait a second," Peg blurts. "It's not *my* library."

"Oh, yes it is," Hannah says. "If Kindler gets to receive the gift, you get the honor. He'll have to stand up in front of everybody and read the words." She looks intently at both their faces. Francis thinks for a minute she's going to ask again what's going on between him and Peggy, but he knows she doesn't need to. He can see the disillusion in her eyes. Hannah stands up. "We've got a deal," she announces.

Francis stands up too. "Don't go. Stay a while. We'll have lunch."

"I'm going. Going to see Miss Oliver's School for Girls' boy headmaster. See if he wants a couple million bucks."

"Thank you," says Peggy. "Just don't put my name in, all right? Mention the curriculum, the library, but not me."

Hannah shrugs her shoulders.

"Promise?"

"All right," Hannah says.

Peggy stands, pulls Hannah into a hug, and over Peggy's shoulder Hannah winks at Francis to tell him: of *course* we're going to put Peggy's name in.

His world saved, Francis can't wait to be alone with Peg. He's going to put his arms around her, celebrate.

"See you guys later," Hannah says.

"I'm coming partway with you," Peg says. "I'm on my way to the library." And then they're both out the door.

THAT NIGHT, from her side of the bed, Peg says to him. "You would have taken it, wouldn't you? You would have played that kind of game."

"No," he responds, saying the words straight up to the ceiling in the dark. "Not after I thought about it, I wouldn't. You made me think about it. I'll give you that."

"Well that's something," she says. She is turned away from him, speaking her words to the wall. "That's something, anyway."

After a while, he says to the ceiling, "And you? You would have risked the gift, wouldn't you? You would have just let it go, if she didn't agree to take it to Kindler."

"Yes," she says. "I would have risked it."

"Well, now I know," he says.

"Because I'm sick of the past," she says. "Marjorie's past. All her worn-out preciousness that she made into a theology that you cling to."

"Peggy, be careful."

"It's too late to be careful, Francis. Because suddenly I don't care whether Fred Kindler brings in boys or not." It's true: she doesn't care, it's not what's important. The realization comes to her as she speaks. "I don't give a damn as long as the school's thriving and he is running it."

He doesn't know how to answer that. He doesn't really believe her.

"As a matter of fact I don't care if the school becomes *all* boys!" she says, exaggerating out of her loyalty to Kindler.

Well, now I know, he says to himself. He won't say it aloud again. He closes his eyes, as if he could sleep.

SIXTEEN

IT'S ONLY NOVEMBER now, Gail Kindler thinks as she watches her husband get into bed beside her. She turns out the light. Two weeks to go before he gets a break at Thanksgiving recess, and after that, eight whole months of the school year left, and already he looks as tired as if it were March. We hardly have time for each other—and when we do, he's so distracted it's as if he were miles away.

But not tonight, she decides. Tonight I'm going to get his attention. She snuggles up so that her head rests on the same pillow as his. He's flat on his back with his eyes closed. "Hey!" she says and drapes her arm over his chest.

His distracted "hey" in return is mere reflex, she knows, his mind far away from this bed, this dark, this heat. It surprises her that he can't ever take his mind off the school even after a lovely windfall of two million dollars to underwrite the deficit! Plenty of time now to build the girls-only enrollment back up. He should be as optimistic as the board was when he told them the news.

She cups her hand against the other side of his face, turns his head to hers, kisses him on the lips.

"You're supposed to kiss back," she whispers. "Those are the rules."

"Yeah," he says. "I'm sorry."

So she flicks on her bedside lamp, then turns back, propping her head on her hand, seeing him squint against the sudden light. "Relax," she says. "Just try."

"Yeah. Relax."

"This," she says, touching his forehead with the tip of her finger. "Not that," pointing downward.

He grins. "Turn over," she commands, and as he does she gets up on him as if riding a horse, straddling his hips, and begins to massage the back of his neck, the tops of his shoulders. "It's a wonder your head doesn't break off in a wind," she says, "your neck's so stiff with tension." She bends down, kisses the back of his neck, nuzzles her tongue behind his ear. "It's night-time!" she says. "You're not in your office. It's not school! It's us!"

"Sure doesn't feel like the office," he says.

"Everything's fixed now," Gail says. "With that Fingerman woman and her big gift."

"Yeah," he acknowledges. "Maybe. A little further down, OK? By the shoulder blades?" She moves her hands further down his back, presses hard, leaning in with her weight. "Ah," he sighs. "Perfect. How much an hour you get for this?"

"I don't do it for anybody who has to pay for it. What do you mean *maybe?*"

"Just maybe. Why don't we do this tomorrow in my office? We'll take our clothes off, I'll lie down on the floor and dictate to Ms.—did you get that *Ms.*? Rice—while you massage."

"I'm busy tomorrow. Maybe Ms. Rice could learn."

"Uh-uh. She can only do one thing at a time."

"Well, now, that's a relief. So why can't you count on the Fingerman gift?"

"Because I think maybe her ex-husband has a very long arm," he says. Then after a pause: "Besides, even with the gift, I'm still not Marjorie."

"Well, screw them!" She wants to bang her fists on his shoulder blades. He's worth a thousand Marjories!

"Hey," he says. "Gail! What's got into you?"

"Nothing." She forces the anger out of her voice, lets her hands relax. "That's just the trouble," she adds softly after a pause. "Nothing, lately." She taps her finger on his back. "That's what I've been trying to tell you."

"I can fix that." He turns over while she turns out the light.

Above him in the ardent dark, she tries to see his face, is full of him, and she remembers in a wave of sadness that they used to wonder if their daughter heard them, when they were doing this, from her bed in the next room, on the other side of the thin wall, in the assistant headmaster's house, of Mt. Gilead school in Ohio—in the long ago. You *really* want to make a baby? she yearns to ask. For that's what she meant, she realizes now, by *nothing*: nothing's inside her—or outside her either—to replace their daughter. Then focus on it, she wants to say. First things first. Quit your job. I'll make the money. Because I don't become my work the way you do. Quit your job. We'll make love all day.

Afterward, while she holds him, it is *her* mind that wanders: she's in her office again with the baby-faced client, the momma's boy, his suit, his leather briefcase stamped with his initials, the pretty tassels on his shoes, who's so sure he knows more about her profession than she does. All right, she thinks, I'll design the damn brochure your way instead of the way I just explained to you three times would save you lots of money and do a better job. I'll take your money. And laugh behind your back.

Why can't you laugh like that about *your* job? she wants to ask her husband. But of course she doesn't, she wouldn't even if he were still awake. Besides, she knows the answer: he doesn't think of it as a *job*. It's never crossed his mind that he's making a living—though *she'd* like to charge about three million dollars a day for feeling suffocated in this hermetic little fiefdom he wants to save. And then the thought arrives, a discovery filling her mind with a too-bright light: soon this time in their life will be over. He doesn't know how lucky he is that it isn't going to work; Miss Oliver's School for Girls will never be Fred Kindler's school—and he'll be free to move on. She feels another wave of sadness. "Whither thou goest," she murmurs. "Whoever you try to become."

In his sleep, he presses tightly against her.

AT ELEVEN-THIRTY that night, an hour after Gregory van Buren goes through his dorm, checking the girls in for the night and saying goodnight to each of them, Sylvia Lapham climbs out the window of her first-floor room to sneak across the campus to the place where her brother has agreed to meet her in his Subaru. "We're not going to a party," he's told her. "We'll just have a few beers and talk." Sylvia's relieved, and glad for this chance to be alone with Charley. She trusts him, now more than she trusts her parents, to know how she feels. In her bed on the other side of the room, Clarissa pretends to be asleep.

Outside in the moonless November night, Sylvia shivers in the cold. She sneaks across the lawns, covered with fallen leaves, and stops behind a faculty house where through an upstairs window she sees a lighted room. A bookcase fills one wall, a fireplace another. Above it, on the mantel, stand a vase of flowers, some photographs Sylvia can't make out from the distance, and a pair of candles. Then a woman moves soundlessly across the window in the warm yellow light, and outside in the cold dark, Sylvia feels as if an arrow has struck her in the heart. She starts to run.

She climbs over a stone wall and crosses a field on the southern edge of the campus. She can just make out the shape of Charley's car, parked up ahead on a narrow dirt road that leads to the river. Soon she's at the car. "Charley!" she says. He's behind the wheel smiling at her through the open window. She runs around the front of the car to the passenger door, opens it, and puts her face only inches from the face of a girl who's looking up at Sylvia from the seat where Sylvia expected to sit. "Surprise! Surprise!" the girl murmurs. She holds a bottle of tequila. There are empty beer cans on the floor by her feet. The girl's face lurches into a crooked smile, and Sylvia knows she's drunk.

"Get in the back!" Charley whispers. Sylvia opens the back door and jumps in on the right-hand side and slams the door as Charley starts the engine. Then the car's bumping over the dirt road toward the river, and she senses someone's in the backseat with her she didn't see when she jumped in. She turns to look at him. He's as far away from her as he can get, scrunched up against the door. She sees big shoulders, makes out a leather jacket in the dark, a white baseball cap.

"That's Robin," the drunk girl says. "Of linebacker fame. Or is it back-liner? Is it backliner, Robin? I can never get it straight. Sports are so boring I can never remember."

"Penny," Robin says, "please, just shut your mouth."

"Now you know my name is Penny," the drunk girl says to Sylvia. "Now everybody knows everybody." Her voice goes up and down as the car hits the bumps. Charley's driving much too fast. Low branches scrape against the roof.

"Charley, slow down," Robin says.

"He can't slow down, he's drunk," Penny says.

"Charley, slow down," Robin says again.

"Drunk with love for me," Penny says.

Charley giggles, drives even faster. Sylvia can smell the wet marshy odor, like rotting leaves, of the river. She wonders if Charley knows how close it is. He'll drive right over the bank!

"Charley, stop!" Robin says. And now Sylvia's sure they are going to drive right over the bank. "Charley! Please!" she yells. Charley giggles again and goes even faster and then suddenly slams on the brakes, and the car slithers sideways in the loose dirt of the road and stops. He turns the engine off. In the sudden silence they can hear the rushing of the river.

"What the hell's gotten into you, Charley?" Robin says. He's still scrunched as far away from Sylvia as he can get. She's grateful for that.

"I've gotten in to him, that's what." Penny says. "Maybe soon it'll be the other way around. Him and lots of tequila," and Charley laughs. Penny slides closer to him, puts her arm around him, pulls him to her, kisses him on the mouth.

Robin gets out of the car, and now Sylvia's alone in the back.

Penny turns back to Sylvia. "You want to watch us make out?" she asks.

"Charley, take me home, please," Sylvia says.

"Oh, in a little bit," Penny murmurs. She puts the bottle down on the floor and spills it, and the smell of tequila fills the car, and then she pulls Charley's head into her chest so his face is nuzzling her breasts. Sylvia looks away, she wants to get out. Just as she reaches for the door handle, she sees Robin by her door. He's reaching for it, and the door swings open. "Let's go," he says. "I'll walk you home." She hesitates. "Really. You'll be safe."

"Oh, you'll be safe all right," Penny says. "That's the trouble with Robin."

Robin reaches into the car, takes Sylvia's hand, and tugs. Sylvia gets out of the car, her hand in Robin's, and they start to walk away from the river. They walk quite a few paces before they realize they're still holding hands. Embarrassed, they let go of each other and walk side by side. He seems huge to her, his shoulders miles above hers as they walk, and it's so dark she can hardly see his face.

After a while Robin says, "Your brother was coming to see you. So Penny and I thought we'd come too. We bought the beer and tequila on the way. Then Penny got drunk and got up in the front with your brother. She can be a pain in the ass when she wants to be."

"My brother got drunk too," she says.

"Your brother gets drunk a lot," Robin says, and then stops walking. "Wait a sec, I just thought of something."

"What?" But before he answers, she thinks of it too. "He's too drunk to drive," she says.

"Yeah," he says. "He'll kill everybody." He takes her hand again, gives it that same little tug he used to get her out of the car, and they walk back toward the Subaru. This time he doesn't let go.

When they get back to the car, Charley's not in it. Penny's passed out in the front seat. "Oh, shit!" Robin says. "Where's that crazy bastard gone?" He reaches into the car, shakes Penny's shoulder. "Where the hell is he?" he yells, but she doesn't stir. Sylvia feels panic rising: Charley's fallen down the bank into the river, he's drowning! "Charley!" she yells.

"Over here," Charley says. And they turn to find him, but it's too dark to see. They stumble through the bushes toward the sound and find him sitting on a boulder. "Where the hell were you?" Charley asks.

"Let's go, Charley," Robin says. He puts his hand under Charley's arm, lifts and steadies him. Sylvia gets on Charley's other side and steadies him too. They walk him to the car, open the back door, and push him into the seat. Sylvia walks around to the other side of the car and gets in beside Charley, and Robin gets in the driver's seat, turns the ignition, and starts to drive. Penny's still passed out beside him.

Sylvia turns to her brother and says, "Put your seat belt on." He doesn't stir. She reaches across him to find the belt, and her face is close to his. His arms come up around her in a brotherly hug. She fixes his belt, then leans to kiss him on the forehead, but he smells like tequila and there's lipstick all over his face, and she feels a wave of disgust and lifts his arms away from her. His eyes are open watching hers, and he tries to keep her in the hug, but he's too drunk and his arms flop down at his sides, and Sylvia moves across the seat as far from him as she can get. In the glow of the dashboard that lights the rearview mirror she sees Robin's eyes. They meet hers and then look away.

Three minutes later, Robin stops the car near the edge of campus where there are no lights. "Thanks, Robin," she says to the back of his head. She wants to say more, but she can't think of the words.

He turns to look at her. "Take care of yourself." She gets out of the car and heads for her dorm. This time she's not sneaking. If she gets caught she gets caught. Then she hears the Subaru move away and realizes that Robin's waited. He's been watching her, hoping she gets back without getting caught. She hopes that Charley's been watching too.

WHEN SYLVIA CLIMBS through the window into her room, she can tell by Clarissa's breathing that she's still only pretending to sleep. She lets Clarissa know she doesn't believe her by being nowhere near as quiet as she would be if Clarissa really were asleep. She rummages around on her bureau for her toothbrush, then stomps out of the room to go to the bathroom, and when she comes back, she closes the door with a bang.

Clarissa goes right on pretending. Her way of letting Sylvia know she doesn't want to deal with her tonight. She thinks Sylvia's been partying with the Park Avenue crowd, Clarissa's name for the kids who get wasted almost every night. They bore her to death. She opens her eyes just enough to see in the dim light coming through the window that Sylvia's throwing her clothes on the floor as she takes them off to get in her bed.

Now Clarissa's too furious to pretend any longer. "Pick your clothes up," she commands in the dark. She knows Sylvia's just trying to get her goat by strewing her clothes all over the floor. They've fought about this before. Clarissa's a neatnik; Sylvia a slob. "Hang them in the closet," Clarissa says.

Sylvia turns on the light.

"Like you promised me you would," Clarissa says. She sits up. She's wearing her green pajamas, pressed and neat, her initials embossed on them, her mother's gift to begin the year.

Sylvia picks up her clothes and hangs them in the closet. She makes a parody of being very neat, folding her T-shirt three times to get it right, creasing her jeans, and hanging each on a separate hanger. "I knew you were awake," she says.

"You better be careful," Clarissa says. "Van Buren's got eyes in the back of his head."

Sylvia doesn't respond

Now Clarissa sits up even straighter in her bed. She doesn't want a roommate who doesn't like it here. Too much like she feels at home trying to explain to all her friends why she loves this school. They just think she's weird. "Why not just quit and go home if you don't like it here?" she asks.

"My parents have paid the tuition; I'm not about to waste it." Sylvia turns from the closet and sits on the edge of her bed.

"All right. Then stop taking chances."

"And anyway, I wasn't doing what you think I was doing."

Clarissa shrugs. She's not the gestapo. What does she care? Getting caught out of the dorm is trouble enough.

"I was with my brother," Sylvia says. She doesn't have to defend herself, it's nobody's fucking business what she does or doesn't do, she just wants Clarissa to know about tonight, that's all, she feels like telling her. So she tells Clarissa about what she was really doing when she snuck out. She likes Clarissa, likes her green pajamas, the way she studies so hard. She's heard the story about how last year Clarissa refused to take Van Buren's final exam because there was an essay question on it about *Huck Finn*. And didn't argue when Van Buren flunked her, not because she misinterpreted the book, an assertion he wouldn't make because he had no essay to assess, but because civil disobedience has no meaning if it doesn't have a price. How can you help not liking that?

"Robin sounds like a nice guy," Clarissa says when Sylvia finishes. "I'm glad he was there for you." Her voice is soft. Her irritation's gone. She turns out the light and lies down.

Sylvia gets in her bed. "Thanks for listening," she says in the dark. She likes hearing Clarissa's breathing across the room from her. This is how it must be for sisters, she thinks.

Just the same, she can't figure out what it is about Miss Oliver's that Clarissa's so loyal to and loves so much. How can she care whether or not boys are admitted; what's all the fuss about? What's so special about going to school with only half the human race? And to have a whole meeting about whether to give that stuff back to some Indians? The Indians haven't even asked for it! She'd love to get up on stage in Morning Meeting and tell everybody to get a life. She'd love just not to be here.

TEN DAYS LATER, on the Monday morning of Thanksgiving week, Fred Kindler sees right away how upbeat the board members are when they gather for the meeting at the River Club. There is good reason for their happiness: just last week the school's lawyers, who have been working closely with Hannah's, reported that they couldn't find any way by which Hannah's ex-husband could stop her from making the gift. It is Hannah's money, they've declared, and as soon as Hannah's ex realizes he's wasting his meager resources trying to prove it isn't, the school will get the gift. It's a sure thing, and it will be wrapped up in only a couple of months.

So now the school has much more time in its race against the deficit!

Fred barely acknowledges this happy news as he starts his report to the board. He moves instead immediately to the grim recruitment statistics. He's a conservative man. The money isn't in the bank yet. Nevertheless, a new attitude, of optimism tempered by realism, of faith in good organization and specific plans, starts to grow around the mahogany table as the meeting progresses. Alan Travelers senses this optimism as he moves through the agenda, acknowledging it to Fred with a subtle glance.

Near the end of the agenda, an important item, under new business, is the Student Council's petition to the board, signed by more than two thirds of the students, to return the Collection to the Pequots. There's a little silence when everyone is finished reading. The members are looking at Travelers. How to deal with this?

But Milton Perkins is staring at Fred. "Why are you bringing us this crap, Fred?" he asks. "First they threaten us with a Declaration. Which I gotta admit I like the nerve *that* took. But then they bring us *this!* Has nothing to do with building the enrollment, or even letting boys in, or any other price of eggs. Just tell them no, for crying out loud, and let's get back to running the damn place!"

"He's probably already told them no, and they're still there," Sonja McGarvey says. "That's why he's bringing us this crap, as you so elegantly put it."

"Process!" Perkins explodes. "Jeezus, process again! Petitions. Protests. Even Hitler couldn't run this nuthouse!"

"Try Eva Braun," Sonja suggests. "Hitler's the wrong gender."

"When I first got on this board," Perkins remembers out loud, "nobody argued with the head. And they never even *saw* the board."

"Was that before the glacier," Sonja asks, "or after?"

"That was when board members gave their money instead of their half-baked opinions," Perkins says.

Sonja starts to say something, thinks better of it, turns to Travelers. "Can we get on with this?" she says.

But Perkins isn't finished. "Sounds like it was written by some god-damn lawyer!" he growls.

Nobody answers.

"Whenever I read anything written by a lawyer, I automatically tear it up," Perkins says. He's grinning now, obviously enjoying himself. It's not clear whether he's making this up or if this is actually what he does.

"All right, Milton," Travelers says.

"Then I send him a bill for three hundred dollars for wasting my time opening the envelope."

"Can we just please get on with the subject?" Sonja asks again.

"We're *on* the subject," Perkins says. "And when the bastard doesn't pay, I take him to small-claims court just to hassle him." Travelers raps his knuckles on the table, but Perkins goes right on: "Then when he sends *me* a bill, I wait until just before he takes me to small claims and send him half—"

"Milton!" Travelers starts to stand.

Perkins put up his hand, relinquishing the floor. "Works every time," he says, winding down. "They never even bill for the second half."

"All right. Now that we know how Milton feels about lawyers, let's address this issue," Travelers says.

"I've made *my* point," says Perkins.

Travelers, with whom Fred has shared his idea, announces, "Fred here has an alternative." Fred takes over and recommends making the Pequots owners of the on-campus Collection. The solution, he says, provides not only a logical answer to a legitimate ethical question but also an excellent public relations initiative that will support the needed enrollment growth. "We can raise money for building the extra room to house the Collection from people who otherwise wouldn't give us a dime, and I believe we can also find some money for financial aid for Pequot children," he tells them. "It's a win-win; let's do it."

It doesn't take long for the board to authorize Fred to put out feelers to the Pequot authorities and move forward with the plan if the Pequots agree. There's a lot of work to do to bring this off.

"I think it's a great idea!" Alan Travelers says just before he adjourns the meeting.

"We still need to put the right spin on it, though," Sonja pronounces. "It's great public relations if we make it very clear we're doing the right thing, and doing it right."

"I agree," says Fred. "We'll do it."

"Christ, what is this, Berkeley, California?" Perkins asks. He hates both the Student Council's idea *and* Fred's for their political correctness. He's not the kind of man who spins. "You open up this can of worms with the Indians, they'll decide they don't want it in anybody's museum. They'll want to just bury the stuff, and then even *they* won't know about their past," he says. "What about that? You thought about that?"

"Let's cross that bridge when we come to it," Travelers suggests, and raps on the table and calls for adjournment, and when everybody but Perkins raises a hand, he ends the meeting.

But, once again, Milton Perkins isn't finished. He's staring across the table at Sonja. "Since it's spinning you want, why give just one little bone back?" he asks her gleefully. He just loves to push her buttons! "Why not give 'em a whole skeleton? We could dig an old alumna up. Find a real big one who died years ago. She'd never know the difference. We could give *her* to the Indians. That would shut *every*body up."

Before Perkins finishes, Sonja is out the door. She's been looking at her watch for the last ten minutes.

"YES, I UNDERSTAND," Lila admits the next morning when Fred tells her the board's decision. "It makes a lot of sense. And Marie's idea was a little crazy." But that's the trouble: she does understand. She wishes she didn't.

"Lila, are you OK?" It's the second time he's asked her. He respects her yearning for the moral purity of Marie Safford's and Sara Warrior's position, would be disappointed if she didn't. "There's a lot of pressure on you, Lila," he says, taking a different tack. "More than on some of the faculty, even."

That's not what she wants to talk about. Pressure. This tension. It makes it worse to talk about it.

"You could have a chat with Ms. Rugoff," Fred persists, mentioning the school counselor. He holds his breath, remembering how angry Francis Plummer got when he mentioned counseling to him.

Lila shakes her head.

"All right," he says, backing off. "It was just an idea."

"I don't need her to tell me what's bothering me," she says, lowering her eyes. "I already know."

"Well, that's good," he murmurs and sits quietly waiting.

"It's hard to explain, and it sounds stupid, " Lila begins. She looks up now, studying him to see if she trusts him enough to reveal this much about herself.

"I bet it won't sound stupid to me."

She sends a little smile to thank him for that. "I wish I could be like Marie," she says, admitting it at last. "The way she cares about what's absolutely right, and nothing else."

"Not even whether it works?"

"Yes!" she says. "Not to give a damn!"

"Its too late, Lila," he says. "You're way past that point." And when she doesn't say anything to that: "How old are you, Lila?"

She frowns. Why's he asking that? "Eighteen," she says. "Why?"

"How long do you think those Pequots lived?"

"In the village that was here? Maybe forty years."

"You're almost halfway there. You'd be a chief by now."

"Uh-uh," she shakes her head. "The chiefs were men."

"Behind the scenes, Lila. The real boss behind the boss."

"No way. I'm not going to be anybody's boss. I'm going to be an archeologist."

"You'll be the boss archeologist," he says. "You'll take the weight."

But he's got that wrong, she thinks. I don't take it. It goes right by the ones who really want it, which I don't, and just comes to me. She could tell him that—if she knew him better, if it didn't sound so proud. "Well, anyway," she finally says, bringing their meeting to an end—she needs to get out of here before he mentions Ms. Rugoff again. "Thanks for telling me. I'll tell the students today in Morning Meeting." But she doesn't stand up, realizes she doesn't want the meeting to end after all. She likes talking to this man, he calms her down.

"All right." He stands, and the meeting *is* over. She's disappointed.

"Thanks, Lila." He shakes her hand. Treating her like a grown-up. A peer. "This is going to work out fine."

"Yes," she says. "It'll be just fine."

THE NEXT PERSON Fred tells is Peggy, of course. He promises that over Thanksgiving recess, which starts tomorrow at noon, he'll begin to work on the plan. He'll do some research and ask around to figure out with whom among the Pequot authorities he should broach the idea. Peggy is delighted. What she started years ago will achieve its most logical and inspiring development. In her mind, she sees the new wing, a true museum, the school now serving not just a private, but a public, purpose. "Why didn't I think of this idea years ago?" she asks.

Because you're human; he wants to quote Rachel Bickham to her. Instead he says: "Who cares who thought of it. We're teammates."

"Yes, and I love being on your team," she tells him. "You're the best thing that ever happened to this place."

LATER THAT MORNING, when Lila makes the announcement, applause breaks out. But when she goes on to tell the students that this good idea was their new headmaster's, the applause is sparse, seems grudging, almost disappointed that it wasn't someone else's: Peggy Plummer's, especially, or Francis's, or Rachel Bickham's, even Gregory van Buren's. So Peggy stands up, shows her true colors once again, tells the school how creative an idea this is, how inclusive, how much it pleases her; and the students, corrected, supply a little more applause.

The twenty or so students who remain unpersuaded sit on their hands until the applause ends. They do so for themselves and for Sara, who isn't here to get this news. She's home by now. She called her parents last night; they arrived this morning and took her home. They'll bring her back on Monday when Thanksgiving recess is over. That way she doesn't have to be there for the turkey the school will serve tonight, the pumpkins, the corn: Indian food white people eat to say thank you to their god for helping them steal the land. Thanksgiving's not for Sara at this school, where a remnant of one of her people lies in a display for all to gawk at.

AFTER THE THANKSGIVING dinner, Peggy again goes to her library for the evening instead of coming home. Levi goes with her, leaving Francis alone in the apartment thinking about Fred Kindler's solution to the issue of the Pequot Collection. He has to admit it is a marvelous idea to invite the Pequots back to the ground on which one of their villages thrived for centuries. So it doesn't surprise him that he thinks right then of the papier-mâché model that Siddy made in the sixth grade of that very village. It's stored away in the attic. Up there with all the other nostalgia that neither he nor Peggy can bear to throw away.

He climbs the stairs. Under the naked lightbulb that hangs from the rafters, he sees the model just where he placed it years ago on an old table. What he notices, which he had not seen as sharply before, is the familiar shape of the ground that Siddy modeled—his son's loving imitation of the ground on which he had grown up, the place in the world he knew best. The revelation fills Francis with longing for his son. Staring at the model, he remembers that Siddy's teacher had told him that this was perfect research. "Everything we know tells us that an Indian village very much like this one existed here on this very spot for years and years and years. On this very spot!" she repeated. He remembers loving her for being so proud of Siddy.

For an instant he *knows* he's been in the village, way beyond mere visualization, its every part familiar, and suddenly he is so lonely for his son he misses a breath, remembering that years ago when he and Peg were very young and they had just brought Siddy into their lives they would wake in the middle of the night and go into his room just to watch him sleep. Siddy chastised him once when he couldn't have been more than seven years old for cutting down a small tree in the backyard that was casting shade on the garden. "There are millions of trees in New England," Francis told the boy. "They are like weeds."

"But Dad, it's *alive!*" Siddy said.

THAT NIGHT HE DREAMS: in the middle of a starlit night the students stand in semicircular rows in front of the library staring at him. Somehow he knows that he has called them there. He hears drums. The library looms behind him in the dark.

One of the girls steps forward. She looks like Lila, but he knows she isn't. She hands him a torch, which a second before had not been in her hand. He turns. The library is a dark cliff in front of him. He reaches toward it with the torch, and it bursts into flames. He realizes, strangely, that he has been smelling smoke since before the flames began. He kneels and weeps. When he rises finally and turns around, all the girls are gone.

He is still dreaming that he is weeping when Peggy shakes him awake. She is staring at his face. "Wake up!" she says. He sits up. She hands him some clothes. "There's a fire," she says. "The library's burning." Her words are a monotone—as if it were someone one else's library, on the other side of the world.

WATCHING THE LIBRARY BURN, all he can think of is that the smell and the crackling sound remind him of campfires. He thinks of marshmallows, their skins wrinkling, turning black. He stands, watching, behind the students, who got there first. Everybody has to stand a long way back. Peggy stands to his right. Soon Margaret Rice joins them, stands to his left. She reaches for his left hand, and he takes it. No one speaks. Finally the fire department arrives and sprays streams of water into the orange glow. The fireman in their heavy coats are dark silhouettes against the flames.

He stands on tiptoes, finds Lila Smythe in the crowd of girls. She turns toward him then, and their eyes meet. He watches her leave her friends, move through the crowd toward him. She stands in front of him. Peggy moves away. "Well," says Lila. "It isn't how we planned things."

"It's too bad," he says. "It was a beautiful library." Just then the building collapses, the roof melts. There's a shower of sparks against the black sky. Someone screams.

"Fire purifies," Lila says. Her eyes are shining. "It will work out. The insurance will rebuild the library, bring in some more artifacts, but it won't rebuild the bones. They're safe. It's a sacred fire." Her eyes are alight with more than the fire.

He doesn't answer, stares at her face. She looks right back. Ashes to ashes, he thinks, the bones at rest. Then he feels a presence behind him, and he turns. Fred Kindler stands there, not ten paces away. He's staring into Francis's face just the way Francis stared into Lila's.

SEVENTEEN

"Don't come home," Peggy says to Francis as soon as Lila goes back to her friends. The words surprise her. As if someone she doesn't know were saying them.

Francis pretends he doesn't hear. He's not even looking at Peggy. He's staring at the fire. The flames are lower now that the walls are collapsed, but still fierce enough to eat the water streaming from the firemen's hoses. The sodden smell of ashes floats in the dark. Some of the students are crying.

"Don't pretend you don't hear me," she tells him. She can't believe she's saying this, for she can see he's grieving too. But Lila Smythe stood two feet away from her and told her husband that it was a sacred fire, and he didn't say a thing, didn't even argue!

He stares straight ahead, but in the glow she sees the shock of her words register on his face. Margaret Rice hears them too. She turns to Peggy, then quickly looks away.

"Just stay away, Francis," Peggy says. Margaret looks at Francis, who gives her a little shrug that seems to say don't worry, she doesn't mean it; then Margaret steps away into the crowd. Francis turns to Peggy, reaching for her hand.

"Find some other place to live," Peggy says. She takes a step away.

"Peg!" he calls after her.

She whirls around, facing him again. "A sacred fire!" she says. "I hope it keeps you warm!" The crowd of watchers makes room for her as she moves away.

There it is, big as life, her first reaction to the library's burning down: she wants him out of the house. She doesn't even ask herself how long she thinks this feeling is going to last. So at five-thirty in the morning, she's packing Francis's underwear and socks, his shirts and khakis in the same ugly duffel bag he took to California, putting his shoes and shaving gear in a backpack. There's a Dewy decimal system for this stuff too, departing fragments, that Francis would just throw in all together if she were to allow him into the house long enough to pack them for himself. He'll come in an hour or two, after he's finished moving around the campus talking to the students, comforting them. She's sure that's what he's doing. Otherwise he'd be here right now, convinced that she doesn't really want him out of the house. So she's locked the door from the inside, a door they've never locked in thirty years. She makes neat piles in the duffel, squaring the edges. In the smell of wet ashes pervading her house, she has more need for order than ever.

At six-thirty the phone rings. It's Fred saying he wants to see her in his office. "So we can get started," he says

"Started?"

"On the new library, Peggy."

You're crazy! she almost says. The fire's only been out a couple of hours. Then she realizes it isn't crazy, it isn't crazy at all; and it's typical of him to know this is exactly what she needs.

"I knew you wouldn't be asleep," he says.

"Give me thirty minutes," she responds. If Francis comes home before she's back from Fred Kindler's office, he'll just have to wait to get his things.

She carries the suitcases and the backpack out of the bedroom, across the living room, and places them next to the front door, divining what Francis will see when she opens the door and allows him only that one step into the house to pick up his things. Her eye goes straight across the room to the mantelpiece where, between two candlesticks, a framed black-and-white photograph sits: her father, and her mother, Ada Louise Boyer—the loveliest name in the world, she thinks. On the front lawn, sprinkled with October leaves, they gaze past the camera at the bright future they still believe is theirs. The photo is the first thing Francis will see when he enters the house, but he won't notice. They're dead, she says to herself, looking away, he never knew them. Next to this, another picture sits, in which she and Francis stand, bride and groom, side by side. In his rented black tailcoat, grinning, Francis comes up to her shoulder. She goes to this, plucks it off the mantelpiece. Francis's grin is aimed right at the camera. She's looking past the camera, out of the picture, to where Francis's father stands. She places the picture on top of the backpack.

She vacuums, she dusts, she turns on the kitchen fan, trying to get the ashy smell out, pulls down the shades on the side of the house toward where her library was, and when she is finished, her house as clean and neat as she can get it, she locks the door to the dormitory, then goes out through the front door, locking it behind her. The key feels strange in her hand. When Francis comes and finds the front door bolted while she's away, he'll stand there for a little while not believing—she can hardly believe it herself—before he gives up and goes away. Then he'll go to

Michael Woodward's house. When he comes back to try again, she'll stand just inside the door, guarding her house.

"I've already called the insurance agent," Fred Kindler tells Peggy. "He's coming right out. He says not to worry; it was completely insured."

What he doesn't tell her was that he wasn't sure it was insured, until he'd called Alan Travelers, the first person he informed. He knew he was being overanxious.

"Of course it was insured!" Travelers exclaimed. "You forget what *I* do for a living." And then, "Oh, my God! You thought Marjorie and old Vincent were *that* unbusinesslike?"

Fred didn't answer.

"OK, I won't go there," Alan said, and then he changed the subject. "Don't let this get you, Fred. Think of it as an opportunity. We've got a chance to build an even better library." Traveler's voice was full of energy. It almost sounded optimistic, and Fred knew that his board chair was trying to keep him pumped up. "Nobody was hurt. Concentrate on that."

"Well, I hope that softens the blow for you at least a little bit, anyway," Fred tells Peggy now. "And I promise you this," he adds. "The new library's going to be even better than the old one. You won't lose a thing."

She shakes her head, a very slight motion, like a hurt boxer clearing his head.

"I'm sorry," he murmurs. "I didn't mean to sound—"

"When do we get started?" Peggy asks. She doesn't want him to have to apologize for trying to keep her spirits up.

"Right now!"

"Thank you! I don't know what I would do if I had to wait till Monday."

They start to work. He asks her to make a list: "Everything you'd want to preserve and everything you'd want to change if your library hadn't burned down and we had all the money we needed." You can't replace a person, he wants to say; you can a library. And you can make it even better.

While she makes her list, he makes one of his own of everything that has to be done, starting with how to handle the newspapers. As soon as the faculty and students get enough sleep after being awake most of the night— it's still only seven in the morning—he's going to assemble them all. They need to be together, all in the same space, after such a disaster; and after they have talked a while, he'll ask them to send all newspaper reporters, and phone calls from reporters, to him. In the meantime, the phones are on the taped answering system that will tell people the switchboard is closed until eight o'clock and if there's an emergency, to please call a number that will ring right here on his desk, so he can answer it himself. Even though, later in the day, the parents will be arriving to take their children home for the Thanksgiving recess, he'll divide the list of parents among the faculty and ask them to call and give exactly the same message to everyone: the library burned in the night; no one's hurt; the cause is unknown. "Emphasize that too," he'll tell them. "Don't speculate with anyone about the cause."

When Peggy hands him her list, he isn't surprised that, except for a few minor details, it describes the library that has just burned down. A few days later, he'll ask her to think some more.

"Thanks," he says. "This is great."

"All right," she says. "What now?"

"Keep making this list. Everything we can think of that needs to be done. We'll put it into sequence later." He steps into Ms. Rice's office. Peggy waits, alone, then sees him return a moment later with a big pad of easel paper. The two of them rip the sheets off and tape them up on the walls around his office. "I always feel silly when I do this," he tells Peggy, speaking as if to himself. "Too with-it and groovy. Like a consultant instead of a guy with a real job, but it works."

That's when she starts to cry.

At first he ignores her, pretends he doesn't see she's crying. Then he reaches for her hand. Peggy doesn't offer it, and steps a little further away from him. That small shake of her head again. "I'm sorry," she murmurs. "I'll be OK."

"Look, I'd be crying too."

She makes a small dismissive gesture with one hand, wipes at her eyes with the other, and forces herself to stop crying. "OK," she says. "Let's get going."

He turns to the sheet he's working on and writes: appoint a committee to decide on the architect. She watches him write that, and on her own sheet, starts writing the names of people who might be on the committee.

After they have worked for several more minutes, she suddenly puts her marker down, turns to face him, and says: "Who did it?" She's been trying not to think about this, but she can't put it off any longer.

"I don't know." He's still facing his sheet of paper, still writing.

"Who do you think?"

"I don't think," he says, still facing the paper.

"I think you should."

"Most people would," he admits.

"Most people would be right." She feels anger rising. How can he not want revenge?

He turns to her then. "I have other priorities," he says. "I'm not going to wreck this community by investigating people, playing detective. I'm going to leave that up to the fire department and the police. They're outsiders. They can be the ones to hold suspicions."

Marie? he wonders. Lila? How terrible that would be! He hates himself for even thinking of them. Thank God Sara went home a whole day before the fire. At least she's not a suspect. He shakes his head to clear it. This is exactly what he told himself he wasn't going to do.

"I'm going to need to know," he hears Peggy say. "I'm not going to be able to let it rest."

"We'll know soon enough," he says.

"All right," she says. "I hope so." Then after a pause: "Anyway, you need to know—"

"Peggy, I don't need to know anything."

"That you only have one person running our dormitory now. You're the headmaster. You need to know that. Francis is going to be living somewhere else."

The sharpness of his disappointment surprises him. Not just for her, but for Francis too—that's what surprises him. "This makes me very sad," he says.

"Me too," she says. "I can't believe I'm doing this."

"I understand," he says.

"The truth will come out someday," she says, because she needs to change the subject. "It always does. I just hope it wasn't any of the students. That would hurt too much." She starts to cry again.

"Maybe it just happened," he murmurs. Which he knows is crazy. But he has to admit that if he knows who did it, he knows whom to be grateful to. For like wars to failing presidents, this calamity provides a chance for him to shine. He'll manage the crisis, build an even better library, bring the Pequots in to establish a more extensive Collection, and house it there. The new library will be *his* accomplishment, it will give him power. He's surprised to discover that he's not ashamed of these thoughts. But he's not about to admit them to Peggy.

"Nothing ever just happens," Peggy says, struggling to stop crying.

"I know," he says and turns back to his work.

EIGHTEEN

IN SPITE OF FRED'S determination to downplay the investigation into the burning of the library, he realizes as soon as the students return from the break that he's in charge of a school in which the only thing anyone can see is the empty space and blackened foundation that loom in the center of campus, where the library used to be.

Who did it? That's the question on everyone's mind. And even more painful for some: Does anyone think I did it?

That question haunts Lila Smythe, who thinks she catches a certain expression, half fascination, half embarrassment, in the sidewise glances of some of her peers. She's sure that at least a few students—and who knows how many faculty?—overheard her when she told Francis Plummer that the fire was sacred. She catches herself every once in a while feeling guilty, as if she actually did cause the fire. Even Sara Warrior, whom everyone knows didn't do it because she was home with her family, feels estranged because she knows that she was the first person everyone thought of—as if she could imagine doing something so terrible! Marie Safford also wonders how many think she did it.

The lead investigator is a somber man in his forties, already bald, a weight lifter in a crisp blue uniform and shiny badge. He wants to give a speech to the students about fire safety in the dorms, which Fred prohibits, angering the man and hurting his feelings. He doesn't understand that his face, associated with suspicion and mistrust, should be as invisible as possible.

When the investigators finish examining the ruins, they report that they've eliminated natural causes such as lightning. Fred's not surprised. Of course it wasn't lightning; it was a clear November night. They don't tell him any more than that, since, officially at least, he's a suspect too.

Fred pushes the investigators to work as fast as they can, and he won't let them interview the students on campus. He rents an office off campus and insists the interviews take place in this neutral space and in the company of Kevina Rugoff, the school counselor. Some parents retain a lawyer to accompany their daughter to the interview. Most of the parents of the interviewed students are angry and hurt. Over the phone and in person in his office they rail at Fred. He lets them tell him how angry they are with him, sometimes several times, assuring them each time that he understands their feelings, before he ends the conversations.

FOR THE STUDENTS, one small light in this darkness is their excitement over the secret they are for the most part managing to keep—especially, they incorrectly assume, from the new headmaster—about the research Karen Benjamin is conducting on the sex lives of the seniors. The students don't know that last summer Karen warned the headmaster about the article. If they did, they would be even more convinced that they'll never see it in the *Clarion.* They expect it to appear sub rosa, Xeroxed and passed around. In fact, they might be disappointed if their new headmaster didn't forbid publication. They expect him to confirm what they already know: how much less daring, how much less heroically committed to the truth he is, than their beloved Marjorie was when *she* was the headmistress of Miss Oliver's School for Girls.

Karen's research focuses as much on the girls' attitudes as on their actual activities or lack of them. For instance, what, short of actual intercourse, qualifies in their minds as sex? She's distributed a questionnaire to be filled out anonymously. The first section elicits objective responses to questions about what actual activities starting at what age, how many partners, and so on. The second section, more subjective, probes the motivations, such as: Why do you refrain from sexual activity (if you do)? Check any answers that apply: (A) Religious or philosophical beliefs. (B) No desire to engage in sex. (C) Lack of opportunity. (D) Timidity. (E) To avoid disease. (F) Other. Or: Why do you engage in sexual activity as you have defined it? Check one: (A) Peer pressure. (B) To stay in a relationship. (C) Pleasure. (D) Curiosity. (E). Generosity: desire to please. (F) Other. After each section there is a space in which the student can write anything she wants.

Karen knows how easily the students could turn her project into comedy. She could do a fair job herself of lampooning it, and she giggles when she imagines the seniors filling out the questionnaires together, agreeing to claim orgies with gangs of sex-crazed people of both genders and all ages and shapes who sneak out of a local prison and invade the dorms each night; and cooking up a sexual life at home on vacation that features practices so grotesque they require positions which could only be achieved with the aid of chiropractors and could only be induced by drugs. Well, if that's how the seniors react, that's what she'll report, but she doesn't think it will happen, and she's right: the seniors trust Karen's skepticism and her detachment, and so most of them fill out the questionnaires as accurately as they can.

She decides she needs a partner in evaluating the questionnaires, some-one less virginal than she, to assure a balanced interpretation. So she enlists her friend Claire Nelson, a senior colleague on the *Clarion* staff, who is poised beyond her years, long legged, raven haired, and so beautiful that people's eyes are always on her. Nothing has happened yet to Claire to dissuade her that the power her beauty gives her to project herself on the world is some-thing she deserves rather than merely a stroke of genetic luck.

Karen stores the answered questionnaires in a safe in the *Clarion's* office, to which she's changed the combination so only she can open it, and on an evening in early December she removes them and carries them to Claire's room, where they can work more privately. She doesn't ask herself why she chooses Claire's room rather than her own.

Karen sits at Claire's desk with half the questionnaires, and Claire, languid on her bed, reads the other half. As they finish each one, they hand it across to the other. After a while Claire sits up on her bed, swings her feet to the floor. "Upper East Side," she says, handing a questionnaire to Karen. She knows it's wrong to try to identify the participants, but that's not what she's really trying to do. Her remark is simply her way into a con-versation. She wants to talk, to *really* talk.

"What?" Karen looks across the room at her friend. She thinks it would be a distraction to be so beautiful. Besides, she knows that there's always a bottle of vodka hidden in Claire's bureau right here in her room. She worries that Claire is an alcoholic. But Claire doesn't consider herself an alcoholic. She just drinks because she likes to. Whatever Claire likes to do, she does.

"New York," Claire says. "It's obvious. I can tell. I used to live there, you know. I can tell by the bragging tone."

Karen knows Claire had lived all her life in Manhattan until last year, when she moved with her father to London. And she knows Claire's mother deserted the family when Claire was eight, but she doesn't know that the real reason Claire's father, a vice president of an international investment bank, managed to get himself transferred so suddenly is that his daughter had been caught having sex with a young teacher by none other than the headmaster of her well-respected independent day school in the city. Claire's father wanted to get her far away from that scene, so he moved to London and enrolled her at Miss Oliver's because he traveled a lot and needed to put her in a boarding school. He'd learned from his daughter's recent adventure the value of a school's acting in loco parentis. Besides, he reasoned, at Miss Oliver's there is a dearth of young men with whom to go to bed.

Claire was caught because the headmaster, much admired by his board of trustees for his thrifty management, made the rounds at the end of every day to make sure the lights were out, and on a Friday evening found Claire and her paramour in flagrante in the faculty room. The headmaster, who might have been in his job a few too many years, and who'd never believed the stories he'd heard about this kind of thing, assumed that the teacher, a year out of college and thus five years older than his victim, was the predator. Or at least he pretended to, for we don't know how well he knew Claire, though he did tell his wife, who's also good at keeping secrets, that what surprised him the most about the scene that confronted him when he opened the faculty room door was that the teacher was more naked than Claire—and Claire was on top. He fired the teacher immediately, of course, glowering and quoting the school's lawyer at anybody who wanted to know why. He was this secretive to protect Claire's honor, a word he'd learned the meaning of long ago studying English novels at Yale, where all the males in his family always went, and where he belonged to Skull and Bones.

"RICH KIDS," Claire goes on. Her voice is filled with contempt. "They do anything they want, but they don't do it because it's fun. They do it because others do."

"We're not supposed to be guessing. It's supposed to be anonymous," Karen says.

"I know, but it's so childish, it's hard not to know. Look at how she's marked it." Claire wants Karen to see how bold and large the marks the kid has made to affirm how wide ranging her sexual activities are and how, just as enthusiastically, she's marked only *Pleasure* as the motivation. Claire doesn't think anybody does it just for pleasure.

But Karen won't look at the questionnaire. She hands it back. The girl who filled this out could come from Toledo, for all they know.

"I don't want to be a voyeur any more than you do, I just wanted to talk," Claire says, surprising herself at this confession. It gives her power away to reveal how lonely she is.

"I'm sorry. I didn't mean that you were," Karen says. She wonders why she's been so slow to understand that Claire's beauty and worldly charm don't bring her friends, they set her apart. The way she never talks about herself creates an aura. For some of the girls their world would be less exciting if that aura melted. They'd rather be paparazzi to Claire than friends. Karen knows it's Claire's fault, that Claire makes plans, creates her aura on purpose. But just the same, she feels she hasn't been a good friend.

"Hey," she says, "if you want to talk, let's talk. We'll finish this later." She starts to reach across the small space to pat Claire on the knee, but Claire draws away from the gesture, retreating back inside herself. "Some other time," she says.

And an hour later, as they finish, Claire says, "You left a big one out when you made the questionnaire."

"What did I leave out?" Karen feels just a little defensive.

"Power." Claire says. She looks intently in her friend's eyes. She's added *Power* in her own handwriting on her questionnaire as her motivation, the only one to do so, and marked the kinds of sex she's had too. But nothing about the teacher. That's still her secret. "Now you know which one is mine," she says. "I really wanted you to know. I get lonely sometimes."

Karen is touched. "You know, I'd kind of figured it out myself," she admits. "Because you'd marked all those things and I knew how—" She pauses. She doesn't want to say "active"; it sounds too clinical. She starts again: "I knew how busy you are," she tries. She pauses again, and then she says, "But I don't think you could be so mean. You wouldn't do it just for power."

"I made him do it," Claire hears herself saying. "I made him want me so much he'd do the worst thing he could do, even though he knew the second it was over he'd wish that he hadn't."

"What?" Karen asks. "Who?" She's fascinated.

"A teacher. That's why I had to leave the school, that's why my dad got transferred. It's why I'm here."

"A teacher!"

"He cried every time we did it. Right after we were finished he'd start to weep. The only time he didn't was when we got caught."

"A teacher did it to you?"

"More like the other way around," Claire says. "I made it happen. *I* fucked *him*."

Karen winces. The word, used that way, makes her think of guns. "What happened to him?" she asks.

"He got fired," Claire says, and gets up from her bed and goes to her bureau and opens the drawer.

"I don't want any," Karen says. She's thinking about the teacher getting fired.

"Oh, sure you do," Claire says. Her tone is very matter-of-fact. She crosses the room with the bottle in one hand, two glasses in the other. She puts them on the desk next to Karen and pours vodka into each. Then she hands one to Karen.

Karen shakes her head. Claire takes a drink. "I didn't mean to get him fired," Claire says. She can see the teacher in her head. He's very tall and thin, his hair's as black as hers, and his thin chest is naked and it's moving in and out with his sobs. "I'm really sorry about that part," she says.

"I know you are," Karen says. "I know you're not mean, but just the same—"

"Yes, just the same," Claire says. She picks up Karen's glass and hands it to her. Karen shakes her head again, and Claire puts the glass back down.

"I don't drink," Karen says.

"You never break the rules, do you?" Claire says. "Why are you so nice?"

"I guess I just don't want to break the rules."

"Of course you do. Everybody does. You just don't think you should. Somebody told you not to, and you don't think you should. Good for you, but I read an article in some magazine saying that kids who never do drugs or booze or sex frequently have big problems in their adulthood. What do you think about that?"

"You just made that up," Karen says.

Claire hesitates. She really did read it in some article, maybe in the *New York Times*, she wishes she could remember where. Maybe she'll find the article and make Karen read it.

"Don't ever do that again with me," Karen says. "You don't need to. I like you just the way you are."

There's a silence then, while Claire thinks about that. And then she hears herself saying: "Yeah, I was just making it up." She fakes a giggle to cover her lie.

Karen giggles too, the tension dissolved. "It really was pretty funny," she says.

Now Claire says, "Please. Do me a favor. Just join me in a little drink." She slides Karen's glass across the desk toward her.

"Because we're friends?" Karen says.

"Yes, because we're friends."

"Or to prove I'm not timid?" She's thinking about Claire's made-up article. Even though it doesn't exist, it could be true.

"We're friends," Claire insists.

"All right, because we're friends." Karen picks up the glass and looks at Claire. How beautiful you are! she thinks, and takes the whole drink down in a single shot. And winces. She hates the taste.

"Thank you," Claire says, and slugs down her own. Then she gets up, caps the bottle, and crosses the room with it to her bureau and puts it away.

"Well," she says. "That's all for tonight. I hope you'll come again."

"I will," Karen says, standing up. "We'll have a little drink to keep each other company."

AT EIGHT O'CLOCK the next evening, Rabbi Myron and Rachel Benjamin, Karen's parents, who are hosting a recruiting meeting, open the door of their home in Brookline, Massachusetts, to Fred Kindler, Nan White, and Francis Plummer. The rabbi is tall and thin like his daughter. He's bald and wears a worn sports coat. He shakes hands with the three of them. Rachel, dark haired and shorter than her husband, smiles at Nan and Francis and takes Fred's hand in both of hers. "Our daughter tells us you're very brave," she says, then she kisses him on the cheek as if she's known him all his life.

The room into which the Benjamins usher them is big and lined on every wall with books. The guests are already seated, eleven teenage girls among them. Eleven potential students!

They have a good plan: after the rabbi introduces them, Fred will focus on the culture of Miss Oliver's School as a life-changing experience. He'll describe what he witnessed in his visits to the school as a candidate, and show how he was drawn to the school, how he fell in love. Then Francis will focus on the excellence of the teaching at Miss Oliver's School for Girls. He'll know when he stands up and looks at the faces in the audience what examples to use. Perhaps how in science the students discover the truth before they learn it, rather than the other way around, maybe history as research, maybe for English he'll teach a poem. Something short and succinct to show how charged language can be. "Two Voices in a Meadow," for instance, by Richard Wilbur, he thinks as his excitement rises and the poem sounds in his head:

> *A Milkweed*
> *Anonymous as cherubs*
> *Over the crib of God,*
> *White seeds are floating*
> *Out of my burst pod.*
> *What power had I*
> *Before I learned to yield?*
> *Shatter me great wind;*
> *I shall possess the field.*

A Stone
As casual as cow dung
Under the crib of God,
I lie where chance would have me,
Up to my ears in sod.
Why should I move? To move
Befits a light desire.
The sill of heaven would founder,
Did such as I aspire.

Yes! He'll recite the poem, then start by seeing if any of them heard how the structure of each verse mirrors the other, and go from there to get the girls thinking and talking, drawing the parents in too. Don't talk about teaching and learning, give them the experience instead. Then tomorrow, he'll mail a copy of the poem to each of the families and ask them to talk about it together. That will keep the school in their head, that will draw them in!

BUT WHEN MYRON Benjamin finishes introducing his three guests, he doesn't sit down and give the floor to Fred. He goes on talking, though it isn't really a talk, it's a meditation in which he discovers—as if he never knew—why he and his Rachel are willing to part from their beloved daughter at a time in her life they can never have with her again. First he lists the teachers' passion for their subjects, mentioning in particular Gregory van Buren, who has engendered in his daughter a love of language and a desire to write, and goes from there to claim that because the teachers expect so much of his daughter she demands even more of herself, reminding himself out loud that the other word for *subject* is *discipline.* He meditates aloud this way for a full twenty minutes or so, never once speaking of the value of single-sex education for girls.

Near the end it comes to the rabbi that great teaching is an act of love, a love that is disciplined, chosen, and that has nothing to do with whether or not the teacher likes the child. "Not like the love of my Rachel and me for Karen, our daughter. That we can hardly help, for she's our own flesh and blood," he says. "So when you choose a school, don't think so much about preparing for the future, getting into college," he tells them, leaping now to their misguided obsessions. "As if your children were squirrels hoarding for the winter. Look for that passion instead, that adoration of life. Tell me, would you withhold an education from a child who you knew was going to die before she was old enough for college?" and then he stops, coming out of his meditation like a man waking up, a little sheepish for having wandered from thought to thought, and being so personal.

What can Fred say after that? Whatever it is will be anticlimactic. Besides, two talks will be enough, three would be redundant. So, though he's disappointed not to give the talk he was so eager to give, he decides that instead of following the rabbi's talk with one of his own, he'll prove the truth of the rabbi's praise of the school by showing these people how committed the headmaster of Miss Oliver's School for Girls is to its great teachers, how much he reveres them and supports them, how much he *trusts* them. He introduces Francis Plummer as Miss Oliver's most celebrated teacher, who embodies the school as much as any one person can. So much more empowering of himself publicly to give the floor to the little creep than have him steal it like he did in San Francisco!

As Francis stands up, it doesn't even cross his mind that he won't talk, as planned, about great teaching at Miss Oliver's School for Girls. But when he opens his mouth to speak he knows he won't. He can see on the faces of the audience that they are thinking about the rabbi's talk, building on his thoughts, making them their own. Francis is disappointed. He wants to give his talk, he wants to teach this poem he loves so much! But he's much too good a teacher not to know that what's needed right now is not for him to talk, but to invite questions about the school in which Myron Benjamin has caused so much interest.

When he begins, it is soon obvious to him that some of the questions are best answered by Nan, or Fred, or even the Benjamins, and so he directs them to the appropriate person. The result is that the questions are answered well; the guests, already inspired by the rabbi, are satisfied that the school is managed judiciously and see how well Miss Oliver's people work together. When Nan finishes her slide show a few minutes later, the audience applauds, and before they leave, several families ask Nan for an application. Clearly, the evening's been a success.

After the guests leave, the Benjamins invite the three recruiters to sit with them at the kitchen table to drink coffee for a few minutes before the drive home. Francis is delighted with this lingering: a chance to savor his satisfaction over his part in the evening's success. He's been a good teammate to Fred Kindler, feels the beginning of his redemption. He leans back in his chair, sips the coffee, feels his muscles relax.

"You did a wonderful job," he hears Fred Kindler say, and for an instant thinks Fred's talking to him, but then he sees that Kindler's directed the comment to Myron Benjamin, sitting close to him on his right. "Coming from a parent rather than a staffer—"

"It was a pleasure," the rabbi interrupts, he doesn't need this praise. But Francis does. His disappointment's a surprise. He's waiting now for Kindler to acknowledge his work too, his decision not to give a talk, his deft handling of the questions.

But that doesn't happen because now Rachel Benjamin is explaining that she and her husband would have started recruiting for Miss Oliver's three years ago, as soon as they saw how Karen was thriving there, if they hadn't heard the rumors that the school might have to close. "That's right," Myron Benjamin agrees. "We didn't want to entice families into a school that might not be able to stay the course for them. But then the changes were made," he says, looking right at Francis now and choosing those neutral words on purpose, "and that was the sign for Rachel and me that the school was going to make it."

"Yes!" Nan says. Fred says nothing, and, for a different reason, neither does Francis.

The rabbi, who could not have survived for fifteen years in his position merely being a man of God and not a politician too, goes on. "It was typical of Marjorie Boyd that after having built this wonderful school she had the grace to step aside," he says, and watches Nan's face, and now he knows that's exactly what Marjorie didn't do. So he turns toward Fred and says, "I followed in the footsteps of a longtime charismatic person just as you have. It wasn't easy," and then he waits for one of them to say what needs to be said so he doesn't have to, and when no one does he goes on. "But I had an assistant who'd been here almost as long as my predecessor, and he said all the right things."

"Like what?" Nan asks, and Francis hears the fierceness in her voice.

"We didn't have any meetings like tonight, where nobody except Rachel and me remembers Mrs. Boyd," Myron Benjamin says, as if he'd already answered Nan's question.

"Like what?" Nan asks again.

"Like telling everybody who remembers Mrs. Boyd that the new headmaster is exactly the right person. That has to be the point of every recruiting meeting, doesn't it? Since everybody who remembers Mrs. Boyd already loves the school." And then he turns to Francis and asks, "That is the kind of meeting you'll be having from now on, isn't it?" and when Francis doesn't answer right away: "Where lots of the people will remember her?"

"Well, is it or isn't it?" Nan says. But Francis still doesn't answer.

Rachel Benjamin turns to her husband then, puts her hand on his. She knows when her husband should stop. "Dear, we need to let these people go," she says. "They have a long ride home," and Myron sends her a little look of thanks and stands up to help his visitors with their coats and ushers them out and into their car.

On the long drive home, Francis burns. It's one thing to support the man, he thinks, but to have to lie, to have to get up in public and praise him when I think he's absolutely the wrong guy for the job. When he made up his mind to fulfill his responsibility as the head's right-hand man, he didn't think of *this. I* didn't choose Fred Kindler, he tells himself. I would have known better. Up front Fred is driving and pretending to listen to the radio, and Nan is pretending to sleep.

The bastard! Francis thinks. The manipulator! Thinking of how Karen's father worked the conversation so that he could nail him. But his anger is hollow, he knows. All the rabbi did was tell the truth. "All right," he says at last, to the back of Fred Kindler's head, "I'll do it."

"Do what?" Fred asks. Francis sees him looking in the mirror to find his face.

"What the rabbi says," Francis answers. He can't bring himself to put it into words.

Fred doesn't answer, just keeps driving on in the dark

"Well?" Francis asks. "Is that how we're going to do it, or not?"

"It's up to you," Fred says. He's damned if he's going to beg Francis Plummer for praise!

And for the rest of the drive neither of them speaks again, and Nan White keeps on pretending to sleep.

LATE IN THE AFTERNOON of December 14, the investigators report that every suspect student's name is cleared. The best evidence they can gather suggests the cause of the fire was faulty wiring. The next morning before the school breaks at noon for winter vacation, Fred announces this fact to the school, going on to tell them how optimistic they can all be when school begins again in January, after we've had a rest and the work of choosing the architect for the new library will have begun. There is a visible relief among the students, but Fred knows, and so do they, that once the insult of suspicion has been made, it takes a long time to melt away.

Soon after the students file out of the assembly, some of them get on a bus to be taken to Bradley Airport. Parents start showing up on campus to drive the others home. One of these is Mavis Ericksen. Before even speaking to her daughter she goes directly to Fred's office, getting there before either he or Margaret returns from the assembly. She's sitting in one of the chairs in front of his desk when he arrives.

"Oh, hello!" he says, failing to hide his surprise and irritation at her barging in like this. She doesn't return his greeting, just crosses her legs and waits for him to sit—as if it were her office, not his—and in spite of himself, his eyes wander to those amazing legs of hers. He can tell she's caught him looking. She's got this little victory already.

"You told me you were going to evaluate Joan Saffire in November," she says. "Well, it's November. Have you fired her yet?"

He hesitates, trying to decide: does he explain to her—as if she didn't already know!—that it's none of her business?

"Well, have you or haven't you?"

"Fired who?" he says, putting his hand to his ear as if he didn't hear her.

"Why are you resisting me?" she asks him. "Who do you think you are?" And when he doesn't answer, "You heard me. Joan Saffire. Have you fired her yet?"

"Oh, Joan Saffire!" he exclaims. "That's who we're talking about." Then, stroking his chin, "What was the question again?"

"Have you fired her!"

"No."

"No?"

"As a matter of fact, I just promoted her," he says, a great big lie, he hasn't done anything of the kind. He doesn't even evaluate Joan Saffire. Dorothy Strang, does that. "Gave her a big fat raise too," he goes on. "Biggest raise I ever gave anyone." He's amazed at himself, he's never acted so crazy. But it's the first real fun he's had in four frustrating months. He's not sure he'll regret this later even when she pays him back. "I think I'll hire her sister too," he says.

She's staring at him.

"Anything else you want to know?" Fred asks. "I have an appointment."

"Who do you think you are?" Mavis asks again. This time it's not a rhetorical question. She wants to know.

"The headmaster," he says, standing up. "I do the hiring. And I do the firing. And you don't."

A look of surprise flits across her face. She graduated from Wellesley, her husband's an MBA from Harvard, they own a big house in Old Lyme, her daughter will get early admission to any college she wants. Everything's always come out just the way she's planned.

"Oh!" she says. "Oh! Oh!" and then she's out the door, her high heels raining on the floor as she crosses Margaret Rice's anteroom.

A minute later, he's in Margaret's anteroom too, on his way home. He's promised Gail they'd drive to the shore together, spend the afternoon walking on the beach. "I'm through for the day," he tells her.

She doesn't answer. But she's smiling at him—a surprise, until he realizes why: Margaret doesn't have any more use for Mavis Ericksen than he does. Mavis was one of the ones who helped get rid of Marjorie, one of the leaders of the pack. He returns Margaret's smile, then leaves the office to begin his winter break.

BOOK THREE

WINTER TERM

NINETEEN

IT IS VERY COLD, and new snow sparkles in the sun as the winter term begins. The occasional storms that replenish the snow, and the days of sunshine in between, preserve this loveliness all through a January that Fred Kindler will remember later as the time when he was most convinced he could save the school.

In the first week of the new term, three of the families who attended the recruiting event at the Benjamins' home visit the school, like what they see, and promise to apply. The school they visit isn't sick anymore with the suspicion that someone inside the community burned the library down, for now that the charred bones of the library foundation are covered in virginal snow, the memory of that grim time before the students' names were cleared recedes. The committee to select the architect has begun its work, and the belief that the new library will be even better than the old one spreads across the campus.

Most important, Hannah Fingerman's two-million-dollar pledge, which the board made public as soon as the lawyers assured them it would be fulfilled, has much reduced the fear that the school will close, and thus one of the reasons for not applying has been removed. Accordingly, Nan White is able to report an increase in the rate of inquiries and of visits to the campus. Though the numbers are far short of those needed to reach Fred's goal of twenty-six new students enrolled for next year, the two million dollars will underwrite the shortfall and provide more time for the marketing efforts to take effect. Even with no increase in enrollment, the school could survive for at least another year, thanks to Hannah's gift.

The beauty of the winter brings no joy, though, to Francis and Peggy Plummer, who are still living apart, Francis continuing as the guest of Michael Woodward in the rectory and Peggy still mothering their dorm alone. They are so dreary and lonely that they live in a state of continual surprise that they are still apart, and this surprise makes them so angry with each other and themselves that it grows more difficult each day either for Peggy to give in and invite him back or for Francis to insist on returning.

If Francis were to bang on the door, Peggy wouldn't refuse him—especially if he brought with him a sincere belief in the rightness of Fred Kindler's leadership, and a relinquishment of his pagan yearnings, two issues that in Peggy's troubled heart have melded into one. But all she really needs is for him to insist on coming home—and then insist some more. When you kick your husband out of the house, he's supposed to try to come back.

Father Woodward, who true to his promise continues to pray for them both and can't bear to see them apart, would love to say to them that their marriage vows have nothing to do with who is loyal to whom at Miss Oliver's School for Girls. But Father Woodward, a dreamer, unversed in politics, who'll never be elected bishop, would fail to convince Francis. Even more than when he came rushing home from the West determined to redeem himself in Peggy's eyes by redeeming himself at school, Francis believes he needs to help Fred Kindler save the school before he can reclaim his marriage. When that is done, he'll bang on her door and won't take no for an answer.

Nevertheless, Father Woodward, who really does believe in Everything, is still convinced of the other advice he'd love to give to Francis not to abandon the spiritual questing that was part of why he went out West. Don't do that to save your marriage, he would say. That's too high a price to pay, for you'd only be bringing part of yourself to her. You tried that for years and were always hungry. But we already know that's not how Michael Woodward works. He thinks people should figure things out for themselves.

In fact, Father Woodward needs to apply this theory to himself. For he is so unselfishly focused on the needs of others that he hasn't figured out yet how closely his own spiritual yearnings have begun to mirror those his friend is determined to ignore. He does know how his heart went out to Francis when Francis told him about his abortive sojourn in the Nevada desert: how grace would not come, and he fled in his car to a plastic motel in Winnemucca. Michael can see himself staying in the desert much longer than Francis did—his own version of the forty days—breathing the spirit that inhabits the earth and quickens us all. But he's not ready yet to understand that within a year or two he will no longer be able to so constrain his beliefs that they can be summarized by anything so human centered, and so specific, as the Nicene Creed. He can't see far enough ahead to know the time will come when he won't be able to lead his congregation as they recite that creed; and therefore, an honest man, he will resign.

But he does know that he won't much longer be Francis's host in the rectory. He will not be co-conspirator with Peggy and Francis in the destruction of their marriage by providing Francis this sanctuary. So if

Francis doesn't soon decide on his own to return to live with Peggy, Father Woodward will make that happen by refusing to let him stay any longer as his guest. He'll kick Francis out of his house just as Peggy kicked him out of hers. If necessary, he'll put Francis's belongings on the front porch and lock the door and tell him to go home.

A very painful moment in these first weeks of the winter term comes, for both Francis Plummer and Fred Kindler, early in a recruiting event in West Hartford, when, as Myron Benjamin told him he should, and as he promised he would, Francis declares that Fred is exactly the right person to head Miss Oliver's School for Girls. Francis hates himself for his hypocrisy, but he forces the words out, going so far as to list the same qualities the board listed in its letter to the community announcing Fred's appointment: absolute integrity, passion for single-sex education for girls, appreciation of great teaching, skills at managing finances and marketing. Francis makes this short speech with considerable aplomb.

But he only does this once. As he speaks, he watches Kindler's expression. It's all the poor man can do to keep from squirming in his seat while Francis talks. Kindler simply doesn't have it in him—he isn't *that* good a politician—to hear words of praise delivered in public by a man he doesn't trust. Well, that's all right with me, Francis thinks, his small admiration for Fred Kindler grudgingly rising one notch. And so without saying a word to each other, they make a pact: never again.

Nevertheless, that recruiting event and the two that follow in January go quite well, and Fred's spirits continue to rise and are still flourishing on a morning a month later in mid-February when he looks up from his desk to see Peggy Plummer in his office doorway.

He jumps to his feet, comes out from behind his desk to greet her.

"Can we talk?" Peggy asks, closing the door behind her.

"Of course we can talk," motioning to one of the chairs in front of his desk. He's puzzled. They've always been able to talk.

"I mean *really* talk." She remains standing in front of her chair.

He moves to the chair facing hers, but, since she hasn't sat down yet, he doesn't either. "I hope I've never been hard for you to talk to," he says.

"Not yet."

"Well, then test me this time," he smiles. Peggy sits down now, so he does too.

"I don't like any of the architects in the competition. Not one of them!" she says. "All their ideas seem so wrong to me."

"All wrong? Peggy!"

"Why change so *much?*" she asks him. "Everybody loved the old library. Some people even called it the new library."

He hesitates, remembering how long her list was under *preserve* and how short under *change*. He should have paid more attention.

"You haven't answered my question," she persists. "Change isn't *always* good."

"Peggy," he begins, "I understand how you feel."

"It's not that," she exclaims. "Don't tell me it is!" She's about to go on, to insist there's nothing wrong with her judgment, she's perfectly open to change—which of course everyone says when you ask—but there's a knock on the door, so she stops talking, and Margaret Rice steps in.

"Yes?" Fred asks, letting his irritation show. The last thing he needs is an interruption. He needs to focus on *this*. Even Peggy Plummer's not going to talk him out of the opportunity to create a better library.

"It's urgent," Margaret says, pointing to the phone, and right away he knows the bad news he's about to hear.

It's a Mr. Singleton, Hannah Fingerman's lawyer, telling Fred that Hannah's ex-husband has decided to contest her right to the funds. Whatever weaknesses Hannah's former spouse has as a businessman, he seems to have considerable resolve as a litigant, according to Singleton, who tells Fred that Hannah's ex has hired a very substantial law firm to work on a contingency basis. It will be a long time before the case is resolved. In the meantime the funds are not Hannah's to give away.

"How long?" Fred asks.

The lawyer hesitates. "A long time; maybe years."

"How *many* years?" One? Ten? Twenty-seven? he wants to ask, but controls himself and doesn't.

"How do I know? It could be five." Singleton sounds exasperated now. "After all, you gave them a great angle to work with, and they found it right away."

"I don't understand," Fred says. He tries to keep his face blank so Peggy won't know what this call's about. Alan Travelers should be the first to hear this news.

"As you know, Ms. Fingerman put very specific language into the gift declaration," Singleton explains. "It stated that the gift was in honor of the anthropological thrust that distinguishes the curriculum of Miss Oliver's School."

"Oh, I see," Fred murmurs, because now he does, and it's all he can think of to say. He knows what Singleton is going to tell him next.

"And then to make matters *worse,* Ms. Fingerman provided the precise ammunition her ex-husband's attorney needed by specifically stating that this distinguishing curriculum emanated from, is based on, and is still inspired by, the Pequot Collection," Singleton goes on, his voice rising exactly one note with each of this triad of phrases.

"Oh, damn!" Fred says.

"I quote," Mr. Singleton says. "Those are the exact words."

"Yes," Fred agrees. "They were."

"I believe she wanted to honor the school librarian, a Mrs. Plummer."

"I guess so," Fred says.

"So, when the Collection went up in smoke—"

"All right, Mr. Singleton, that's enough. You don't have to explain."

But the lawyer's too amazed at the stupidity of others to stop. "Without that specificity in the language we would have a slam-dunk case," he complains.

"Really, Mr. Singleton? Well then where in the world were *you?*"

"Not involved, I assure you," Singleton answers huffily. "Ms. Fingerman has fired her attorney and engaged me. And I can't resist pointing out that your school attorney was also careless."

I doubt that he knew the library was going to burn down, Fred wants to say; but of course he can't, not with Peggy there.

"It's important to be prepared for every possible contingency," Mr. Singleton lectures, as if reading Fred's mind. "If that had been the case, the school would be receiving these funds in a few weeks from now at the most."

That's all Fred can take, he's about to burst. He cuts the lawyer off: if Peggy weren't here, he'd be standing up and yelling into the phone at this pompous twerp. He'd be quoting Milton Perkins on lawyers. "Thank you, Mr. Singleton," he says instead. "Keep me informed," and hangs up abruptly.

"You OK?" Peggy asks.

"Yeah," he says, and she knows whatever it is, he doesn't want to talk about it.

"So where were we?" he asks.

"Later" she says, starting to stand. "You've got something heavy to deal with, I can tell."

He waves her back down. "It can wait a few minutes," he says.

And then it dawns on her. How could it have taken her so long to guess? She saw how his face fell. "I think I know what you just learned," she murmurs, and Fred moves his hand in front of his face in that dismissive gesture that she knows drives Francis crazy, letting her know that she's guessed right and that he's not going to talk about it. He never really counted on the gift coming through anyway, he tells himself. Always felt a little dishonest for pretending that he thought it would. It was just a teaser, a promised rescue waved in front of our eyes to make us happy for a few short months, and then yanked away, he thinks. Yet, God, he's disappointed!

Besides, he's determined not to put Peggy off. She's going to grieve even more when she finds out that the library's burning down is what delays, maybe even cancels forever, the gift that was going to save the school "Peg, I'm going to be honest with you," he tells her, changing his mind about gentling her. The time to be assertive is now, it's the kindest way. "We're not going to base our decision on which architect we pick—"

"You don't have to tell me you're going to be honest," she interrupts. "You could never be anything else."

Now she's worried she's going to cry. But not in front of him, she won't do that to him. She hates it when women use tears for leverage. "I'm out of here," she says. "You've got enough on your plate." She flees through Margaret's office and goes straight to her apartment. She needs to be alone to think.

Maybe it's the shock of learning there isn't going to be any two million dollars to save the school that keeps her from seeing that she's acting just like Francis. Her emotions are all a jumble, she doesn't want things to change. It isn't only nostalgia for her library that makes her want to beg Fred Kindler to replicate it. When the library was standing, she and Francis were together. How can she ask Fred to fix that?

One thing she is clear about: she's not going to sit around waiting for something to happen to fix her marriage. She's going to do something, and do it soon.

AFTER LEAVING A MESSAGE for Alan Travelers, Fred steps out into Margaret Rice's anteroom. "I'll be back in ten minutes," he tells her. "I need a little walk."

"Have I guessed right what that lawyer fella told you?" she asks.

At first he thinks she must be gloating. Then he knows she isn't. In spite of the grudge she harbors, she wants the same thing he does. "No comment," he answers.

"Damn!" she says

"Yes." he says. "Damn."

"Well, take a good walk. You deserve a break," she says, to his surprise. "I'll take care of Gregory until you get back," she adds, reminding him that he has an appointment—*another* one—with the head of the English department. "Maybe while he waits for you he can explain to me why *Moby Dick* isn't as boring as everybody but English teachers knows it is," she says, surprising him even more with a hint of a smile.

Ten minutes later, while Gregory waits in Margaret's anteroom, Fred talks to Alan, who has returned his call. It doesn't take long. Travelers is not the type to spend time bemoaning events he can't control. "I'll call an emergency meeting of the board for the day after tomorrow in the afternoon," he tells Fred. "That will give us time to get as many members as possible together to decide what we should do, and we'll do it in our New York offices. That's the easiest place to gather trustees from around the country at such short notice."

"Good," Fred says.

"And Fred?"

"Yes?"

"I can't tell you how glad I am that in times like these we have you to be the boss."

"Thanks, Alan. I'll have a recommendation ready for the meeting."

"No, you won't, Fred. Let us do that."

"That makes me feel like a chicken, Alan."

"So be a chicken. We need you around."

"Well, I'll think about that."

"Don't think about it. Just do it. It's an order."

Fred doesn't answer.

"And in the meantime just hang in there, my friend," Alan says. "Just keep going as if nothing's happened. I know you will." Then he hangs up.

FRED STANDS UP as Gregory enters, but he doesn't come around his desk. The last thing he needs right now is to have to pretend he interested in one of Gregory's legion of worries. But didn't his board chair just remind him that it's his job to keep on as if nothing's happened?

Gregory sits in one of the chairs facing the desk. "Good morning," he says, and draws breath for small talk.

"Good morning," Fred responds, and glances at his watch.

Gregory looks disappointed, lets out his breath.

"Yes?" says Fred.

"I've come to report on *Clarion* affairs," Gregory tells him. "As faculty advisor," he adds.

"And?"

"Thus to facilitate your decision."

"My decision?"

"Yes. It won't be difficult once you've heard what is in the article."

"Which article?"

"You haven't heard?"

"The head's the last to hear certain things, Mr. Van Buren," Fred says. "But I can guess which article." Well, here it is at last, he thinks. He's been waiting for this shoe to drop since his talk with Karen Benjamin in September.

"Karen Benjamin's done research," Gregory tells him. "Lots of it. She's given every senior a questionnaire about sex. She's written an article."

"About sex?"

Gregory makes a face, a stagy gesture that irritates Fred. "How many are sexually active and how many are not," Gregory explains.

"Really?"

"It's quite detailed, I'm afraid."

"Really? Is it a good article?"

"Of course not! I think it's disgusting!"

"Disgusting? You mean it's pornographic? Explicit?"

"No, it's not *pornographic*. It's just not the kind of thing—"

"That should be in a school newspaper?"

"That's right." Gregory is beginning to look confused.

"Especially of a *girls'* school."

"Oh, yes, especially a girls' school!" exclaims Gregory, his face brightening.

"Well, then, tell her she can't print it," Fred says.

Gregory's face goes pale. "Me?" he asks.

"You're the advisor to the *Clarion*, Mr. Van Buren," Fred says. He's beginning to enjoy this.

"The headmistress, uh, Mrs. Boyd used—"

"To make all these decisions," Fred finishes Gregory's sentence again. Gregory nods.

"Which you thought was kind of dictatorial, I believe. And you didn't even agree with her when she let the kids print this kind of thing, am I right?"

"Yes, but—"

"Well, *I'm* not a dictator, Mr. Van Buren. "I'm a delegator. You've told me, rather often, that you like that about me. And you're the advisor to the *Clarion*, and you don't think that Karen should print the article. So here's your chance."

"But—"

Fred stands up. "Just do it," he says. "Just tell her your decision. Make sure she knows it's *yours*. And make it stick." He puts his hand on Gregory's elbow, ushers him to the door.

He has to admit he feels a little better now.

GREGORY GOES STRAIGHT to the *Clarion* office to see Karen. He's so nervous he needs to get this over with.

Karen's sitting at her desk when he enters the office. She looks up at him. "Good morning," she says. "I've been expecting you."

Her greeting sounds like a challenge to him. Moreover, she's sitting down at *her* desk in *her* office, while he's standing up, like a supplicant.

"Karen—" he begins.

"Could you sit down, please Mr. Van Buren?" she interrupts. "You make me nervous standing there."

"Sit where?" Gregory huffs. "All these chairs have papers piled up in them."

"How about that one?" Karen answers brightly, pointing to the chair nearest her desk. "Here," she says, reaching for the papers Gregory has picked up from the chair.

"Actually, you look nervous too." She knows what he's here for, and she's going to make him pay!

He doesn't answer.

"I like it messy like this, don't you?" Because she knows he's a stickler for neatness. "When things are messy it means people are busy."

"No, it doesn't," Gregory finally speaks. "It just means they're messy."

Karen shrugs. "What can I do for you?"

He draws breath, starts to answer; she cuts him off. "How'd you like my article?"

He doesn't answer

"It's good, isn't it?"

"It's inappropriate."

"But I asked whether you thought it was *good* or not."

He hesitates. She's not about to give him time to frame his answer. "You know it is," she says, smiling. "It's everything you taught. Well organized, great quotations, a subject everyone is interested in, everything substantiated—facts, figures."

"Karen, you know very well it's not appropriate. This is a school."

"Just tell me, is it good or isn't it?"

He nods, starts to speak.

"It tells the truth, doesn't it?"

"I don't know whether it does or not," Gregory hedges. "I don't really want to know about the students' sex lives."

"That's my point," Karen says. "It does what good reporting does: tells the people who want to keep on not knowing what they need to know about what the people who are written about already know."

Gregory doesn't say anything, he's taking in her comment, as he does in his class when somebody makes an interesting point. "All right," he finally concedes. "You've won that point."

"It's a model, isn't it? If it were for a magazine, not a school newspaper—"

"Yes, it's very good."

"Thank you. That's what I wanted to hear. From you. If you told me it wasn't good, I'd write it over. Anybody else, and I'd tell him he's wrong."

"All right," he says. "I've told you. It's very good."

"And you're here to tell me the headmaster says I can't print it."

"No, Karen, not the headmaster."

"It's not surprising," she says.

"You didn't hear me, Karen. *I'm* telling you."

"No, you aren't," she says. Her voice is neutral. There's no anger in it; she's just telling a fact. *"You're* not telling me. Because *he* told you to tell me."

Gregory looks stunned, as if he's been slapped in the face. "How do you know?" he challenges.

"Hey!" she says. "Big Momma's gone. The new guy wants everybody to grow up. And you tried just now. But it was too late, wasn't it? Because you'd already gone to him." She can see by his expression that she's guessed right.

"You're being insolent," Gregory warns.

"If *I* were the advisor to the *Clarion* and some kid wanted to print an article I didn't think should be printed, I wouldn't go to the boss about it first," Karen says. "I wouldn't even tell him. I'd make my own decision."

"You're being very impolite," Gregory repeats.

"Sorry," she says. "I didn't plan to be impolite. It's just that it's true, that's all," she adds with a little apologetic shrug. She feels a small sadness taking the place of her resentment. It's not the first time this year that she's had the sense she's caught up with him, some of the other teachers too, ex-heroes. She doesn't need them anymore, it's time to graduate and say good-bye. "Really," she says. "I apologize."

"I accept," Gregory answers—his best tactic at this point, and adds, as if he were still in a position to dispense comfort, "I know it's a disappointment not to print it."

"Hey, forget it," she says.

There's a silence now they both find embarrassing, which he has the grace to end by standing and moving to the door. But at the door he turns back to her because he can't resist. "You really ought to clean this mess up," he says.

"OK, I will," she responds. "And guess what?"

He waits.

"I could print it anyway, you know. Underground. Just Xerox it and hand it out."

"I hope you won't."

"I won't," she says, remembering her conversation with her new head-master about this issue, how straight he was with her, how clear and realistic. How *authentic*, she thinks. "You can count on it," she adds. "I won't sneak."

"A wise decision," Gregory says as firmly as he can. "A very adult decision." Then he leaves.

THAT NIGHT WHEN Sylvia sneaks out, Clarissa doesn't bother to pretend to sleep, and Sylvia makes only a little effort not to be seen as she runs across the campus to the spot where she expects Charley to be waiting for her in the Subaru. In the back of her mind, she knows she wants to get caught so she'll be kicked out.

"We're going to blitz tonight," Charley told her on the phone. "Party city!" Why is he talking that way? she wondered. He never talked that way before. But he hung up the phone before she asked. It's not the party she cares about. It's the chance to talk with Charley, to be alone with her brother, for the half hour it takes to get to Trinity.

Fifteen yards from the car she can tell even in the dark that it's Robin, not Charley. She walks the rest of the way, gets in the car beside him.

"Hello. I thought you'd like a real date," Robin says.

She knows he means a date with a brother isn't real. It's a huge disappointment. He's not my brother anymore, she wants to protest. "Well, OK. Thanks," she says instead. They have very little to say to each other on the way to the Trinity campus.

Inside the fraternity house, the room is crowed with dancers. The rock band is across the room from the door, playing so loud it's impossible to talk. There's a big shiny aluminum beer keg in each corner of the room. Sylvia looks for Charley, can't see him anywhere. Robin takes her hand, and they squeeze further into the room and begin to dance.

She likes moving to the rhythm. Her unhappiness lifts and flies away. It gets hotter in the crowded space, bodies bump into each other. "I smell weed," she shouts at Robin. "Get me some." But he shakes his head. All right, she thinks. I've got all night. She lets herself go, swaying her hips, rolling her shoulders, waving her arms above her head. Opposite her, Robin's graceful for such a big guy, dancing just as hard as she is. But there's a serious look on his face, a frown in his forehead, as if he were concentrating to avoid mistakes, and suddenly she doesn't want to be with him anymore. She wants to dance with someone uncaged and crazy. "I need a beer," she yells, but he shakes his head. She dances further away from him. She's dancing alone now. Or maybe she's dancing with everyone, she doesn't care which.

A few minutes later the band stops to take a break, and she pushes her way through the crowd to one of the kegs. There's a puddle of beer at her feet. She doesn't like the smell of it. She fills a plastic cup and chugs it down, then fills it again and chugs that too.

"Careful," she hears behind her and knows it's Robin. She ignores him, takes another slug. She doesn't really like the taste any better than the smell. She'll just get a little loose so she can really dance.

She turns around. "Where's Charley?" she says.

"I don't know," Robin says. "Making out someplace, I guess." He takes the cup from her.

She reaches for her cup of beer. He moves his hand so she can't get it. "You're my date," she says. "Not my father." The band starts up again, and she doesn't hear his answer. He takes her hand, leads her to the middle of the room, and they start to dance again.

While she dances she watches the front door. People keep coming through it, crowding the room even more, but none of them is Charley. It's hotter in the room now, and she dances even harder. Robin grabs her hand, tries a fancy move, spins her around. He's frowning again. "You're trying too hard," she yells over the music. "This isn't a job."

He spins her again and lets go, and she pretends to think he wants her to dance with someone else and moves away from him. Next thing she knows she's dancing with a boy who's half Robin's size. He's short and pudgy, but his eyes are sparkling and she likes his smile. He's got black hair and a film of sweat on his face over acne scars and dances much better than Robin. He's in the zone, on the beat without thinking, and she moves with him. Some of the dancers nearest them stop and watch. The crowd hoots and cheers, and, lost in the music, Sylvia is as happy as she's been for weeks.

When it stops, the boy puts his arm around her waist and pulls her to him. "Hey, hey, hey!" he says "What a great dancer!" Their hips touch; she feels his sweat. Her own too, her blouse is soaked through. "That was great!" the boy says and lets her go, moving off.

She heads back to a keg. Near it a girl is passed out on a sofa. Next to her, a boy sits stroking her hair. The sofa is ripped, the innards showing. Sylvia fills a plastic cup and chugs it. The boy on the sofa gets up and stands beside her. "Where'd you come from? Who robbed the cradle?" he asks. Silvia fills her cup again, turns to the boy, looks him in the face, and chugs the beer down.

"I can do that too," the boy says. He fills a cup, faces her, and chugs it. "Now, what else can you do?" he says.

She gives him a little smile, fills her cup again, and very deliberately pours the beer on his head.

He doesn't move a muscle. He grins while the beer runs down over his hair and onto his shoulders. Then he fills his cup and, just as deliberately, empties it on her head.

She doesn't move either while the cold sticky beer soaks her hair and runs down over her shoulders into her blouse. Then she fills her cup and pours it on his head.

Now a little crowd gathers to watch. They cheer with each pouring.

This game seems to Sylvia to go on forever. The group of watchers gets bigger, the cheers louder with each pouring. Suddenly she feels dizzy. She feels her lips twitching, her eyes rolling in their sockets. "Oh, shit!" she hears the boy say. "She's going to barf." He drops his cup, escapes back to the sofa. Sylvia turns away, gets out the door, and throws up on the lawn.

The next thing she knows she's sitting on a bench on the lawn, shivering with the cold, and Charley's standing over her. A girl stands next to Charley. "You passed out," Charley says. His lips are red with lipstick and the girl's lipstick is smeared. "Robin's getting the car," Charley says. "Bringing it as close as he can so you don't have to walk. He'll drive you back to school."

"No, you," she says.

Charley turns to his date.

"That's fine, Charley," the girl says. "I don't mind. But I'm going to drive. You're a little drunk."

A minute or so later, Robin brings the car up into the driveway. "We'll take her home," Charley says to him.

Robin frowns and shakes his head.

"I'm driving," the girl says, and Robin smiles and gets out of the car. After all, who wants to be with a girl who's throwing up? He helps Sylvia into the backseat. "You'll be all right," he says. "Next time be more careful."

Sylvia's sick once more on the way home. She just has time to get her head through the window. She makes a mess on the outside of the car door.

"That's all right," Charley says. "I'll just get a hose and it'll be fine."

"Don't worry about it," the girl says kindly. "It happened to me once too." Sylvia realizes she doesn't know her name. She's too tired and sick and embarrassed to ask.

When they get back to school, Charley holds her arm while they sneak across the campus. He leaves her by the window to her room. This time Clarissa doesn't pretend to be asleep. "It's three o'clock in the morning!" she says. Sylvia doesn't answer. "You smell awful," Clarissa says. She sits up, turns on the light.

"I'm sorry," Sylvia says.

"I'll help you with a shower so you don't fall down and drown," Clarissa says.

"No, I'm all right." Sylvia goes into the bathroom, turns on the shower, and gets under it with her clothes on to get the smell out. Then she strips and showers and comes back to the room. The light's still on, and Clarissa's sitting up.

"You're going to flunk out if you keep this up," Clarissa says.

"I know I am," Sylvia says. She has a history test tomorrow she hasn't studied for, and a paper due for Mr. Van Buren the day after that she hasn't begun. Clarissa turns the light out, and Sylvia gets into bed. She wants to think about Charley and that girl, both smeared with lipstick. But the room whirls around and around, and she can't think about anything. Finally at dawn she falls asleep.

"CLOSE HER DOWN then," Milton Perkins mutters two days later, thirty stories above the street in New York City. "She's run her course. Just close the old girl down."

"Well, that's the question, isn't it?" Travelers asks in a somber voice.

"Well, *isn't* it?" he repeats.

Two chairs to the right of Perkins, Sonja McGarvey reaches across Barbara Tuckerman, a rigidly erect silver-blonde in her fifties, and lightly lays her fingers on Milton's hand. The red of Sonja's fingernails flashes against the starched white of Perkins's cuff. "Please, Milton," Sonja says, her voice as quiet as if she and he were the only people in the room. Perkins turns to her, his face registering mild surprise, and Barbara Tuckerman slides her chair back from the table, as if escaping from a scene that should take place in private. "A coed school is better than no school at all," Sonja says. "I really want you to believe that." Perkins doesn't take his hand away, and he does keep his suddenly gentle eyes on Sonja's face. But he moves his head from left to right and back again, as if rejecting a gift.

"Oh, come on, surely there's another alternative," Barbara exclaims. This is the first meeting she has attended since Fred's appointment. "I believe emphatically that we should simply soldier on as Miss Oliver's School for Girls," she announces. "And I repeat, *for Girls*. We've been doing it for years."

"You got two million dollars?" Perkins asks her, and Sonja just looks away and rolls her eyes. Fred wants to yell, That's exactly the problem: you've been doing it for years!

Instead, he uses the excuse of Barbara Tuckerman's naïveté—which he's not sure isn't fake—to sum up the situation all over again. Some of these people have been drifting so long, he needs to stick it between their eyes. "We need twenty-six new enrollments for next year," he reminds them. "We can hope for fifteen, but I can safely predict only ten. Now without the Fingerman gift to tide us over, if we do only get ten, we'll run out of cash around the beginning of next year's winter term. If we get lucky and get fifteen, we can last about two weeks longer. We just won't have any more money!" There! he says to himself. How's that? Do you understand *that?*

"Oh, our poor school!" Charlotte Reynolds moans.

"This is what we get for letting Marjorie do *our* job," Mavis Ericksen declares, and when no one responds: "Well, it's true isn't it? Why do you think John and Charlotte and I got ourselves on the board?" she says, pointing down the table at John Williamson, who joined the board the same time she and Charlotte did. "If the alumnae knew how the rest of you let that ridiculous Boyd woman go on and on, they'd sue you."

"All right, Mavis," Travelers tries to interrupt. "Let's not go there."

"They'd take you right to court and get every penny you've got—if they didn't shoot you first."

"And they'd be right!" Charlotte says.

"But I'll be goddamned if I'm going to vote to let boys in!" Mavis finishes.

"So I move that we close the school at the end of this year," Perkins says. His voice is calm, resigned.

Silence.

"Well?" asks Perkins.

"Let's not go quite so fast, Milton," Travelers says—though he knows they have reached the moment of decision. He doesn't want anyone even to suspect they haven't studied everything, examined every possible way out of this. So in the way of most boards when faced with such a calamity, they spend an hour and a half going over all the numbers again as if they didn't already know everything the numbers could possibly tell them. As expected, they learn nothing new; and so they turn to the concept of operating with a skeleton crew, and Fred explains once again what they already know about critical mass: how, since foreign language teachers don't teach math and math teachers don't teach English—and so on—a certain number of teachers is needed, no matter how few students there are to support them. Finished with this, with hopes even more rapidly descending, they examine the possibility of closing part of the campus, even renting some of the buildings out, the theater, for example, to the local amateur repertoire company, which happens, Sonja, informs them, having already looked into this at Fred's request, to have the use of Fieldington High School's auditorium for free. She and Travelers and Perkins and also new member John Williamson have examined every possibility of creating revenue via use of campus—including the tax implications— and even selling timber from the seventy-acre wood lot. They go over all of it again with the rest of the board, and at the end no one contradicts Sonja when she sums it up as a pipe dream to think that any of this can save the school.

In the ensuing silence Perkins says again, "I move we close the school at the end of the academic year."

No one says a thing.

"That gives the kids time to find another school and the faculty to get hired someplace else," Perkins adds. "We should make the decision now; it's only fair."

"Is there a second?" Travelers asks.

Silence again. Fred and Travelers look at each other. Travelers makes a tiny gesture with his eyebrows, acknowledging the moment.

"I move we accept boys," says Sonja.

"Just a minute," Travelers says. "We have another motion on the table."

"Yeah, well it's not getting any action, is it?" Sonja says.

"Why isn't it?" murmurs Perkins. "What's everybody afraid of?"

"Any second to the motion to close the school?" Traveler's asks again. He looks around the room.

Silence.

"The motion fails," Travelers announces.

"I move to accept boys," Sonja repeats.

"Second?" Travelers asks.

"Hold it. I'm not through yet," Sonja says.

Travelers waits.

"And change the name to The Oliver School."

"Get rid of *for Girls*?" Barbara Tuckerman exclaims.

"Right. No more *for Girls*—and gear Fred's marketing campaign to a coed school. Use all the same strategies he's using right now. You know damn well that'll work. Coed schools are turning kids away in droves. So the students have signed a pledge not to come back if boys are admitted? So what? Half of them will change their minds and come back anyway. We get some boys, and we enter the much bigger market of girls who want to go to school with boys. You know damn well we could get twenty-six more students in that market. Hell, just with the boys, we'll get twenty-six—"

"Second?" Travelers interrupts. "Then we can discuss."

"I abstain!" Barbara Tuckerman blurts.

Travelers looks at her for what seems like minutes. "We're not there yet, Ms. Tuckerman," he says at last.

"Let's call the question," says Sonja.

"We can't," Travelers says. "We don't have a second." He looks around the room again. "All right," he says when no one offers a second, "I'll second the motion—just to get it on the table so we can at least discuss it."

"I'm not sure you can do that," says Sylvia Updike, the alumnae representative to the board. "Can the chair second a motion?"

"I'm doing it. Discussion. Please."

"Oh, goody!" Sonja says. "We can discuss all the details while the school goes broke. Let's start with the price of urinals."

"We can start with the fact that the boys we take won't be the best students," Beverly Monroe challenges. Ms. Monroe has recently retired from a long career in admissions work in independent schools. "I just want to point that out so it can be part of the consideration."

"Is that really why you're bringing it up?" Sonja asks across the table. "Or is it just some more bullshit?"

"Careful, Sonja," Travelers warns.

Ms. Monroe blushes. "Well, it's true," she murmurs.

"I agree. It's true," says Charlotte Reynolds. Sonja stares at her. "Well, it's *probably* true," she says.

Mavis Ericksen turns to Fred. "Mr. Kindler, is it true or isn't it?"

"It's true," Fred says. "The best will go to schools that have been coed for years." He hates this topic. Talking about kids as if there were a "best" and a "worst."

"You mean second-line? We're going to take second-line boys in?" Barbara asks.

"Beggars being choosers," Sonja mutters. "Jesus!"

"Any other discussion?" Travelers asks. No one answers. "Really?" he asks. "No questions, no thoughts? All right, then, we'll call the question. All in favor signify by raising your hand." Sonja puts her hand up. So does Travelers—obviously with reluctance. Everybody else's stays down. Travelers looks surprised. "Both motions fail," he announces.

"Big surprise!" Sonja says

"Scaredy-cats!" Perkins growls.

"I said, I abstain," Barbara Tuckerman says. Several people nod. "See?" says Barbara. "People are abstaining. They're not ready. It's natural."

"This is no time for abstaining," Travelers declares. "I won't accept—"

"Alan, let's go around the table," Fred suggests. "Ask each person to say whatever she or he is thinking right now."

"I think we ought to hear what *you* think," Barbara Tuckerman interjects. "You're the headmaster. What's your recommendation?"

"The *board's* supposed to make these decisions," Alan Travelers says. "You people need to do your damn job!"

Now there's a big silence in the room. "That's right," says Sonja. "Time to step up to the plate," and Milton Perkins nods in agreement.

"We're not leaving here until *we* decide," Travelers declares. "Does everybody understand that? We're staying right here." Now it's very quiet in the room.

John Williamson turns to Travelers then. "There is a question that we *should* ask the headmaster," he says.

Travelers frowns. Either way, he clearly doesn't want this decision to be pinned on Fred—especially if the decision is to admit boys. He doesn't need a head whom everybody hates.

"It's a question for the educator," Williamson says. "The professional. It's not about which way he'd vote if he could."

"All right, ask it," Travelers says.

Williamson turns away from Travelers now, and faces Fred. "Haven't we learned enough about how to educate girls at Miss Oliver's that now we could apply that knowledge to the benefit of girls *and* boys in a coed school?"

"Of course we can," Fred says.

"Of course we can *what*?" Mavis says.

"Of course we can apply—" Fred begins.

Mavis cuts him off. "You traitor!" she hisses. "You son of a bitch!"

Travelers stares hard at Mavis.

Mavis stares right back. She starts to say something.

Travelers cuts her off. "Sonja, make your motion again," he commands. And Mavis starts to cry.

Sonja puts the forefinger of her right hand on the thumb of her left, "Admit boys," she says over the sound of Mavis's sobs. She moves to the forefinger, "Change the name to The Oliver School."

"Eliminate *Miss* too!" Charlotte exclaims.

"Yes, eliminate *Miss,* why the hell not?" Sonja moves to the second finger. "And continue with the present marketing strategies but geared to coed."

"Second?" asked Travelers.

"I second the motion!" Williamson says.

"You *too?*" from Mavis, crying.

"You promised!" Charlotte says.

"Discussion?" Travelers asks.

"We got you on to get rid of Marjorie, not to let boys in!" Charlotte says, leaning across the table at Williamson.

Travelers raps his knuckles loudly on the table. "All in favor of the motion signify by raising your hand."

Everybody except Mavis Ericksen, Milton Perkins, and Charlotte Reynolds raises a hand.

Travelers hesitates, looking straight at Fred. Then he moves his eyes around the room. "The motion passes," he announces. "This is an historic moment. Thanks for doing your job."

Mavis Ericksen gets up from her chair. She leaves her papers on the table and charges out of the room. She slams the door behind her. Fred is sure she'll go straight to Sandra Petrie. "This meeting is adjourned," Travelers announces.

LATE THAT EVENING, back at the head's house after the drive from New York City, Fred hears a message left on his answering machine, and knows right away that if Gail had thought to check for calls, she would have deleted it, and he never would have heard the enraged and drunken voice stumbling over the wires: "You . . . you Quibling. Quidling. Quisling!" It's Barbara Tuckerman's voice. The prim, erect, perfectly dressed Barbara Tuckerman who moved graciously back so Sonja McGarvey could lay her hand on Milton Perkins's hand, is saying: "Thadz wha you are a fugging quisling, a real pansy, weak . . . weak." Big sigh here. Fred imagines her running a finger down a list of epithets and thinks he hears ice tinkling in a glass. "Sonabitdch," Barbara chooses from her list. "Knew the minud Mavis told me you didn' have tha guds to fire that Safford bidch we had tha wrong person." Then in the background he hears a man's voice, obviously her husband's: "Honey, please." The voice is gentle, and now Fred feels very sad. He should hang up, he knows. But he's fascinated. "Don't. You're making a fool out of yourself," the husband says, but then Barbara's voice goes even louder, drowning him out: "Shid! We'd a been better off if we'd stayed with Barjorie Moyd. At leasd she wasan a man!" Fred hears her draw a new breath, she's thinking what else to say, she's going to start all over again. He hangs up the phone.

"And I didn't even make the recommendation!" Fred says to the empty room. Then he pushes the delete button and heads for bed.

TWENTY

NOW AT EIGHT-FIFTEEN the next morning, the entire school is in the Marjorie E. Boyd Auditorium, the big doors in the back are closed, and Fred Kindler is stepping toward the lip of the stage. "Good morning," he says into the silence. There's almost no response. The students sit warily silent, bulky in their winter coats, and most of the faculty stands along the back wall near the doors, ready to retreat. If news can't wait for a regular Morning Meeting at the usual time, it must be bad. Fred nods his head. He agrees: it's much too tense in here for pleasant greetings. He introduces Alan Travelers, then sits down on a chair onstage, and feels a small relief when all the eyes come off him and on to Travelers. The board chairman stands now and calmly begins to talk.

"Yesterday the trustees resolved that beginning next September, male students will be admitted to this school," Alan Travelers says, and then he pauses. He's not going to rush through this; he'll stand here and absorb the anger, take the heat. But the response is silence and staring eyes, so he goes on, "This was the *board's* decision," he declares. "It was not the head-master's, or the faculty's, or the alumnae's; it was the board's." He pauses again. The auditorium is silent; so he finishes, explaining the factors that compelled the decision, citing the numbers twice to make sure they're understood. He accomplishes this in less than three minutes. He's clear, firm, and wholly unapologetic, and when he's finished, no one says a word, no one stirs.

Then Fred gets up and stands by Alan's side. It will be his job now to control the riot.

But there isn't any riot. For a few seconds that last forever, the students sit, and the faculty stands by the closed doors in the rear. Then Fred sees Francis Plummer turn, open one of doors, and bolt across the frozen lawn. Then the other teachers follow Francis, and the students begin to move down the aisles, and then the auditorium is empty, except for Alan Travelers and Fred Kindler, side by side on the stage.

"Well," Alan murmurs, "that was a strange reaction."

"No, it wasn't," Fred answers. "I should have predicted it." For this was exactly what happened at Mt. Gilead when it was announced the school would close: the students fled to their dorms.

Outside the auditorium, moving away from it as fast as he can, Francis stops in his tracks. For a crazy instant he thinks he'll turn around, rush back into the auditorium, tell the crowd that's coming out the doors now to turn around too and take their seats again. Then he'll climb up onto the stage, push Travelers and Kindler aside, and declare the decision void. Who has a better right than he?

But of course the fantasy dissolves as soon as he tries to think of what words to use, and he tosses it away as the absurdity it is.

Why isn't he gathering the faculty to organize a strike? he asks himself, why isn't he leading a demonstration, engineering a coup, instead of turning suddenly into a mere well-adjusted, practical man? Then it dawns on him that he's been trying hard for the last six months to become a practical man who can adjust to the facts—and besides, he's living apart from his wife, and maybe he has only grief enough for that. So he heads for a dorm to comfort the students. Before the day is over, he'll go to all the dorms except the one he wants to go to the most. For this would be the worst time, he thinks, to force himself on Peggy.

What he doesn't know is that Peggy waits for him there. Foolishly perhaps, for after all, she's the one who kicked him out. When he doesn't come, she goes through her dorm alone, speaks to each girl, and has never felt so lonely.

Fred wants to hide in his office, but makes the rounds of the dorms, showing his face, taking the heat. A few girls tell him they understand that this really was a board decision; most are too angry even to speak. Some are simply numbed by the discovery that the world is a treasonous place. He explains the board's decision over and over, trying hard to be as factual and unapologetic as Alan Travelers was.

That morning, Mavis Ericksen telephones Sandra Petrie. She needed the time since the board meeting to design a plan to present to Sandra. Otherwise some of the ideas in the plan might be Sandra's, and Mavis wouldn't be in control. Though Mavis could never admit it to herself, the real reason for her enmity toward Marjorie was not the way Marjorie ran the school; it was that Mavis couldn't control her.

The conversation is awkward. Mavis and Sandra hate each other. Sandra was fiercely loyal to Marjorie and resents this newcomer who worked so hard to get rid of her. But that's the reason that Sandra can ask Marjorie to lead the alumnae to rebel against the admission of boys and Mavis can't.

"All Mrs. Boyd needs is to have people like you invite her back," Mavis says.

Sandra hesitates. She got beat up pretty badly the last time she tried to fight back. She's not sure she's ready for another battle. She reminds Mavis that Marjorie is in Europe, and won't be back for a month.

"I know that," Mavis reassures her. "There's plenty of time after she gets back. And we can get the word out to some of the alumnae that we're doing this. They'll be ready when Mrs. Boyd steps in to lead them. And I'm sure Barbara Tuckerman will go with you. I haven't asked her because you're much more persuasive than I could ever be, and you should talk to her. And anyway, I really couldn't call last night, could I?" She knows that Sandra will understand: Barbara is usually drunk in the evenings.

A moment of silence passes while Mavis holds her breath; then Sandra says, "OK, we'll do it. I'll call Barbara right away and as soon as Marjorie returns, the two of us will pay her a call."

"Bless you!" Mavis says. "Let me know what I can do to help."

By noon, almost every student in the school, and about half the faculty, show up wearing T-shirts with the word NEVER! emblazoned in red letters across the front. And that afternoon, placards begin appearing on walls and other surfaces, including the trunks of trees. Some are hand printed, some computer produced, some obviously created in the art studio. All of them say FOR WOMEN ONLY!

The next morning, Gail Kindler gets up early to join her husband on his morning run. This, before his day begins, is the best time to be with him, to get his attention off the school and on to his family, though she knows it's really not a family anymore, it's just a couple. When they have a child—or is it if?—there'll be three, a family again, and he'll have to pay attention.

While he has one more sip of coffee, she goes outside to wait for him and almost trips on the little modeled bonfire, unlit, piled with books and sticks of kindling and little logs. She can feel the hostility of this insult that someone has snuck out of the dorms in the middle of the night to build on their doorstep, but for a few seconds she doesn't know what it means, and then, of course it comes to her. It's about the article he squelched.

So he's a book burner, a Nazi, because he wouldn't print an article about some teenage girls who like to fuck? We'll, she thinks, he'll never see it. She kicks the wood and the books off the side of the steps into the laurel bushes by the side of the house. Just in time. When he comes through the door, eager to run, he's already looking straight ahead, in the direction they will go: across the campus and to the path that goes along the riverbank where he loves to run.

She knows he's running slower than he usually does so she can keep up with him. Her hips hurt. He chats easily, points out a flock of geese grazing on a field across the river, speculates about why they don't migrate south in winter anymore, comments on the hardness of the frozen ground. She doesn't answer because she's breathing too hard; if she weren't, she would be crying.

They circle back to their house, and he goes straight in, so intent now to take a shower and get to his office, she thinks he wouldn't see it if it were still on the steps, actually burning.

That afternoon, Gregory van Buren tries to persuade Fred to outlaw the T-shirts and have the placards removed. "I'm not the gestapo, Mr. Van Buren," is Fred's weary response. He doesn't even bother to point out that for every placard removed, several others would inevitably appear in the night and chooses not to confess that besides, he admires the students for their resistance. Why should they give up?

Though the letter to parents, alumnae, and friends of the school announcing the board's decision to admit boys came from Alan Travelers as chair of the board, the majority of the responses are addressed to Fred. It doesn't surprise him that the board is still considered mere decorative support for a royal head. But the heat of the letters, especially from alumnae, is a shock. These assaults on him are so *personal!* Hate, he discovers, is just as intimate as love. Reading the letters, he feels soiled, as if the contempt and rage expressed in them are a filth that will stick to his skin, and yet they fascinate him. He has to struggle not to read them twice before he throws them away.

By one week after the board's announcement, most of the alumnae have canceled their pledges, totaling almost six hundred thousand dollars over the next three years—unless the decision to admit boys is reversed, and all but fifty-seven reenrollment contracts—a number close to matching the number of undergraduates who did not sign the Declaration—are withdrawn, leaving behind the five-hundred-dollar deposit.

Nevertheless, Fred, who is still wondering what Mavis and Sandra are going to do, doesn't give up. Sticking to the plan, he calls alumnae and parents in each of the cities from which Miss Oliver's draws its students to ask them if they will host gatherings at which he and Alan Travelers can explain the decision. Each of them refuses.

Only then does he begin to confess to himself that he is running out of ideas.

TWENTY-ONE

IN AN AFTERNOON in the middle of March, three weeks after the announcement, Francis is hurrying to be with Peggy, who's waiting for him in a coffee shop downtown. She wouldn't be there at all if it weren't for Eudora, who yesterday gave her some advice she really needed: "Peggy, don't be an idiot. Tomorrow's his birthday. At least take him to lunch."

"You take him to lunch," Peggy answered. "You and Michael. I'm too angry."

"More confused than angry, I bet," Eudora murmured, and when Peggy didn't answer: "All right, then at least meet him for coffee. One of you has to make a move." Eudora remembers what it's like when there's no move you can make and you have to wait for time to melt regret. She was angry enough with her husband for going away on a reserve Marine Corps training exercise just two weeks after their marriage, and then he got himself killed on it! After that, all she could do was feed her anger and grief a relentless diet of huge peanut butter and jelly sandwiches and hot fudge sundaes, all the goodies she'd been refraining from to snare a man like him. She grew so round and smooth that he wouldn't have recognized her if he had awakened from the dead and returned to her.

Now Peggy's glad for Eudora's advice. She couldn't bear not to be with Francis on his birthday. All she knows is she still loves him, she wouldn't be so hurt and angry if she didn't. Just the same, she hasn't the foggiest idea how she's going to act when they are together.

She's got her eye on the door. She sees him before he sees her. And then she does know what she's going to do. She's going to ask him to return to their house. That's the move she's been waiting to make! She won't go on with this sadness one day more.

Nevertheless, she doesn't want to wave to him. The least he can do is find her for himself. She knows that's stupid, but she still doesn't wave, and then she sees his eyes light up and stay on her face as he moves toward her and sits down with her at the table.

"Hello, Peg," he says and touches her hand.

"Happy birthday," she says. But now she knows that what she wanted was for him to bend over her and kiss her cheek before he sat.

"How are you, Peg?" he says. He's still touching her hand.

"I'm OK," she says.

"Peg, I miss you," he says. And she waits for him to say more. But he doesn't, because he wants her to admit she misses him, and then the waiter shows up.

"You want some coffee, Francis?" Peggy asks, taking her hand away. "I'm going to have some coffee. "Two coffees, please," she tells the waiter. "One decaf for me, and one regular for my friend." The word surprises her, though she doesn't mean much by it. It's just a little dig. Just a little revenge, and then she can forgive him and ask him home.

"Friend!" Francis asks. The waiter, looking embarrassed, hurries away.

"Well, you are my *friend*," Peggy says mildly. "Aren't you my friend, Francis?" She knows it's crazy and can't help it, and is amazed to learn how much she needs to punish before she forgives.

"I don't do that to you, Peggy. I never do that to you."

"Do what? What do I do to you, Francis?"

"You know! You know damn well!" Francis's whisper's getting loud. He'd come here full of hope, and the first thing she does is insult him, and now he's too furious to care how loud he is. "Sarcasm, that's what! Not saying anything straight. Hiding behind your rhetorical questions. That's what you do. Hit, and then pretend you haven't."

"Not so loud, Francis. Everybody's listening." She keeps her face bland, expressionless—as if she were commenting on the weather.

"See! See what I mean!" he barks. He's not even trying anymore to disguise that they're having a fight. Nor does he care how stupid this is, how much they'll regret it later.

The waiter returns with the two coffees. Peggy points across the table at Francis. "My *acquaintance* there gets the regular," she reminds the waiter, who puts the two coffees down and flees. Francis is staring at her across the table, and she can see the hurt all over his face. Later she'll remember that look and know this is where she should have stopped, she'd punished him enough. Right now, it goads her on.

"You ran away!" she hears herself saying. What else can she do but hark back to the summer? Otherwise he gets away with it. With everything! she thinks, her fury mounting. "For a whole summer," she tells him. "You took a powder. Is that a rhetorical question? Is that straight enough?"

"Peg, this is nuts!"

"And what about him? How do you think *he* feels?"

"Who? Who the hell are you talking about *now?*"

"What do you mean, who are we talking about now? Who do you think?"

"Kindler? What's he got to do with this?"

She stares across the table at him. "Ask that again," she says. "I dare you. Ask it again," and when he doesn't, she adds, "It's your fault that we had to let boys in."

"Don't say that!"

"I'm saying it."

"That's the worst thing you've ever said to me," Francis tells her.

"Pay the check, Francis," Peggy says, putting some cash on the table, then standing up. "I need to go."

By the time she goes through the door, she realizes she isn't angry anymore. She's amazed at how fast it happened. She'd give a billion dollars to do the last ten minutes over. She'd ask him back before he even sat down. Now she can't ask him back at all. She doesn't remember ever feeling quite so sad.

AN OLD MAN at the table closest to Francis catches his eye, then lifts his chin, pointing it toward the door where Peggy's just exited as if to say: follow her. Don't let her get away! Francis acknowledges this with a faint smile, but he doesn't move. He's not about to chase after her, begging forgiveness. Besides, something's worrying him at the back of his mind, something that brings relief along with this sadness. That's the real reason he's not moving: he needs to sit here and figure it out.

It's your fault that we had to let boys in, the worst thing she could say, that's true.

But boys *aren't* going to be admitted. The alumnae won't stand for it, he imagines himself responding. Either will the parents. The words come to him before he knows they're true.

Dreamer! he hears Peggy answering. When are you going to grow up?

But the words *are* true. "They *won't* stand for it!" he says again, discovering another reason he didn't start a riot when Travelers announced that boys would be admitted: "I knew it wasn't going to happen," he says—out loud this time, and the man at the next table sends him another worried look.

Francis puts a ten dollar bill on the table—a big tip for his own good luck—and stands up. The old man smiles, relieved that Francis is going to rush after his wife after all. But that's not why Francis is moving so fast, almost tripping on a rug to leave the restaurant. He's going to rush back to campus, go straight to Fred Kindler's office—and tell him how to save the school.

"REALLY? YOU WANT to see him?" Margaret Rice asks. Francis nods in assent, ignoring her surprise that he's here of his own free will. "All right," she says, gesturing toward the open door to Fred Kindler's office, the signal that anyone's welcome. "Go right in." Then, to his back as he steps toward Kindler's office, Francis hears Margaret murmur, "Try not to have a fight this time, OK?"

The remark surprises him. Since when did Margaret want to keep things peaceful for this guy? He steps into the doorway and waits for Kindler to acknowledge him. But Kindler, who couldn't possibly not know that Francis is there, keeps his eyes on some papers on his desk; so Francis has to knock on the wall beside him.

At last Fred looks up and stares. "Yes?" he says. He doesn't even try to keep the animosity out of his voice. He stays behind his desk, doesn't stand up.

"I have an idea," Francis says.

"Really? What is it this time?"

Francis steps into the office and starts to close the door behind him. "Leave it open," Fred Kindler commands.

I don't particularly want to be in the same room alone with you either, Francis thinks, and walks across the rug to the two chairs in front of Kindler's desk and sits down in one of them. Fred watches.

"I don't know why no one thought of it before," Francis begins, striving to sound relaxed.

"Well, I'm sure I'll be able to tell you why," Kindler says.

Francis sits and waits. He's going to hold his temper.

Kindler looks at his watch. "I don't have a lot of time, Mr. Plummer."

"How many more girls do we have to enroll for next year than we did this year to break even?" Francis asks.

"Is this a quiz, Mr. Plummer? I thought it was going to be an idea."

That's it for Francis. He jumps to his feet "If you don't want this idea I'll take it to the board and *they'll* tell you to do it. How's that? You want it that way or this way?"

Kindler leans back in his chair, puts his hands behind his head, and stares at Francis. "Isn't there something I should do first? Before I tell you which way I want it—as you so gracefully put it? I mean shouldn't I be running to the auditorium now?"

Francis doesn't answer.

"To see who's starting a riot *this* time."

Francis is about to explain that he didn't know any more than Kindler did that Sandra Petrie was on campus. But once again he finds he can't.

Who is he, Richard Nixon, that he has to explain he's not a crook? So instead he accuses: "You actually believe that I would do that, don't you? You think I'm low enough that I could set you up."

"Can you give me some reasons why I shouldn't?" Fred Kindler asks.

"Yeah, I can. But I won't. You can believe whatever you want."

"That's right," Kindler says. "I can."

"And so can I. But I have an idea that will work and you *are* the head-master."

"All right, I'll listen to it," Kindler relents. He's feeling just a little chagrined now, unprofessional, to be so ruled by his feelings as to have accused without any facts. Every time he even gets near this guy, he screws up!

Francis sits down again. "Obviously, if we could recruit enough girls to make budget, we wouldn't have to admit boys," he begins—a neutral remark to cool things off.

"Mr. Plummer, please! That's what we've been trying to do," Fred says, exasperated all over again.

"Yes, and it hasn't worked."

"Your point, Mr. Plummer? Today! Please."

"It hasn't worked because we haven't given the problem to the alumnae and the parents."

"What do you think I've been trying to do?" Fred asks, surprised by how defensive he feels. "I'd give my eyeteeth to find a way to explain why we have to have boys."

"You didn't hear me," Francis says.

After a little pause, Fred murmurs: "No, I guess I didn't" because now, with just this little hint, he's beginning to get the drift of this idea—and, like Francis, wonders why in the world he didn't think of it months ago.

"You've told them what the options are: One: Admit boys. Two: Close the school. You've announced to them that you've chosen the first option. They've rejected both of them."

"No. They've chosen the second option, Mr. Plummer." Though he's caught Francis's drift, and knows it's right, Kindler can't resist arguing and wants Francis to be wrong. "The alumnae have withdrawn their pledges, and the parents have supported the Declaration and refused to enroll their daughters. They've chosen to close the school."

"No, they haven't. That's just how it looks. They can't even imagine this school's not existing anymore." Francis pauses, studies Fred's face. He can tell: Kindler's taking it in. "They could imagine it if it were their problem.

But you're still holding on to it, you haven't given it to them. So it's still *your* job to contemplate a world without Miss Oliver's, not theirs." Now Francis is in his accustomed role again, giving advice to the head. He feels the rightness of it, and knows too—a more pressing feeling—a huge regret. That he gave this up!

"All right, I get your drift, Mr. Plummer," Fred begins.

But Francis wants to make sure—after all, there's a lot this guy doesn't get—so he explains some more: "You go to the alumnae and the parents, and you tell the girls too, just how many girls we have to have enrolled next year and the year after that, and how much money we have to raise by what time if they want to save the school as a school for girls only. You give them very precise goals: how many girls we have to enroll, how many dollars we have to raise by a specific date each year, and challenge *them* to go out and raise the money and recruit the students within that time." Francis rushes on, explaining. The strategy is so powerful and encourages him so much that he fails to realize how much easier this would go down with Fred Kindler, and how much it would help his and Peggy's marriage, if he gave this idea to her, and had her take it, as hers, to the headmaster—who isn't listening anymore because he's understood the strategy from the first minute that Francis Plummer began to talk and knows it's perfect and wishes he could focus on the joy of it, this gift that will bring him everything he wants, instead of his resentment that he's not being given it by Alan Travelers, or Peggy Plummer, or Rachel Bickham, or even one of the kids: Lila Smythe, for instance—let alone thinking of it himself. Instead of having to sit here and get it from *Francis Plummer.*

"We tell them we can't do this by ourselves," he hears Francis finishing. "We need you. It's your school, and if you love it as you say you do, then get out there and tell everybody you know to send their daughters here, raise the money, do it. And they will, you know," he adds. "They will, and we'll have Miss Oliver's School for Girls forever. Because they'll never stand for letting boys in here."

Yes, Fred says to himself, and if they don't get it done by the deadline, we'll have no other option than to let boys in and they'll just have to shut up about it. *And it won't be my fault, I'll still be able to lead!* "All right," he says aloud. "It's a good idea. We'll do it."

"Fine, I thought you'd like it," Francis says, not sure whether he means to be sarcastic or not. He starts to get up.

Fred motions with his hand in front of his face in the gesture that Francis hates so much. "Sit down, please Mr. Plummer," he says, and

Francis sits down again. "Why did you wait so long to come to me with this?"

Because you're the wrong head, Francis longs to say. Completely the wrong style for us. But he holds his tongue and tells the truth instead. "I just thought of it half an hour ago." Later he'll wonder if he would have thought of this months earlier at the beginning of the summer, if he hadn't gone West instead.

Fred sits very still, his eyes full on Francis's face. "All right," he murmurs, "since *I* didn't think of it at all."

Francis shrugs to show he doesn't care whether the headmaster believes him or not.

"I'll call the board chair this afternoon and tell him your idea," Fred Kindler says.

"Don't make it *my* idea." Francis corrects. "*You're* the head. The alumnae and the parents will need to think it comes from you. They need a strong headmaster."

"Which in your opinion they don't have?"

Francis doesn't answer.

"All right, Mr. Plummer, we won't go there."

Francis still doesn't answer.

"But I will act on your idea."

"Good," Francis says and stands up. He starts to reach across the desk to shake Fred's hand, but then decides he won't. He doesn't want to watch Kindler force himself to accept the gesture. So he turns and heads for the door.

"Mr. Plummer?"

Francis faces back. He sees that Kindler has caught him deciding not to shake hands. This is what he'll remember about this, Francis thinks. That I wouldn't shake his hand.

"Thanks," Fred says. "It's a good strategy. It will work."

"Yes it will," Francis answers, "thank you for listening," and moves to the door.

"Close the door after you, please," Fred Kindler says. "I have a phone call to make."

IT ISN'T UNTIL he gets home that Francis realizes that not only will the strategy he's invented save Miss Oliver's School and its single-sex mission, but it will most probably also save Fred Kindler's headship. In the first place, it will work, he says to himself, and even if it doesn't, it will be the alumnae who have failed, and they won't be able to blame it on him. At first he's stunned by this realization; and then he's surprised that he's not more disturbed by it than he is, and then it comes to him that if he's right and Kindler is the wrong person for the school—which he's sure he is—then he'll figure it out for himself and go away on his own. The guy's not a phony, there's not a dishonest bone in his body—and then for the second time this day, he wonders why he's been so slow to understand the obvious. Oh, well, he says to himself, if Peggy knew what we've just done, she'd say I was growing up.

But Peggy's not going to know. Or anyone else. It's his and Kindler's secret.

TWENTY-TWO

ONE WEEK AFTER Francis brings his idea for saving the school to Fred, Marjorie Boyd's tour of Europe comes to an end. She is surprised to be so disappointed to be home again.

Marjorie has been looking forward to establishing her life in the Hartford apartment she rented soon after she was fired and knew she would have to move off campus. It's a fine apartment: new, painted in colors she chose herself, with a view of the river, and far enough away from Miss Oliver's for her to be out of Fred Kindler's hair, while close enough to feel at home. But as she unpacks her bags, she knows she doesn't want to live here.

Almost as soon as she arrived, her phone began to ring. Old friends welcoming her back. She wishes they'd wait a bit. She needs time to think, to discover why she's disappointed.

"Marjorie, welcome back," a voice on the line says. "This is Sandra Petrie."

For an instant Marjorie can't remember who Sandra Petrie is. She was expecting Francis and Peggy Plummer.

"Marjorie, are you there?" The anxious voice jogs Marjorie's memory. "Yes, I'm here, Sandra."

"Oh, it's so good to have you home!" Sandra gushes.

"Thanks, it's good to be home." Now Marjorie's on her guard.

Sandra understands Marjorie's tone. The old headmistress has so much integrity she won't come to a meeting to hear complaints about Fred Kindler. But she'll come to a lunch with loyal friends. Once she's there, she'll hear what's happening and understand that she's the one who has to save the school. "I'd love you to come to lunch tomorrow at my house," Sandra says. "I'll gather Barbara Tuckerman and Harriet Richardson. We'll have a nice intimate lunch, just the four of us. We're dying to see you again and hear about your trip."

Marjorie hesitates. Just thinking about being with these people depresses her. She remembers Sandra and Barbara as students. She educated their daughters. Harriet Richardson has been a friend for years and a dutiful trustee. But now she doesn't want to see them.

"Please come. We've missed you so much," Sandra says, speaking the truth.

Marjorie has no desire to offend, and doesn't want to lie that she has another appointment. She hasn't had to bend the truth for anyone for months. "Well, thank you very much, I'd love to come," she says.

"Oh, wonderful!" Sandra says. "It'll be such fun!"

EARLY IN THE MORNING of the next day, the last full day of winter term, Fred Kindler, Milton Perkins, and Alan Travelers bounce across Long Island Sound to East Hampton on a little commuter plane to visit with Mrs. Jamie Carrington, president of the Alumnae Association. She will be the first to hear of the new strategy.

Jamie Carrington sends a chauffeur to meet them at the airport in a dirty, beat-up 1960 Plymouth convertible, and though it's a cold March day, she sends it with the top down. The chauffeur, who introduces himself merely as "Jack," doesn't shake hands. He wears jeans, moccasins with no socks, and a cracked leather jacket.

"This is what we get for saying we're going to let boys in," Perkins says, grinning at Travelers as he and Alan get in the backseat, and Fred sits up front next to Jack. "But it ain't too bad. I was expecting a hit man." And just before Jack starts the car, Perkins leans forward. "Jack," he says to the back of Jack's head, "it's kinda cold. Maybe you could put the top up."

"I can't; it's broken," Jack announces to the rearview mirror.

"No, it isn't," Perkins says mildly. "It's just your boss dicking around with us."

"Hey, it's broken!" says Jack. Then, apparently losing his resolve, he softens his voice. "I'm sorry, sir. It really is broken. I was going to come in the Mercedes like always, but Mrs. Carrington, she told me no, take the little one and stay in my old clothes from changing the oil—so I did."

"Yeah, well maybe after she hears our plan she'll send us back in a hot tub," Perkins says.

"It happened once before," says Jack.

"Oh, yeah?" says Perkins.

"She didn't trust the guy her daughter was dating," says Jack.

"Well, nobody said she was dumb," says Perkins.

"And I was going to meet him at the station. He was coming from New York."

"We going to get a punch line, Jack?" Perkins asks. "We're freezin' our balls off here."

"She told me to tell him to hitchhike. So that's what I did. I drove to the station just so I could tell him to hitchhike. The guy thought I was joking.

But when he tried to get in the car, I just drove away." Jack's laughing now at the memory. "You shoulda seen his face!" he says.

"Really?" Perkins says. "So *we're* not doing too bad here." He puts his hand on Jack's leather-clad shoulder. "Drive on, Jack. We'll just sit back and pretend we're Eskimos."

TWENTY MINUTES LATER they stand on Mrs. Carrington's big front porch, shivering from their ride. Travelers rings the doorbell. "Remember, you speak first," he says to Perkins. "You can let her figure out you never were for letting boys in, you got outvoted. That'll warm her up. We save Fred here for last."

"Yeah," Perkins says. "Good."

They hear footsteps approaching the other side of the door. Travelers puts his hand to his left to touch Perkins's elbow; to his right he touches Fred's elbow too. Fred has a sharp sensation of the three of them joined. "Here goes," Travelers whispers. The door opens.

Mrs. Jamie Carrington isn't anything like what Fred expected. He expected "cute." Why else have a name like Jamie? What he discovers is anything but cute. In her mid-forties, the woman frowning at them is tall and stiff-backed. She's dressed in a blue silk shirt, tight jeans, and high heels, her dark hair streaked with gray.

"Good morning," Alan Travelers says, putting out his hand. "This is—"

"I know who you are," Jamie Carrington says, refusing Travelers's hand-shake. Her voice is a surprise: dark and low, like an angry man's. Without another word, she turns her back to them and starts to walk away. They follow her down a long hall to an office, where she sits down behind a desk.

There are only two chairs next to the desk. There's a long silent moment in which Jamie Carrington watches with apparent scientific interest her three visitors make the discovery that one of them is going to have to stand up. Fred starts to point this out, she shrugs, and then he sees a big armchair way across the room in a corner. He crosses the room, picks up the chair, hugging it to his chest, and wrestles it across the room. He puts it down next to the other two chairs and sits down in it. Travelers and Perkins sit too, pretending to ignore the insult.

"I have fifteen minutes," Mrs. Carrington announces.

"You owe us more than that," Milton Perkins says.

"Fifteen minutes," she repeats.

"All right, Jamie," Perkins's voice is soft. "You owe *me*."

"You!"

Perkins nods. "Me!" he repeats.

She looks away from him.

"We've been down a long, long road," Perkins says very quietly. "We've given lots and lots of bucks. Both of us. Me even more than you." She starts to say something. He puts his hand up. "I'm the only one who's given more than you."

"Yes!" she blurts. "Precisely! The only one. You matched me every time and then some. Precisely."

Perkins hesitates, frowning, trying to understand. Then a dawning: "Oh," he exclaims. "*That's* what you thought!"

"That's what I *knew!* The minute I heard what you had done, I knew. Why else?"

Perkins is shaking his head back and forth. "Not for that reason," he murmurs as if only to himself.

"You traitor!" she says. "You sneaky old crook!"

"Just a minute," Travelers says. "I can't tolerate—"

Perkins puts his hand out, places it on Traveler's shoulder. "Hold it, Alan," he says. "We're about to get to the bottom of something."

Carrington turns on Travelers. "Yes, hold it. I don't have the slightest intention of conversing with *you.*"

Travelers stands up. He's had enough. "Well, then, we're leaving," he says. "This meeting isn't going to get anyone anywhere. Fred, Milton, let's go."

"Sit down, sit down, you're rocking the boat," Perkins says.

"All right," says Travelers, still standing. "You tell me why."

"Yes, why?" Fred asks, standing too. He's already thinking of other alumnae to approach.

" 'Cause now we know," Perkins says. "This lady thinks I gave more money than she gave so I could win, so we could get away with—"

"Well, didn't you?" asks Jamie. "Didn't you? Well, it's not going to happen. No boys! Do you hear? You bastard!"

"Oh, for Christ's sake, Jamie, shut up," says Perkins very quietly as if he were asking for a cup of coffee. "Close your mouth and open your brain."

She just stares.

"The way it usually is," Perkins says, "when you're not so excited." Then after a little pause: " 'Cause we're here to tell you were *not* going to let boys in the old place. You're the first to know. We've got a plan, and you're it, Jamie, that's why we're here."

"A plan?" she says. "That's why you're here?"

"And don't try to tell me you can't give any more. You've got lots more, and you're going to be giving it, just like me. You could sell this castle you've been getting lost in since you were born, and the house in Baja and the one in Vermont. People like us only give what's leftover."

"You're not going to let boys in?"

"That's right. No boys."

"Never?"

"Jamie, get a grip."

"Oh!" she says.

"Let Fred here explain," Perkins says.

Travelers and Fred both sit down again, and Fred explains the scheme. He starts with the reasons for the first decision, but when he sees the frown begin to return to Jamie's face, he zips through that part and focuses on the new plan. He watches her face grow more and more relaxed, sees her nod in agreement, repeats the idea in a different way and concludes.

Jamie takes her eyes off him the minute he finishes.

"So," Travelers says. "The idea is that Fred as head, you as president of the Alumnae Association, and I as president of the board will send out an invitation together to the alumnae to attend meetings at the school and in our major cities, where we will put the challenge to them."

"All right," she announces. "I'll sign it."

"And we hope you'll communicate personally with key people to urge them to come."

"OK! OK! I said I'll do it." Carrington puts her hand up, cutting Travelers off. Then she turns directly to Perkins. "I'm sorry for what I said, Milton," she says.

"Hey!" Perkins says. "It's over."

"It's a good plan," she says.

"You bet," he says.

"I'll do it," she repeats. "I'm yours."

"Thank you!" Travelers exclaims.

"Wonderful!" Fred says.

But she doesn't look at either Fred or Travelers. It's as if they're not in the room. She reaches across the desk and shakes Milton's hand. "You're right." she tells him. "We've been down a long road together."

Perkins looks embarrassed.

"So I'll sign the letter, call some people, and then I'll get back to you."

"Get back to Fred here, not me," Perkins says, his hand finally released. "He's the head."

Jamie shakes her head. "I'll get back to *you*," she says, looking directly at Perkins. Then she stands, still refusing to look at Travelers or Fred. "Jack's outside waiting," she says. "He'll take you to the airport now."

"In the Mercedes, right?" Perkins asks.

She smiles at him. "For *you?* Of course."

Travelers gets up out of his chair. "Thanks for supporting our plan," he forces himself to say, and puts out his hand to shake. Jamie Carrington just looks at him.

"Yes, thanks," Fred murmurs, standing up too. But he's damned if he's going to offer to shake her hand. Nor is he going to say good-bye. He heads directly for the door. Travelers follows.

Perkins lingers for a moment, and Fred hears him say, "Wise up, Jamie. You're blaming the wrong people."

"If you say so," she says.

"I say so," Perkins answers.

PERKINS SITS UP front this time in the big warm Mercedes. Jack tries to start a conversation, but no one wants to talk. Finally, Fred says, "I guess I know what kind of signal I got from her."

"Me too," says Travelers.

"Forget it," Perkins interrupts, turning around to Fred. "Choose the signals you want to see, not the ones you don't. You're the boss."

"Milton's right," Travelers says to Fred as Jack pulls up to the entrance of the little airport. "You're the boss, and you brought us this great plan. It will energize everybody, and *you're* the one who thought it up."

"Yup," Perkins says. "You've saved our bacon, Fred. And the next time we come back here, Jamie's going to be so happy that the school's full and with no boys in it she'll send Jack here to get us in a—" he hesitates, then turns to Jack. "In a what, Jack?"

"I don't know," Jack says, grinning. "Maybe a yacht?"

As FRED KINDLER, Milton Perkins, and Alan Travelers are boarding their plane on the other side of Long Island Sound to come home, Marjorie Boyd gets out of her car in Sandra Petrie's driveway and walks around to the back of the house to look at the view. She holds her hand on the bun she wears at the back of her head to keep the wind from blowing it apart. Down the hill, a little to the north and on the other side of the river, lies the campus of Miss Oliver's School for Girls. In the distance the white clapboard buildings glimmer in the sun. Girls, tiny in the distance, walk the paths, and the lawns, brown from the winter, sweep to the river's edge.

Once again, she is surprised. It's not nostalgia that overwhelms her but disbelief. "I used to be the head there," she says aloud into the wind.

She walks around to the front of the house, hoping that Sandra and her guests weren't watching her. When the door opens to her knock, it's not just Sandra who greets her but Harriet and Barbara standing in the doorway; three pairs of expectant eyes staring into hers, and she wants to step back away from them.

Each of them hugs her, gravely. "I'm still devastated," Harriet Richardson finally says. "For you and the school. So angry I can hardly speak."

"Please, ladies," Marjorie says. "I hope that's not what we are going to talk about."

"Of course, not!" Sandra exclaims. "We want to hear about your trip." She leads them into her living room. "Sit down there so we can look at you," she says, smiling at Marjorie and pointing to the biggest chair. Marjorie sits in it; three other chairs face hers as if she were on stage. "Well, where should I start?" Marjorie asks.

"At the beginning, of course," Barbara says.

Marjorie begins with the plays she saw in London, while Sandra pours white wine and everyone pretends not to notice Barbara put her hand over her glass. When Marjorie gets to her time in Paris, Barbara asks her if she looked up Sidney Plummer, who is still living there, supporting himself by working in a wine cave.

"No, I didn't," Marjorie admits. "I would have loved seeing him. He's my godson, you know. But being with Siddy would bring back all my memories of the school. I took this trip to get away and start a new life."

It seems to her that each of them leans forward, and she realizes they've misinterpreted her. They're waiting to hear her tell them that she can't forget, that she's angry and bitter and still wants to be the headmistress of Miss Oliver's. Well, she does feel that way, sometimes—but less and less, and anyway she won't talk about it. She resumes talking about her trip, how exciting it was, how refreshing, and sees their disappointment. They ask a few more questions and tell their own travel stories because they don't know what else to talk about.

But Sandra doesn't give up. "It's time for lunch," she announces. "We'll go into the dining room now."

As soon as they're seated at the table and Sandra's served the salad, she turns to Marjorie and says, "Do you know what's been happening at the school?"

"I know the library burned down," Marjorie answers.

"Oh, my dear, that's the least of what's happened," Harriet says.

They wait for Marjorie to ask what happened, but she doesn't

"They are going to admit boys!" Barbara announces.

"I thought they might," Marjorie says mildly.

Everyone stares.

"Maybe they had to," Marjorie says, as if she were making an off-hand comment. "Maybe they had no choice."

"Of course they had a choice," Barbara says, clearly bewildered.

"Please, Marjorie," Sandra says. "I know you're trying to be ethical."

"I'm not trying. I can't help it," Marjorie says. Maybe that will shut them up. She's just as surprised at how angry she is at them as they are by the way she's acting.

"I understand exactly how you feel," Harriet says. "I experienced what you are presently experiencing. But the very reason for the school's existence was at stake, and then I realized that it had been planned all along and they had brought in this Kindler person for the express purpose of bringing in male students, and I finally decided it was a higher ethic—"

"What do you want?" Marjorie says. "Get to your point." She can't believe she's being so impolite to Harriet Richardson.

"Ladies, just say it," Marjorie says when no one answers. Because she knows they can't just say it. They expected her to get angry to hear boys were to be admitted, and say it for them: that she would lead a revolution, stage a coup. "I know what you want me to do," she tells them. "And I won't. You should have known I wouldn't. So let's change the subject."

There is a lengthy silence. None of the women looks at her. They feel a more painful betrayal than when she was fired.

"I think I'd better leave," Marjorie says, and stands up from table. She starts to walk away. Sandra gets up to beg her to stay. But Marjorie says, "No, that's all right. You stay here and talk." When she gets to the dining room door, she turns back to them. "They wanted me to change, and they were right. But I didn't want to, so I didn't." She puts into words what she is now willing to admit. "If I'd understood what was happening, I would have simply told them, 'No, I don't want to change.' I would have resigned before they asked."

As she drives home, she makes a decision. She'll break the lease to her apartment, get away, find a very different place to live, a larger scene. New York City! She's still got lots of time for some new career there, she's only sixty-three. She's not about to ruin her memories by living in them.

When Sandra gets home, she calls Mavis to tell her what happened.

"Well, then, we'll have to try something else," Mavis says.

TWENTY-THREE

SYLVIA LAPHAM SPENDS the last afternoon of spring vacation with her parents, nailing shingles on the roof of a studio they are building for a Dartmouth professor. She's proud of being so sure-footed on the sloping plywood. To the west she can see across to the Vermont side of the Connecticut River to the hill where her family's house is hidden in the trees. She can't imagine her parents living anywhere else, doing any other kind of work, though she knows, because she made them tell the story over and over again when she was a little kid, that twenty years ago, they moved up here from New York without the foggiest idea how they were to make their living. Well, this is what they chose to do, she thinks proudly: build post-and-beam buildings whose frames don't have a single nail in them and are solid as a rock and beautiful. She knows how hard they worked to learn this specialty and build this business. Now they have more offers for work than they can accept.

Maxwell Lapham, Sylvia's father, goes up and down the ladder to bring the shingle bundles up. A big man with a red beard and red hair under a floppy fedora hat, he wears an intense expression and lifts the bundles easily. Mary Lapham is much smaller than her husband, less tightly wired and, Sylvia notices, more nimble on the roof. Her hair is black, shining in the sun. Sylvia's proud of how well she teams with her parents; she knows what to do without their telling her.

They work until it gets too dark, and when they get home, Sylvia goes to her room to pack for her return to Miss Oliver's in the morning. Her parents go to the kitchen to make dinner together.

In her bedroom as she begins to pack, Sylvia's already homesick, and her desire to stay home feels overwhelming. If she could stay home with her parents and be their only focus now with Charley away at college, she could prove to herself that she's no less beloved in her their eyes than he is. And after that happens she would dare to ask her mother and father who her biological parents are. When she first learned she was adopted, she didn't want to know. It would make her feel as if all her life she'd been living in someone else's home. Now she wishes she'd gotten up the nerve to ask the question during her vacation. There's no way she's going to ask it tonight and then leave and deal with her feelings about it alone. She needs to be at home.

She packs dispiritedly, grabbing her clothes from her bureau drawers and closet and tossing them into her suitcase, shirts and shoes and skirts all jumbled together, making an even bigger mess than she usually does because tomorrow when she transfers it to her room at school, it's guaranteed to piss Clarissa off.

And while her daughter packs in her room, Mary Lapham looks up from her work to gaze out the kitchen window at the Connecticut River flowing south toward where her daughter will go tomorrow. "I feel like we're selling her down the river," she says to her husband, who's scrubbing potatoes at the sink. Miss Oliver's School for Girls can insist until it's blue in the face that it is an independent, not a private, school, but Mary will continue to think of all such schools as private, antidemocratic havens for the privileged, who should be supporting public schools. And a boarding school to boot! Why would anyone who loves their children even dream of sending them away when they're still so young? It's lonely enough with Charley away at college.

"Well, it's hardly selling when the one going begs to go," Maxwell says.

"We should never have given in," Mary answers.

"Hindsight is easy, Mary," he says. "Forgive yourself. You remember how disturbed Sylvia was when we told her she was adopted."

What Mary remembers now is saying to Charley, "We thought you'd like a little sister" and seeing the look on her daughter's face that said she'd always thought she *was* Charley's little sister, until that instant when she found out she wasn't. "Now that we know how much she hates it at that school, we should let her stay home."

"She's never told us that she hates it."

Mary ignores his remark; he's just being stubborn. Sylvia isn't going to admit that she was wrong, that she's wasting her parents' money, that she was running away only because she didn't know what else to do with the way she felt. "There's no fiat from heaven that she has to go back," Mary says.

Maxwell leaves the sink and puts his arms around Mary. "Please, dear," he says. "We've been over this so many times before. She needs to finish what she started."

In his embrace, Mary doesn't answer. She knows he's right. That's what they've always taught their children: no matter how hard it gets, you stay the course.

BOOK FOUR

SPRING TERM

TWENTY-FOUR

FIRST THING on the first day of spring term, the whole school assembles in the auditorium at Fred's request, and while everybody is wondering what the bad news is this time, Fred stands on the stage and announces, "I have great news. The plan has changed. Boys will *not* be admitted to our school." And then he rushes on to explain before the roar of gladness drowns him out. "The board, at my suggestion (for Alan Travelers commanded him, several times, to put that in), has challenged your parents and the alumnae and, yes, each of you, to go out there and talk about this school and recruit and recruit and recruit until we're full again. And if everyone works together—and I know everyone will—then we'll *never* have boys at Miss Oliver's School for Girls!"

There's a moment of silence as if no one is breathing, and then a roar even louder than he expected, and the students are standing up and hugging each other and in the back two teachers are dancing with each other. Halfway back on the aisle Francis Plummer is standing too. Fred looks him straight in the eye. You told me to pretend it was my idea, he wants to say. Well, that's what I'm doing. Francis returns the stare, but he's the first to look away.

"Isn't it great news?" Fred says to the school, when at last the noise dies down enough. Because, by God, he's going to celebrate too! "Isn't it wonderful?"

Suddenly there's very little noise. The cheering has stopped, and the students are staring at him. Why are *you* celebrating? they obviously want to know. You're the one who tried to let boys in.

He stares back at them. "I do think it's wonderful," he says bravely. "And it is a great way to start spring term." Silence again. He can see how restless they are. They want to celebrate—but not with him. "I'm proud of you for signing the Declaration." Silence again. They don't believe him. "I really am," he says, and still there's silence.

So he dismisses them, and they troop out of the auditorium, buzzing with the news. Then he leaves the stage and walks down the aisle and follows them out. It's warm outside on this early April day.

The students and the faculty gather in clusters on the lawns. They talk loudly, laughing, celebrating. He stands on the steps of the auditorium watching them. From one of the faculty clusters, Rebecca Bickham looks across the lawn to him, smiles, and gives him two thumbs up. Then he walks, alone, to his office.

HE SPENDS THE NEXT few days waiting to see how many people respond to the invitations and checking the enrollment data—especially the reenrollments. Very few come in. He persuades himself that these undergraduates and their parents are waiting to see how the alumnae react to the challenge before they commit. And he continues to spend a good deal of his time walking around the campus to make himself visible, show his face. For that's how you build trust: through personal connections—like he had at Mt. Gilead, where the students hung out in his office so much, telling him things they'd never tell their parents, and kidding him about his funny clothes, that it was hard to get his work done. But now at Miss Oliver's the students keep their distance even more than before. Nevertheless, he shows his stubborn side, never stops trying to reach out to them.

The members of Sam Andersen's spring term dig for Pequot artifacts on the Oliver campus is one group with whom Fred's reaching out is successful. Lila Smythe and Sara Warrior are among the fifteen students who show up each afternoon at the fraction of an acre they have roped off to begin with on the northeast corner of the campus, a hundred yards from the river. They welcome him each afternoon when he stops by to say hello and are especially glad when he has the time to put on some old clothes and join them at their work. Lila is always glad for a chance to be in Fred Kindler's company, and Sara is grateful to him for giving his blessing to the agreement Andersen made with her father that any artifacts they find will be brought to him, so he can make the legal arrangements to make them the possessions of the Pequot Nation.

At the end of two weeks, Nan White comes to Fred's office to report on the progress of the new strategy. She seems nervous. Normally he meets with her in her office—on her turf, but she has insisted this meeting take place in his.

"Out with it," he says.

"It's just not happening."

"How many for the meeting here at school?"

"So far, exactly seventeen."

"Didn't we figure there were at least eight hundred alumnae within two hours' driving range of the school?"

"We did."

"How many for New York?"

"On April 17, there were eleven—if you count spouses. On April 28, three."

"Philadelphia?"

"Zero."

"Zero!"

"Zero. Evidently they all got together to refuse."

"All right," he murmurs. "I guess I don't have to ask about Chicago, Cleveland, and San Francisco."

"Pretty much the same. Altogether we have fewer than a hundred."

"Well, well, well," he says, trying to smile. "I hope United Airlines will give our money back."

"Don't give up yet," Nan urges.

"You don't sound convinced." And when Nan doesn't answer: "What does Jamie Carrington say?"

"She doesn't say."

"What do you mean, she doesn't say?"

"I talk with Mr. Perkins, not with Jamie Carrington. I don't care what *she* thinks, or Mavis Ericksen, or anybody else says. I don't work for them. I work for *you!*"

"Thanks," he says. He has to turn his face away for an instant. Mavis! he thinks. Of course. Revenge. He'd give anything to know what passed between Jamie Carrington and Mavis Ericksen. He can only guess that Mavis called people up to urge them not to serve as hosts, but he doesn't really believe that even if she didn't, the results would have been much better. Mavis is only a small part of this.

Then feeling as if maybe he is wandering too far from where he needs to be: "You don't work for me, Nan," he reminds her. "You work for the school."

"Sometimes I hate this school!"

"Me too," he says. "Funny, isn't it."

Outside, through the French windows in his bright sunny office, the campus flows with girls going to classes. The lawns have turned a deeper green in the last few weeks. Buds are swelling on the maple trees. "Well," he says. "It's pretty obvious what my next move has to be."

"Don't you dare!"

"Long as *I'm* the head, it isn't going to work."

"Not another word! I don't want to hear one more damn word like that!"

"You know, I got the signal right away at Jamie Carrington's house. I did my best to ignore it. I'm associated with the move to let boys in. I'm tarred with that brush. So they won't follow me in the other direction. That's all there is to it."

"It's just not fair!" Nan says.

"No. But it's the truth, isn't it?"

Nan doesn't answer. She doesn't take her eyes off his face either. She's struggling not to cry. He appreciates that. He really doesn't think he could handle it if she started to cry. "It's the truth, isn't it?" he asks again. "Come on. You're a professional. You need to say what you really think."

"All right," she says very quietly. "I think you might be right."

He has to work hard now to keep the hurt from showing on his face. After all, he asked for it. "So," he says, standing up, "I'm going to think about it. Very seriously."

"If you do, I will too," she exclaims, her voice breaking. She can see the hurt, plain as day around his eyes, and in the thinness of his smile. "I leave here the minute you do!"

Don't do that, he starts to say. The school will need you more than ever. But he can't get the words out, it's too much to ask. "I'm going for a walk," he says. "I need some air."

When Fred comes back from his walk, he finds that Nan has left him a note. "Please don't make that decision yet," it says. "Promise me you'll try one more thing first: get Francis Plummer involved in selling the new strategy. I'd hate it if you didn't try *everything*—even this!—before you make that decision."

TWENTY-FIVE

FRED SWEEPS NAN'S note off his desk and into the wastebasket. How in the world can you ask me to do that? he imagines asking her. Then he leans back in his chair and stares out the French doors at the campus. It's not just having to ask Plummer for help that swells his resentment so. It's the knowledge that people would follow Plummer's leadership and spurn his! Now he wonders if he can even look Francis Plummer in the face.

He gets up from his desk and walks restlessly around in his office. He knows what he has to do. Try *everything,* he says to himself, repeating the words in Nan's note. It's a comfort to know from her underlining that word that this is just as distasteful to her as it is to him. Then he opens the door to his office. "Get in touch with Mr. Plummer, please, Ms Rice," he says. "Tell him I want to see him in his next free period."

THIRTY MINUTES LATER, Francis is sitting in a chair in front of Fred Kindler's desk, staring at the Mickey Mouse watch and the monstrous exclamation point beside it, and thinking about how surprised he is that the goofy watch on the wall doesn't insult him anymore. Instead it makes him sad, sorry for Kindler, and he wants to explain how off-key it is. But you don't talk about style with this guy. He's all substance.

As if substance was ever enough!

"We need you to do something for us," he hears Kindler say, and takes his eyes off Mickey Mouse and shakes his head to clear his thoughts. He knows Kindler would say "*I* need" to anyone else.

"No?" Kindler says, misreading Francis's head shaking. "You're telling me you won't do what we need?"

"Wait a second," says Francis, very flustered now. "I mean, no, I didn't say I wouldn't—"

"You're sitting there shaking your head!"

"Not for that! I was just clearing my thoughts."

There's a long awkward silence. Francis still doesn't know why Kindler summoned him. For a minute it looks to him as if Kindler can't remember either, or, more likely, he is so disgusted that he'll just say the hell with it—whatever it is—and cancel the meeting.

"We need you to send a message to the alumnae," Fred says.

Francis waits for Kindler to explain. He's embarrassed to see how much it pains him to admit he needs his help.

"Because they still think you're God almighty," Kindler says.

Francis turns his face, looks out through the French doors. He thinks maybe he'll just get up and leave.

"Sorry," Kindler says, quietly, "I didn't mean to descend to that. They think of you as the fine teacher that you are. That's what I should have said."

Francis listens for sarcasm in Kindler's tone. He doesn't hear any, and feels even more embarrassed now. Praise from Kindler, however reluctant. That's awkward. And—he has to admit—a little welcome too.

"It really is something to be proud of," Kindler says.

"I am," says Francis almost under his breath.

"Good," Kindler says, and nods his head, and sits perfectly still behind his desk. Francis sits still too, returning Kindler's gaze.

"Our strategy's not working," Kindler says at last.

Francis still says nothing.

"At least my part in it isn't exactly turning people on. To them I'm the guy who wants to let boys in. Among *other* things." There's that damn self-pity again, Fred Kindler thinks, and wishes he could have the words back. But it's too late, and Francis Plummer's heard them. As if he were trying to tease pity, maybe even mercy, out of him! He'd rather die.

But Francis hears no self-pity. He's too busy thinking about how he wouldn't be in Fred Kindler's shoes for a million dollars if anybody asked him—which nobody who really knows him would.

"So we want *you* to write a letter to all the alumnae, telling them you are behind this idea a thousand percent and you want to see them all at these meetings," Fred says. "We want you to be there at every meeting. You have more clout than anybody else around here. It's as simple as that."

Out of what's become his habit, his knee-jerk reaction, Francis spends a lively instant seeing himself refusing. He has the power now. He can do anything he wants.

"Mr. Plummer?"

"Of course," Francis says. "Fine. I'll do it."

"At your invitation, they'll come. We all know that," Fred says. He leans toward Francis, studying him. "And you are going to open each meeting, introduce me, tell them you think I'm just a *dandy* head. Right?"

Francis nods.

"The rest of us will do the real work of running the school. You just do the selling." Kindler's remark isn't meant to be an insult. He's just describing the facts.

But that's exactly why Francis takes it as an insult—and is almost proud of himself for ignoring it. "All right. I understand," he says. "I'll do it."

"Thank you," Kindler says. "This whole plan was your idea, and it is a good one. Your part in it will make it work."

Francis is grateful to Kindler for saying this. "*We'll* make it work," he says. "Both of us. It will save the school."

Kindler nods his head, agreeing. "I believe it might," he murmurs. And he adds, "Please go to Nan White's office the first minute you can. She has the details." Then he stands up. It's clear he wants this meeting to be over.

"I'll go right now," Francis says, and stands too and offers his hand. This time Kindler takes it and they shake. "I wish I'd thought of this before," Francis says again.

Fred doesn't answer. What can he say? He didn't think of it at all.

THE ATMOSPHERE in Nan White's office is so icy, it takes Francis completely by surprise. He's always felt comfortable with Nan—that is, when he's been aware of her, a mere administrative functionary miles away from the heart of the school where he resides. Now, as he enters her office, she looms large.

Nan studies him for what seems like forever without saying a word, and when he tries to start the conversation by acknowledging why they are together in her office, she cuts him off and runs through all the details of the plan.

"That's it," she says. "That's the whole plan." Her expression is rigid.

"You're not going to ask me how I like it?" he jokes.

"No," she says. "I don't give a damn."

No one talks to *me* like that! he starts to say, but checks himself and says nothing.

"Why didn't you get behind Fred Kindler in the *beginning?*" Nan stares at him. "It was all up to you, and you didn't do a thing."

And before he can answer, she says: "If you're thinking of telling me it's complicated, don't."

Francis checks himself again. He's not going to waste his time by giving in to his anger; he's going to write the letter, just do his job. He starts to stand up. "That's right," Nan says. "Go write that letter. Bring it back to me, and I'll correct it."

"*Correct it!*"

"Yes. *Correct it.*"

On his way out, Francis closes the door gently behind himself.

Later it will occur to him that checking your feelings, holding them inside where they burn, is what a leader has to do. Every day.

TWENTY-SIX

Several days later, when Lila Smythe arrives early at the dig, she's glad to see Fred Kindler dressed in his old clothes. She approaches him while he's talking to Sam Andersen. Fred turns to her and smiles, obviously glad to see her.

"I need a partner today," she says, handing him a trowel.

"Well, now you've got one," he says, happy for her invitation, and adds, "We've been partners all along."

She smiles, acknowledging this recognition, and Sam's gaze travels between the two of them. "It's true," he murmurs. How much these two have made happen! Every new direction, every critical event, finds them at the center. It's natural they would gravitate to one another.

Kneeling beside Fred as they trowel the earth, excavating carefully, Lila feels the same calm trust in him she did that day in his office when she confessed her ambivalence, how she longed for Marie Safford's vehement moral purity and chose compromise instead, and he told her she'd always have to live with such ambiguity because she'd always be a leader. She remembers how much she wished that meeting wouldn't end. Partners! she thinks, savoring his remark. Peers!

Near the end of the session, two students in another part of the dig find several artifacts: a bone fishhook, a shard of pottery, a notched stone hoe whose handle rotted away long ago. That evening, Sam Andersen phones the good news to Sara Warrior's father. He's delighted to receive it.

The next morning, a week before the series of meetings for explaining the new strategy is scheduled to begin, Nan White reports to Fred (cc to Francis Plummer) that Francis's letter has produced only four additional acceptances. Fred isn't surprised at these sparse results. He knows the reason. If I just went away they'd come in droves, he tells himself. But Francis is surprised—and angry. When I invite you to come to meetings to hear about how you can save the school, you goddamn better come, he fantasizes shouting. Who do you think you are?

For the next three days, while the buds on the big maples turn into leaves, and only two more people accept, this failure weighs on Francis. His frustration mounts until he finally decides to write another letter, much more strongly worded—and more than that—to make a very strategic list of fifty people and get on the phone with each of them. He goes to Fred Kindler's office to tell him of his plan.

Francis hears no anger, only resignation, in Kindler's mild "good morning" as he sits down across the desk from Kindler. The breeze coming through the open doors brings the smell of clipped grass from the first mowing of the year, and across the lawn Francis can see the gray foundation walls of the new library. When the construction workers arrive at eight o'clock, this silence will be ended, and the exhaust of their machines will pervade the air. That's fine with Francis. The sooner the new library's up, the sooner Peggy will stop grieving the old one. Then he realizes that this must be what Kindler is thinking too.

Fred follows his glance. He's proud of himself for convincing the board not to use the insurance money that resulted from the fire to prop up the school's desperate finances instead of for building the new library. "This is a time we need to be bold," he told them. Not to replace the library would have been a clear signal that the board was sure the school would fail, a self-fulfilling prophecy. "It's coming fast," he says now to Francis, thinking that if he resigns, the new library will be the only visible mark he leaves behind—and he won't even be here when it's finished. "They're right on time. They don't dare not be. They know I'd shoot them," he says.

"I bet they do," Francis says, making sure his tone makes clear he means it.

"This fall, she'll cut the ribbon," Fred Kindler murmurs. He's not looking at Francis. He's still gazing across the lawn at the construction site.

Francis knows Kindler means Peggy will cut the ribbon. "I appreciate that," he says. He's very embarrassed. "Instead of some big donor," he adds.

"Perkins would be the one," Kindler says, turning his attention back into the office—but not really to Francis. "He's given more over the years than anyone." What he doesn't tell Francis is that Milton Perkins is also anonymously funding the architects' fees. "But Peggy's cutting the ribbon," Fred Kindler says. "It's Milton's idea as much as mine."

"Well," Francis repeats. "I appreciate it."

Kindler looks at him squarely. "I have to tell you something."

Francis waits.

"I don't care whether you appreciate it or not." Still no anger. Just a statement of fact. Fred Kindler has cut his losses.

"OK," Francis, shrugs.

"It's for Peggy. It has nothing to do with you."

Francis doesn't respond and keeps his face expressionless. He's going to take whatever Kindler hands out. For the sake of the school. That's his mantra now. Be Kindler's partner, no matter what.

"So?" Kindler says. "You wanted to see me about something?"

"I need to write another letter," Francis urges. "They need to hear twice. And I'm going make a bunch of phone calls. Then I think more will turn out."

Behind his desk Kindler is shaking his head. "I don't think that's going to work."

"Let's try."

"I'm thinking of an alternative strategy."

"Oh? What's that?"

Kindler studies Francis. "This time, Mr. Plummer, you will not be among the first to know."

There's a little silence while Francis wonders what's he supposed to say to that—and then he knows what Kindler's not telling him. You're going to resign! he almost says, but catches himself. Kindler's steady eyes stay on his face, and Francis forces himself not to look away.

Kindler's raising his eyebrows now—as if to ask him why, since now he knows, he doesn't just get up and leave?

But Francis doesn't move. Too much to take in all at once: this is exactly what he's has been hoping for. Then why does he feel so disappointed? "Look, I just wish we could have—" he begins.

Kindler puts his hand up. "Please don't."

"All right," Francis says. He starts to stand up. He's surprised to discover how sharp his regret is. No more chances to be what he should have been since the day Fred Kindler came. No chance to rectify!

"There is only one thing I want from you now, Mr. Plummer: that you not repeat this conversation to anyone."

"I won't," Francis says.

"Do I have your word?"

Just a little while ago, that question would have angered Francis. Now it makes him sad. "You have my word," he says.

Halfway to his classroom, Francis thinks maybe he should turn around, go back to Kindler's office, and urge him to reconsider. The idea shocks him. Kindler's leaving is everything he's wanted for a year. But he keeps on walking. He knows he wouldn't be urging Kindler to stay for Kindler's sake or for the school's but for his own. To give him another chance to redeem himself. Well, he's had his chances, and they're gone. Besides, Kindler wouldn't listen.

Not to him, he wouldn't.

TWENTY-SEVEN

FRED STARES AT FRANCIS'S back as he goes through the door. Then he stares at the door, not seeing it, until long after Francis has disappeared.

How unseemly that Alan Travelers, the chairman of the board, for God's sake, is not the first to know! How grotesque that Francis Plummer finds out first! Before even Milton Perkins, the other board members, before Rachel Bickham, Peggy Plummer, even Lila Smythe!

Nevertheless, he's not surprised that Plummer figured it out. It was as if Plummer wanted his resignation so bad he could read his mind and find it there. And then that look of regret when he finally got exactly what he'd been hoping for—and wondered if he wanted it after all. That's what Fred Kindler thinks about as he sits very still at his desk still staring at the door.

In fact, Fred realizes, Plummer found out even before Gail did. It wasn't until Plummer guessed it that Fred realized he had made the decision. Right up until he said he was *thinking* of an alternative strategy, those words were true, and the minute he said them he knew he wasn't merely thinking about resigning anymore. He'd made up his mind.

Last night, he told Gail he was considering resigning. He wasn't surprised at her neutral reaction. She'd already lost the place she loved the most, the one that felt like home, when they'd left Mt. Gilead. No other move would hurt that much. "Here I go again," he told her last night, "dragging you around."

"Please do," she said.

Now in his office, he gets up from his desk, goes into to Margaret Rice's anteroom, and asks her to cancel his appointments for the day. Then he'll go straight to Alan Traveler's office to submit his resignation.

"Everything all right?" Margaret asks softly.

"Everything's fine," he lies. He's still surprised she's not his enemy anymore.

He reenters his office, closing the door behind him, sits down at his desk, turns on his computer, and writes his resignation letter. He's surprised at how fast it comes. As if he already knew the words.

Dear Alan,

After much thought [and much prayer, he writes and then erases; what he chooses to pray about is his private business] *I have regretfully come to* the conclusion that it is in the best interest of the school that I resign effective at the end of this academic year.

I think you know how much I have always admired this school, and how much in my short tenure here I have come to love it in a very personal way. And let me put in writing now what I hope I have conveyed to you in our many conversations: that I am deeply grateful for your leadership and support. While the sadness of leaving will subside in time, my joy and satisfaction in the partnership you and I and other board members have enjoyed will be permanent.

My sense is that the school has made some steps toward maturity during my time here. I'll leave the judgment of that to others.

I have no doubt, however, that the recent decision to retain the historic commitment to single-sex education for girls, and the inclusion of the alumnae and parents in the drive to bring that commitment to fruition, is precisely the right one. I am just as strongly convinced that this critical initiative requires a school leader who comes fresh to the scene, in no way associated with our recent short-lived consideration of admitting boys.

This is the single reason for my offering you my resignation. It is compelling. Therefore, please accept my resignation effective at the end of this academic year.

Sincerely,
Frederick Kindler, Head of School

Now, as he reads over his letter, his statement that the school has taken some steps toward maturity under his leadership seems off-key to Fred. He deletes the sentence, along with the *however* in the first line of the next paragraph. For though Alan Travelers will agree with this claim, this letter will be published to the whole school community—which will not agree. Instead the community will take the statement as his ungraciousness in failure, and an insult to Marjorie Boyd. No one wants to hear him imply that Marjorie's school was immature.

But when he reads the revised version, the deletion sticks in his craw.

Being *gracious* means he has to be *dis*graced; he has to pretend he didn't get anything done, and just slink away? He can't bring himself to do that. He's the one who brought the truth out about the finances and forced the board to deal with the realities, instead of drifting. That's *something*. And then the little interior changes, unrecognized by most—which shows how much they were needed—like sending the message that people need to be successful or be fired by firing the beloved but incompetent business manager, and resisting the personal agendas of powerful people by *not* firing Joan Saffire; and insisting that people be on time; and replacing Francis Plummer with Rachel Bickham and Peggy Plummer as wise counselors. If he doesn't make some claim to at least a little success, his resentment will overwhelm him. So he types the sentence back in, changing *steps toward maturity* simply to *progress,* prints the letter, slips it into an envelope, which he puts in his inside sports coat pocket, and heads for his car.

"No," SAYS ALAN TRAVELERS a half-hour later in his office. "I won't accept it. It's as simple as that. You've got a three-year contract. You're stuck with us; we're stuck with you." Then he crunches the letter into a ball and tosses it in his wastebasket. "That's that," he says. "Time for lunch."

In the restaurant Fred insists. "It's not going to work with me as the head."

"Shut up and read your menu," Travelers says.

So they order and talk of other things, and the waiter brings their meals, and then they try to eat and can't.

"Suppose we bring Perkins into this?" Fred says after a while.

"Milton? Why?" Though of course Alan Travelers knows. He's been Perkins's friend for years.

Because he's a cynic, Fred wants to blurt; then, still inside his head, corrects himself: a realist, remembering how unsentimentally Perkins was willing to close the school rather than surrender its mission. He's sure that Perkins loved Marjorie, admired her, and was grateful yet willing to push her out the door. Out loud he says, "If Milton doesn't agree with me, I'll consider changing my mind."

"Consider? That's pretty vague isn't it? How about tearing up the letter and going back to work?"

"Let's see what Milton thinks," Fred says.

"All right," Travelers concedes. "I'll invite him to lunch tomorrow. Meantime you go back to work, get all excited again, and change your mind."

"Nope. Call him right now. I don't want this thing left hanging. Besides, he's bored as hell sitting around that club. You call him now, he'll be in your office before we get back."

Travelers throws his napkin down on the table and stands up. "All right, but he's going to have a fit," he says. "You better be ready with the CPR." Then he heads for the phone.

Fred was right: Milton Perkins is waiting for them in Alan Travelers's office by the time they get back from lunch. He turns from the window where he's been standing, watching the river, as Fred and Alan enter. Fred feels Perkins's eyes on his face and wonders if he's guessed.

"Let's sit down," Travelers says, pulling one of the chairs out from a table in the center of his office. "Otherwise you're going to fall down when you hear the news."

Perkins sits down, keeps his eyes on Fred.

"Fred here wants to resign," Travelers says.

"*Wants* isn't the right word," Fred says, still standing.

"Sit down, Fred," Perkins says softly. "Tell us about it." Fred sits down, and so does Alan.

"He's just a little discouraged, that's all," Travelers says. "Who wouldn't be?"

"No, Alan," Fred says. "That's not the point."

Without taking his eyes off Perkins, Travelers cuts Fred off. "We're not going to give up, do you hear? And I'll not have this man destroyed. I'm not going to let—"

"Hold it, just hold it for a minute." Perkins leans forward. "You just said that Fred wants to quit because he's *discouraged?* He wouldn't do that. You know him better than that."

"I'll give you that," Travelers concedes after a pause. "I take that back. You bet. But he can have a dumb idea once in a while, just like the rest of us."

"Milton, the numbers just aren't there." Fred says. "No one's accepting the invitations."

"That's not your fault!" Travelers interrupts. But Perkins, sitting very still, doesn't take his eyes off Fred, and waits for him to finish.

"The strategy isn't going to work with me as the headmaster," Fred says to Perkins. He's weary of this; it already feels as if he's been over it a thousand times.

"'Cause they put you with letting boys in," Perkins finishes.

"That's right," Fred says.

"And with them losing Marjorie," Perkins adds.

"That too," Fred says.

"Well, Jesus! Talk him out of it, Milton!" Travelers says.

"I can't," Perkins says mildly. "He's right."

Travelers stares at Perkins, speechless.

Then Milton turns to Fred and says, "You're a hell of a guy, Fred. Most everybody else would have to be told."

TWENTY-EIGHT

EVEN THOUGH the light's not on in Sylvia's side of the room, Gregory van Buren sees at first glance that that's not Sylvia in the bed. It's a laundry bag stuffed with clothes under the covers made to look like a person sleeping. He's seen this many times before on his nightly check, and probably been fooled by it once or twice. But he's never seen it so carelessly done as this. It looks exactly like what it really is: a laundry bag stuffed with clothes under the sheet. He understands right away that Sylvia wants to get caught.

"Where is she?" he asks Clarissa, who is studying at her desk on the other side of the room. Her desk lamp is the only light that's on.

Clarissa shakes her head. She doesn't want to tell.

"On campus?"

The look Clarissa gives him lets him know that Sylvia's not on campus. She understands the reason for his question: if Sylvia is on campus, partying probably, doing booze or drugs or both, she's in big-time trouble with the school, but at least she's safe. "All right then, she's off campus," he says. "I'm going to call her parents and notify the police." He turns to leave the room.

"She's with her brother," Clarissa blurts.

He turns back. He looks at his watch. "Well, then, I'll wait one hour. If she comes back before that, tell her I want to see her right away."

Gregory is surprised at himself. He's always been a stickler for the rules. But then there's another thing he's a stickler for: not giving youngsters what they want just because they want it. The child obviously wants to be expelled. So that's exactly what won't happen. Just the same, he's nervous as he waits in his apartment. Who knows what's she's doing? He looks at his watch. The hour's almost up.

Just in time, she knocks at his door. He feels a huge relief. She's here! She's safe! He's been imagining terrible things. Drunken sex with some friend of her brother she doesn't even know, or bleeding to death in a mangled car her brother's crashed into a tree. Now he's angry at her for making him so worried, and he doesn't stand up. He'll be the king on his throne, she the frightened subject. "Come in, Sylvia," he tells her through the door.

He sees right away she's perfectly sober, another relief. "You're home early," he says sarcastically. And yet it's only midnight. She could have stayed out till dawn.

"Come in and sit down," he says. He points to a chair facing his. He can tell by the way she holds her shoulders, and by the calm look on her face, that she's not the least bit afraid of him, not at all ashamed of what she's done. She thinks she's gotten exactly what she wants by getting caught.

"Have you called my parents yet?" she challenges.

"No. Should I have?"

"You haven't?"

"No, Sylvia, and I probably won't."

"What, then?"

"What would you like to happen?"

She doesn't answer.

"Do you want to go home?"

She looks surprised. "You haven't even asked me where I went," she complains.

"Forgive me if I'm not curious. You're here now," he says. "And safe. That's what I care about."

Oh, I thought all you cared about was books, she starts to say, and stops herself. She wouldn't have said it as an insult, merely as a statement of fact. But she *is* surprised he cares about her. She doesn't believe he doesn't want to know what she was doing tonight. "We went to a rock concert. My brother drove. He had a date," she says. "He got me one too with a guy I danced with another time I snuck out," she adds to make sure he knows that tonight is not the first night she should have been expelled. She doesn't say how bored with each other she and the boy who'd been so great to dance with were.

"Tell me about your brother," Gregory says.

That stops her for a minute. "He goes to Trinity," she says at last.

"I know he does," Gregory says. "It's in your folder."

"He's not really my brother," she says. "I'm adopted, and he's not."

Gregory nods his head. He knows that too. Sylvia starts to cry, and Gregory understands that Sylvia's problem is over his head. "I think you should go see Miss Rugoff in the morning," he says as gently as he can.

She shakes her head, still crying.

"All right, see someone at home."

"How can I do that if you don't kick me out?"

"Sylvia, this is a school, not a prison," he says, but she shakes her head, so once again he tries another tack. "What do your parents expect?" he asks.

She's frowning now. Why is he asking me that? "They expect me to finish this year and come back next year and graduate."

"I see," Gregory murmurs. "And do you plan to spend all *next* year attempting to get yourself expelled?"

She gives him a little grin through her tears.

"Well, then?" he says.

"Well, then, what?" she says, feeling stubborn.

"Sylvia, please, fill in the blank. When you don't want to attend a certain school, the alternative to being expelled from it is—"

"You mean I should just quit?"

"*Resign* might be a more appropriate word," Gregory says. "But either word would indicate you're not a victim, and you're not being devious."

Sylvia thinks about that for a little while. "I'm sorry if you think I was being devious," she says.

"Oh, I don't know if you should be sorry," Gregory muses. "You thought you didn't have a choice, and now you think you do. That's hardly an occasion for regret."

"Well, all right," she says. "Maybe I'll call my parents and ask them."

Gregory gives her a questioning look.

"All right, I'll tell them," Sylvia says tentatively. She sees that he's not satisfied and realizes she isn't either. "Yes, I will. I'll tell them!" she says again, firmly. She's stopped crying now.

"A wise decision," Gregory says. "Will you finish this year?"

"Of course! I'm not crazy enough to waste the credits. There's only another week of classes, and then I'll go, and I won't come back next year. I'll graduate from my high school at home."

"Another wise decision," he says.

"I'll call my parents tomorrow," Sylvia says. "Thanks for not turning me in."

He shakes his head.

"I mean thanks for helping me make my decision," she corrects.

Gregory smiles and stands up "I think you've had a very productive evening, and I've enjoyed our conversation."

She stands too, amazed at this teacher. He seemed so pompous and stuffy before, and boring. She steps forward, puts her arms around him, gives him a hug, and feels his body stiffen. How shy he is, how scared of his feelings! She steps back, thinking she's made a mistake. Then she sees he's glad she hugged him. She feels a rush of compassion and knows she trusts him. Except for Clarissa, she realizes, he's the only person she's made a connection with at Miss Oliver's.

A few minutes later as Gregory lies in bed, it comes to him that in Marjorie's time he wouldn't have made the decision he made tonight. He would have turned Sylvia in to Marjorie, and she would have decided her punishment. That punishment would not have been expulsion. Marjorie would have persuaded Sylvia to stay. Well, Gregory says to himself, Marjorie was wrong about a lot of things.

TWENTY-NINE

IN THE LAST WEEK of May, Francis gets a message from Alan Travelers's secretary: he needs to drop whatever he is doing and come to Travelers's office right away to meet with the executive committee. She doesn't tell him why, and Francis doesn't ask.

Maybe he's going to be fired, he thinks as he drives north along the river's edge toward Hartford. Maybe Kindler's changed his mind about resigning and is going to get rid of him instead. He wonders whether if Peggy knew he'd been summoned by the executive committee, she too would guess that he's about to be fired. If he were living with her, she would know, and they would talk about it. They always told each other their worries, and comforted each other, he tells himself. He shakes his head. Liar! he thinks. He knows damn well the problem between them didn't start with Marjorie's dismissal and Fred Kindler's arrival. Those events just brought their trouble to the surface.

Then he realizes the board wouldn't do the firing. Heads do that, not boards. But it's no consolation.

A homeless person sits on the sidewalk holding a God Bless sign near where Francis parks. Impulsively, Francis gives him ten dollars—another ten-spot offered for propitiation to the Gods. "God bless you, sir," the homeless man says, as if reading his sign, and Francis, feeling a sudden intimacy with this derelict stranger, has a strong desire, which of course he squelches, to tell him everything that's happened lately at Miss Oliver's School for Girls.

Five minutes later he's twenty stories up, entering Alan Travelers's office, and Travelers, Milton Perkins, and Sonja McGarvey are sitting side by side, Travelers in the middle, on the other side of the conference table in the center of the room. Francis moves toward them like an actor moving upstage into the lights. Travelers is pressing his hands together—a narrow tent in front of his mouth. He's frowning. Perkins is the only person to stand up. He's smiling. "Good to see you," he says. "How's the teaching business going?"

Before Francis can answer, Sonja says, "Please, let's just skip the bullshit. Let's get this over with." She doesn't look at Travelers when she says this; her eyes bore into Francis, her expression full of disgust. Francis feels his nervousness leaving, anger rising in its place, and stares back at Sonja. He's no more ready for bullshit from her than she is from him. He sits down across the table from the three of them.

"You got any idea why you're here?" Perkins asks, sitting down again. The gentleness in his tone surprises Francis.

Francis shakes his head. The idea persists: they're going to fire him.

Travelers reaches for a stack of papers. He takes the top one off, slides it across the table's polished surface to Francis. "Read this," he says.

"Yeah," Sonja says. "I'm sure you'll be surprised."

It's two pieces of expensive paper, joined on their left margins to make a four-page booklet. On the top page he reads: *An Important Announcement to the Oliver Community,* and Francis knows what he's going to read inside, he's seen so many of these! Marjorie used to pin them to the bulletin board in the faculty room when they came in from other schools. "To keep everybody informed," she used to say. But everyone knew what she was really saying: "Look! Heads roll everywhere. But *I'm* still here!"

He lifts the top page, opening to the two inside pages. On the left a letter from Fred Kindler. On the right, Travelers's response. He reads Kindler's letter three times before he moves his eyes to Travelers's letter:

Dear Fred,

It is with more sadness than I can ever convey to you in one short letter that I accept your resignation.

As you know, when you first tendered it, I refused to accept it. The idea of our school's losing a leader of such integrity was more than I could fathom.

But when you insisted, I had at least to consider your offer—because, Fred, it was you who was insisting, you who described your reason as compelling. I have so high a regard for your leadership, your wisdom, and your dedication that what compels you to make a decision for the good of the school you have served with so much honor compels me to its consideration.

Therefore, after much consideration, I accept your resignation. I wish you and Gail much happiness. The school to which you journey next will be most fortunate.

Yours in admiration,
Alan Travelers, Chair of the Board of Trustees

Francis keeps his eyes on the letter. "You win!" he hears Sonja whisper. "Congratulations!" He looks up at her. But he sees the words on the pages he's just read more clearly than he sees her face. "Don't even think about trying to pretend you're surprised!" he hears her say. "You've been working for this for a whole fucking year!"

"Sonja, let it go!" Travelers commands, and Sonja shrugs, looks away.

Francis makes no answer to Sonja, surprised he doesn't have her by the throat. In fact, his huge regret, grown even more painful now that he's read these confirming letters, leaves little room for anger, he can only feel so much at once. He turns away from Sonja—as if she were merely a nuisance—and asks of Travelers, "Have you mailed them yet?" For if not, there's still some hope. But as soon as the question's out of his mouth he wonders why he asked it. Kindler's not going to retract.

"Not yet, it's incomplete still," Travelers says. And then shuts up. He's studying Francis's face.

And now Milton Perkins does the talking. He leans across the table to Francis, white shirt cuffs shining at his wrists against the blue of his suit coat. "Awful late in the year for this to happen," he observes.

Francis says nothing.

"Isn't it?" Perkins asks, smiling now, and waiting for Francis to agree.

Francis still says nothing. He has no idea what's coming next.

"Too late to find a permanent head," Milton says. "We need an interim."

"That's you," Travelers says to Francis. "You're the one. We need *you* to run the school."

THIRTY

"IF YOU SPEND ONE more second pretending you're surprised, I'm going to barf," Sonja says, and this time Travelers doesn't object. For Francis Plummer has sat there like a stone and hasn't said a thing for so long that Travelers is sure he's faking. But in fact, Francis is in shock.

Yesterday Sonja at first refused to go with Alan and Milton to Fred Kindler's office to tell him that Francis Plummer would be the next headmaster—if only for a year. Of course it was the right and courteous thing to do: tell Fred Kindler before calling Plummer in and appointing him. But *Plummer!* "How can we tell Fred Kindler that?" she asked, though she agreed with the decision: the alumnae would follow him, it made a lot of sense. She didn't want to see Fred's face when they told him.

But of course she relented. Sonja McGarvey didn't get where she is by ducking the hard jobs. She remembers how Kindler turned his head away and looked out through those big French doors in his office yesterday when Travelers said the name: Francis Plummer.

Then Kindler turned his head back, and she could tell he wasn't surprised. Bitter yes. Crushed. Humiliated. But not surprised. She admired the way he kept his face blank. But she saw his shoulders stiffen.

Travelers saw it too. "I know this must be hard," he said.

"I understand," Fred said. "It makes a lot of sense." He didn't tell them he'd already been through this once: when he had to ask Francis Plummer to write those letters—for exactly the same reason that this decision makes a lot of sense. He wanted to ask whether the decision was unanimous, or whether there was argument among the board members, but of course he couldn't.

"It was a reluctant decision," Travelers said, as if reading Fred's mind. Almost the truth. He wasn't about to go into it. Because most of the reluctance was in the executive committee, his and McGarvey's and Perkins's, who nevertheless knew what would work for the school.

Near the end of the meeting Sonja said to Fred, "I wish you'd fired the little prick," and realized she was about to cry. Sonja McGarvey shedding tears, that would be a sight! She's grateful to Milton Perkins for rescuing her—and Fred—from that grotesquerie by standing up to end the meeting. He'd seen what was about to happen.

"Try to get a little distance, Fred," Perkins said.

"Thanks," said Fred, standing up and shaking each of their hands. He meant thanks for Milton's good advice—which it was still much too early to be able to follow, and thanks for telling me first—but mostly thanks, Milton, for ending this meeting.

Now, a day later in Travelers's office, Sonja takes her eyes off Francis and turns to Travelers and says, "Alan, tell Superman here why we chose him." She's going to get this much revenge at least.

"Because the alumnae will follow you," Travelers says.

Francis waits for more, but Travelers's mouth is shut. All three are watching him.

"Well?" asks Travelers.

"If that's the only reason—" Francis says, then shuts his mouth.

"Well it *is* the only reason," Sonja says.

Now all Francis can see in the room is Sonja's face. He leans forward into the table, and this time he can imagine himself reaching across it and squeezing her throat. "Maybe it is," he says. "But I *am* surprised. Whether you believe it or not, I didn't plot for this." I'm a teacher, not a head, he wants to yell. Besides, he doesn't give a damn what she thinks, he just doesn't want to hear her talk. "Don't open your mouth one more time," he tells her. "Do you hear? Just keep it closed." Sonja stares back at him, then looks away.

"All right," Perkins says into the silence. "You didn't plot. That clears the air. That's good."

"Fair enough," Travelers says. "We assume you'll accept."

"I need a day to think," Francis says. His own words surprise him. He needs a day to think? Is he crazy? After being told, as if he couldn't figure it out for himself, that the only reason for the offer is that the alumnae will follow him—and only till they find the one that's right!

"We hoped for an answer today," Travelers persists. "The school needs the certainty."

All three watch intently as Francis considers. "You'll get it tomorrow," he answers at last. "I'll consider it very carefully, and if I think it's what the school needs, I'll accept."

"Don't you think we can decide what the school needs?" Travelers asks.

"Not as well as *I* can," Francis answers mildly, standing up and moving toward the door. "I've been working here for thirty-three years." He doesn't wait around for Travelers to respond.

THIRTY-ONE

LESS THAN HALFWAY home it dawns on Francis: there's no way he can say yes to Travelers! Even if he wanted the job. Even if he thought he was right for it—which, of course, he doesn't. For how in the world could he tell Peggy that he's going to take Fred Kindler's place? For the good of the school? he can hear her ask. *The good of the school would have been your helping him. And now you're taking his place?* He'll never even tell Peggy what the board asked him to do. Nobody else either, of course. And he'll call Travelers this afternoon and refuse.

But first he'll tell Fred Kindler. He should be the first to know. He hurries to Kindler's office.

"WHY NOT?" Kindler asks from the other side of his desk. "You scared?"

Taken aback, Francis doesn't know what to say. "Forget I said that," he hears Kindler mutter.

Francis doesn't respond. He's still trying to let Kindler know he can say anything he wants.

"You'll have plenty of help," Kindler says. "There's lots of *good* people."

"That's not the point," Francis says, ignoring the sarcasm.

"Lots of good people," Kindler says. "Rachel Bickham, for one. And your own wife."

Francis shakes his head.

"You've been asked to *serve!*" Fred Kindler's voice is hard. "You can let them really run the school. "You can be the figurehead. It's the image, you know." He pronounces the word as if it were a disease.

For all his intentions, Francis bristles. "If I did it, I wouldn't be a figure-head!" he says, and Kindler raises his eyebrows.

"I'd do the goddamn job!" Francis blurts.

"Then, do it!"

"No. I'm not the right person."

"I'll give you that!" Kindler says. "Finally we agree on something." Then after a pause. "Who is?"

"Rachel Bickham. You know that." Francis's words surprise him. He never thought about who should do the job—only that he shouldn't—until just now when Kindler asked the question. "We both know that," he adds.

Kindler leans forward, puts his eyes on Francis. "Yes," he says. "We do." He sweeps his hand across his empty desk. "But she's new. Only been here five years. Nobody calls *her* Clark Kent, and besides, she didn't take sides."

"That's one of the reasons—besides being who she is," Francis urges and adds, "Comes fresh to the scene. You said it yourself in your resignation letter that's what we need. Five years around here is pretty fresh."

"So?" Fred Kindler asks.

"So that's what I'm going to tell Travelers. I wanted to tell you first."

"You'll have to tell Milton Perkins. Travelers has resigned." Fred Kindler's tone is matter-of-fact. As if this news were inconsequential, and not surprising.

Francis feels Kindler's eyes boring into him. He makes himself look back. Kindler's sitting there waiting for his reaction, but he doesn't have any, he's hardly spoken ten words to Alan Travelers. Then it begins to dawn. "Oh!" he says. "He's associated with admitting boys too."

"You catch on fast," Kindler says.

"The same way you are—"

"You catch on to some things faster than others."

Francis ignores the remark.

"Alan Travelers is a wonderful person," Kindler exclaims. "He deserves better!"

"So do you," Francis blurts, and Kindler looks surprised. "That's the other thing I came in here to say," Francis adds lamely. It's not exactly true; he would have liked to put it a different way, but this is what comes out. Across his desk Kindler stares mildly at Francis's face.

"I'm sorry," Francis finally says. "I could have helped you more. Maybe we could have made it work." He doesn't say that he still thinks Kindler's the wrong person for this school. That's not for him to say. Never was. All he wants to do now is to acknowledge his own failure. "I regret my actions," Francis forces himself to say. He's going to speak slowly, say it all. "I apologize."

But Fred puts his hand up in front of his red mustache, like a traffic cop, cutting Francis off. "Part of me appreciates your wanting to get your feelings off your chest, but another part says to me that maybe you shouldn't get them off so fast. Maybe you should live with them for a while." He stands up. "And that's the part I'm going with for now." What would his struggle be worth if Plummer got off so easy?

But he's already acknowledging to himself his resentment that by identifying Rachel Bickham as the best person to be the interim head, it is Francis Plummer—again!—who came up with the right idea.

"All right," Francis says, standing up. He turns, walks across the office toward the door.

But Kindler discovers he doesn't want this meeting to end, not yet, and has to call Plummer back. Damnation! "Mr. Plummer?" he says to Francis's back.

Francis turns.

"Thanks for refusing the offer," Kindler says. He wants to acknowledge that Plummer is putting the school ahead of himself.

But Fred Kindler should know that the only way Francis would interpret his thanks would be as one more insult to go along with all the rest. What Francis hears is his gratitude for admitting that he isn't worthy and would ruin the school if he were its head.

Nevertheless, Francis says nothing as he turns away again, and closes the door behind him.

"WELL, I NEVER PUSH a job on a man who doesn't want it," Milton Perkins says to Francis, who has just phoned to tell him he won't take the position.

"Rachel Bickham?" Perkins says a minute later when Francis tells him who should be the head. "Fred thinks so too?"

"Yes, he does," Francis says.

"Well, he ought to know. And *we* know she's a star. We'll talk to her."

"Good. She's perfect for the job."

"Nobody's perfect for anything," Perkins says. "But we'll talk to her."

Francis nods his head as if Perkins could see him.

"You're going to keep this under your hat till we get it squared away, right?"

"Of course," Francis says. And hangs up.

THIRTY-TWO

OUT OF THE BLUE that afternoon Rachel Bickham gets a call from Milton Perkins telling her he wants to see her as soon as possible. He doesn't offer the reason, and she knows better than to ask over the phone. It's obvious something big is up. She'll find out what when she gets there.

Of course, by the time she's halfway to Hartford, she's guessed: Perkins is going to tell her that Fred Kindler has resigned. The realization makes her very sad—and not a little angry—that good man deserves much better than this. But she's much too aware to be surprised. It's clear to her that no one—certainly not a *man*—who directly follows the thirty-five-year tenure of any head, let alone the charismatic Marjorie Boyd, could possibly succeed as the head of Miss Oliver's School for Girls. The person to follow Marjorie would inevitably be the sacrificial buffer between the past and the future. She wishes she'd seen that more clearly when Fred Kindler was interviewing for the job. She would have told him.

Of course he should have known himself. But that's another thing she admires in him. That he's no politician. But a man of faith. And hope.

Now she thinks she knows why Milton Perkins is singling her out to hear this news before the rest of the community: Board Chair Alan Travelers, along with some other board members, must be interviewing Francis Plummer for the interim head's position, while Milton Perkins takes her aside to test the waters in case Francis refuses. It just goes to show you never know what's going to happen next.

And yet, however amazed she is—and sad for Fred Kindler—at how fast everything is happening, she's not surprised that she is the one the board will choose if Francis Plummer refuses. You can't have as much impact as she has, be as natural a leader, without knowing it.

Milton is waiting for her in the foyer when she arrives, and leads her out to the terrace overlooking the river behind the club. "More private out here," he says. They sit in deck chairs facing each other, his back to the river, she facing it. Over his shoulder she sees the glint of the sun on the water. "I don't suppose you have any idea why I've asked you here," he says, studying her face.

She doesn't answer. That's up to him to figure out.

"Fred Kindler's resigned," he says.

Even though she's already guessed, she's shocked to get the news. Milton is watching her. "That's terrible news," she says at last.

"You think so?"

"Yes, I do. It makes me very sad. And *very* angry."

"Good, I thought it would," he says. And waits for her to speak.

But she doesn't. Your move, she thinks. Not mine.

"We need an interim head," he says. "To run the school next year."

Rachel answers, "Of course you do."

"We need one right away," Perkins says. "Like tomorrow. We need everyone to know there's a boss. That there's someone in charge. With a plan."

"Yes, we do," Rachel says, beginning to feel impatient.

"You need to know that Alan Travelers has also resigned," Perkins says.

"He has? Why?" And then, before Perkins can explain, she figures it out. "Oh, of course."

"Yeah, pretty wacky isn't it?" Perkins asks, smiling a little and shaking his head, and she can see the sadness in his face "You'd think a school could be free of politics." And Rachel thinks, Really! A school! How could you think that? And Perkins, seeing the look on her face, says, "Don't worry, that's what I wish, not what I think."

"Well, that's a relief," she says.

"Anyway, I'm the chair now."

"That's also a relief," she says.

"We want it to be you," she hears Perkins say. "We want you to take the job" and waits for the rest: if Francis Plummer refuses. But Perkins says nothing, just watches her face, and then at last he says, "We asked Francis Plummer first."

"I thought you would," Rachel murmurs. It sounds a little dumb, she knows. She should be answering him. But in spite of her knowing this could happen, she's shocked and it's all she can think of to say.

"Just so you know. From me. Now. Not later from some jerk."

"Thank you."

"He turned us down. Doesn't think he's the right one." And then, as if talking to himself, "Somebody tells me he's not right for a job, I always agree, who the hell am I to argue?" And when she doesn't answer—because what can you say to that?—and she's wondering if she'll have to give up *all* her teaching, and deciding—already! to put the girls in uniforms, and hearing the groans, Perkins says, "He says, *you're* the right one."."

"That's good, I'm glad he does," she says. She knows she'll have to answer soon. She already knows she's going to say yes.

"So does Fred Kindler."

"Well, if Fred Kindler thinks so, I do too!"

Perkins smiles. "So you're accepting? You're going to run this fun house for us?"

"Yes, I accept!" Rachel says. "Assuming the board approves."

"They'll approve," Perkins answers. "Unless they want to find a new chair. It's not as if we have a lot of time." Then after a little pause, "Besides, I'm the guy with the money," and breaks into a grin.

"Well, then, if *that's* how it is," Rachel hears herself say. If Perkins can do whatever he wants, so can she. "You want me now, you keep me." The words surprise her as she says them. The idea has just come to her. It's outrageous and she loves it.

"What?" Perkins says.

"I'm not going to be your head just because I'm convenient," she announces. "You've got to want me enough now to want me permanently." There are only twenty-two people of color—her mom would say colored people— who are heads of school in the whole National Association of Independent schools. This time the arrogance is going to come from the other direction!

"Jesus!" says Perkins. "I'll be goddamned!"

She starts to say, If it doesn't work out, I'll get out of your way before you have to ask, just like Fred did. Then thinks better of it. That's a promise she'll make to herself, she doesn't owe it to anyone else. "You don't want to be picking a new head every year," she says.

"Jesus!" Perkins says again. He's smiling, his face is lighting up. Rachel Bickham's right. The school won't survive a whole year of not knowing who's going to be the permanent head. Make a bold, decisive move right now, forget all the fancy bullshit process stuff—asking everybody what they think. He doesn't give a damn what anybody thinks, it's what he thinks that counts. He stands and sticks out his hand. "You're a hell of a lady!" he tells her.

Rachel stands too, to take Milton Perkins's hand. "You obviously agree," she says. This is actually happening!

"You bet I do!" They are standing face-to-face, her hand in his. "You think I'm going to announce that we don't know who's minding the store when I can announce *this?*" Then he lets go of her hand and takes her elbow, and they walk side by side, he in his blue suit, she stately in her summer dress, to her car. In a world where we don't think about the color of our skins, you'd think they were a father and daughter walking across the lawn.

"I'm going straight to Fred Kindler's office," she tells him when they get to her car. "I want him to be the first to hear—and from me."

Milton Perkins nods, smiles, and opens the door for her. "I think he's going to like your news," he says.

FRED ISN'T SURPRISED an hour later that it's Rachel Bickham standing in the doorway to his office. It would have to be either Rachel or Milton Perkins—they're both too classy to let anyone else know what has been decided before he does.

"Well, aren't you going to ask me in?" Rachel says, smiling.

"Of course! Sorry to be so spacy." He doesn't know how to tell her that his head is so full of all the feelings brought up by what he's sure she's going to tell him that for a minute he can't focus on the simple act of inviting her in.

Just inside the door, she puts her long fingers lightly on his shoulder. "I'd space out too," she says. It is just what he wants her to say, and he's grateful.

He watches her sit down in one of the chairs in front of his desk, stretch her long legs out in front, put her arms up on the back. He sits in the chair opposite her. "I think I can guess what you're going to tell me," he says. "I hope I'm right."

"You are," Rachel answers.

"Oh, Rachel." he says. "Congratulations!"

"Thanks. From you that means a lot." Then Rachel takes her arms from the chair back, pulls her legs in, puts her elbows on her knees, and leans forward. "Are you all right?"

"I'm all right."

"You are?" she asks, studying his face. "Because I don't think I would be."

Her questions make him feel shy all of a sudden; he has to make a conscious effort not to look away. "It hurts a little," he admits.

"I bet it does!"

"But your news makes it better."

"Good," she says. "Thanks. I could have worked for you," she goes on, looking at him even more intently now. "I could have worked for you for a long, long time. I felt good working for you," and before he can thank her for saying these words, which he knows she means, Margaret puts her head in the door.

"I think this is one you better take," she says, pointing to the phone.

"Later," he says, but Margaret shakes her head and he remembers the last time she insisted that he interrupt his meeting to take a call. He picks up the phone.

It's Hannah Fingerman's lawyer again. "You have no idea how lucky you are," he says.

"I don't understand," Fred says. He thinks the lawyer means that's he's lucky to have quit as head of school. Well, he doesn't feel lucky at all. How does he know? he wonders.

"We threatened him, and he called off his suit, and so we win," the lawyer says.

"Threatened? Who?" Fred asks.

"Mr. Fingerman. Who else? I mean, he was the one with the motivation, wasn't he?"

"Wait a minute," Fred says.

But Mr. Singleton's too proud of himself to wait. "The police let him off after one or two interrogations," he says. "Even though he gets two million dollars out of it. They were convinced he didn't do it, that he's not the type to run around hiring arsonists. Particularly since there's no evidence of arson. They think it was a wiring problem that started the fire, but they aren't absolutely sure, right? So we were able to convince Mr. Fingerman that we could put a lot of pressure on the police, stir up a lot of trouble by letting the media know how much money he's been able to keep because the library burnt down. They'd have to haul him in again, maybe he'd end up in court."

"Oh, come on, you know he didn't do it," Fred says. What he really means is he doesn't believe any of this, he can't afford to.

"Of course I don't think he did it, Mr. Kindler," the lawyer says. "But I believe we could make an awful hassle for him, and I know he's a softie who doesn't like to fight. Otherwise his ex-wife wouldn't own all the businesses he started, would she? But when I absolutely knew we won is when Mr. Warrior called me to tell me that you've found some artifacts."

"Oh!" Fred says. "He did?" He's already guessed what's coming next. "But we've only found a few," he says.

"So what? If you look long enough, you'll find lots," the lawyers says, "and that's another reason to persuade Mr. Fingerman to capitulate. Because you're obviously going to make another Collection, which will provide the same distinguishing element to the curriculum its predecessor did. Thus the help for his case collapses, doesn't it? Besides, maybe he still loves his wife. Anyway, you've got your two million dollars now. Congratulations."

"Whose idea was this?" Fred asks.

"I was the one who convinced him the new Collection destroyed his case," the lawyer says, and Fred knows it was Sara's father's. He wonders if it was Milton Perkins who laid the threat of suspected arson on Hannah's husband. And then decides he doesn't want to know.

"Persistence pays, Mr. Kindler."

"Yes, it does," Fred says.

"So now the school will get the gift," the lawyer says. "It'll take a month or two, but it's going to happen. There's nothing in the way now. It's certain."

"That's wonderful news," Fred says.

"Yes, I thought you'd think so."

"Well, thanks," Fred says. "Thank you very much."

"Is something wrong?" the lawyer asks. "You don't sound as happy as I thought you would."

"Everything's fine," Fred says. "It's extremely good news. Thank you very much."

"Fine, we'll stay in touch."

"Yes, we will," Fred says, and hangs up.

"Anything wrong? Rachel asks the same question the lawyer did. She can see the shock on his face.

He wouldn't know how to answer even if he thought he should. Besides, his instinct is telling him she shouldn't know—or anyone else—not until after she's officially appointed interim head. If she finds out now she'll think he has another chance to succeed and change her mind about taking his job. "Everything's fine," he says, and when she doesn't answer he knows she doesn't believe him, so he adds, "Really. It's good news, actually."

"Well, that's good," she says as brightly as she can. And then, as much to get his mind off whatever the bad news was as to tell him the exciting news about herself, she says, "Fred, guess what: I'm not the interim! I'm permanent!" I'm the *real* head!" She tells him about her conversation with Milton. "He didn't have much choice," she says. "I had a pretty good hand to play."

"Rachel, that's wonderful!" he says, after he gets over the surprise. He wants her to know how glad he is for her, how right for the school the boldness of this stroke. "You're exactly the right person at exactly at the right time," he says. But in an instant another thought arrives: she has his treasure, and she has it with a security that he never did, and in spite of his regard for Rachel, he's crushed again. Now he wants to be the headmaster of Miss Oliver's School for Girls more than he ever did.

Later, thinking back on this moment, he will be proud of how forcefully he set aside this grief so he could be gracious to Rachel. "Exactly the right person!" he says again, repeating this truth. "How clear it all is."

"Nothing would have ever gotten clear if you hadn't come along to define the issues and stick them in our faces," she says, standing up to go. She reaches, takes his hand, pulls him up out of his chair, and hugs him. "You need to remember that."

"Thank you, Rachel," he says, and hugs her back. Her words are a blessing, and he's glad for the school that she will be the head.

Just the same, he envies her. And she's a friend! It's exactly how he doesn't want to feel.

THE NEXT DAY the board unanimously approves Perkins's recommendation of Rachel Bickham. They are relieved by the handy and worthy solution she provides, just as he predicted they would be.

And besides, if it doesn't work, they can always fire her.

On Thursday, one day before graduation, the package of letters goes out: Fred's resignation letter to Alan Travelers, Travelers's regretful acceptance, and from Milton Perkins's the announcement that the brilliant, young, and *female* Rachel Bickham will be the headmistress. To show how fortunate the school is, the newly appointed board chair, celebrated for his steadfast loyalty to girls-only education, also sends Rachel's stunning curriculum vitae.

Before classes that same Thursday morning, Fred Kindler gets the word around to the faculty that he wants to see them in the faculty room. As soon as most of them arrive, he tells them of his resignation. He makes it standing up and doesn't wait for their reaction. Instead, he turns and leaves before any of them can think of what to say.

Then at Morning Meeting he tells the students. A few of the girls break into smiles, and several make silent gestures of applause. A few others, surprising him, frown, shocked and disappointed. But mostly there is silence. Then Milton Perkins stands. He doesn't say anything in praise of Fred Kindler, doesn't say how grateful the school should be, what a hell of a guy he is—because Kindler has made him promise not to. He simply announces that on July 1, 1992, Rachel Bickham will become the headmistress of Miss Oliver's School for Girls. There is an instance of silence. And then the girls stand up and stamp their feet, and cheer.

Before the cheering's over, Karen Benjamin discovers she's walking up the aisle toward the stage. The decision's made so fast she feels as if she's had nothing to do with it, as if it has arrived like startling news from another land.

Peggy Plummer watches Karen move toward the stage. She guesses Karen's going to do the right thing by Fred Kindler. Good for you, Karen, she thinks. If Karen doesn't, Peggy will.

Karen climbs onto the stage and stands in front of the podium, then looks down straight at Fred Kindler in the front row. "Mr. Kindler, come up here," she says.

Taken by surprise, and filled with dread, Fred doesn't move in his chair. The last thing he wants is to be onstage again.

Karen beckons him. He shakes his head. "No. Please don't," he says just loud enough for her, and the people nearest him, to hear. He wants to melt away, out of sight.

Karen walks along the lip of the platform to the steps, climbs down, crosses to Fred, and takes his hand. For an instant, he resists. But how churlish it would be to refuse her gesture! He lets her tug him to his feet. The next thing he knows, he's walking hand in hand with her to the steps and then up them and onto the stage and everyone is staring at them. All right, he thinks. I'll just get through this.

Karen lets go of his hand, steps away from him, and stares out over the audience. "Stand up," she says. At first only a few stand. "Up!" she commands. People begin to stand, some immediately, willing to do what's right, others slowly, resentful for being bossed around. "Good," Karen says when everyone is standing. "Thank you. Now we're going to do what we should have done before. We're going to thank Mr. Kindler for being our headmaster." She turns to Fred and claps her hands, applauding him.

Peggy Plummer, of course, leaps immediately to her feet when Karen says "Stand up!" and cheers loudly and claps her hands, and so do Rachel Bickham, Eudora Easter, and Michael Woodward. The applause of Gregory van Buren, Francis Plummer, and yes, even Margaret Rice, is also clear. Lyla Smythe claps her hands loudly, a grave expression on her face. The girls near enough to her to see her applauding follow her example, convinced that if Lila applauds, they should too. But from most of the school, the applause is merely polite, and a fair number refuse to applaud, or even to stand. The overall effect is dispiriting: a community failing to be gracious when graciousness is most needed. Many will look back on this moment as one of the lowest in the year.

Now Fred knows even more clearly how few friends he has and how many enemies at Miss Oliver's School for Girls. It's a brutal message. He can't get off the stage fast enough. He turns to Karen. "Thank you, Karen," he says. He wants to tell her how much more her respect for him matters than the contempt of all these others. But this is for her ears only, and he can't say it because the meager applause has died to almost nothing, and the whole school would hear. He won't demean himself by returning the insult he's just received.

He can see that Karen's trying not to cry and wants to soothe her. It's all right; this is just what happens, he would like to say. But he can't say that either in front of all these people. He goes down the steps and takes his seat.

Fred's right. Karen is so furious she could cry. She stays onstage. She's not about to let it end this way! She thinks back to the riot that the hysterical Petrie woman started that day in September—it seems like years ago—and how the next day Fred Kindler walked across this stage in his funny suit and disappeared behind the podium he was too short for while everybody mocked and laughed. And then he stepped out front, red mustache flaming on his face. He just stuck his face out there! Braving them. And they shut up. He took the weight. She wants to be like that.

"You people need to grow up," she says. "This whole school needs to grow up. You don't have the foggiest idea what's going on. But *he* knows," pointing to Fred Kindler. "That's why we blame everything on him." And then the example she'll use to prove her point comes to her. "Take that article I wrote," she says. "Remember that? You thought he was the one who banned it. Well, just to show how dumb you are, he wasn't. *"I* was the one who decided not to publish it." It's not a lie, she tells herself. Just doing this makes it true. She sees Gregory van Buren three rows from the front. He's staring at her. In the front row, the headmaster's staring at her too. She thinks she sees him starting to stand up, then change his mind. Sit down, she wants to tell him. I can do this. Let me honor you just this much. Let me show how right you were, that even I could understand. Then she watches the headmaster turn his head to rove over the audience. He's looking for Van Buren. This is complicated, she thinks. This is really complicated!

"It was my decision not to print the article about our sex lives," she tells all the faces out there staring at her. "So if you want to be mad about it, be mad at me," she adds, raising her voice. "Or at yourselves for being dumb enough to think an article like that should be in the *Clarion*. But not at Mr. Kindler. Why be mad at him? He's the best thing that ever happened to our school."

Gregory van Buren puts his hand up, but she ignores him. "It would have been bad for the school, so I killed it," she says. "And I threw it away," she adds, thinking now I *am* lying. "I should have told you then. It would have stopped your bitching and moaning."

Gregory van Buren is standing up.

"What?" she says

But Gregory isn't talking to Karen; he's talking to the students. "It was the right decision," he announces. "If Karen hadn't made it on her own, I would have made it for her," he tells the students. No one says a thing. No one dares. Because he's staring them down. He's got his face right out there in front of them just like Kindler did. And he's staring them down.

And Fred Kindler's watching—watching and smiling.

ON FRIDAY MORNING the calls from the alumnae start to come in to Nan White's office. Yes, they say, we'd be delighted to come to the meetings, you can count on us to recruit for the school, we'll never let it die. For now with the right person at the helm, and two million dollars to give us the time we need, how can we possibly fail? In Friday afternoon's mail, the reenrollment contracts start to arrive.

It takes Nan White a long time to find the heart to take this news to Fred.

THIRTY-THREE

IN THE SPLENDOR of the noontime sun, Fred Kindler walks across the dais to the microphone to begin the graduation ceremony. The graduating class sits in the honored position to the left of the dais, their white dresses glistening in the sunshine. And in the faculty section, Francis and Peggy Plummer sit next to each other, their sides almost touching. To sit apart at such a time would be an affront to tradition. Three seats away in the same row, Eudora watches them and is encouraged. "We save the school, we save everything," she remembers telling Peggy, it seems like years ago. Soon she'll know whether she was right.

As Fred begins to speak, Francis reaches for Peggy's hand, as he has done for thirty-four years at this point in this occasion. She lets him hold it, but doesn't squeeze back, a tentative grasping to match her indecision. For she's not weeping now as she did a year ago, sobbing all through Marjorie's final speech; she's wondering what it would be like to follow Fred Kindler, to work for him at whatever school is lucky enough to land him as its head. It's only when she realizes how far these imaginings could take her away from Francis—who she thinks wouldn't even consider teaching anywhere else but Miss Oliver's—that she begins to weep.

And Francis has none of the anger that last year made him squeeze Peggy's hand so hard it made her wince. He can only feel regret that he didn't do better for Fred Kindler, and sadness that he can't weep with Peggy for his parting. It doesn't occur to him that that's not what she's crying about, nor does it occur to him to tell her that he was the one who saved the school with his idea to give the responsibility to the alumnae and parents. He wouldn't do that to Fred Kindler—or to Peggy's opinion of him. He has accomplished that much at least. So now he's free to try to save his marriage.

Fred's graduation speech is even briefer than Marjorie's used to be. He has no desire for the last word. When it is over, he sits down to mild applause.

For the next two hours the faculty confers the diplomas in the sacred way. Karen Benjamin is the first in the order, her name having been the first to be pulled last night from Daniel Webster's hat. Gregory van Buren calls her name, and she bounces across the grass to stand while Gregory says the memorized words. They boom through the mike: "Only when love and need are one / And the work is play for mortal stakes / Is the deed ever really done / For Heaven and the future's sakes." And then Gregory hands Karen a scrapbook. It contains every article she ever wrote, pasted in order of their appearance in the *Clarion*—and also the one that was never printed. Karen hugs Gregory long and close, then troops back to her seat, holding the scrapbook up like a sports trophy for her parents to see.

Fred's being chosen by Lila Smythe for this special moment in her life will be among the warmest of the memories he'll take from his time at Miss Oliver's School for Girls. When he calls her, the last in the order, he introduces her as the "author of the Declaration, the staunchest one of us all" and hands her a photograph of Gail, himself, and their daughter, who is identified by the note appended. "So that you know us," the note goes on. "So you'll stay in touch." Lila stands in the sunlight looking at the picture of the girl, two years younger than her. Tonight when she's alone, she'll cry for Fred Kindler. Right now, she smiles and steps into his hug. "Always," she says. "Wherever we go."

Near the end, Milton Perkins goes to the mike and asks Fred to stand next to him. Fred feels a huge reluctance, and hesitates. When he finally stands, the sun seems piercingly bright, the faces in the audience are hard to see. So he doesn't know that all alone in the audience, Myron and Rachel Benjamin, Karen's parents, are standing up to show their respect. And though he feels Perkins's hand on his shoulder and knows that Perkins must be praising him and thanking him—and God knows, praise from Milton Perkins is praise he treasures!—the words don't register. They will later, after he's gone and has time to reflect. That's the way it always is. All he is aware of now is how eager he is for the end.

Perkins finishes to polite applause. When Fred sits down again, he feels a sudden relief. It's over. The line that marks the end's been crossed.

MICHAEL WOODWARD is sitting on the steps of his front porch when Francis gets back to the rectory. "Oh!" Francis says. "You're not at the church."

Michael just raises his eyebrows. "And you're not at the graduation luncheon," he replies.

"No. I'm not," Francis says.

"Well, that's a first," Father Woodward says.

"I came to get my things," Francis says.

Father Woodward flushes. "Oops!" he says. "I made my move too early." Then Francis sees his suitcase and his backpack behind Michael, on the porch by the door. "Eudora helped me pack them," Michael says. "She knows I'm as much a slob as you are." Then he stands up, crosses the porch, picks up the suitcase and the backpack before Francis even takes a step, and hands them to Francis. "Find out why she loved your father so," he says, breaking his dictum to let people figure things out for themselves.

Francis puts his things in the same dented yellow car he took out West and drives across the town to Peggy's house. He's too realistic to think of it any other way. She'll still be at the graduation luncheon when he gets there. He'll put his things in Siddy's room instead of theirs—as if for this beginning to come only halfway home—and wait for her. When she finds him there, she'll be glad.

But neither of them can know whether they will heal their marriage.

He only knows how he will try: he'll confess he doesn't need a parent anymore and try to learn why she loved his father so, and then he'll beg her to broaden her vision enough to include his pagan spirituality, his totemic connection. He'll try again—a thousand times if he has to—to tell her his turtle story. For she needs to earn a broader view, having spent her life at Miss Oliver's, a hermetic, tiny scene. Maybe he can help them both broaden their views. After all, he's the one who's been on a vision quest.

"LET'S GO DOWN to the shore tonight," Gail says in the afternoon sunlight of the back lawn of the head's house, surrounded by the empty tables. Just seconds ago the last guests of the graduation luncheon departed. Yellow jackets buzz around the little mounds of strawberry shortcake left on the plates, and the wind picks up some paper napkins, strews them across the lawn. She wants to be alone, with him, in some other place than this.

They leave in the early evening. They take the smallest, most rural roads they can find. "Let's imagine we've already left," Gail says. "We're in a new place."

During dinner, which they eat outdoors on the deck of a restaurant that looks out on the mouth of the river, that's just what they do. Over martinis, they locate the fantasized new school in Italy, on the shore of the Mediterranean, to which Fred has been called with much fanfare to found a brand-new international school. By the time the lobsters and the bottle of white wine are gone, they have described the head's salary as beginning at three hundred thousand dollars with mandatory two-month summer vacations and a huge travel allowance. All the students are brilliant and charming, and there are no pathological geniuses on the faculty. "Like you-know-who," says Gail. By desert they are speaking in broad Italian accents and calling the waiter Mario.

After dinner, driving back to the bed-and-breakfast, Fred says to Gail, "I think Maine would be more reasonable. Or North Carolina. Maybe Rhode Island?" He's trying to say, as humorously as possible, that his spirits have suddenly descended, the buzz of the wine faded. Next to him, Gail pats his knee. "Let's take a walk on the beach," she says. "A nice long walk in the dark with my very resilient husband."

A little while later, in the empty parking lot of a state beach, they step out of the car into the smell of the sea. The sand blown off the dunes onto the macadam is gritty underfoot. They shiver, take each other's hands, and walk toward the dunes, pale hills in the dark.

When they reach the crest of the dunes they are a little out of breath. Below them the beach is a wan ribbon, and beyond that the little waves coming out of the dark make a rhythmic hissing. The moon makes a river of light along the black water. "Beautiful!" Gail whispers. She puts her arm around his waist.

They descend to the beach and stand with a dune just behind them. The waves hiss louder, the sea smell is even stronger, and the moonlight touches the phosphorescence stirred by a school of minnows in the thin water at the beach's edge. "Oh, the glory of it!" Fred murmurs, "the glory!" and feels a lightness. The leadership of the school has just lifted away and opened his eyes to the world.

Gail pulls him closer. "This is as good a place as we'll find," she says.

He knows what she means and turns to her. Yes! this is it, he thinks. He can already imagine the new life springing in her, and they lie down together, like impassioned teenagers, with no other place to go.

ACKNOWLEDGMENTS

I am grateful to:

Tom Jenks for superb editing.

The Carol Edgarian-Tom Jenks writing workshops
for brilliant teaching.

John Miller for designing a cover that makes me
want to be a teacher again.

Mimi R. Kusch for getting rid of all my mistakes.

George Eckel and Dick Bradford for reading draft after draft—
and sending me back to do another.

Peter Tacy and Rick Childs for believing in the book
and finding an agent for it.

The late Robert Ducas, literary agent, for continuing
to the very end. And for his exquisite taste!

Diane Sampson, Rachel Belash, Jessie-Lea Abbott,
Rod Napier, David Mallery, John Faggi, Joanna Lennon,
Steve Weiner, Joanna, Wendy, John, Sally Davenport,
Barclay Palmer, and all the others who dared to read and comment
on the manuscript: What would you have said if you had hated it?

Peter Buttenheim, the king of loyalty,
for keeping my spirits up.

And finally, all those who work in schools,
for spending their lives the way they do.